ONE STOP

Company Secretary

'niversity of Ulster

²C, JC⁻   'N

ONE STOP

Company Secretary

Sixth edition

DAVID MARTIN

ICSA
PUBLISHING

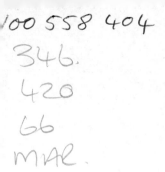

Published by ICSA Information & Training
16 Park Crescent
London W1B 1AH

Typeset in 10 on 12.5 pt Meridien by Paul Barrett Book Production, Cambridge
Printed and bound in Great Britain by Hobbs the Printers Ltd, Totton, Hampshire

British Library Cataloguing in Publication Data

A catalogue record for this book is available from the British Library.
ISBN: 978 1860 724268

Contents

Preface

Each year, in presenting around 80 seminars, I have the pleasure of speaking to and with around a thousand directors and/or company secretaries. These executives are representative of their colleagues in the many organisations on whom the wealth and success of the nation depends. Their prime roles are to maintain the success (and expansion) of their companies, in the process creating employment and making profits which are taxed by the Government to fund the demands and needs of society. They operate within an increasingly complex legislative regime perpetrated by law-makers, some of whom seem unable to understand business in general and the operation of limited liability companies in particular. Indeed the vast majority of those responsible for this legislative minefield have never run a business, operated at a senior level in one, or even have any personal first-hand experience of business – merely an often out-of-date or erroneous perception of one. Yet they expect those who do have that experience not only to run their organisations but also to comply with around 3,000 additional new laws each year, creating, in passing, a legislative morass so complex that it is doubtful if any of those responsible for their business could honestly state that it is and they are entirely legally compliant. Ignorance of the law is no excuse, and someone in each organisation needs to be responsible for this compliance facet of company existence.

The person who should try to keep the company legal (and its directors legally compliant) is usually the company secretary, whose position as 'keeper of the company's conscience', legal interpreter and adviser and board's confidant, is vital. Quite a task, given the legal scenario set out above, to which task is added at present the need to deal with the considerable challenges in the Companies Act 2006 (CA06), which will be not be fully in force until October 2009 – a large tranche having been postponed for a year to give Companies House (CH) time to complete their own preparations. This means that the Act has undergone a gestation period of 11 years, during which period many millions of words were spoken and written (and reinterpreted and rewritten) about it. What has been eventually created is a monster – CA06 is the largest single piece of legislation ever passed by the UK Parliament, although along the way it seems to have lost much of the 'original thought' that it was stated would be incorporated when the consultation process was launched in 1998.

During that process, some uninitiated person dreamed up the idea of companies being able to operate without a company secretary, thereby removing the person who is:

- the focal point for legal matters and interpretation;
- someone to whom the board have every right to look for guidance on matters legal (literally to keep them legally compliant and enable them to avoid falling foul of legislative requirements);
- the logical point of contact for third parties with the legal persona that is a limited liability company;
- the custodian of the board's confidential data or 'secrets' (from which the word 'secretary' is derived);
- the logical person to construct the legally required written record of board meetings (i.e. the minutes, which may assume an even greater importance as a result of the right to launch derivative claims given to shareholders under CA06);

and

- in essence, the keeper of the company's conscience.

Many of those involved in the consultation process pointed out (as just one example of the downside) this concept of 'doing away' with the company secretary would mean an LTD with a sole director could be left with just one officer, whereas deeds etc., require two signatures. The response was to allow a sole director to appoint someone as a witness. When it was pointed out that a third party would not know the status of this witness (as they do a company secretary since the latter's details are lodged at CH), it was proposed that details of authorised signatories should be lodged at CH. Since, if the position of company secretary was left untouched, you would not need such a ramshackle concept of 'authorised signatories', common sense prevailed at the last minute and the 'abolition' of LTDs' company secretaries was itself abolished and the position is now optional for LTDs.

Abolitionists might have been wise to have considered the New Zealand experience. Nine years after companies were given the option of not having a company secretary, only just over five per cent of New Zealand companies have done so! This is entirely understandable, since if there is no company secretary, the duties normally and properly undertaken by such a person must still be fulfilled – ideally by a director, even though the two jobs have entirely different parameters and pressures.

When I was studying for the ICSA examinations many years ago, I sought unsuccessfully to find a practical guide to enhance the theory of the course studies and to help me understand (and to carry out) the myriad practical day-to-day requirements of a company secretary. This title (now in its sixth, fully revised, extended and completely updated edition) is the result of many years' hands-on experience of actually doing the job for a variety of companies (both in-house and for clients of my consultancy), and is very much the title I sought all those years ago. It is aimed at those seeking practical hands-on guidance and is designed for those who undertake the role of company secretary as add-on responsibilities to other administrative duties, and yet lack any formal training (in this area) to help them cope with these challenges.

The book is written in ordinary, everyday English, and is arranged in the expanded index format, so that a reader should instantly be able to find user-friendly guidance to specific subjects. This 'subject-holistic approach' leads inevitably to some duplication. As a plain guide to both traditional and new requirements such content should suffice in over 90 per cent of the cases where guidance is required. In the other areas it would be wise to seek specific legal advice – in which case the book should enable the reader to ask the right question, without which there is little hope of ever obtaining the right answer. I hope it is helpful in undertaking a fascinating role.

David M Martin
Buddenbrook Consultancy
June 2009

Using this book

1 To provide immediate access to the topic, each subject is dealt with comprehensively within its own section, cross-referencing to other sections where appropriate (effected by setting the name of the referral section in upper case e.g. 'see AGENDA').

2 Throughout a public limited company is referred to as a 'PLC', a private limited company as an 'LTD', Companies House as CH, SAIL for the Single Alternative Inspection Location, where registers can be kept, and the various Companies Acts as 'CA' followed by the last two digits of the year they were enacted, thus the Companies Act 2006 becomes 'CA06'.

3 This edition assumes CA06 is fully in force and, to aid ease of use/ reference, sections under CA06 have been cross-referenced (where applicable) to the corresponding sections in CA85.

4 Traditionally the forms for information required to be filed at CH have been given numbers corresponding to sections in the most recent CA. For CA06, however, all the forms have been redesigned (and reclassified) losing the direct link in the format of their presentation with sections in the Act – although the appropriate section is referred to on each. In this book the new reference letters and numbers are given with the previous form number under CA85 as well as the appropriate section of CA06. The new forms cannot be used until October 2009 although they can be downloaded via the CH website.

5 CA06 allows optional dilutions (e.g. LTDs are not obliged to appoint a company secretary, do not need to hold an AGM, only need give 14 days' notice of special resolutions, etc.). However a company's articles of association are its constitution and rules. Such dilutions can only be used providing the articles are silent about them or do not prohibit them. Thus if the articles refer to an LTD holding an AGM each year then it must (unless and until it changes its articles) continue to do so. In short, CA06 does not overrule a company's articles as far as these dilutions are concerned.

6 CA06 will be fully in force on 1 October 2009, and companies formed after that date (in fact it may not be possible to form a company between 1 and 4 October, as CH is closed) will be completely subject to the new Act. This may pose a challenge to those administering existing companies when they set up a new company unless they

bring the articles of the existing companies into a similar format and content of the company formed under CA06.

7   Traditionally, any meeting other than a company's AGM has been called an extraordinary general meeting (EGM). CA06 specifies that meetings other than the AGM are simply called general meetings. However, companies registered under Acts prior to CA06 may have articles based on drafts accompanying previous Companies Acts – e.g. Table A of CA85. Such articles refer to EGMs. CA06 does not override the articles and thus unless (and until) the articles of those existing companies are changed, requirements regarding EGMs continue to apply.

8   Since 1856 each company's constitution has been comprised of a memorandum and articles. A company formed under CA06 will have a memorandum (which cannot subsequently be altered), consisting only of its address, and details of the promoters. If such a company wishes to adopt 'objects clauses' they must be set out in the articles (which will henceforth be referred to as the company's 'constitution'). If an existing company does not change its articles, the objects clauses of that company will be deemed to be part of its articles. Existing companies changing their articles will be required to incorporate their objects clauses in the revised articles.

9   The current definitions of 'companies' sizes' are:
Small: Does not exceed two of the following criteria:
- turnover: £6.5 million net;
- balance sheet aggregate: £3.26 million;
- 50 employees.

Medium-sized: a company that exceeds the above parameters for a small company but does not exceed two of the following criteria:
- turnover £25.9 million net;
- balance sheet aggregate £12.9 million net;
- 250 employees.

Large: exceeds the medium-sized parameters.

10   All references to companies (other than in case studies) are for example only and not representative of any real company.

11   Use of the masculine includes the feminine.

12   Brief case studies have been included to demonstrate the effect of points just referred to in the text. Such studies also demonstrate the law in action. Courts cannot change the law but if, in promulgating a decision, they change our understanding of what the law means, that has virtually the same effect.

13   Opinions expressed in this book are those of the author, not of ICSA Information & Training.

STOP PRESS

On 5 June 2009, the Government created a new Department for Business, Innovation and Skills (BIS). The new department has been created by merging the Department for Business Enterprise and Regulatory Reform (BERR) with the Department for Innovation Universities and Skills (DIUS). The merger results in a single department '...committed to building Britain's future economic strengths'. The original press release covering the change can be found at www.berr.gov.uk/aboutus/pressroom/page51711.html.

References to BERR appear throughout this book and the reader should treat the names BERR and BIS as one and the same.

Table of cases

Agenda and notice

INTRODUCTION

A board meeting has been described as a 'maze'. If so, the agenda for a meeting can be compared to a map, essential to help find the best (and swiftest!) route through that maze. An agenda also provides control over the meeting's content. Furthermore, if meetings are not convened properly by means of a notice (possibly containing the agenda) and attended by the required QUORUM, decisions taken may be invalid and the meeting may fail to achieve its purpose(s). The specimen sets of articles (for a PLC and for LTDs limited both by shares or guarantee) that accompany CA06 state: *'every director must be given reasonable notice of a meeting of directors'*. Such notice is meaningful only if the matters required to be considered are listed, and although this is not so vital for general meetings (since very often they are fairly routine and formal events), advance planning for both is essential.

Targets and aims

All meetings should have targets – unless one has a target, how can aim be taken? As Sir John Harvey Jones stated in his bestselling management book, *Making it Happen*: *'You've got to have a clear idea of where you want to take whatever it is you've got.'* In order to focus the attention (individual and collective) of the meeting's members on the subject matter, and to try to avoid the meeting descending into what can otherwise become a meandering discussion, a list of targets or aims should be identified for each meeting. An agenda for a regular meeting can provide additional short-term aims, even though longer-term, strategic aims may be set out elsewhere. In convening and running a routine meeting, these longer-term aims may, to some extent, be taken for granted. An agenda can act as a directing force at and on the meeting, creating latent pressure on the meeting members to work towards the attainment of such targets. Thus, although a board of directors might have adopted as the overall targets of the company:

- maximising profit to at least £X million in the current financial year without utilising additional capital;
- keeping employment costs to no more than X per cent of gross margin;
- earning Y per cent return on capital employed;

- achieving output of Z per cent of previous financial period;
- maintaining quality and service, to levels as defined; and so on,

these are outline statistical guidelines or long-term strategies, within which it is possible to adopt and use a number of shorter-term alternative actions or tactics. The horizon and timetable of action of the board are essentially long-term, but there will understandably be deviations in the short term. Under s. 172 of CA06, boards are explicitly required to consider (and balance) not only the long-term consequences of their decisions, but also the interests of what have been called the company's 'stakeholders' – e.g. the company itself, its shareholders, employees, customers, creditors and suppliers, society and the environment.

Reflecting specific aims, or a synopsis of them, at the start of the agenda can act as a valuable reminder to all members of the meeting of its – and their – priorities, i.e. *'This is why we are here.'* Agendas require careful consideration and compilation – more attention than, experience indicates, they are often given. The benefits of a comprehensive and detailed agenda include:

- guidance through the meeting's 'maze';
- assistance to the chairman in achieving the meeting's aims;
- guidance to all participants of what is required to be achieved; and
- (possibly an invaluable side benefit for the company secretary!) a first draft of the legally required record of the meeting – the MINUTES (see below).

See also sections on ANNUAL GENERAL MEETING, (extraordinary) GENERAL MEETINGS and BOARD MEETINGS.

Annual General Meeting

Under current law, every PLC must hold an ANNUAL GENERAL MEETING each year within six months of the company's FINANCIAL YEAR END (i.e. its accounting reference date). Under CA06, LTDs are no longer required to hold an AGM, unless their shareholders or members (or the directors) require it; but if they do, it must be held within ten months of the company's year end. However if the articles of an LTD registered under an earlier CA require there to be an AGM, then such meetings must continue to be held until the articles are changed – or the shareholders pass a resolution not to hold such meetings. Everyone entitled to attend (i.e. all members) must be given adequate notice of the meeting.

To convene the AGM of a PLC, the required notice must be given; notice can only be waived in whole or part if all the members agree (see ANNUAL GENERAL MEETING). Under CA06, the AGM of an LTD requires 14 days' notice (although the articles need to be checked in case a longer period of notice, is required e.g. the traditional 21 days). Notice for an LTD's AGM can

Example	Draft agenda for an annual general meeting

ANY COMPANY LTD

NOTICE

Is hereby given that the

XXTH ANNUAL GENERAL MEETING

of the members of the Company will be held at 9.30 a.m. at the [registered office] on Friday, 14th March 2XXX, for the purpose of considering the following business:

1   Notice of Meeting.

2   Apologies for absence.

3   Directors' report for the year ended 30th September 2XXX.

4   Profit and Loss a/c for the year ended 30th September 2XXX and Balance Sheet as at that date.

5   To consider and if thought fit authorise payment of a final dividend of X% (Y pence per share) to ordinary shareholders on the register as at [date].

6   Retirement and proposed re-appointment as directors of:
    a) Ms C Smith
    b) Mr B Jones

    who retire by rotation and, being eligible, offer themselves for re-appointment.

7   Retirement and proposed re-appointment as a director of Mr A Robinson who was appointed a director on 1st January 2XXX and retires and offers himself for re-election.

8   Appointment and remuneration of auditors.

By order of the board

[Name]
Secretary   15th February 2XXX

A member entitled to attend and unable to do so may appoint a proxy to vote in his place. Such proxies should be sent to the registered office of the company to arrive not later than 48 hours before the commencement of the meeting.

be waived if 90 per cent (a level which can be increased to 95 per cent by the articles) of the voting strength of the members agree.

Whilst accidental failure to give notice to one or more member will not usually invalidate the meeting, every effort should be made to ensure that members' addresses are kept up to date and the agenda/notice is sent in accordance with the requirements. With their shareholders' authority, companies can now serve such notices on their members by electronic means.

Case study	Faxed notices of AGM
	In *PNC Telecom plc v Thomas*, the court held that it was valid to serve notice of a meeting by fax. This was the first occasion on which this matter was challenged in court.

At the meeting, certain standard business is required to be transacted (although other business can also be transacted if it is timely – for example a special RESOLUTION). The ARTICLES OF ASSOCIATION must be checked for requirements. If business other than that covered in the draft agenda below is required to be considered, then full details must be given; for example, a special resolution or special notice of an ordinary resolution require specific periods and types of notice.

Notes

I   If the company secretary is also a director when issuing the notice of the meeting he should sign 'On behalf of the board'; otherwise the meeting is convened 'By order of the board'.

2   The ARTICLES of some companies require a proportion of the DIRECTORS to retire ('by rotation', as it is termed) at each AGM and to offer themselves (if eligible) for re-election. (If a company's articles incorporate regulation 84 of Table A of CA85, only non-executive directors are required to retire by rotation, although experience indicates that many LTDs operating under such rules do not realise this and rotate both executive and non-executive directors.)

3   Any director(s) who has/have been appointed since the previous AGM must retire at the next AGM and may (if eligible) offer themselves for re-election. The purpose of this process is to ensure that members' authority is eventually obtained for all board appointments.

4   Special rules apply regarding the appointment at a general meeting of anyone other than the retiring AUDITORS.

5   Only members and auditors have a right of attendance at a general meeting, although non-shareholding directors have a right of attend-

ance (and to address the meeting) should their removal be one of the items of business.

(Extraordinary) General Meeting

Traditionally, any meeting other than a company's AGM has been called an extraordinary general meeting (EGM). CA06 specifies (for companies formed under that Act) that meetings of members other than the AGM are simply called general meetings, although the requirements are identical to the previous requirements for EGMs. Many existing companies have used as

Example	Draft agenda for a(n) (extraordinary) general meeting

ANY COMPANY LTD

NOTICE

Is hereby given that a(n)

(EXTRAORDINARY) GENERAL MEETING

of the members of the Company will be held on Wednesday 18th June 2XXX at 11 a.m. at [registered office] for the purpose of considering the following business:

1   Notice.

2   Apologies for absence.

3   SPECIAL RESOLUTION: that the share capital of the company be and it hereby is increased from £10,000 to £2,000,000 by the creation of:

   a)   990,000 new ordinary shares of £1 each ranking in all respects *pari passu* with the 10,000 existing ordinary shares of £1 of the company,

   b)   the creation of 1,000,000 [X]% net p.a. Cumulative Redeemable Convertible Preference Shares of £1.

4   SPECIAL RESOLUTION: that the name of the company be changed to ANY OTHER COMPANY LTD.

By order of the board

[Name]

Secretary   20th May 2XXX the basis for their articles the pro forma drafts accompanying previous CAs – e.g. Table A of CA85 – and such draft articles (and therefore the articles of those companies) refer to EGMs. CA06 does not override the articles of companies formed under earlier legislation and thus unless (and until) the articles of those existing companies are changed, the requirements regarding EGMs will continue to apply.

EGMs are usually convened for specific purposes, although there is nothing to stop such business being conducted at the AGM providing the timing is appropriate and any special rules regarding the business to be considered are adhered to.

Notes

1 An (extraordinary) general meeting requires 14 days' notice (Longer notice may have to be given if a special resolution is to be considered. Although under CA06 only 14 days' notice (formerly 21) is required of special RESOLUTIONS, a company's articles may require a longer notice period.)

2 To be passed at a meeting a special RESOLUTION requires a minimum majority of 75 per cent of those voting (whether present or by proxy) and must be filed with the REGISTRAR OF COMPANIES within 15 days of being passed. In filing, a specified layout must be followed – the minutes of the meeting are not acceptable. (If a special resolution is required to be passed using the WRITTEN resolution alternative, it requires the support of 75 per cent of ALL the votes – not just the votes that are cast, as is the case if it is considered at a meeting.)

Registrar's notification

Special resolutions (and any resolution required by the company's articles to be passed by unanimous agreement of members which would otherwise be a special resolution) as well as any ordinary resolutions which:

- increase the authorised share capital of the company;
- authorise the director(s) to allot shares;
- authorise a voluntary winding up of the company;
- revoke an elective resolution

must also be filed with the REGISTRAR (within 15 days) using a specified format.

Allotment and transfer of shares

INTRODUCTION

Many companies limited by shares are formed with just one or two shares being issued to the company promoter(s). These shares are then transferred to the first shareholder(s) of the company. For a company formed under a CA other than CA06, subject to the capital authorised in the MEMORANDUM and any limit on the directors' powers contained in the ARTICLES or in a SHAREHOLDERS' AGREEMENT, or by resolution of the shareholders, the directors can issue additional shares. The process of issuing shares and allocating them to those wishing to subscribe for the shares is termed "allotment'. Companies formed under CA06 do not need to have an 'authorised share capital', and will simply have the capital that the directors determine is required for the company from time to time (unless the shareholders constrain the directors' powers in this regard).

Authority

The total value of, as well as the denominations of, the share capital of all companies limited by shares have always hitherto been stated in the company's memorandum. Whilst shares in the defined CLASSES (ordinary, preference, deferred etc.) could be issued up to the maximum stated in the memorandum, before any shares were issued in excess of those figures, the shareholders' authority was required (i.e. to increase the authorised share capital). However, for companies registered under CA06, 'authorised share capital' as a concept (and, in effect, limitation) is abolished, and a company will be able to have whatever share capital its directors wish, subject to any restrictions imposed on them by the shareholders. Thus (unless the shareholders have inserted a control mechanism in the articles) the share capital would then be able to be increased by resolution of the board.

Under many company articles (and/or SHAREHOLDERS' AGREEMENTS) however, shareholders may have retained a right of pre-emption (a requirement that before shares are issued to a third party, they must first be offered to the existing shareholders, usually in the proportion that their shares bear to the total). This would mean that the board may be precluded, without shareholder approval, from issuing shares without first gaining shareholder agreement. Other restrictions could include a prohibition on the issue of shares that would result in any one holder owning more than (say) 50 per cent of the total and thus having effective control of the company.

The usual exceptions to a pre-emption rule are as follows:

- shares issued for employee share schemes;
- issue of non-participating preference and similar securities, or of any other non-equity securities;
- allotment of shares for a non-cash consideration;
- allotment of shares under a renounceable letter of allotment.

Issues of shares in these categories do not need the members to waive their pre-emptive rights.

Administration

Shares which are not fully paid (that is, the full issue price has not yet been paid in respect of those shares) must be numbered and such numbers must be referred to in all transactions, so that the 'status' of the shares is obvious. However if the shares are all fully paid, they do not need to bear a distinctive number. Each time a new share is required to be allotted, the authority of the board is required and a record of the resolution to this effect should be entered in the minutes. Entries should also be made in the register of members (i.e. either the details of the new shareholder(s), and their shareholding, or the addition of new shares to the holding of an existing shareholder). In addition under s. 555 of CA06 (formerly s. 88(2) of CA85) a return of allotments (using form SH01) must be made to the Registrar within 28 days. The following board minute might be appropriate:

Example	**Board minute**
	Board Meeting: 1st December 2XXX
	It was resolved that the following shares be and they hereby are allotted to the shareholders stated, amounts in respect of the subscription monies referred to having been received from each person. It was further resolved that the secretary should issue the appropriate share certificates in accordance with the articles and make the necessary entries in the share register.

New shareholder	Number of shares	Cash rec'd
A. Bloggs	1,000 Ordinary shares of £1	£1,000
B. Jones	2,000 Ordinary shares of £1	£2,000
J. Smith	10,000 Ordinary shares of £1	£10,000

Controlling who owns the shares (i.e. keeping an LTD 'private')

A major advantage of LTDs is that they can quite legitimately include in their articles rights reserved to their directors, not only to monitor who holds the shares in the company, but also to prevent someone unacceptable to the board becoming a shareholder (hence the reference to or definition of such companies as being 'private'). The board of an LTD can block a transfer of shares (or an issue of new shares) to prospective shareholders who they deem to be unacceptable. If an LTD wishes to re-register as a PLC, this right of the directors to prevent shares being transferred to a holder who is unacceptable to them must be abandoned.

Payment

The original subscribers to the memorandum of a PLC must pay for their shares in cash. But shares in LTDs are not always issued for cash – sometimes they can be issued in exchange for the rights to property, or a patent, or a new process, etc. If shares are issued for consideration other than cash, then such assets must be passed to the company within five years of the shares being issued. If a transfer of the asset does not take place, then the allottee is liable to pay cash for the shares (and any premium) plus interest. If shares are to be issued in exchange for an asset then the value of the asset must be assessed by an expert (defined as a person capable of acting as an auditor) and stamp duty may need to be paid.

A PLC cannot allot shares unless at least 25 per cent of the value of such shares (together with any premium) has been paid in cash. In addition a company cannot use the designation 'PLC' unless it has an issued share capital of at least £50,000 (a figure originally required in CA81 but maintained unchanged in CA06).

Share transfer

Once shares are allotted, shareholders can hold or transfer their shares by completing a signed (and, if required, stamped – see below) stock transfer form and their share certificate(s). However if a shareholder dies, or is sectioned under the Mental Health Act, or is declared bankrupt, since they no longer have 'capacity' to sign a stock transfer form, ownership can be passed to another person under 'share 'transmission' arrangements. In these cases the authority to deal with the shares is vested in the shareholder's personal representative(s) (executor or administrator), committee or receiver, or trustee in bankruptcy, respectively.

Share registration work is involved and complex, and most listed PLCs with a large number of shareholders and/or companies with active share registers tend to place such work with specialist companies (particularly subsidiaries or divisions of the main clearing banks). For a small LTD, particularly those that are family-owned, share transfers may be relatively rare.

Stamp duty

Until March 2008 stamp duty had to be paid on all share transfers. Apart from some exempted transactions (which bore a fixed £5 duty), the amount of the duty was in proportion to the value of the shares changing hands (*ad valorem*). This meant that it was first necessary to establish the value of the shares – a relatively easy requirement for companies whose shares were listed on a stock exchange, but far more difficult for non-listed companies. In such situations it is usual to ask the auditors to prepare a valuation. For transfers on or since 13 March 2008, any transfer in respect of shares where the value is less than £1,000 is exempt from paying duty.

The following transfers (which formerly had to be stamped with a nominal £5) are now also exempt from stamp duty, subject to confirmation (by a certificate required to be completed on the reverse of the transfer form) that the transaction falls within one of the categories, that is the transfer is:

- of property in the name of a trustee to a new trustee;
- by way of security for a loan;
- to a beneficiary under a will;
- to a beneficiary from an intestate's estate;
- to a residuary legatee;
- on, and in consideration of, marriage;
- by liquidator;
- not on sale and not arising from sale, where no beneficial interest passes (e.g. from one nominee to another nominee);
- by way of gift.

Record and title

The issue of a share certificate acts as both receipt for the money subscribed and evidence of title to the shares. However, the articles of some companies stipulate that share certificates are only valid as evidence of title if they bear the common seal of the company. If a company wishes to dispense with the use of the SEAL (or simply not to use one), either its articles should be changed to ensure share certificates can be issued validly without being sealed, or alternatively a 'securities seal' can be retained purely for the purpose of authenticating share certificates.

Single member company

If a transfer of shares results in the company having only one member (i.e. creating a SINGLE MEMBER COMPANY, or SMC), this fact and the date of the event must be entered in the folio in the register of members for the sole member. (Should an SMC issue share(s) to an additional person, then the fact that the company is no longer an SMC, and the date, should be added to the entry in the share register for the former SMC.) The articles of a company that becomes an SMC should be examined for any implications – e.g. the quorum for meetings may be stated as 'two', which is obviously an impossibility.

Reduction of share capital

Provided there is nothing in its articles to prevent it (and if there is a bar, the articles must first be changed), a company may by SPECIAL RESOLUTION reduce its share capital. Since this could prejudice the interests of the creditors, in addition to passing the resolution (for a PLC), the permission of the court must be obtained under a scheme of arrangement regarding the reduction. The reduction can only proceed with the court's permission. However, under s. 643 CA06, court permission is not necessary for LTDs (although if they prefer, they can opt to use the court procedure). Following the passing of the special resolution, the directors must sign a solvency statement confirming that each director has formed the opinion that

- there is no ground on which the company could be unable to pay its creditors or discharge its debts;
- during the year ahead the company will be able to pay its debts as they fall due;
- (if it is intended to wind the company up in the following year) the company will be able to pay its debts in full within a year of the commencement of the winding-up process.

Two copies of the special resolution or the solvency statement must be sent to CH within 15 days of the passing of the resolution.

Buying back shares

There are strict rules regarding share buybacks, and the advice of the AUDITORS should be sought. A company can buy back up to 10 per cent of its shares and hold them 'in treasury'. During their time 'in treasury' the voting power of such shares is suspended and they do not rank for dividends. They can of course be reissued at any time and will then be treated in exactly the same way as other shares. Shares in treasury can also be cancelled, which would result in (and thus requiring the authority related to) a reduction in capital. Legal and accounting advice should be taken.

Annual general meeting

INTRODUCTION

A meeting of the shareholders (the AGM) must be held each year by all PLCs. The AGMs of most listed PLCs tend to have a much higher profile than a similar meeting of the average LTD, since not only do they tend to have a range of shareholders but also their results may be of interest to the media. It is usually the sole occasion in the year when the corporate entity is 'on display', and needs careful planning and attention to detail to ensure that the company is portrayed as competent, efficient and in as advantageous a manner as possible. Under CA06, LTDs need not hold AGMs unless their articles stipulate this, or their members or directors require it.

Convening and content

A PLC must give 21 clear days' notice of its AGM to all shareholders. However as a result of the EU's Shareholder Rights Directive (effective August 2009), if the shareholders of a listed PLC have agreed and the company offers to all its shareholders the *'facility for shareholders to vote by electronic means'*, then it need give only 14 days' notice.

An LTD which is required (or whose directors or members have opted) to hold AGMs, must give 14 days' notice (s. 307 CA06) or a longer period if the articles so require. 'Clear', for English and Welsh companies, means the day of the meeting and the day the notice is deemed served are in addition to the required period. For companies registered in Scotland, the day of the meeting can be counted as one of the days of notice.

Under the Stock Exchange listing agreement, listed PLCs are required to give their members 20 business or working days' notice (i.e., they must exclude weekends and public holidays). Ideally, to avoid claims that insufficient notice has been given, it is prudent to give more than the above minimum notice periods. In addition, items sent by first class post are not deemed to be served until 48 hours later, and thus this period should be added to the calculation of the 'days' notice' required. Notice is not normally validly served on a day on which there are no postal deliveries (that is, weekends and Bank Holidays). As an extreme example therefore, notice of a meeting despatched on Thursday 22 December might not be deemed properly served until 27 December (assuming that is not a Bank Holiday), which would then become day one of the 21 'clear' days' notice. The meeting could not be properly convened until 17 January – 27 days after posting. For a listed PLC the meeting could not be held until 24 January, i.e. 34 days after posting.

Shareholders of LTDs can waive the whole or part of the notice period for a general meeting, provided the holders of 90 per cent (unless the ARTICLES require a higher percentage – up to 95 per cent) or more of the voting rights agree.

For PLCs, notice of the AGM can be waived only if there is unanimous consent of all members. Notice of (extraordinary) general meetings can be waived, providing 95 per cent of all the votes are in favour.

Business

At the AGM the following business must be transacted, but this is not exclusive, and if other matters are timely, there is no reason why they should not be included in the notice/agenda and considered at the meeting.

- **Receipt and consideration of the accounts and balance sheet and audit report.** In smaller companies, experience indicates that there is a widespread misconception that a company's shareholders approve the report and accounts. In fact it is the *board* that must approve the report and accounts and then present them to the members. If the members purport to vote not to 'approve' the report and accounts, such action has no effect on those documents, which remain the version that must be filed with the Registrar of Companies within the required time limit. Thus using the word 'approve' in the wording of the resolution is dangerous since it implies (if the members can 'approve' the accounts) they also have a right to 'disapprove' or reject them, which they cannot (or if they purport to do so, it has no effect on the status of the accounts which must be filed at CH).
- **Approval of any DIVIDEND on the shares**. Shareholders have control over a final dividend only. Normally the payment of interim dividends is the prerogative of the board and needs no shareholder approval. However, shareholders can approve, reduce or reject the amount of a final dividend recommended by the board. If the board feel that shareholders might reject the final dividend, this is easily avoided by the board resolving to pay an interim (or second interim) dividend on their own authority. However, there is no obligation on the board to pay a dividend at all. (Obviously, if the company was profitable and there was no reason for not paying a dividend, the shareholders' recourse would be either the DIRECTORS: REMOVAL or application to the court.)
- **Election or re-election of directors**. If the ARTICLES require a proportion of the directors (often a third) to retire at each AGM, the third of the directors who are the longest serving must retire and, assuming

they wish to do so, can put themselves forward for re-election by the shareholders at the meeting. Directors appointed since the last AGM also have an obligation to retire at the next following AGM and (if they wish) to seek re-election by the shareholders. The requirement to retire by rotation is on the decrease for companies other than charities, some guarantee companies, and listed PLCs (where under the Listing Agreement a proportion of directors are required to retire and seek re-election each year).

- **Election or re-election of AUDITORS.**
- **Authorisation of the directors to agree the remuneration of the auditors,** although normally the shareholders delegate this task to the directors. Companies whose turnover is less than £6.5 million are no longer legally required to have their accounts audited (unless they are also subject to the requirements of the charity or financial services regulators). The EU is suggesting that companies with a turnover of less than €1,000,000 should not need to file accounts at all (see AUDITORS).

Preparation

The AGM is the one occasion in the year when the company could be said to be 'on show'. Where many members (particularly those not also on the board) are likely to attend the meeting, attention needs to be given to every aspect of its presentation, in the widest sense of the word. Using a checklist such as the following may be appropriate. Obviously progress should be monitored by the board/company secretary on a regular basis, with all preparations being checked in detail, say, one month prior to the event.

CHECKLIST Preparation for annual general meeting

Item	Responsibility
Decide date and time	Board
Visit venue, check facilities	Co. sec./ board
Book venue (6–12 months ahead) – check:	
✓ room and overflow facility	
✓ air conditioning/ventilation	
✓ acoustics/amplification	
✓ accommodation, including catering/toilet facilities	
✓ noticeboards/room directions	
✓ tables for signing in	
If product/photo display required	Marketing dept
✓ display tables or electronic equipment	

Stipulate to venue management :	Co. sec.
✓ timetable for arrivals	
✓ serving tea/coffee	
✓ lunch (if required) ·	
✓ likely departure	
Delegate items to staff :	As allocated
✓ greeting arrivals (especially 'speakers')	
✓ ensuring arrivals sign in (taking attendance cards)	
✓ ushering to seats	
✓ care of registers & proxies	
✓ acting as teller(s) (in event of VOTING AND TAKING A POLL)	
✓ care of statutory books, service contracts, minute book	
✓ liaison with catering	
✓ spare copies of annual report, publicity handouts	
Arrange 'speakers'	Co. sec.
✓ 'tame' members (and back-up in event of absence), who will actually propose and/or second the various resolutions to avoid it looking like too much of a one-person show (i.e. the chairman's)	
Anticipate and prepare for any hostility	Chairman
✓ liaise with advisers (see VOTING)	
✓ preparation of and answers to awkward questions	
✓ If chairman is new to running formal meetings:	
✓ preparation of chairman's crib (i.e. a script to cover each part of the meeting – see BRIEFING THE CHAIRMAN)	Co. sec.
Promulgate timetable and checklist	Co. sec.
✓ briefing on preparations, likely problems etc. (i.e. a meeting scenario) for board and advisers	
Liaison with:	Finance director
✓ auditors (have a right to attend and may read the Audit Report)	
✓ solicitors, stockbrokers (for listed PLC)	Co. sec.
✓ public relations (and, through them, media representatives	Corporate PR
✓ Company registrar (including printing of DIVIDEND cheques and tax vouchers, and arrangements for granting authority to post)	Co. sec.
Transport arrangements for directors, staff, guests, major shareholders etc.	Transport mgr.

Arrange for display of products/tour of premises (either   Director
actual or electronic):

✓ Press release: Corporate PR

✓ if required, draft and agree with chairman in advance,
   possibly amending should this be required following
   the meeting.

Style

Those attending will have received the ANNUAL REPORT which, for a listed
PLC, must include a chairman's statement. Both report and statement will
have used (whether deliberately or not) a certain style and tone, which
should normally be reflected in the AGM's presentation. If the company is
reporting on a very successful year and has strong plans for the future, the
tone taken at the AGM could be confident and assertive. If the year has been
difficult and such difficulties still exist, a 'determination in adversity' type of
approach might be best adopted.

Documentation

Notice

The prime documentation for the AGM is the AGENDA and NOTICE of the
meeting, which is usually included by custom in the annual report although
there is no requirement for this and it could be sent separately, which some
listed PLCs now do, particularly where an informal letter inviting (i.e.
urging) shareholders to attend the meeting accompanies the notice.

Letter of invitation

An increasing number of listed PLCs, particularly those with numbers of
private (i.e. non-institutional) shareholders send a semi-personal 'letter of
invitation' to shareholders to attend the meeting with the formal notice.
This may also explain the logic and reasoning behind business to be transacted – e.g. changing the ARTICLES etc.

Intention and attendance cards

Companies with large numbers of shareholders, many of whom may wish
to attend the meeting often send their shareholders 'intention of attending'
and 'admission' cards. Shareholders are urged to return the 'intention' cards

in advance, simply to provide a likely 'number of attendees' total, knowing which is useful for security, accommodation, catering etc. Using 'admission' cards on arrival can aid swift admittance, and also assist identification when there is a need for increased security vigilance. Obviously no shareholder without a card should be barred from entry – processing their admittance may simply take more time.

Proxy

Proxy cards will have been sent with the agenda or notice of meeting and should be lodged with the company (specifically with the company secretary or the share registrar of the company), and these should be checked and an analysis of the support for and opposition to each resolution passed to the chairman before the meeting. The proxy cards themselves should be available at the meeting and those processing attendance need to be able to cross-reference the proxy cards with the attendees' lists, in case someone who has already lodged a proxy then attends in person. There is nothing wrong with this, but obviously their votes must not be counted twice. The value of the proxy card as a source of up-to-date information, for example regarding addresses, should not be overlooked. A 'change of address' notification could form part of the card.

A member of a company can appoint more than one proxy. Thus a shareholder could appoint a proxy for several tranches of the same holding (e.g. 100 different proxies each acting for 1 share of a holding of 100 shares). Whilst this could be useful for voting on a show of hands, since all one hundred votes would then be counted, this is fairly pointless since the proxy (if they disagree with the result of a show of hands vote) is usually empowered to demand or join in the demanding of a poll, in which case all the votes are counted.

Some listed PLCs have changed their ARTICLES OF ASSOCIATION so that voting at general meetings cannot be effected by a show of hands (which only grants one vote per person) but only by poll (one vote per share), thus ensuring all resolutions reflect the true voting strength.

Informal communication

Since such meetings may be fairly formal, a custom has been growing with listed PLCs for members of the board to make themselves available at the AGM venue, say, 30 minutes before meetings (and/or for some time afterwards) so that shareholders can talk directly to them. At least one leading listed PLC invites shareholders to send in details of any 'shareholders' topics' for consideration at the AGM. The advantage of 'drawing' any hostility from the more public domain of the meeting in this way should not be underestimated, although directors of listed PLCs need to be careful regarding any comments they may make at such meetings, to avoid falling foul of insider dealing legislation. For most LTDs the AGM is likely to be a less formal event, and such informal contact can be achieved relatively easily and with fewer 'leakage' concerns.

Developments

Some companies have been investigating holding their AGM at more than one location (e.g. using a number of regional meeting points) to save excessive travel of shareholders based remotely from the meeting location. Such meeting points would then be linked by closed circuit television to the central location where the board (and perhaps a high proportion of shareholders) might be present.

Case study	Meeting remotely
	In *Byng v London Life* the Court of Appeal held that that a shareholders' meeting could be held in more than one place provided there were *fully functional mutual audio-visual links* in all locations. Thus it would not be possible to hold a general meeting validly using only an audio or written (e.g. e-mail) link.

Using two or three locations is possibly appropriate, but any more could pose considerable problems. Before taking advantage of such a ruling, legal advice would need to be taken, and it might be preferable for the ARTICLES to be changed to avoid any challenge, and to address the situation regarding the possible invalidation of the meeting should one or more of the links between the venues break down.

Members' right to convene

General meetings are usually convened by the board. However members can also require a meeting to be convened. See (extraordinary) GENERAL MEETINGS.

Annual report

INTRODUCTION

Every company must produce a report each year giving an account of its progress (or lack of progress) for its members. Since the document must also be filed with the REGISTRAR OF COMPANIES, effectively the report is made to the world at large. The requirement to file information with the Registrar protects (at least in theory) the interests of those who have advanced credit to the company. Thus creditors may wish to (and many do) inspect the accounts included with the Report to check the perceived 'safety' of their debts although, since the accounts do not have to be filed for several months after the end of the financial year, this right and the 'opportunity to check' may be regarded as somewhat academic, as the results are considerably out of date. An 'unlimited company' is not obliged to file its accounts (unless it is part of a group which includes other limited liability companies), since the liability of its shareholders to its creditors is unlimited (thus, if the company fails, the unpaid creditors can proceed against the shareholders personally).

Content

The annual report of a high-profile listed PLC requires considerable investment in both time and money, but, since it can be as much a public relations document as a document of record, this may be cost-effective. Although the required content is in principle virtually identical for an LTD, usually a far more modest document will suffice for such companies.

(a) The chairman's statement

Listed PLCs must under listing requirements include in their report, a lengthy chairman's statement. Indeed this is often virtually the focal point of the whole document. The statement usually includes comment on:

- the financial and other results;
- any recommended final dividend;
- significant developments and changes;
- competition and market conditions;
- political and economic developments;
- capital expenditure and requirements;

- training and managerial development;
- staff contribution;
- CORPORATE SOCIAL RESPONSIBILITY;
- CORPORATE GOVERNANCE;
- ENVIRONMENTAL OBLIGATIONS;
- future expectations, and so on;

and then provides a detailed review of each part of the company.

CHECKLIST   Preparation of chairman's statement

✓ Decide on theme and style.

✓ Collate background data from previous statements, interim statement, media comment and interviews, results of direct competitors.

✓ Collate data on external factors – political, economic, environmental etc. – which have impacted/could impact business.

✓ Assess impact of results on current and future prospects.

✓ Report on capability of personnel current and anticipated and steps being taken to ensure adequate skills supply.

See also BRIEFING THE CHAIRMAN.

(b) Report of the directors

This is a legally required statement, and the advice from the company's AUDITORS should be sought to ensure compliance with the latest requirements. The contents include:

- statement of the principal activities of the company;
- summary of the trading results;
- transfers to and from reserves and any movements in assets in the period under review;
- notes regarding the dividends paid and proposed;
- details of acquisitions and disposals;
- details of all who have been DIRECTORS during the year under review and, for those seeking re-election at the AGM, of any SERVICE CONTRACTS;
- details of the AUDITORS and a note regarding their re-election or replacement;
- statements concerning developments in employment, employee involvement, disabled employees and health and safety;
- statements regarding donations made, separating political donations from others;
- a statement regarding major shareholdings (if any) in the company;

- a statement regarding the development of the business;
- information regarding any share option and/or share ownership scheme(s);
- information regarding any activities of significance that have taken place since the date of the balance sheet;
- a statement that the directors take responsibility for the financial statements and accounts.

(c) Annual accounts

The directors must provide a complete package giving a true and fair picture of the financial state of the company. In addition, unless the company is exempt, or is under the audit threshold, the accounts must be backed by an auditor's statement to that effect. The accounts package will normally comprise a profit and loss statement, funds flow statement, balance sheet, details of accounting policies and any change thereto, plus full supporting and explanatory notes.

(d) Notice and agenda of the annual general meeting

Whilst most annual reports include the AGENDA and notice of the ANNUAL GENERAL MEETING, this is not a requirement. However, there is logic in such inclusion, as the accounts and balance sheet, together with a note of any dividend proposed, must be given to the members. (Under CA06 an LTD is not obliged to hold an AGM, unless its articles or the directors require it or the shareholders vote to require one.)

(e) Auditors' statement

The accounts must be accompanied by a statement, drafted and signed by the company's auditors, indicating that the accounts give a true and fair view of the state of the company's financial affairs as at the date of the balance sheet. If the auditors feel this is not the case they may wish to qualify their statement and will state the scope of such qualification within their report. Companies whose annual turnover does not exceed £6.5 million (and which are not charities or involved in financial services) are not required to have their accounts audited. In excess of 90 per cent of the companies able to take advantage of this relaxation have indicated they will continue to have their accounts audited, for a variety of practical reasons, particularly if they want to borrow money, since almost certainly any prospective lender will insist that the accounts are audited.

(f) Directors' biographical details

Listed PLCs are required to provide full details of all prospective appointees to the board and of directors retiring by rotation, together with details of the sub-committees of the board on which they sit. An increasing number of companies provide personal details of all their directors in every report.

(g) Statement of compliance with requirements of the Combined Code of Corporate Governance

Currently this is only required of listed PLCs (see CORPORATE GOVER-NANCE). A company that does not comply with the detailed requirements must provide an explanation for its non-compliance.

Business review

The business review could be described as the 'son of operating and financial review', which after two years' preparation was scrapped without warning during the pre-budget review of November 2005 – to widespread condemnation from those who had spent time and money preparing for the requirement. As a form of response, s. 417 CA06 requires companies to publish a business review, the purpose of which is to inform members and help them assess how the directors have performed their duty to promote the success of the company having regard to employees, community and the environment. The requirement affects all but small companies even though the original requirement affected only PLCs and large LTDs.

The review must contain:

- a fair review of the company's business;
- a description of the principal risks and uncertainties facing the company;

and be a fair analysis of:

- the development and performance of the company's business; and
- the position of the company's business at the end of the financial year.

For the purpose of understanding the performance, development or position of business, it must also provide analysis:

- using financial key performance indicators; and
- where appropriate, using other key performance indicators, including information relating to environmental and employment matters.

(These last two items of non-financial information are optional for medium-sized companies.)

Listed PLCs must also state:

- trends and factors likely to affect the company's future development;
- principal risks and uncertainties facing the company;

- information concerning environmental matters, employees and social and community issues;
- details of key contracts (that is 'significant relationships with major suppliers which are likely to affect (directly or indirectly) the value and performance of the business').

Directors are personally liable for the content of the report and could be held liable to compensate anyone for any loss they suffer as a result of any untrue or misleading statement in, or any omission from, the report, if they knew (or were reckless as to whether) the statement was true – or knew the statement to be a dishonest concealment of a material fact. (See OPERATING AND BUSINESS REVIEW.)

Additional obligations for listed PLCs

Listed PLCs are required to comply (or explain any non-compliance) with the combined code of CORPORATE GOVERNANCE. Thus a listed PLC's annual report must comply with the recent additional contents requirements, namely, disclosure of:

- the manner of the board operation; the types of decisions taken by the board and those that are delegated to management;
- the names of the chairman, deputy chairman (if applicable), the chief executive, the senior independent director and the chairman and members of the various board committees (i.e. nomination, audit and remuneration);
- the number of board and board committees meetings; and individual attendance at both by directors;
- the names of non-executive directors that are independent (and the reasons for that assessment);
- any significant commitment(s) of the chairman outside the company;
- the manner in which the board, its committees and members are evaluated;
- the procedure by which the board (especially non-executive directors); understand the views of the company's major shareholders.

The following must also be stated:

- how the board's nomination committee carries out its work in finding new board appointees and explaining whether the advice of external advisers has been sought regarding the appointment of the chairman or deputy chairman;
- how the board's remuneration committee complies with the requirements of the Directors Remuneration Report Regulations 2002;
- whether any executive directors serve as non-executive directors of other companies and, if paid, whether the directors retain such earnings;

- statements explaining the directors' responsibility for preparing the accounts and (from the auditors) their reporting responsibilities;
- that, subject to any qualifications, and/or with assumptions used, the business is a going concern;
- that the board has conducted a review of the effectiveness of the internal controls used by the company;
- details of the work of the board's audit committee and, (if applicable) the reasons for not using an internal audit function;
- should the board have refused to accept a report and recommendations from the audit committee regarding the appointment/retention of the external auditors, the reasons for that rejection;
- details of any non-audit work the external auditor carries out for the company.

In addition, the following information is required to be disclosed either in the annual report or on the company's website:

- the terms of reference of the board's committees (nomination, remuneration and audit) explaining their roles and authority;
- the terms and conditions of appointment of the non-executive directors;
- a statement, if any remuneration consultants were appointed, of whether they had any other connections with the company.

Where there is a resolution regarding the re-election of directors/auditors, the company must provide:

- such biographical details that will enable shareholders to take an informed decision on their election or re-election;
- the reason(s) for someone being elected to a non-executive directorship;
- if the re-election of a non-executive director is to be considered, the chairman's confirmation that the performance of the person has been evaluated and has been found to be effective;
- if the re-election of an auditor is to be considered and the audit committee's recommendation is not accepted by the board, a statement showing both the recommendation and the reason(s) for the board opposing the recommendation.

Preparation

The preparation of an annual report is a lengthy and complex operation, particularly for a listed PLC, where it is customary for the document to be presented to a high standard, including a pictorial review of the activities, products etc., in addition to the legally required contents. (Such documents approach what could be described as 'corporate brochures', and are often used for promotional purposes.) The main areas requiring attention are:

1 Determine impression to be given (e.g. forward-looking, high-quality, retrenching, expansionist, etc.).
2 Determine theme and, if reports are written by a number of executives, ensure this theme is used consistently.
3 Determine type of report required in relation to company, and brief those invited to contribute.
4 Calculate budget and gain approval.
5 Prepare draft layout and content and gain approval.
6 Suggest and gain approval for size, paper, typeface and style, since each individually and collectively give an impression of the company.
7 Appoint project leader.
8 Prepare detailed timetable, allowing flexibility.
9 Check space requirements with auditors (e.g. new or revised accounting requirements may mean a greater space being required to display financial data).
10 Prepare proforma report and obtain quotation from typesetters and printers based on proforma and specification.
11 Agree timetables with all involved (including accounts staff, public relations advisers, auditors, designers, typesetters and printers, registrars and despatch).
12 Agree timetable with chairman/board who will need to give final approval possibly at short notice.
13 Publish timetable and contact names/telephone numbers to all involved.
14 Agree proofing turnround and discuss procedure with those involved. Advise printers of numbers of proof copies required and destination in each case.
15 Communicate each step with all involved. Ensure those writing items for the report are chased for copy as deadlines approach.

CHECKLIST Timetable for the production of the annual report

Item	D: Despatch Day
✓ Prepare budget and timetable (in liaison with interested parties)	D minus 100 days
✓ Prepare editor's brief, board specification and commitment to theme, style, design, concept, etc. Prepare mock-up.	
✓ Prepare proforma and send to auditors to assess space requirements	D minus 95
✓ Notify public relations advisors of publication and check possible clashes (e.g. are major companies or competitors likely to report around the same time?)	D minus 90
✓ Photographer/illustrator specifications drafted	

✓ Chairman's Statement 1st draft	
✓ Executives' Reports 1st draft	
✓ Employee Report 1st draft	
✓ Proxy and other cards 1st draft	
✓ Chairman's Statement, etc. 2nd draft	D minus 80
✓ Photographer/illustrator commissioned *	
✓ Analyse numbers of report required	D minus 70
✓ Chairman's Statement 3rd draft and copy to typesetter/printer	D minus 60
✓ Liaise with Registrars & provide checklist	
✓ Liaise with corporate public relations (PR)	
✓ Liaise with brokers	
✓ First proof back, checked & returned to printers	D minus 50
✓ Second proof to company/auditors	
✓ Photographs reviewed and agreed	D minus 40
✓ Third proof (colour) to company/auditors	
✓ Preliminary announcement	D minus 30
✓ Insert figures in third proof for printers	(Hold period: D minus 30 to D minus 25) **
✓ Commission Dividend Warrants	
✓ Final proof checked by company/auditors agreed	
✓ Print order given. Printers liaise with registrars re mailing addresses	D minus 20
✓ Report despatched externally	D minus 1
✓ Report despatched internally	D day

* Some companies retain a photographer to capture events during the year so that illustrations are available when the report is being created.

** A 'hold' period provides time for an objective consideration of the production when no deadlines are pressing. In practice, it tends to be used to catch up on earlier slippages in the timetable!

Approval and filing

The board must formally approve the company's individual (and any consolidated) accounts and balance sheet and the directors' report and business review. A director must sign the balance sheet but the directors' report can be signed either by a director or the COMPANY SECRETARY. The signatories' full names must be shown on the printed copies. The accounts and balance sheet are then presented to the members of the company in general meeting and (a black and white copy) must be filed with the REGISTRAR OF COMPANIES within the following time limits (as required under CA06):

- by the end of the sixth month (after the financial year end or accounting reference date) for PLCs;
- by the end of the ninth month for LTDs.

Failure to file accounts within these strict time limits renders the company liable to a fine (currently ranging from £150 to £15,000, depending on the status of the company and the delay in filing) and, for those responsible, to prosecution.

Companies can (and listed PLCs must, under s. 430 of CA06) post their results on their website and, with the permission of individual shareholders, can use the provision of such electronic information as a substitute for providing shareholders with a hard copy of the above statutorily required information. (See ELECTRONIC COMMUNICATIONS.)

The accounts of a newly incorporated company must be filed not more than nine months after incorporation or not more than three months after its first accounting reference date (FINANCIAL YEAR END), whichever is the later.

Summary financial statements (SFS)

Research indicates that very few recipients actually read annual reports, and even fewer understand them. The Chartered Accountants of Scotland Institute once stated that many accounts are capable of being understood only by their compilers. Thus, for some years listed PLCs have been able to produce an SFS for those shareholders not wishing to receive the full report yet wanting to see the salient points of the results. An SFS must contain:

- details of developments of the business during the year under review and since the year end;
- profit and loss account;
- balance sheet;
- comparative figures;
- details of directors;
- events since year end;

and must state that a member has a right to apply for a copy of the full report.

The SFS must:

- state that it is a summary;
- contain an auditor's statement that it is consistent with the full report;
- state whether the auditor's report of the full report was unqualified or not; and
- be signed by a named director on behalf of the board.

A company whose articles incorporate Table A of an earlier CA may find that their ARTICLES OF ASSOCIATION do not allow them to send an SFS in place of the full accounts, and before they do so, they must first change their articles.

Requesting an SFS

Shareholders must be asked their preference, by either the passive or the active method. The passive method entails sending both SFS and annual report to the shareholders with a reply-paid card. To receive subsequent full reports the shareholder must return the card indicating this.

The active method entails canvassing the shareholders in advance as to their choice; if they do not reply then they should be sent the full report.

Employee reports

In the interests of employee communication as well as the movement to encourage more employees to become shareholders, there was a need for a report capable of providing information to non-financially aware employees. Some companies (even those that produce an SFS) also produce employee reports. The overall aim of an employee report can be stated as being *'to present the financial results, statistics, and facts in a way that they can be understood by everyone – not just accountants'*.

Whilst the following checklists have been framed for use when producing simplified reports primarily for employees, the precepts apply also to the production of an SFS and, it could be argued, to no small extent to try to make it easier to understand the full report.

CHECKLIST Content of employee report

✓ Statements of the aims of the business and of the report.
✓ Statement by the chairman – in ordinary user-friendly English, avoiding or explaining jargon.
✓ Highlights of the year.
✓ Simplified balance sheet, with an explanation of terms used.
✓ Simplified profit & loss a/c or added value statement.
✓ Statement of sales and profit, particularly expressed on a per employee, or a localised or divisional basis.
✓ General information regarding products or services, employees, share schemes, environmental and community matters, etc.
✓ Organisation chart and developments.

In all cases, graphics and illustrations which support and complement the above, should be used, as most readers can understand trends and proportions far more easily if expressed in graphic form than in a line or list of print. Using graphics should help achieve better reader comprehension.

CHECKLIST   Use of graphics

✓ Keep it simple – avoiding making one illustration do too much.

✓ Either use base lines of zero or clearly indicate that the zero has been suppressed. Using a base that is other than zero (that is, 'suppressing the zero') can have the effect of seriously distorting the impression of movement in the subject matter. For those used to dealing with statistics, inserting what is called a 'lightning' mark in the vertical axis to draw attention to this, may be acceptable; but for any target audience not used to statistics it is inexcusable, as the effect is often to confuse rather than explain. (It must be said that suppressed zeros are widely used, sometimes deliberately without any lightning marks to warn the unwary viewer that the variations in the graphic are accentuated.)

✓ Two-dimensional representations may result in greater clarity than three-dimensional representations. The problem with three-dimensional representations is that it can be difficult to establish the exact location of the base line. If so the dimensions of the relative items may also be confusing.

✓ Ensure all illustrations or graphics are of a decent and appropriate size.

✓ Ensure accuracy of all representations. A pictorial message can be far more powerful than text commentary. Inaccuracy in what are powerful visual images can mislead the reader as well as undermine the integrity not just of the item in question but of the whole report.

✓ Percentages are not generally understood (as one politician stated recently, *'Half the population do not know what 50 per cent means'*) and may be best avoided unless both figures which indicate the percentage difference or change are stated.

✓ Use bold colours – but not too many, or they may overwhelm the message.

✓ Check that colours have not been used in a way that indicates a 'code' (e.g. that two or more entirely disparate items are not represented by the same or a similar colour).

✓ Photos, illustrations and graphics should be given captions unless they are placed in immediate juxtaposition with the copy they support and are referred to in such copy (and thus need no further explanation).

✓ Ensure the whole document is enticing – particularly both back and front covers.

✓ Named employees and products should be well-featured.

✓ All copy should be specially written for the report. It should avoid (or explain) jargon, not shirk bad news or be couched in patronising terms. Above all, hype should be avoided.

Follow-up

Having produced an employee report, care should be taken with distribution to ensure all employees are given a copy, ideally, at the same time. In addition, briefing meetings should be held with as many of the target audience as possible to ensure that questions generated by the report and its contents can be answered. The publication of such a report should be seen as part of a long-term aim of improving communication – one of the requirements of new legislation regarding employee consultation. Consistency of reporting may be as important as the content.

Abbreviated reports are required to carry a statement to the effect that the results are an extract from the full reports and accounts for the company which have been lodged with the Registrar of Companies. (See s. 427 CA06.)

Postscript

As noted above, many reports are not easy to understand – very often the requirements of the target audience are overlooked. Their compilers should bear in mind the comment that their aim in compiling the report should not be so much as to make it easy for a reader to understand the content as to make the content impossible for the reader to misunderstand!

Annual return

INTRODUCTION

Once shareholders were granted the legal protection of limiting their liability to the nominal value of their shares, should their company fail, companies were obliged to make certain information public – the price of limited liability protection being disclosure of information. Such disclosure is achieved by means of records, available for public inspection or reference, being kept on every company, by the REGISTRAR OF COMPANIES at CH. Data on changes to the status, control, results and direction of each company is required to be filed – mainly on forms either made freely available by the Registrar or downloaded from the Registrar's website. Public disclosure (by making such records available to all-comers) then enables anyone with an interest in a company (particularly its creditors) to inspect such information.

Annual obligation

To ensure that these public records are up to date, each year every company must provide a return of the salient information regarding the corporate entity to the Registrar. The return must be filed accompanied by a payment of £15 (or £30, if filing in hard copy) and a declaration signed by a director or the company secretary. The return must be filed within a set time limit – failure to file the return by the 'due date' can result in the officers of the company being fined and prosecuted, and even in the company being struck off the register. The 'due date' is the date not more than 28 days after the 'return date'; whilst the 'return date' is any date convenient to the company which is not later than the anniversary of the 'return date' to which the previous return was made up. Thus the return date of a subsequent return can be brought forward but not postponed.

The return

The form (AR01) which now constitutes the annual return has been completely redesigned as a result of CA06. It is divided into a number of parts. There is also a new distinction between 'traded companies' (companies whose shares are traded on the main Stock Exchange), and 'non-traded companies' (LTDs and PLCs whose shares either are not quoted/listed, or are traded on the Alternative Investment Market). For non-traded companies, addresses of their shareholders are not required.

Part 1

This consists of three pages requiring details regarding:

- the name of the company and its registered number;
- the date to which the return is made up. A return can be made up to any date no later than the anniversary of the date of the previous return. However, the Registrar has powers to prevent a change of return date if the last two returns have been filed late;
- details of the principal business activity (in accordance with the trade classification code or a description of the main business activity if the code 'cannot be determined');
- the company type (i.e. PLC, LTD by shares, LTD by guarantee etc.);
- the address of the registered office. Currently the registered office can only be situated in the country in which the company is registered. Thus a company registered in England and Wales can only have its registered office in England or Wales, and a company registered in Scotland can only have its registered office in Scotland, and a Northern Ireland company must have its registered office in Northern Ireland. However under the draft 14th Company Law directive, the EU proposes allowing complete transferability of registered offices within its boundaries. Any change of location of the registered office must be notified to the Registrar on form AD01 (under s. 87 CA06; formerly s. 287 CA85);
- details of a designated office (the SAIL or Single Alternative Inspection Location) where the company records can be inspected. This must have been advised using form AD02 and if not, that form must accompany the annual return;
- details of which records are held at the SAIL. However if all the records are held at the registered office none of the boxes need to be completed.

Part 2

This requires the company to provide details of its officers:

- an individual who is the secretary;
- the secretary's service address (which can be the company's registered office);
- (if applicable) a corporate secretary;
- if there is a corporate secretary, where the location of the register concerning that body is kept, either within or outside the EEA;
- individual directors of the company (if these details are different from

the file at CH then the appropriate form (e.g. CH01) must accompany the return);

- the service address(es) of each director (this can be the registered office of the company; from 1 October 2009 only the service address needs to be shown for every director);
- (if applicable) a corporate director;
- if there is a corporate director, where the location of the register concerning that body is kept, either within or outside the EEA.

Part 3

Requires details of the share capital of the company, both in sterling and any other currency.

Part 4

Requires details of the shareholders. Private LTDs and non-quoted or listed PLCs need only provide a full list of shareholders if one did not accompany the last two returns. Because they are 'traded' companies, quoted or listed PLCs must provide a list and details of all shareholders holding 5 per cent or more of each share class.

A 'traded' company is one whose shares are traded on a 'regulated market' i.e. the main Stock Exchange market. Companies listed on the Alternative Investment Market, and private LTD companies are now designated as 'non-traded'. For non-traded companies, shareholders' addresses must not be shown; if they are, the return will be rejected. Electronic filing of a non-traded company's return will not allow the entry of shareholders' addresses.

Part 5

Is a signatory clause with space for the signature of the presenter, followed by a 'presenter information', completion of which is voluntary, and a number of continuation pages in case the space provided for earlier data provision was insufficient.

If paying by cheque (made payable to 'Companies House'), it is suggested that the company number to which the return refers should be written on the reverse of the cheque (since many cheques that accompany returns are drawn on bank accounts other than that of the subject company, and if cheque and return are separated, it may be difficult to link them again).

Continuation pages

There are a number of extra pages if space in the main return is insufficient.

Completion problems – and fining for lateness

The Registrar states that nearly 30 per cent of the previous version of the annual return contained incorrect information and had to be returned. In addition it was claimed that a considerable number of envelopes for hard copy filings contained a cheque but without the return – as well as a number containing the return but without a cheque. CH also claim to receive a number of entirely empty envelopes! Having the presenter's contact details enables speedy return of the document and may allow resubmission without infringing the time limit within which the return must be filed. A substantial proportion of all returns are filed late, which can incur a fine. In 2008 the Registrar levied just under £55 million in penalties for late filing of required documentation (mainly annual returns and accounts).

If filing by hard copy, it is advisable to keep a photocopy of the return. The original should be sent to the Registrar with a covering letter (in duplicate and with a stamped return envelope) or with a POST 31 form (available from CH) asking for a receipt. In both cases the Registrar attaches an adhesive barcode to the document and returns it. A company's first return, if not made up earlier, must be made up to the anniversary of the date of the company's incorporation.

Returns *must* be filed with the Registrar within 28 days of the operative date if a penalty is to be avoided. Late or non-filing an annual return is a criminal offence. Thus if a return is late or not filed, the Registrar can take action to require compliance with the obligation including prosecution of the directors, and, if judgement is granted, those responsible may be given a criminal record and a one-off fine of up to £5,000 plus a fine of £500 for *each day* the company was in default (that is for each day the return was late).

Electronic filing

The majority of annual returns are now filed electronically. Companies wishing to use this facility are required to register via the Registrar's website and to obtain (by post) an authentication code. The payment fee can be collected by credit card transfer or via the account system (currently used for the CH Direct service – see REGISTRAR OF COMPANIES).

Articles of association

INTRODUCTION

Since 1856, the constitution of a limited liability company formed under company law has been set out in 'external' and 'internal' contracts entered into by the member(s) and made public. The external contract exists between the members and the outside world, in that it states what the company was set up to achieve – its objects or aims. For existing companies, the company's objects are set out in its memorandum of association; but if companies are formed under CA06 and wish to adopt objects clauses, these will have to set these out in their articles. The internal contract exists between the shareholders and the directors and officers they appoint to run their company and is set out in the articles of association. At one time during the consultation on CA06 it was suggested that the contents of these two contracts should be revised and amalgamated to form a single document – the company's 'Constitution' – but this has not been entirely followed through (although the MEMORANDUM for a company formed under CA06 will be a very skeletal document, and all the 'rules' will be within the articles). In addition, under CA06, companies (other than charities) will no longer need to adopt objects clauses.

The articles are the 'rules' under which those that own the company expect those they have chosen to run their company – its officers – to run it. Hence the board (and particularly the company secretary advising them) need to be familiar with the articles' requirements. In the event of any question concerning the control of the company or the operations or activities of its directors, an immediate query should be 'What do the articles say?'

Adoption

All companies are legally required to have articles – under s. 17 CA06 these are referred to as the Constitution of the company. Although there is no required format, every CA has contained model sets of articles. Unlike previous CAs (which contained model articles), model articles for PLCs and for LTDs limited both by shares and by guarantee do not form part of CA06, but are available separately. If a company feels that it can operate with such standard rules, it simply adopts these instead of drafting its own set of articles – indeed if no articles are adopted, the Act's set of articles as at the date of the company's registration apply by default as far as is possible (s. 20).

Although it is administratively simple to adopt a pro-forma set of articles in its entirety, many companies 'cherry-pick', using the sections they require, and drafting their own articles either in substitution for those they discard, or simply devising their own additions or versions of individual regulations. The 'standard' forms of articles are really intended only to be used as a base to facilitate customised versions.

A company can include virtually any provision in its articles, although legal advice should be sought (for example, to ensure any restrictions are feasible and not illegal), and, once adopted, such provisions become binding. The original articles are adopted by being signed by each subscriber to the MEMORANDUM (each signature needing to be witnessed) and filed with the Registrar as part of the INCORPORATION of the company.

Notes

1   If, in drafting articles, only a selection of the regulations from the pro forma is used, it is helpful to set out in full the contents of those sections plus any customised articles. Unfortunately for many LTDs registered under earlier Acts, the articles simply cross-refer to 'Table A' (or 'Table C', for a guarantee company), leaving the reader to source (hopefully the correct edition of) the appropriate table before they can comprehend the full requirements placed on their company. Even then, this is no simple task, as two detailed documents need to be read as one.

2   By the time CA06 is fully in force there will be around three million UK companies most of whose articles will be based on the Tables set out in CA85. Table A of CA85 was drafted in the early 1980s, when, for example, only 10 per cent of UK companies owned or leased a computer. It is unlikely that operating a company with such articles is entirely appropriate for many companies at the end of the first decade of the 21st century! Since, if the directors act in breach of the articles, they can be held personally liable for such acts (and must account to the company for any profit they make), regularly reviewing the articles (and updating them if necessary) is essential.

Changing the articles

To change its articles a company must obtain the approval of its members by means of a special RESOLUTION (i.e. one that requires the approval of at least 75 per cent of the votes cast in person or by proxy) at either the AGM or at an (extraordinary) GENERAL MEETING or by WRITTEN RESOLUTION (which needs support from 75 per cent of the *total* voting strength, not just of the votes cast). Such resolutions must be filed with the Registrar within 15 days of being passed.

If the change is minor (or only affects part of the articles), the wording of the special resolution could simply include details of such change, although companies formed under Acts other than CA06 who wish to change their articles must now incorporate their objects clauses (direct from their memorandum, or as revised with the authority of the shareholders), so this would also have to be set out in the notice. However, as a result of CA06, the availability of the new drafts, and the requirement to incorporate the objects clauses, it may be felt more appropriate to change – and thus update – the entire articles. This may be particularly apposite for groups with subsidiaries registered under earlier Acts. If a group wishes to set up a new subsidiary after 1 October 2009, it must be formed under CA06. The company secretary (or other person responsible for compliance) will then have the challenge of dealing with different sets of articles derived from different legislative enactments.

To change the articles, the reasons for each change and its effect should be outlined in the notice to the members, with the advice that a copy of the proposed new articles (or the whole revisions) is available to those who wish to inspect it (if one is not sent with the notice). Once approved, the redrafted articles must be lodged at CH.

The proforma articles for an LTD limited by shares accompanying CA06 are much shorter (only 53 sections, or 86 for a PLC) than, for example, Table A of CA85 which contains 118 regulations. Companies wishing to use the new draft may wish to retain some of the large number of items have been omitted. Some of those for consideration for retention are included in the following checklist.

Checklist   CA85 Table A regulations (in brackets) for consideration for retention when using CA06 drafts as basis

(a) Granting the right to the company to have a lien over shares where the shareholder has not paid in full for the amount due (CA85, Table A reg. 8). Alternatively consideration could be given to reserving the right to disenfranchise shares where calls made have not been paid.

(b) The administration by which the board can make calls on shares issued partly paid (reg. 12).

(c) How shares are to be transferred (regs 23 and 25-31).

(d) If an LTD wishes to continue to convene AGMs the provisions concerning such meetings need to be added (regs 36-63).

(e) If an LTD wishes to continue to operate with a company secretary, it might be as well to make this clear (reg. 99).

And so on.

Companies are not allowed to:

- make any article unalterable;
- increase the size of the majority required to authorise a change in its articles beyond that required for a special resolution (that is 75 per cent of the votes cast when voting in person or by proxy or, if by written resolution, 75 per cent of the total voting strength);
- increase the financial liability of its members without their written authority, or to require members to subscribe for additional shares. However where there are different classes of shares, a company may be able to incorporate article(s), the effect of which could be to restrict the rights of holders of those shares. Legal advice should be sought if this is required as the law gives protection where such interests might be prejudiced.

Knowledge of the articles

At one of the first conferences I attended as a newly qualified company secretary, the then Registrar of Companies addressing us, stated: *'You company secretaries have a duty to memorise your companies' articles'* – a chore few might relish, particularly if looking after a group of companies with several subsidiaries and a range of different articles! Nevertheless, there is an element of truth in the advice, since it is important that company secretaries (or the directors, if there is no company secretary) have a good working knowledge of their company's articles – or at least have a summary of the principal requirements. If there is a group of companies it may be convenient if they are given, at least as far as possible, the same articles – at least it is only one set to memorise.

If the board or individual directors fail to act in accordance with the requirements of the articles, they are deemed to be acting *ultra vires* – beyond their powers – and can be held personally liable as such for any losses incurred by the company.

Case study	Acting *ultra vires*
	In *UK Safety Group Ltd v Hearne*, a managing director (one of six directors) decided he needed to delegate his sales responsibilities to a sales director. He met a young ambitious man – a good salesman – who seemed ideal for the post. Since the managing director was concerned in case this appointee, after he had performed the job for a short period, might set up →

Case study	Acting *ultra vires* – *continued*

his own business in competition using the contacts (especially the customers) he would make from working for the company, his advisers devised a watertight contract including a 'garden leave' clause which would minimise this effect. When the appointee agreed and signed the contract, the managing director appointed the young man as a director.

After a couple of years the sales director left and started his own business. Relying on the 'garden leave' clause in the contract the managing director went to court to prevent a breach. The company lost the initial action since it was pointed out that the sales 'director' had not been properly appointed. The articles stipulated that directors could only be appointed at a 'properly convened and constituted Board meeting' – which had not taken place.

In making the appointment, the managing director had exceeded his authority and was acting *ultra vires* the company's articles. Accordingly the shareholders could hold him liable for any loss occasioned to the company. Under CA06 it is made easier for shareholders to sue directors – see DERIVATIVE CLAIMS.

(During the case, the managing director stated *'but we sent the form to Companies House'*, to which the judge replied: *'That's just a piece of paper'*! Whilst CH must be advised, they have no means of knowing whether an appointment has been correctly made.)

It is not only directors who could lose out because the requirements of the articles are not known and therefore ignored.

Case study	Restriction in Articles

In *Cottrell v King*, C held 75 per cent of the shares and K the remaining 25 per cent. When C died, the shares in his name were automatically transmitted to his widow, who became the new majority shareholder. Mr King objected and it was realised that the articles stipulated that on a member's death their shares

➡

Case study	Restriction in Articles – *continued*

had first to be offered to the remaining member at a price to be determined by the auditors. The dispute finished in the High Court, which held that the transmission to Mrs Cottrell was void and that she had to transfer C's shares back to the estate of Mr Cottrell. The executor of the estate had then to offer the shares to King. If King agreed to buy the shares (at valuation), the proceeds would be passed to Mr Cottrell's executor and Mrs Cottrell (and any other beneficiary) would cease to have any interest in the company.

Ironically, since he had held 75 per cent of the shares, whilst he was alive, Mr Cottrell could have changed the articles by a special resolution taking out the provision – unless, of course the obligations under a SHAREHOLDERS' AGREEMENT precluded him taking such action.

Notes

1 Since they must be filed at CH, a company's articles are a public document. Company law must be observed in framing the articles (i.e., one cannot put in the articles commitments beyond those allowed under the law), however in companies where the shares are tightly held (e.g. by say no more than four shareholders), there would seem to be nothing to stop them entering into a SHAREHOLDERS' AGREEMENT to, for example, require the level of support for special resolutions to be 80 per cent rather than 75 per cent (meaning in that example that all four shareholders – assuming they had equal holdings – would need to agree).

2 Recently some PLCs have obtained shareholder agreement to alter their articles (burying fundamental alterations amongst relatively unimportant changes) so that should the shareholders wish to challenge the directors, they are forced (by the wording in the revised articles) to use arbitration. This means that publicity is denied to those wishing to challenge actions. Such a development is hardly in the spirit of the transparency and accountability of CORPORATE GOVERNANCE requirements (to which such companies are subject), and in theory might mean that even DERIVATIVE CLAIMS might be transferred from the public arena of the courtroom to the private room of the arbitrator.

Auditors

INTRODUCTION

Other than companies that are dormant or exempted (as defined below), the accounts of companies are required to be audited, that is, independently verified by authorised accountants. If a company subject to audit does not appoint auditors, it must notify the Secretary of State, who can make such an appointment. If such notice is not given to the Secretary of State, those responsible can be penalised. Auditors are required to report to the members, although, particularly with smaller companies, the auditors often become virtually board nominees reporting to, working with and being guided by the board. In view of a number of cases where companies have attempted to hold their auditors liable for the contents of the accounts they have audited, there is now a requirement to acknowledge in each set of accounts that it is the responsibility of the *directors* to ensure accounts are prepared in accordance with the law, and that it is directors who must answer criticisms regarding such accounts.

Qualification

An auditor must have a recognised accountancy qualification. The qualification of auditors is supervised by Recognised Qualifying Bodies (RQB) and their operation is regulated by Recognised Supervisory Bodies (RSB). To be able to operate as RSBs and RQBs (a single body can act as both), organisations need to be approved by the Secretary of State. Only registered auditors are eligible to audit the accounts of companies. If accounts are audited by an unregistered auditor, the Registrar can reject the accounts and require them to be properly audited. Since the costs of such work may be borne by the directors personally, it is important to ensure that the appointed auditors are registered.

By virtue of their appointment by the members, auditors are required to hold an independent view of the activities of the company and the board and to report on it to the members. Although they may need to work closely with the board and company secretary, their first duty is to the members, and should there be irregularities, it is their duty to bring these to the attention of the members. An auditor has a right to notice of, and to attend and to speak at a general meeting of the company.

Appointment and term

The first auditors are appointed by the board of directors at any time prior to the first ANNUAL GENERAL MEETING (which must be held within 18 months of the date of incorporation of the company). At the first and subsequent AGMs, auditors are appointed (or reappointed) by the members.

Auditors hold office (other than in the period leading to the first AGM or from their appointment) from the conclusion of one AGM until the conclusion of the next – or, if the company does not hold AGMs, from appointment until they or the members wish to bring the appointment to an end. If an auditor resigns the directors can appoint another to fill this casual vacancy and that appointee holds office until the conclusion of the next following AGM. On occasion it may be administratively convenient for a company to appoint replacement auditors. For example, if a parent acquires a new subsidiary, it may be logical for the parent company's auditors to become the new subsidiary company's auditors.

When an auditor resigns he is required to lodge at the company's registered office a statement of any matters that he feels should be brought to the attention of the members and creditors. In addition, notice of the resignation must be given to the REGISTRAR OF COMPANIES within 14 days. If the auditor has lodged such a statement, the company has 21 days to take the matter to court to gain authority to have such a statement suppressed, and, if so must notify the auditor that it has taken such action. If, within 21 days of lodging the statement with the company, the auditor has not received a statement that an appeal has been made to the court he must lodge his original statement with the Registrar. The court has the authority either to suppress the statement or to require that copies be distributed to the members.

To ensure that matters are brought to the attention of the members, a resigning auditor who feels that members should be aware of such matters, can call upon the directors to convene an (extraordinary) general meeting. This request must be actioned within 21 days of the auditor's request and be held within 28 days of the notice of the meeting. The auditor also has the right to have a statement distributed to members attending such a meeting and to be heard at the meeting, although no further action can be taken, unless a member(s) wishes to press the point.

Removal

A serving auditor can only be removed from office by resolution of the members in general meeting. Special notice (see RESOLUTIONS) must be given of this ordinary resolution. If the resolution is passed, the Registrar must be notified within 14 days – even if the change is made at the AGM at which the auditor's reappointment would otherwise be proposed.

If a member wishes to propose that the current auditor not be reappointed then he must give notice of this proposal (which can only be made once in each year) to the company at its registered office. The proposal requires special notice which means that the auditor is given seven days to respond to the original request and then the request and any representations from the Auditor must be sent to the members giving 21 days' notice of the meeting to consider the proposal. If the resolution is passed, then the auditor's office terminates at the end of the current financial year. If, however, such a notice is lodged within 14 days of the issue of the accounts for the previous financial year, the auditor's appointment may cease with effect from the end of the financial year being reported upon.

Rights

In addition to the right to attend and be heard at general meetings, auditors have rights of access to all records of the company (including the minutes of board meetings, since they need to check whether there are any commitments made by the board which could affect the results) necessary for them to be able to complete their audit, and to require directors and staff of the company to provide information, and answer their questions. The auditors must also be sent a copy of every written resolution. Failure to comply attracts a £500 fine.

Payment

Fees paid to auditors must be determined by company in general meeting, although it is usual for the members to delegate the responsibility for this task to the board. Auditors' fees must be disclosed in the accounts, split between charges for audit and any other work, for example, taxation advice and calculations, consultancy, etc.

Exemption from audit (and its retention)

Under company law, the following companies are exempt from the requirement to have their accounts audited:

- a charity whose gross income does not exceed £250,000 (although such a company may have to have its accounts audited to comply with charity law);
- a small company (as defined), provided it is not a PLC, bank, insurance company or broker registered under the Financial Services Act 1986 or the Trade Union and Labour Relations (Consolidation) Act 1992.

This relaxation of the requirement for companies to have their accounts audited applies to over 100,000 companies (in addition to the number that previously were not subject to audit when the turnover threshold was £1,000,000). Whilst initially attractive, the suggestion of dispensing with an audit has been taken up by few of those entitled (well under 10 per cent). There are several reasons for this. The role of the directors is to take risks and to drive the company forward in accordance with the law. Some however can be tempted to overlook legal and accounting convention practices. Knowing that such practices could be challenged by the auditors can act as a brake on such activities. Without this 'audit brake', such practices might go unchecked – and potentially unnoticed – until the company fails. Even where there is no dishonest intent, genuine mistakes are unlikely to be corrected without an independent view.

Those potentially prejudiced by the accounts not being audited?

1   *Trade creditors*. Accounts are publicly published to protect the creditors' interests. Without any external checking of the directors' figures, such protection disappears. The lack of audited accounts could also inhibit the subject company being able to obtain future credit from suppliers (who will have only unaudited accounts to rely on when assessing credit-worthiness).

2   *Shareholders* (who are not directors) who may be unhappy at relying on the figures without the benefit of the auditors (who they appoint) checking them. In addition, without an independent check, they could be precluded from action (e.g. removing the directors) by the fact that a worsening situation has been concealed – probably until it is too late.

3   *Banks and finance houses* and any other organisations that have advanced credit to the subject company. Those asked to lend money to the company could insist that an independent audit is conducted before granting a loan – probably at a far higher cost than the regular audit. Future borrowing might only be permitted if supported by directors' personal guarantees.

4   *Non-executive directors* could be at risk, since they may lack knowledge of some internal developments, yet have personal liability should the company trade wrongfully or fraudulently.

5   *Regulatory authorities*, who will not know whether the published results of companies with non-audited accounts have been prepared in accordance with the requirements.

6   *The directors* themselves may find difficulty calculating the company's tax liability (and to ensure the company gains all the exemptions and allowances to which it is entitled – and complies with the latest

disclosure requirements) without the advice of the auditors. In addition, they should derive some comfort from an independent check that others in the company are behaving correctly.

7   *Insurers*. Credit insurance may be impossible to effect without audited accounts, as also might be employment risks insurance.

8. *Employees*, whose reputation and future employment prospects are dependent on the existence of the company and on their employer's honesty.

Comment

To save an audit fee probably costing less than £8,000, most companies otherwise entitled may think this exemption is not worth using. Since research indicates that well over 90 per cent of those companies entitled to opt out of the audit requirement do not do so, this seems to be a deregulatory move more in perception than reality.

The EU is proposing to exempt companies whose turnover is less than €1,000,000 (around £890,000) and who have fewer than ten employees from the need to file accounts. This could put such companies at an even worse disadvantage than companies which do not have their accounts audited – at least in the latter there are unaudited accounts available.

Authority, control and delegation

INTRODUCTION

Unless a signatory to a contract has authority to enter into the contract, its validity may be challenged or it may be rendered void. However if it was reasonable for the third party to believe the other party had authority, the contract may be binding. To ensure authority is delegated and granted to the appropriate levels, that there is adequate and clear control of delegated authority, and that only properly authorised persons commit the company contractually, it may be advisable for a company, virtually regardless of size, to adopt a delegated authority chart. Indeed it is arguable that without one, should there be fraud and the company lose as a result, shareholders could hold the directors culpable for not having taken suitable precautions – i.e. the shareholders could make a DERIVATIVE claim, prosecuting which is made easier under CA06. It may also be advisable to provide suppliers with appropriate guidance so that they are aware who in the company has authority to commit the company. In its absence, adoption of such a control mechanism may be urged by the company's auditors.

Members

The ultimate authority in the company belongs to the members in general meeting. A properly approved members' resolution contains the highest authority to bind the company, for example changing the rules under which the company operates, which are contained in its MEMORANDUM and ARTICLES of ASSOCIATION, both of which, since they are filed with the Registrar, are public documents. Such changes need the approval of a majority of the votes in general meeting (either a simple or a 75 per cent majority of the votes cast, depending on the subject matter).

Directors

The authority of the board is derived from the members via the articles or resolutions. The members are obliged to appoint directors by company law – and can also remove them. Board authority itself operates on the basis of collective responsibility. Decisions are taken 'by the board' in meetings and evidenced by minutes of those meetings – compiling which is a legal obligation. In dealing with third parties, it may be convenient to pass a resolution at a board meeting and, as evidence of such authority, provide the third party with a copy of the appropriate minute. Usually the extract from the minutes will be required to be signed by the chairman to evidence its authenticity (i.e. certified as a true copy).

Example	**Extract from the minutes of a board meeting**
	Board meeting of J. Bloggs & Company Ltd
	held on 29th November 2XXX at [address]
	Minute 157 – Brazilian contract
	It was resolved that the company enter into a contract with Sao Paulo Construcciones for the supply of steel [amount/brief specification] for a 10-storey office block for a contract price of [sum], on terms to be agreed in discussion and that T Smith [a director] be and he hereby is authorised to agree terms and sign the contract on behalf of the company.
	Certified a true copy of Minute 157 ....
	J Bloggs, Chairman
	Date...................

Under such a resolution, collective authority of the board is granted to the contract itself, whilst T Smith is granted individual authority to actually agree the terms of the contract and to sign it on behalf of the company.

Seal

Although many contracts require only a signature, possibly witnessed, some require the authority of the attachment of the SEAL to the document. Even though under UK law companies can dispense with a seal (see below), those seeking to do business abroad may find there are some countries that not only insist on the seal being used but also that the contract be notarised – i.e. signed by a notary public).

Generally any contract which must be evidenced by a deed will require the affixing of the company seal or, because CA89 allowed companies to dispense with the use of their seal, by being signed 'as a deed' by two directors or a director and the company secretary, or, in Scotland (only), by a director and an authorised countersignatory. The seal is the signature of the company and the manner of its use is set out in the ARTICLES OF

ASSOCIATION. It is usual for the seal to be witnessed by two directors or by one director and the company secretary, and for details of each document to which the seal is affixed to be entered in a register of sealings (which is not a legally required register, but one that has considerable practical advantages as a central record of contracts entered into). If details of all items sealed are entered into the register, which is subsequently brought to a board meeting, it saves explanation of all the items (since sequential numbers in the register can be recorded rather than the full details – which can be referred to by members if required outside the meeting). This procedure enables the seal to be used between board meetings, but subsequently grants the authority of the whole board to each individual use. To evidence this, the chairman should initial below the most recent entry in the register and authority can be evidenced by a minute such as the following draft.

Example	Draft minute
	Sealing [Minute number] Authority was granted to the affixing of the seal to deeds and documents numbered 112-118 in the Register of Sealings which was tabled at the meeting and initialled by the chairman.

Notes

1   The seal can be witnessed by a countersignatory (other than a second director or the company secretary) only if the articles allow this.
2   Using a register allows any director not involved in witnessing sealings to check the details of the contracts entered into, although it may be helpful for the company secretary to give a brief outline of the items whilst the register is being initialled at a board meeting.
3   Fuller guidance regarding the use of the SEAL and the recent dilutions of such use will be found in that section.
4   Section 47 of CA06 allows the board under deed to delegate authority to execute deeds on its behalf (either generally or for a specific purpose) as its attorney to a single named person. This would need a board resolution and might also need to be reflected in an authority chart.

Notarial certification

A considerable amount of UK trade is now with the 'BRIC' countries (Brazil, Russia, India and China), recently the four fastest expanding economies in the world. Increasingly in these countries organisations dealing with UK companies require contracts to be certified by a notary public that the person signing the contract has authority to do so. In such cases it may be necessary to provide an 'audit trail' to prove to the satisfaction of the notary that the person signing a document is who they say they are, holds the position stated, and is authorised to sign. To assist in this respect, retaining a local notary and arranging for the notary to meet the directors and company secretary may assist, as the notary can then, at least in part, rely on personal knowledge of the signatories (i.e. that the person before them is who they say they are, and holds the position claimed in the company).

Officers

Directors are officers of the company, and as such have authority to bind the company. However, for their own protection as much as that of the company, it may be advisable to adopt an authorities chart (see below) to delineate the levels of authority attaching to each director (or manager). Like the directors, the company secretary is an officer of the company and is often referred to as its chief administrator and 'keeper of the company conscience'. Every PLC must have a company secretary, who can also be a director. An LTD may have a company secretary, although under CA06 this is not compulsory (subject to any requirement for the company to have a secretary in the company's articles). By virtue of the appointment, the secretary has authority to bind the company in terms of such administrative duties (ostensible authority), but may not be able to enter into new commercial contracts without the authority of the board. If, however, it has been customary for the secretary to sign particular contracts for some time, authority to continue to sign such contracts may actually be derived from what has gone before and been accepted previously. Under 'actual' authority the secretary can sign (for example) a contract of employment, the terms of which have been approved previously by the board.

Since such an arrangement may be somewhat imprecise, it may be preferable to enter brief details of each contract in a contracts register, entries in which, like the register of sealings, are periodically approved, once again giving the authority of the board to the 'signings'. Obviously there is nothing to stop these two registers being combined.

Other signatories

The value of the delegated authorities chart, which itself should be regularly reviewed and approved by the board, is that it not only sets out limits of authority for those lower down the chain of command (and can help reduce the likelihood of fraud, or at least exploitation of loopholes), but also grants the express authority of the board to those signing. It helps demonstrate that there is effective control regarding the delegation of authority. It is essential for internal use, but can also be used as a control mechanism by providing it externally, to suppliers.

Case study	Assumed authority
	In *Pharmed Medicare Private Ltd v Univar Ltd*, two employees, described as 'managers' of an organisation, placed a number of small orders which were fulfilled by the seller and paid for by their organisation. The two employees then placed a much larger order under a pro forma invoice. There was then a dispute about paying for the goods, with the buying organisation stating the seller should have known that the two 'managers' who placed the orders did not have authority to do so. The seller successfully claimed that the employees concerned had ostensible authority, since all previous transactions entered into by them had been honoured by the buying organisation (i.e. it had paid for the goods ordered by its 'managers'). (Of course, using an authority chart – provided to suppliers as well as internal executives – could have avoided the whole dispute.)

Example	Authorities chart
	BUSINESS NAME AUTHORITY LEVELS
	It is essential for the proper control of the organisation that approval is granted to contracts by suitably appointed personnel, and for the allocation and disposal of money and stock assets of the organisation, that authority is granted at an appropriate level. Employees may only commit the company in accordance with the stated levels.
	→

Example	Authorities chart – *continued*

CONTRACTS

All contracts between the company and third parties, other than those covered by items set out below, must be channelled through the company secretary's office, to ensure correct status (i.e. whether they are to be regarded as a Deed or not) and approval.

The company secretary will arrange the passing of suitable board resolutions granting approval to specified person(s) to sign on behalf of the company. Sufficient time to obtain such a resolution should be allowed.

CASH COMMITMENT

Capital projects

Authority for all projects (no low cut off) (All items must be supported by a Capital expenditure – Capex – form)	Board
Repairs and renewals, purchase of furniture and fittings (All items must be supported by a Capex form)	
Up to £1,000	Manager-level
Over £1,000 and up to £5,000	Director
Over £5,000	Board

Vehicles

(Supported by Capex form, for new allocations, or replacement form for write-offs and replacements) All purchases to be in accordance with Policy	Board

Example	Authorities chart – *continued*

Expense items

Up to £500	Manager-level
Over £500 and up to £1,000	Senior manager
Over £1,000 and up to £5,000	Director
Over £5,000	Board

Committed expenditure

Rent, rates, utility costs:

– where no change or increase is less than rate of inflation	Manager-level
– where change has taken place	Director

Bought ledger

Raw materials, services etc., in accordance with budgeted level of production	Purchasing Manager
Not in accordance with level of production	Director

Personnel matters

Recruitment – as per plan	Director
– additional to plan	Managing Director
Wage adjustment	
– Annual review	Board
– Other than annual review, or for new staff, or replacement at other than at old rate	
Salary up to £20,000 p.a.	Manager-level
Salary over £20,000 p.a.	Board
Warnings – written (grades ...)	Director
(grades ...)	Managing Director
– verbal	Manager
Dismissal	Managing Director

(No hearing which could result in dismissal will take place unless the requirements of the ACAS code (or equivalent) have been followed.)*

→

Example	Authorities chart – *continued*

In course of business

Credits (cash or stock), samples, etc.

In accordance with policy and less than £1,000	Manager-level
Over £1,000	Director

Gifts, donations (cash or stock)

In accordance with policy and budget	Personnel Manager

Stock write-off and/or authority to dispose in stated area (e.g. to market trader, staff shop, by gift, etc.)

Up to £1,000	Sales Manager
Over £1,000	Sales Director in liaison with Finance Director

**Personal expenses
(inc. telephone bills etc.)**

Up to £500	By level above level submitting the expense claim (i.e. using the required company form)
Over £500	By level two levels above person submitting expense claim

Removal expenses

In accordance with range of reimbursement agreed at time and may only be authorised by a board member. All invoices should be submitted in the name of the company to allow recovery of VAT.

Loans

Loans to assist a new employee during the first weeks of his/her employment

→

Example	Authorities chart – *continued*

| (i.e. during the working of the 'week in hand' arrangements) | Personnel Manager |
| All other loans | Board |

Tips and inducements

Other than normal business entertaining and acknowledging special service, the provision of inducements bribes etc. in the name of the organisation is expressly forbidden, being a criminal offence. Any instance where this is expected or required should be referred to [name] for guidance.

Price fixing

It is illegal for any organisation to conspire with another to fix the price of any product or service – indeed even discussing prices might infringe the rules. Sanctions include imprisonment. On no account is any employee permitted to discuss prices with a competitor or to enter into any arrangement regarding prices, no matter how informal. Any instance where this is expected or required should be referred to [name] for guidance. Breach of this rule is gross misconduct (i.e. can generate dismissal).

Issued by Finance Director on [date]. To be updated 6-monthly

(Next review due ...)

* Inserted to draw attention to the fact that breach of the code could create an unfair dismissal and the employer could be liable for considerable financial penalties.

(Figures have been inserted purely for illustrative purposes.)

Notes

I   Whilst delineating and defining levels of authority is fairly obvious as well as being a sound control mechanism, it can be overlooked that in the event of dissent and dismissal it may be necessary to advise third parties that a former employee no longer has authority to bind the company. If a dispute has resulted in summary dismissal for instance, those with whom the employee dealt (particularly if selling or buying) should be advised immediately by e-mail or fax.

2   The reference to outlawing tips and inducements is included partly because the company wishes to act ethically and partly due to the impact of the Anti-Terrorism, Crime & Security Act 2001, Part 12 of which strengthened the laws on bribery and corruption. As a result, any bribery or corruption conducted by UK companies overseas is (at least in theory) now subject to the same restrictions and penalties that would be applied if such acts were committed within the UK. The Government has stated that it would not prosecute for minor infringements of this new law – e.g. a small gratuity to facilitate the issue of a visa. Whilst this appears sensible, some may be excused for thinking this undermines the whole point of the Act. In addition, in 2006, the then Prime Minister stopped an investigation into the alleged offering of inducements by BAE Systems to the Saudi Arabian government as *'not being in the national interest'*. This intervention has been claimed by the Foreign Affairs Committee on Human Rights to have created a backlash in terms of damage to the UK's international reputation for fairness and probity – and its fight against corruption. This was evidenced by the most recent edition of the Corruption Perception Index (published by Transparency International), which reviews perceived levels of public sector corruption in Government, and ranked the UK 16th (down four places) in its league table of 180 countries. The publishers commented: *'the weakening performance of some wealthy exporting countries … casts a further critical light on government commitment to rein in the questionable methods of their companies in acquiring and managing overseas business. Continuing … foreign bribery scandals indicates a … broader failure by the world's wealthiest countries to live up to the promise of mutual accountability in the fight against corruption.'*

The Law Commission has proposed new laws concerning the practice of giving bribes. There would be two entirely new laws – one prohibiting the giving of bribes and another prohibiting the taking of bribes. In addition there would be new laws prohibiting the bribing of a foreign official residing or doing business in the UK and negligently failing to prevent bribery by an employee or agent. The latter is particularly relevant to companies who would need to ensure that their internal rules outlaw such practices – and that such rules are stringently policed.

3   The reference to price-fixing is included to draw the attention to those involved in placing contracts (buying or selling) that there are criminal penalties for those that breach the Competition Act as enhanced by the Enterprise Act. Directors and company secretaries of organisations involved in 'hard core' price fixing can be imprisoned for up to five years.

4   Whilst this authority chart may help minimise unauthorised commitment of a company's resources, cash spend may not necessarily be the best criterion in terms of *risk* to the company. Two contracts might

have the same cash value but one (if, for example, the specification is incorrect) could involve the company in substantial loss, whereas the other may not. For example:

- Contract A is for the supply of office furniture. Risk here is virtually nil since if the items are wrong, very often they can be replaced – probably without charge and certainly without any knock-on effect.
- Contract B is for the supply of computer software to a specification generated by the company. If incorrect, there could be serious financial and other consequences to the company.

It may therefore be advisable to incorporate an added dimension – *'risk to the organisation'* – to the authority levels, requiring the originator of the order to obtain a higher level of authority where the perceived risk (for example) exceeds the value of the contract.

5 Whilst this is essentially a document aimed at enhancing internal controls mechanisms, there is little confidential about it and there may be some logic in providing a copy (and regular updates) to suppliers, so that they are advised who can bind the company and to what financial level.

Board meetings

INTRODUCTION

Members own the company and have the right and legal duty to appoint officers to run it. Despite the obligation placed on the officers to run their company in accordance with the law, which would imply that they must meet, strangely enough there is still no explicit legal obligation for the directors to meet (although at least one agreement between them each year is implied, since the board must approve each year's accounts). However, boards that fail to meet (or, at least to formally record the decisions they take) may find it difficult, if challenged, to demonstrate that they have exercised their required duty of care and that their decisions were reasonable in the circumstances. Under proposed EU legislation, a board of a listed PLC would be required to meet at least four times each year in order to consider certain prescribed business. In addition, CA06 places specific duties on directors, compliance with which may need to be evidenced as well as repeating the previous requirement that minutes of all directors meetings must be taken and preserved – although the period of preservation of such records is now shortened to ten years (a period which many observers may feel is too short).

Attendance

In practice, many boards do meet regularly in something approaching formality and (probably far more often) informally, to take decisions regarding the operation of their companies – on both a long- and short-term basis. The only persons with a right to attend board meetings are the directors, although very often others may be present to give reports, answer questions etc. However, such persons should take no part in the decision-making process of the board. As noted, there is no explicit legal requirement for directors to attend board meetings – the obligation is implied. Indeed, since directors cannot abrogate their legal liability for the actions of the company, if nothing else, convening and attending such meetings could be described as self-interest. However, the internal company rules may require such attendance. For example, reg. 81 of Table A of CA85 states that any director who does not attend board meetings without reason (or the permission of the board) for six months can be removed from the board by the other members.

Of course directors have a collective responsibility for board decisions, whether present or not. Hence, for their own protection if nothing else, they should regard such attendance as mandatory.

The secretary has no right of attendance at a board meeting, although any company secretary regularly excluded from board meetings should question the board's motives behind such exclusion and consider whether he is comfortable with the situation. After all the secretary is an officer of the company and liable – at least potentially – as such. In such a situation, resignation should be a real consideration. In addition, part of the company secretary's role should be to compile MINUTES of the board's decisions. If the company secretary is not present, someone else needs to be appointed to do this, since compilation and retention of the minutes (for at least ten years) is a specific legal requirement.

To quote a Chinese proverb, *'big meetings take small decisions, small meetings take big decisions'*, and there is little doubt that, with too many present at a meeting, it can become difficult to obtain a consensus. Recent research at the Medical University of Vienna indicates that any meeting of eight members is the *'worst total for decision making, [because] there will be neither consensus nor a majority view'*, whilst meetings with more than 20 members tend to create too many subgroups.

Administration

An important aspect of the responsibilities of the company secretary is to convene, organise and ensure the effective operation of board meetings – and to make and keep a record of the decisions taken. Meeting administration, however, starts with the compilation of the dates of future board meetings – possibly looking at least six months ahead (with a larger company/board, perhaps 12 months or more), on a rolling six-month basis. Although this means directors should already know the dates, nevertheless specific notice of each meeting, with an AGENDA, should be sent to all entitled to attend. Even if it is known in advance that a director will be unable to attend, an agenda plus supporting papers should still be sent to him – not least since directors (including non-executives) should wish to keep themselves updated on all subject matters, reports etc. concerning the company. Indeed all directors have a legal obligation to keep themselves informed on company matters, and have a legal right to notification of board meetings.

Case study	Keep updated
	In a hearing following the collapse of Barings Bank after the devastating losses caused by an employee's illegal trading in its Singapore office, the court stated that *'directors [including non-executives], collectively and individually [have] a duty to acquire and maintain a sufficient knowledge of the company's business to enable them to discharge their responsibilities.'*

Agenda

Careful preparation of an agenda can assist the efficient execution of a meeting. A well-planned agenda has a number of advantages. It provides:

- for all present, a reference guide or 'map', enabling progress through a meeting;
- a means of concentrating the mind on what needs to be achieved (i.e. what decisions need to be taken);
- for the chairman, an aid to what is required, possibly with suggested wording for more formal resolutions etc.; and
- for the company secretary, a useful outline of the first draft of the minutes (since much of the wording of a detailed agenda may be replicated – at least in part – in the minutes).

There are at least two approaches that can be adopted when drafting an agenda – skeletal and detailed.

Example	Skeletal agenda for board meeting
	ANY COMPANY LTD
	AGENDA for BOARD MEETING
	Thursday 16 December 2XXX at 10.00 a.m.
	At [address]
	Apologies for absence
	1 Approval of Minutes of Board Meeting held on 15 November
	2 Directors' interests
	3 Finance: i) Latest Management Accounts (enclosed) ii) Stock results (to be tabled) iii) Stockholding (see Accounts) iv) Capital expenditure (application forms attached)
	4 Current trading Managing Director's report on 6 Months to end Oct. to be distributed by 7th December
	5 Strategy for 2XXX/2XXY financial year (final report attached)
	6 Personnel Personnel director's report on Staff Absenteeism →

Example	Skeletal agenda for board meeting – *continued*

7   Property
   i)   Shop acquisitions (see capital expenditure approval forms)
   ii)   Rent reviews (details provided)
   iii) Disposals

8   Safety (report attached)

9   Sealing (Items XXX – XXY)

10 Dates of meetings in 2XXX – 22/2, 22/3, 24/4, 22/5 and 20/6 (others to be arranged at meeting)

11 Other business

Although such an agenda is perfectly adequate, it provides no detailed guidance regarding each item requiring a decision. A more detailed agenda such as follows may assist in this and allow the members to prepare themselves more adequately for the meeting.

Example	Detailed board agenda

ANY COMPANY LTD

For a meeting of the Board to be held on Thursday 30 March 2XXX in the Boardroom at 10.00 a.m.

Apologies for absence

1   MINUTES of Board Meeting held on 29 February (copy attached)

2   DIRECTORS' INTERESTS

3   SHARES
   a)   Resolution to approve share transfers in favour of Mr PQR
   b)   Consider recommendation that share registration work of the company be placed with Share Registrars Ltd. (Report and contract attached)

4   FINANCE
   i)   Consider Management accounts to 28th February 2XXX. (Complete set to be distributed by Finance Dept by 25th March)

→

Example	Detailed board agenda – *continued*

    ii) Consider recommended change to calculation of depreciation charge. (See attached report from Finance Dept on effect)

    iii) Capital expenditure a) Proposed purchase of (units)
                             b) Capex project 13/2XXX

    iv) Cash flow. (Projection for remainder of 2XXX attached)

    v) Bank Mandate. (New format in terms of attached draft is required to be adopted.)

    vi) Borrowings. (The secretary to table a report concerning negotiations with the bankers regarding sourcing additional borrowing.)

Draft resolution required to be adopted: THAT the chairman and Mr UVW be and they hereby are empowered to sign such documents and take such actions to provide the company's bankers with the documentation they require in order to facilitate the advance of the additional borrowing requirement

5 CURRENT TRADING
Managing director's report (see enclosed confidential report)

6 PERSONNEL
    a) Wage negotiations for review 1st July 2XXX (see report from divisional director (personnel) attached)
    b) Impact of recent employment protection legislation (secretary to report at meeting with recommendations to be tabled.)

7 PROPERTY
    i) Board approval required for items X, XX, XXX in attached report.
    ii) Progress on sale (facility)

8 SAFETY MATTERS
    i) General report (attached)
    ii) Report re [new project] implementation

9 SEALING
Approval required for items 345 to 361

10 BOARD MEETINGS IN 2XXX
Consider additional dates as follows 28th April, 30th May, 30th June, 28th July, 31st August, 29th September, 25th October, 23rd November, and 21st December.

Note: See section on MINUTES for an example of the record of the meeting convened by such an agenda.

A detailed agenda such as the above should aid the efficiency of the meeting. For example suggesting a form of words for a formal resolution such as is shown in item 4 (vi) may save valuable board time drafting such a resolution on the day. If the agenda and the reports tabled are kept with the minutes it can also show what information was before the board at the time of the decision-making process.

Composition

A meeting's length tends to be proportionate (and sometimes disproportionate!) to the number of people present. If that number is swelled by persons whose contribution is unnecessary, the effectiveness of the meeting may be diluted and its duration extended needlessly. Effective contributions that are concise yet comprehensive should be actively sought. Setting a time limit on the meeting (or on each item of business) may encourage this and may minimise time being wasted on trivia. Conversely, applying such guidelines too strictly can mean sufficient discussion does not take place. Every director has a right to be heard on every subject – and of course has a vote. The chairman also has a vote and often under the articles may have a second or casting vote, in the event that there is a stalemate. The model articles under CA06 for an LTD limited by shares grant the chairman a casting vote, but companies not using these articles need to check the authority.

Board alliances – and disputes

The most effective and successful companies are probably those where the board, whilst there may be individual differences, acts as a cohesive team with shared aspirations and plans. Inevitably from time to time differences may arise and the director who wishes to gain approval for a pet project will be somewhat short-sighted if he does not attempt to gain support from colleagues in advance of consideration of the matter at a board meeting. Seeking support, even if entails a 'quid pro quo' from the other party, may be a sensible way of approaching the matter. Few people like losing out or ending up on the wrong side, particularly in a public forum, and such public defeat may be avoided by broaching the subject with colleagues in advance, gaining their reactions and either toning down or altering aspects of the suggestion or, if there seems to be little support or total animosity, dropping the idea altogether. Such a strategy has a number of advantages:

- It grants the member the reputation of being a good team player. Reputation and respect can help win arguments in meetings and dealing with a possibly controversial matter outside the meeting, particularly if it concerns or is raised with the chairman, may well earn the instigator some prestige for future use, even though the actual subject matter gains no support on the present occasion.

- It avoids embarrassing the person, as it could were it to be raised in open meeting. The position of that person, particularly if he is the chairman, is thus protected. He can explain opposition or reaction in private, and possibly even in confidence, to the instigator, away from the pressure of the meeting.

- It enables the instigator to gain some measure of the depth of feeling likely to be encountered were the matter to be raised in meeting. If the reaction is very hostile he can back off immediately.

- The concept itself is brought into the open. Whilst it may not gain support this time around, repeated references to the idea may ultimately win over those formerly antagonistic to it, particularly if later events are used to illustrate its advisability.Occasionally however, despite all endeavours, antipathy can surface at a board meeting even leading to a situation where one member finds himself completely at odds with his colleagues. He may feel so strongly that he wishes his dissent to be noted in the minutes. Most chairmen will try to avoid this, not least since it is evidence of the breaking the cohesion of the board team, but if the director is adamant then a suitable minute must be included.

It may be preferable for the company secretary to avoid becoming involved in such 'negotiations', other than answering questions in a neutral way.

Motivating members

The role of chairman combines that of 'first among equals' with that of leader, and this dual role should always be recognised. In the latter endeavour the chairman should ensure the best of each member is brought out. Unfortunately it can be easy for a dominant person to take over the meeting and for less dominant members to be overshadowed to such an extent that they make little or no contribution. If this occurs, then the chairman's responsibility is to encourage the quieter members to make a contribution, even, if necessary, silencing others in order to allow them to do so. In this the chairman may find it helpful to adopt the following guidelines:

- Ensure everyone knows why they are present. In this the chairman may need to restate the meeting's objectives. He may also state the time within which he would like to see the business conducted. Such strictures must be promoted positively, the aim being to complete the business properly, recognising that time is scarce and valuable.

- Treat every member as an individual with rights to make the points they wish. This may require the chairman to invite a contribution by name from 'less forward' member(s).

- Encourage every member to identify with the body as a whole and to relate to every other member. This will take time and, with some members, can be difficult.
- Encourage a sense of pride in the meeting and its achievements. Without being excessive, the chairman should praise achievements, whether these be joint or individual. As a nation we in the UK tend to criticise too much and praise too little, even though praise (which costs nothing) can be the most powerful motivator and incentive. It is also helpful when trying to manage a meeting, since this 'feel good' effect can stifle or neutralise what could otherwise be objections.
- Ensure all members are treated fairly and given a chance both to explain their views and attitudes and to argue their cases. Obviously this in turn requires the opposition to have a chance to do the same. If members see that each is allowed his own turn to put forward arguments, the temptation to filibuster or use other means by which the arguments of others are not heard should be reduced.
- Ensure members feel that business which they feel is important does receive the attention it deserves. This may be difficult in the early life of a meeting and the chairman needs to be tactful in accepting or rejecting business requested by members. If it is entirely germane to the business in hand, it may be worth considering, even if that in turn means the meeting overruns its allotted time span. If it is not appropriate, a tactful suggestion ('perhaps we could have an initial chat about that after the meeting') might solve the problem without disincentivising the member.

Dealing with opposition

Whilst most business and most boards operate with mutual respect and consensus, from time to time opposition may arise which despite prior attempted pre-emption may surface at a board meeting. This will need careful handling by the chairman although having some advance notice of a potential problem may assist. If determined opposition is expected then the meeting should be seated perhaps more informally than usual. Seating everyone in comfortable chairs may reduce the capacity for opposition (although it can also generate a relaxed approach which could impair efficiency) or ensuring that seating position is determined by the chairman. This could provide an opportunity for the dispersal of those who are likely to oppose. This does not mean banishing them to the far corners of the discussion table as this may enable them to regroup and even solicit support from uncommitted members. If there are three people who seek to oppose, then at least one, preferably the leader, should be seated very near the chairman which may enable the latter to control him. If the meeting uses the principle of the House of Commons, where before speaking a member has to catch the

Speaker's eye, so that to speak, the chairman has to grant permission, even if only by the briefest of nods, then the person located nearest the chairman will then have the greatest difficulty, by sheer juxtaposition, in catching his close neighbour's eye!

Other opposition members need to be spread amongst supporters of the chairman. In this way, their apparent strength or weight will be marginalised, they will find it difficult to communicate between themselves, which may be necessary in order to regroup or seek an alternative tactic. In addition, if they are each seated next to a strong supporter of the business, the opposition may feel inhibited about making their protest at all, or continuing it in the face of experienced or heavy opposition. The layout set out in the diagram [below] shows how opposition groups can be split and to some extent neutralised.

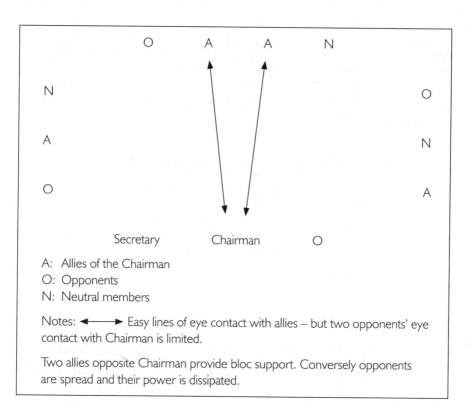

A: Allies of the Chairman
O: Opponents
N: Neutral members

Notes: ◄────► Easy lines of eye contact with allies – but two opponents' eye contact with Chairman is limited.

Two allies opposite Chairman provide bloc support. Conversely opponents are spread and their power is dissipated.

Considering the data

Reports, etc., should accompany the agenda, or a note regarding late or delayed submission be appended. Tabling a bulky or complex report at a meeting should be avoided – since decision-taking on its contents could be uninformed.

Case study	Acting recklessly
	In *Gwyer & Associates v London Wharf (Limehouse) Ltd*, a director of a company in financial difficulties made no effort to ascertain what were the interests of his company before voting on a board resolution. The court held he was not only negligent, but also in breach of his fiduciary duty to exercise his discretion independently and *bona fides* in the interests of the company. It went on to state that where a company was on the brink of insolvency, the directors owed a duty 'to consider as paramount' the interests of the creditors.

On occasion, because of time pressures it may be impossible to provide directors with enough 'reading [or consideration] time' before needing a decision on a matter. In that case a brief synopsis of the main points and effects should also be presented. Ideally, however, directors should avoid taking a decision on a material matter when they have not had time to consider the full implications.

Example	Summary sheet for late/tabled items
	Organisation name
	Report title..................... Date of report....................................
	Author/sponsoring dept..
	Date to be considered by meeting..
	Subject matter..
	....
	Recommendations I ....
	2..
	3..
	Synopsis of facts/ contentions supporting recommendations ......
	....
	....
	.... →

Example	Summary sheet for late/tabled items – *continued*
	Synopsis of facts/contentions contesting recommendations .... Implications for organisation if not proceeded with .... * .... Implications for organisation if not proceeded with NOW ...... * .... Capital expenditure implications .... Skill/personnel implications .... Safety implication... * These questions are posed to delineate the likely impact of the recommendations of the report and as a guide to those asked to make a decision when they may not have had a chance to study the report and consider such implications.

Notes

I Where there are time constraints and the matter is material, it may be practicable, rather than holding a meeting, to obtain approval of all the directors by means of a written resolution. This entails drafting a resolution and sending it to each director asking them, if they agree, to sign to that effect and return it to the chairman or secretary. The individual signed copies should be preserved in the minute book.

In all cases, however, the procedure should balance the need for urgency with the overriding principle that each director should be given as much information as possible and have the opportunity to requisition an emergency meeting of the board to discuss the matter prior to the commitment of the company. Alternatively the board could conduct their business by using the telephone or teleconference facilities.

It would be best if these methods of arriving at board decisions were referred to in the articles to avoid shareholders from challenging the validity of decisions arrived at in this way and/or that all such decisions are subsequently recorded in writing with each director required to sign such a record.

2 The term 'material' may need to be defined. This could range from 'contracts in the ordinary course of business' to 'contracts not in the ordinary course of business'. Financial limits should be set where appropriate.

Procedural guidelines

The level of formality of the meeting will differ widely according to company custom. For example, it was once fairly common (though not a legal requirement) for board members of many companies (particularly charities) to sign a book of attendance, and to address and speak through the chairman, and some boards still operate a system whereby a director is only allowed to speak once on a subject. Whilst this latter restriction may assist in forcing members to marshal their thoughts and arguments it militates against subsequent constructive thoughts. Ideally a board should operate as a dynamic – ideas from one person creating reactions and new ideas from others. Restricting a director's input to just one opportunity to make a point will almost certainly stultify such creativity.

Decisions reflect the 'collective responsibility' doctrine of board work, and once everyone has had their say (each person entitled to be present has a right to be heard on each subject), the chairman should summarise arguments, before taking the 'sense' or decision of the meeting – usually by consensus, but if necessary by vote. The following guidelines attempt may be helpful although boards operate in different ways and they need to be customised to fit specific requirements.

Example	Guidelines aimed at improving meeting efficiency
	Requirements to be issued to all meeting members and those submitting information to be considered at the meeting
	A Timetable
	1 A timetable for use of all required to attend, submit data to and draw information from the meeting will be prepared on a rolling six-month basis and issued by the meeting convener.
	2 Other than in the most exceptional instances, the timing of meetings will not be changed, and any member unable to attend a meeting must inform the meeting convener as soon as possible.
	3 An agenda with supporting data should always be issued at least one week prior to a meeting. →

Example	Guidelines aimed at improving meeting efficiency – *continued*

B Data required

1 All information and reports should be made available to the meeting convener at least seven working days before the meeting.

2 All data should be submitted with the stated number of copies required. (The 'stated number' should be the number of persons entitled to receive the agenda plus any required to be sent out for information, plus, say, one spare for each five persons on the distribution list.) Where it is usual for a number of documents to accompany the agenda, colour coding such documentation for ease of reference could be considered.

3 If data is not available to meet the submission deadline an indication of the availability date should be given, the chairman should be informed and a note of the expected date of receipt/issue entered on the agenda. Those submitting data late must make every effort to convey it directly to meeting members prior to the meeting with the required number of spares to the meeting convenor. Asking for data to be allowed to be tabled at the meeting, particularly if it consists of detailed, involved or lengthy reports, is best avoided. It may result in the item being 'left on the table' for consideration at a later meeting.

4 Documentation will be presented in agenda order.

C Presentation

1 Every item prepared for the [board/committee] will be required to have a standard covering sheet (see the example above).

2 Subsequent sheets may be presented in the most suitable format.

3 The utmost brevity, commensurate with the subject matter, should be employed. Commentary should be avoided and facts and suppositions, and opposing data, suitably differentiated must be presented clearly.

4 Source(s) of data should be referenced, and a summary used, rather than including such data as part of the submission.

Example	Guidelines aimed at improving meeting efficiency – *continued*
	5 The conclusions and recommendations, as required to be set out on the first page of the report, must be clearly evidenced within it. 6 Plain English should be used, with jargon avoided. Where jargon is unavoidable, a glossary accurately defining the terms used should be included. **D** *Supporting commentary* 1 At the meeting, the report's originator or person responsible for the subject matter should be prepared to speak to the report, to answer questions from other members and generally to assist the meeting to come to a suitable decision regarding its content and/or recommendations. 2 Should the meeting require amplifying documentation, this must be provided in the same format as that used in the original report, and submitted for the next following meeting. 3 Proposers should endeavour to speak only once to support or promote the subject matter and should therefore cover all salient facts in their short presentation. This will entail marshalling all facts, data, comments and so on, balancing brevity against comprehensiveness, highlighting only the most important aspects and avoiding repetition, other than when necessary as a result of other members' questions. 4 Other meeting members should similarly endeavour to speak only once, putting forward their objections or comments in the same manner as set out in D3 above. 5 After such proposal and counter-comments, if the subject is of sufficient importance, the chairman may wish to encourage a short general discussion on the subject, otherwise the next move will be to summarise the content and take the sense of the meeting. **E** *Decisions* Board decisions will be communicated externally by the meeting convener and/or the sponsoring member. If approved or referred back for reconsideration the decision will be supported by a copy of the minutes dealing with the subject which will include any conditions, timing, capital expenditure, and so on.

ICSA guidance

The Institute of Chartered Secretaries has published a code on Good Boardroom Practice, as follows:

1   The board should establish written procedures for the conduct of its business which should include the matters covered in this code. A copy of these written procedures should be given to every director. Compliance should be monitored, preferably by an audit committee of the board, and breaches of this procedure should be reported to the board.

2   The board should ensure that each director is given on appointment sufficient information to enable him to perform his duties. In particular, guidance for non-executive directors should cover the procedures:
    - for obtaining information concerning the company;
    - for requisitioning a meeting of the board.

3   In the conduct of board business, two fundamental concepts should be observed:
    - each director should receive the same information at the same time; and
    - each director should be given sufficient time in which to consider any such information.

4   The board should identify matters which require the prior approval of the board and lay down procedures to be followed when, exceptionally, a decision is required before its next meeting on any matter not required by law to be considered at board level.

5   As a basic principle, all material contracts, and especially those not in the ordinary course of business, should be referred to the board for decision prior to the commitment of the company.

6   The board should approve definitions of the terms *'material'* and *'not in the ordinary course of business'* and these definitions should be brought to the attention of all relevant persons.

7   When there is any uncertainty regarding the materiality or nature of a contract, it should normally be assumed that the contract should be brought to the board.

8   Decisions regarding the content of the agenda for individual meetings of the board and concerning the presentation of agenda items should be taken by the chairman in consultation with the company secretary.

9   The company secretary should be responsible to the chairman for the proper administration of the meetings of the company, the board and any committees thereof. To carry out this responsibility the company secretary should be entitled to be present at (or represented at) all board meetings and prepare (or arrange for the preparation of) minutes of the proceedings.

10 The minutes of meetings should record the decisions taken and provide sufficient background to those decisions. All papers presented at the meeting should be clearly identified in the minutes and retained for reference. Procedures for the approval and circulation of minutes should be established.

11 Where the articles of association allow the board to delegate any of its powers to a committee, the board should give its prior approval to:
- the membership and quorum of any such committee;
- its terms of reference; and
- the extent of any powers delegated to it.

12 The minutes of all meetings of committees of the board (or a written summary thereof) should be circulated to the board prior to its next meeting and the opportunity should be given at that meeting for any member of the board to ask questions thereon.

13 Notwithstanding the absence of a formal agenda item, the chairman should permit any director or the company secretary to raise at any board meeting any matter concerning the company's compliance with this Code of Practice, with the company's memorandum and articles of association and with any other legal or regulatory requirement (e.g. for listed PLCs, CORPORATE GOVERNANCE requirements).

Meeting without meeting

The advent of computerisation and electronic communications has inevitably led to the increased use of tele-communicating meetings. The advantages are considerable in terms of reduced costs and time of travel etc. (as well as the advantage of being seen to help 'reduce global warming', etc.) – although the costs of the hardware obviously offset this.

Whilst the perceived cost/time saving may encourage the participants to prepare adequately and complete the business swiftly, in fact the reverse can also be the case – some of those involved leaving things to the last minute, since they don't need to prepare for a trip! Some users report feeling that having only to worry about the reduced image of the screen is a relief. However this may highlight one of the inherent drawbacks of remote meetings – one can see the screen, but not what is just offscreen. In addition, whilst with a one-to-one meeting there may be few drawbacks, if there are members in several locations, trying to keep focus on several screens at once can be difficult.

Above all, what is lacking is the social aspect of the work ethic, and many using the system report missing the interplay with others which is inherent in the work situation. Some people are only able to operate really effectively when face-to-face with their colleagues – addressing a screen is not the same. It has been said that 93 per cent of the message comes not from the words but from the body language – at least some of this may be difficult to 'read' on screen.

Further, a tele-meeting lacks finite boundaries, which are often one of the means of binding the participants together. Using a room for a meeting can create an entity with latent pressure to produce, determine or decide. The lack of such pressure, as well as the knowledge that *'we can always call another one again'* may also allow, or even encourage, delay in decision-taking. In addition, the social aspect of discussion which is often carried on over refreshments or lunch cannot be overlooked – try that via tele-conferencing!

There is an obvious use for such remote meetings; whether they are for the board must be questionable, not only for the above reasons but also for concerns over security and confidentiality.

Briefing the chairman – general and media

INTRODUCTION

As well as needing to be briefed on handling meetings (see BRIEFING THE CHAIRMAN – MEETINGS), the chairman needs to be fully briefed when it comes to recording or reporting strategy, tactics and philosophy, either in writing, via the chairman's statement in the ANNUAL REPORT, or when interfacing with the media. Assistance in assembling background information – an obvious role for the COMPANY SECRETARY – may be necessary not least to ensure that previous statements still support the present stance of the company, and, if not, that changes are explained.

Chairman's statement

Although there is no legal requirement to include a statement from the chairman in a company's annual report, many companies do, including all listed PLCs (which are obliged do so under the Stock Exchange listing agreement), and its omission is likely to generate questions and create uncertainty. Indeed the chairman's statement of the annual report of a listed PLC will probably receive the greatest attention of the whole report. Great care must be taken in compiling a report, the sources for which can include:

- **The results for the year.** Commenting on the results, and more importantly, the outlook for the future should be undertaken with caution. The inclusion of too definite a statement, or too optimistic a view of trading and/or prospects (perhaps unlikely at present) may return, with considerable embarrassment, to haunt the board when reality turns out to be somewhat different. In the event of any subsequent takeover bid, such a statement may even be regarded as a 'profit forecast' which, if not then achieved, could have serious repercussions in terms of censure from the Takeover Panel – and may even create a personal liability to those who may have relied on the 'forecast' when buying shares.
- **Previous written statements**. Great store is set by companies having strategies, despite the virtual inevitability that such strategies need to be changed to reflect changing situations. At present the only constant is change. However, too great, too soon a divergence from a previously announced strategy may, in the absence of severe and/or

obvious problems, pose questions of competence and managerial ability. Subsequent statements thus need to pick up earlier indications and show progress, or explain deviations. Such explanations need to be entirely believable (see examples of questionable statements below).

- **Previous media interviews or statements**. Once again, whatever has been said publicly needs to be reinforced by the statement, or, if there has been a deviation, an explanation should be provided.
- **The outlook for the industry** and/or economy in which the company operates. Companies do not exist in a vacuum, and their progress will almost inevitably be affected by external occurrences which must be addressed.
- **Developments** of the product and/or service and/or the skills available to the company to make progress. Attention to these points seeks to demonstrate to the reader that the board is aware of and is reviewing its responsibilities on a long-term basis.

Qui s'excuse s'accuse

There is little doubt that some statements made to investors by chairmen (such statements being of course, on behalf of the board) are less than accurate. Perhaps such 'explanations' should have been previously questioned by the board members and the company secretary. *The Times* published a number of what it called *'the most preposterous excuses for poor results'*, including:

- a ban on the importing of Indian prawns (which was very odd, since when the same ban was lifted, *'market instability'* was then blamed for the decline continuing);
- (collectively) high interest rates, a hot summer, a deadline for self-assessment tax forms, flooding at Easter and the 'Diana effect' (i.e. a sales downturn following Princess Diana's death);
- the Islamic month of Ramadan (because super-rich Muslims departed the casino tables) – an excuse which seemed to ignore the fact that Ramadan is celebrated every year;
- the fall of Saddam Hussein (for a 50 per cent reduction in the sales of motor caravans?);
- the World Cup (potential purchasers were supposed to be glued to their TV sets rather than buying sports strips).

Excuses like these not only stretch credulity, they also insult the intelligence of the target reader. In any event, the impact of such events is part and parcel of the challenge of running any company – boards should expect the unexpected. They prove their effectiveness by overcoming adverse events – or turning them to their advantage. It should be relatively easy to manage a company when the economy is booming and demand is high, but the real test of management is when elements are adverse – good operators achieve good results despite problems, poor operators blame someone or something else!

Dealing with the media

The media is under great pressure to seek information – particularly from high-profile and consumer-known companies – and retain copies of several years' statements to use for background information. Unless media contacts are cultivated and personal relationships are built up, however, the media will normally have little commitment to the company, other than as a means of obtaining a story to fill column inches or broadcasting time.

Before dealing with the media, representatives of the company, and especially the chairman, need to be coached in how to organise and communicate the messages they wish to promulgate. Any spokesperson needs to have considerable personal knowledge of the company, which can be augmented by detailed input from time to time by those personally responsible for particular areas, divisions, subsidiaries etc. However, such background briefing, whilst essential, may not be sufficient. An excellent chairman, the normal spokesperson for normal corporate matters, may not necessarily make an excellent interviewee when issues – particularly bad news – are under investigation by an inquisitive media. Another reason for choosing

Case study	Joking destruction

Perhaps the best-known instance where a joke had a devastating effect on the fortunes of a company occurred when Gerald Ratner, chairman of the listed PLC that once bore his name, in a presentation at the Institute of Directors jokingly compared some of the products his shops sold to human waste, and having *'not much more value than a Marks & Spencer sandwich'*. Within a few months, 80 per cent or more was wiped off the company's share price, 200 of the company's shops had either to be closed or had their names changed, Ratner himself had to resign as chairman and later as a director.

In a few short words Ratner created a dual insult: not only was he rubbishing his own company's product, he was also rubbishing the customers who were buying such goods. Even if not meant to be taken literally (it was after all only a joke) this is hardly the way to make friends and influence people – or to instill the confidence on which so much of business thrives.

a spokesperson other than the chairman is that should a mistake be made in the initial briefing, the chairman may be able to smoothly correct such misinformation. It may be difficult to do this if the chairman himself made the error!

Very often, tone is as important as content. Certainly the situation should never be underestimated, mass reporting of one's comments can have far-reaching implications. Generally, humour should not be attempted, other than by the very experienced and confident. Equally, a spokesperson must never become angry – remember the catchphrase: *'Lose your temper, lose the argument'*.

Checklist – Media briefing/interviews

1 As comprehensive and complete a brief as possible must be prepared. A complete synopsis of company data, performance, products, problems, plans and so on, should be available and kept updated.

2 The point or aim of the interview must be discovered and appropriate responses and statements prepared particularly if the subject matter is likely to be controversial or embarrassing.

3 The spokesperson needs to have total control of the brief, of all facts and of prepared responses, and to be able to speak knowledgeably concerning the subject matter. Any hesitation, lack of confidence or inadequate knowledge will be communicated to the listener or viewer and may create doubt of knowledge or veracity – or both. In this respect it may be better to admit *'I don't know'*, rather than to try to 'flannel' or bluff the way through an answer.

4 Three or four simple messages that the organisation wishes to promote should be developed, possibly with 'changes of direction' sentences, so that if the interviewer leads off in one direction, the spokesperson may be able to 'steer' the answer to the company's preferred message. This approach needs to be controlled, since a constant (or apparent) 'refusal' to answer the question may lead to a far more inquisitive or confrontational interview.

5 The spokesperson must be ready for the 'off the cuff' and unrehearsed question deliberately introduced and designed to catch the unwary and to lead them to make an unprepared or unwise comment or answer.

6 The spokesperson must be able to keep calm and be patient under pressure (especially under deliberate goading), to be able to think quickly to fend off or deflect aggression and criticism, to retain control, and, above all, never to lose their temper.

7 Most live media interviews last a minute or less, and thus it may be possible to get across only two or three authoritative comments. Spokespersons need to be calm, alert and interested and serious, and not humorous, flustered, or flippant. To some extent, particularly on television, the manner in which a message is delivered can be more effective than the content.

8   The spokesperson should take time to think about the questions, asking for them to be repeated if necessary.

9   False statements should not be allowed to pass unchecked, the record should be corrected.

10 The spokesperson should be positive, not defensive. It may be better to 'own up' to a bad performance or event with a promise to 'improve' or rectify, rather than trying to defend an untenable position. The latter alternative will normally display the company (and the spokesperson) in a poor light regardless of the circumstances, and the impression will be 'they have learned nothing from the mistake', so nothing will change. This is particularly important when there has been loss, injury or death. It is essential that genuine sympathy is expressed.

Media relationship

Rather than leaving it until there is a problem resulting from a RISK, it may be preferable to adopt a 'media relationship policy' and work towards cultivating well-briefed contacts. This is particularly important where the

Example	Media relationship policy
	1. The company recognises the natural interest that will be evinced by the media in its operations and will make all information, other than that which is regarded as confidential, regularly available.
	2. [Name and deputy] will act as dedicated spokespersons for the company and will be briefed continually by those responsible for each [division, product, etc.].
	3. Any other employee being contacted by media representatives, should refer the matter to the dedicated spokesperson.
	4. When interfacing with the media, the spokesperson will endeavour to be truthful at all times, and to try to ensure that all information is correctly reported.
	5. All media contacts will be regularly briefed so that they have background knowledge of the company, updated continuously.
	6. In the event of a serious occurrence the senior manager responsible must brief the spokesperson immediately so that the latter is prepared to answer media questions.

product has a high profile or the company is, for example, a major employer in an area.

Research

No briefing or interview will be successful unless adequate preparation and research has been carried out. Thus, attention to items such as those set out in the following checklist is necessary.

CHECKLIST   Preparation and research for briefing

✓ Identify the areas of operation in which the media could be required to be briefed and updated concerning progress and all related aspects.

✓ Identify the target audiences and the information the media will seek to satisfy those audiences.

✓ Establish who is to deal with the ongoing enquiry and how they are to be briefed and updated regarding progress and all related aspects.

✓ Encourage the spokesperson to create links with media representatives, establishing names, positions, main interests or 'angles', deadlines, bias, and so on.

✓ Examine all stories and reports concerning the company and its products to ensure the correct image is being created, attempting to use the contacts to correct any false impressions.

✓ Continually originate questions that the company least wants asked, and, more importantly, develop some hopefully satisfactory answers to them (and become conversant with both, updated as necessary).

✓ Prepare and update a synopsis of all the successes of the company so that good news is available to leaven the bad.

Media releases

From time to time (and only when there is a real piece of news to impart) a media release can be issued. The media receive such a mass of information that only the most newsworthy will capture their attention. Strict parameters should be observed.

CHECKLIST   Media release

1   The subject matter must be really newsworthy – not to the organisation but to the target readers/listeners/viewers of the media targeted.

2   Newsworthy subject matter must be made attention-worthy. Thus the release should both capture initial attention and provide all the relevant information in an easy to read (and use) form. If the first paragraph does not grab the reader's attention, no matter how good the rest of the document, it is unlikely to be read. If the release is written in a way whereby the editor can use it (or more likely a part of it) without much editing, re-writing or recourse to the contact named (see below) then it stands a better chance of being used.

3   The release should be as brief as possible commensurate with the subject matter. Further, the language used should be simple, straightforward and should avoid jargon. Trying to 'pad out' a short release with extraneous information may damage the message and result in the whole thing being discarded.

4   A release is not the place to build a climax. The most important point should be featured first or prominently. Everything else should support or explain this 'headline' material.

5   A release is not the correct conduit for organisation promotion – if attempted, it will fail. The purpose of a release is to provide information that it is believed will be of interest to the readers/listeners/viewers as a news item – not as promotional puff.

6   A quote from the chairman or managing director, or better still from a household name customer or equivalent may add interest.

7   If the release features a product and it is feasible to do so, include a sample with it. As a (poor) substitute, a photograph might be used. If a number of photographs are available, reference to this in the release and a crib of what is available might generate interest providing obtaining the photo is made easy and in a form capable of being used by the editor. If samples are sent, the greatest care should be taken to send the best quality items.

8   If providing advance information about a forthcoming event ensure that the information is 'in advance'. Giving less than a week's notification is unlikely to generate any interest.

9   Keep a careful note of the correct names, positions and addresses of all those on the mailing lists – and keep all the details updated. Sending a release to the wrong person, or the right person with the wrong title, or to either at the wrong address reflects poorly on the issuing organisation.

10 Always incorporate a contact name and telephone number and ensure that the contact is available on that number at the times stated after the release has been issued.

The golden rules for issuing media releases can perhaps be summarised as the four 'ONLYs':

- Only issue a release when it features something of interest to the target audience.
- Only issue a release if it passes the 'blind man's test'. This comprises reading the release once only to someone who knows nothing of the subject matter and will have no chance to re-read it and asking them to state the story. Unless they can repeat the salient facts the release needs to be re-written – and probably shortened.
- Only issue a release to the particular part of the media whose target audience are likely to be interested in the item.
- Only issue the release if there is someone always on call ready and prepared to answer questions and provide additional data should the target media channel require this.

Briefing the chairman – meetings

INTRODUCTION

Whilst most chairmen will be sufficiently experienced and well able to deal effectively with meetings, inevitably some are not and they, as well as anyone required to 'chair' a general meeting for the first time, may welcome being provided with briefing notes, even if these are used more as back-up rather than as a 'word for word' script or crib.

Annual general meeting

Handling a board or advisers' meeting (whether formal or not) should be well within the average person's capabilities. However the legalistic over-tones of statutorily required meetings, with certain forms of wording to be adhered to – particularly where referring to proposed resolutions – may cause concern. As officer, servant of the board and chairman's confidante it may be appropriate for the company secretary to prepare guidance and even a complete crib for use at a meeting.

Example	Chairman's crib for annual general meeting
	Crib for XXth annual general meeting to be held on (date)
	At (time) call meeting to order with a few introductory remarks such as:...
	'Ladies and Gentlemen I welcome you to the .....th AGM of .... LTD/PLC. I will now start the formal proceedings, following the conclusion of which you will be able to meet members of the board and other executives and chat informally over some refreshments. We have, as you can see around you, provided displays of our products and services and I hope you will find these of interest.
	The notice of this meeting was despatched to all members of the company on (date) and I will ask the secretary to read it. *(Secretary reads notice.)* →

Example	Chairman's crib for annual general meeting – *continued*

The first item on the agenda concerns the consideration of the directors' report with the report and accounts for the (12) months ended (date). Those accounts and the balance sheet as at that date have been audited by your auditors Messrs (Name) and I request Mr/Ms (name) a partner of that firm of registered auditors to deliver their audit report).'

(Auditor reads report)

'May I propose that the Report of the Directors, together with the annexed statement of the company's accounts for the (twelve) months ended and the balance sheet as at that date duly audited be now received and adopted.

Has anyone any questions or comment?' *(Pause)*

(If questions are raised it will be necessary to deal with them and/ or if they are of a technical/financial nature pass them to finance director to deal with.)

'Following on from your consideration of the report and accounts may I also propose that a final dividend of (amount) per cent, or (amount) pence per share on the ordinary shares of the company payable on (date) be now declared for the (twelve) months ended (date). I call upon (name) to second these proposals.

All those in favour please raise your hands *(pause)* Anyone against? *(pause)* *(Assess and declare result.)*

I therefore declare the motion carried.

Item 2 concerns the re-election of the retiring director(s). The director(s) retiring by rotation is/are and I have much pleasure in proposing that (name) be and he hereby is re-elected a director of the company. I will ask (name) to second that proposal.

All those in favour *(pause)* and against *(pause)* *(Declare result.)*

I declare Mr (name) duly re-elected a director of the company.

Item 3 concerns the re-election of Messrs (auditors) as auditors of the company and I call upon Mr (name) to propose that resolution and Mr (name) to second it.

All those in favour *(pause)* Anyone against *(pause)*? *(Declare result.)*

Example	Chairman's crib for annual general meeting – *continued*

'Item 4 authorises the directors to fix the remuneration of the auditors and I will ask Mr (name) to propose that resolution and Mr (name) to second it.

All those in favour *(pause)*. Anyone against *(pause)*?' *(Declare result.)*

Is there any other ordinary business for consideration?

I therefore declare this xxth AGM closed. Thank you.'

Notes

1 There is no need for either the notice of the meeting or the audit report to be read, and doing so is rare. The advantages are that the time taken reading the notice should cover the arrival of latecomers; whilst reading the audit report should at least identify the auditor to the shareholders.

2 Legally the shareholders only *receive* the report of the directors and the accounts, both of which must be approved by the board. Even if the shareholders purport to reject both, their status is unchanged and they must be filed with the REGISTRAR OF COMPANIES within the required time limits.

3 Only if the dividend proposed by the directors is 'final' do the shareholders have any control; they can either approve, reject or reduce it. Shareholders cannot increase the dividend over the amount recommended by the directors. If the directors feel (however unlikely) that a recommended final dividend is likely to be reduced (or rejected), then it may be preferable to consider paying a second interim dividend (which does not need shareholder approval), and not recommend a final dividend in respect of that year's results.

4 If more than one director retires by rotation, separate proposals are required for each unless a proposal to deal with all such re-elections as a single resolution is first passed by the meeting. Proposals may also be needed to re-elect any directors who have been appointed since the previous AGM. Re-elected directors may wish to express their thanks to the meeting.

5 Other than the proposal of a vote of thanks to the chairman/board it is unlikely that anything else can be discussed by the meeting since notice of such business will not have been given. However, if every shareholder entitled to be present, is present and everyone agrees to waive notice the meeting can consider other matters.

(Extraordinary) general meetings

For companies formed under CA06, the word 'extraordinary' in relation to any meeting of the shareholders other than the AGM has been dropped – such meetings being simply referred to as general meetings. However, all companies that have as their articles, in whole or in part, a Table from a previous Act (e.g. CA85) may make reference to an EGM, which will continue unless and until their articles are changed.

By its very nature (that is, not being 'ordinary' and non-controversial), it is more likely that business at such a meeting can provoke greater attention and even disagreement and dissent. This is more likely to be the case should the company be experiencing financial difficulties, and thus unpalatable measures need to be considered. There follows a draft condensed version of a chairman's brief developed jointly by the then chairman and secretary for an EGM of a company in serious financial trouble and where the former chairman/managing director had been forced to resign to allow a capital restructuring to be put in place in an attempt to save the company. The EGM having been properly convened, the former chairman (who was still a shareholder) then submitted an item (too late for inclusion in the notice) for consideration by the meeting. Rather than risk the need to convene a further EGM (and the costs and dilution of effort at a difficult time that this would entail), the new chairman requested the meeting (at which all members were present) to allow consideration of the matter (which it did), although the proposal was then voted down. It was fortunate that all members were present, as, had fewer than the holders of 95 per cent of the shares been present and thus able to waive notice of the item, it is unlikely if it could have been properly put to the meeting at all.

Example	Chairman's crib for extraordinary general meeting
	The commentary and advice to the chairman are shown within square brackets. [Mr Chairman – I have assumed that voting will be by show of hands, in which case a simple majority of hands carries the resolution – i.e. each shareholder has one vote. It is, however, possible under the articles for any shareholder to demand a poll, in which case the meeting must be adjourned whilst we conduct a →

Example	Chairman's crib for extraordinary general meeting – *continued*

poll where the votes in accordance with number of shares held will decide the outcome. If a poll is demanded we also need to appoint tellers. I have prepared three sets of voting slips in case polls are required.

I have also primed several shareholders so that each time you ask for a seconder you should always find someone ready to second your proposal.

I have prepared a handout which details all the resolutions and proposals to be placed before the meeting (including a synopsis of the additional matter put forward for consideration by Mr K) and will give one to each member as they arrive. This should make it easy for them to follow the business as it proceeds.

[Call meeting to order at 12 noon]

Chairman : 'Ladies and gentlemen, my name is [X]. At a meeting held on 4th February, the board elected me its chairman. This extraordinary general meeting was convened by the board by a notice issued on 28th January which I propose we take as read – does anyone object to that?'

[Pause – then, assuming no objection ...]

'Subsequently a shareholder holding in excess of 10 per cent of the shares, as is required by the articles, requested that a further item of business be considered at this meeting. We will deal with that request later.

Since the first item on the official Agenda concerns myself I shall vacate the chair and ask Mr Y to deal with it.'

RESOLUTION 1 – Confirmation of appointment of 'chairman'

Y : 'Thank you Mr Chairman. Ladies and gentlemen, as you will see the first item on the agenda concerns the proposal to confirm the appointment as chairman of Mr X. Neither this nor items 2 and 3 need shareholder approval nor are they required to be dealt with at a general meeting, but in view of the financial situation of the company and the dissent that has prefaced this meeting, it was thought this would be advisable. Accordingly I would like to propose that Mr X's appointment as chairman of

Example	Chairman's crib for extraordinary general meeting – *continued*

the board be and it hereby is confirmed. Do I have a seconder? All those in favour?

Anyone against? I declare the motion carried and hand the meeting back to the Chairman.'

RESOLUTION No 2 – Confirmation of appointment of managing director

CHAIRMAN :'Thank you. At the meeting which appointed myself as chairman, a majority of the directors also appointed Z as managing director. I would now like to propose that Z's appointment as managing director be and it hereby is confirmed. Do I have a seconder?

All those in favour? Anyone against? I declare the motion carried.'

RESOLUTION No 3 – Confirmation of appointment of secretary

CHAIRMAN : 'The directors also requested Mr Y to assume the role of company secretary in addition to acting as a non-executive director and I would like to propose that Mr Y's appointment as company secretary be and it is hereby confirmed. Do I have a seconder? All those in favour? Anyone against? I declare the motion carried.'

RESOLUTION No 4 – Creation of additional share capital, alteration of memorandum

'The next two items on the agenda concern the creation of additional share capital which is necessary so that the major restructuring of the company on which we have been urgently working for some weeks can take place. Copies of the formal resolution which must be filed with the Registrar of Companies have been given to you and I would now like to propose

THAT the share capital of the company be increased from £10,000 to £2,000,000 by the creation of:

a) 990,000 new ordinary shares of £1 each ranking in all respects *pari passu* with the 10,000 existing ordinary shares of £1 of the company,

Example	**Chairman's crib for extraordinary general meeting** *– continued*

AND

b) the creation of 1,000,000 Cumulative Redeemable Convertible Preference Shares of £1.

The notice refers to a coupon rate of 10 per cent, but on reflection the board feels that the rate needs to be left for individual negotiation. Does anyone object to this?

[Assuming no one objects (and having canvassed all the shareholders and found that no-one currently does), the motion itself can then be put to the meeting.]

'Do I have a seconder? All those in favour? Anyone against?

I therefore declare that resolution carried.'

RESOLUTION No 5 – Change of auditors

[I have checked with the retiring auditors who have no objection to making way for the new auditors. They have confirmed that with the steps currently being taken by the board, including the matters that are to be dealt with later in the meeting, they have no intention of lodging any statement requesting that any matters be brought to the attention of the shareholders.]

'Your Board originally requested ABC to act as auditors, a role they carried out until the end of 2XXX, when it was felt more advisable to appoint auditors located nearer to the company. Messrs ABC have indicated their willingness to resign. As part of the investigation carried out by Mr Z, an audit-type investigation on the activities of the company to 31st December 2XXX was completed by Messrs DEF, and I now propose that Messrs DEF be and they hereby are appointed auditors of the company until the conclusion of the first Annual General Meeting which must be held within the next few weeks. Do I have a seconder? All those in favour? Anyone against? I declare that resolution carried.

RESOLUTION No 6 – Company strategy

'The next item concerns the restructuring of the company and the strategy for the next two years, details of which are included in a report from Mr Z, copies of which have been sent to you. The restructuring report, and the "audit" report contained within it were prepared very urgently and within a →

| **Example** | **Chairman's crib for extraordinary general meeting**
– continued |

very short time span. Inevitably, some shortcuts have needed to be taken and the board is aware of a number of errors which need to be rectified at an operational level. We are asking today for shareholder approval in principle to the plan which entails amongst other things, the conversion of shareholder loans with which I will deal later.

I would like you to confirm your acceptance of this plan with those comments in mind, and without discussion since the matter is so urgent we need to move to the next item. However if any shareholder does wish to make any comments …'

[You will have to play this by ear. Since all the shareholders have already received a copy and we have spoken to several and dealt with a number of their queries, this may go through 'on the nod' – which is hardly surprising bearing in mind the pressure evinced by the shareholders to nominate Mr Z as the replacement MD. You can expect Mr K to object of course but unless he can be specific and concise I suggest you request him to put his comments in writing for the attention of the board when it comes to implement the plan. In any event, and as I am sure Mr K knows, the voting strength is overwhelmingly in favour of acceptance.]

PROPOSAL No 7 – Conversion of loans made by shareholders into share capital

'The next item concerns the conversion of loans made by us all to the company as part of our shareholding investment. Although it may be arguable that it is permissible for such loans to be counted as shareholders' investments, the advice the board now has, including that from its new auditors, is that these loans do not constitute part of the shareholders' investment and that if their total is excluded from that category, the company is insolvent and should not continue trading. We need everyone to agree today to convert these loans into ordinary shares, and unless this is done, we cannot see that new money can flow into the company which is the only way the company can survive. Thus the directors view this matter as a question for shareholders of *"convert your loans into shares or the Board will have to recommend that the company be put into receivership."*

Example	Chairman's crib for extraordinary general meeting – *continued*

If the loans are not converted your investment is lost, whereas if they are converted, there is a chance of saving the company and thus your investment. This is not something on which we can vote since it must be an individual decision, although the protection of everyone's investment depends on everyone agreeing to convert. I must stress that as one of the largest investors and, in terms of my shareholder loan, one of the largest creditors of the company I am prepared to convert my loan into shares immediately after this meeting. Any comments?'

[Again you will have to play it by ear. I have forms that will enable shareholders to either a) convert loans into ordinary shares, or b) convert some loan into shares and some into Cumulative Redeemable Convertible Preference Shares (CRCPS) or c) invest new money in Ordinary shares and/or CRCPS. You will need to try to 'insist' that before people leave they sign a form.]

PROPOSAL No 8 – Item put forward by Mr K

'The last item concerns a request made by Mr K for an alteration to the articles. Before we can consider the item itself (which we have set out on the handout) you will note that the short notice given in respect of this item needs to be agreed. The board think it would be advisable for everyone to agree to consider the item and thus I would propose that proposal (8) be considered by the meeting notwithstanding that short notice was given – those in favour? Any against? I declare the motion carried in which case we may now deal with the proposal put forward by Mr K that the articles of association be changed as set out in the wording of the resolution. Mr K do you wish to make any comments regarding this resolution?

[Again you will have to play it by ear but at the end of any discussion, you may like to comment – the board's view being entirely against the proposal – and need to put it to the vote – in favour, against, declare result. I suppose it is just possible that we might have a demand for a poll here, although my canvassing indicates little support for a proposal that really could have the effect of restricting the actions of the board in its efforts to save the company.

Example	**Chairman's crib for extraordinary general meeting** *– continued*
	If there is any argument, you could make the point that the chance of saving the company is slim, and it may be the only way forward is to transfer ownership of part or all of the company which would almost certainly mean the offer of additional shares. Since no existing shareholder is willing to put more money into the company it is difficult to see the point of the proposal.]
	'That concludes the business of this extraordinary general meeting – may I thank you for attending.'

Notes

1 As stated within the above crib, the confirmation of the appointments of chairman of the board, managing director and company secretary are not matters for the shareholders, and this course was adopted only to try to test and gain support for the actions of the newly constituted board in a difficult situation. Had such support not been forthcoming, attempts to save the company would probably have been abandoned immediately by the board.

2 The question of issuing convertible preference shares with a variable coupon rate requires legal advice. In fact here, against the advice of a number of people involved (including the author who was the newly appointed company secretary referred to here), it was put to and approved by the meeting, although the issue was never actually implemented as the board (failing to obtain additional finance) had to invite the lending bank to put the company into administrative receivership within a few weeks of the meeting.

3 The value of canvassing support, particularly in difficult situations like these, cannot be over-emphasised. Whilst not wishing to stifle fair criticism and comment, the will of the majority needs to prevail (subject to ensuring there is no oppression of minority rights) so the company can make progress.

4 Using a handout, particularly as here where there was an extra item of contentious business, should aid attention, and thus the flow of the meeting.

5 The preparation of such a script/crib (providing advice on each item), and the canvassing of support, took several hours but since the meeting went without a hitch the aim was achieved. The concept was to

try to pre-empt every alternative, or to provide an answer for every possibility and or concern.

Postscript

Despite the approaching insolvency, the meeting ran extremely smoothly, not only of course because of the crib, but also because everyone realised the seriousness of the situation. However, there is no doubt the advance preparation and consideration of what was hoped would be all eventualities, was a contributory factor.

Charging assets

INTRODUCTION

As the chief administrative officer of the company, the company secretary has responsibility for company assets. Such assets need to be protected from theft and damage and records of transactions concerning them produced for the AUDITORS. In addition, there may be a need to record the acquisition and disposal of certain assets in the board minutes, and, for a listed PLC, the approval of shareholders needed for major or material acquisitions and disposals.

Valuable assets may not only be used in and for the purposes of the business but can also be used as security for loans to generate working capital for use in the business. However, in these cases, the lender of funds will usually wish to protect their position by securing their loan and requiring the company to create a charge (or mortgage) over the asset in the lender's favour. The effect of this is that the company cannot dispose of the asset without first repaying the lender (or gaining their explicit permission); whilst should the company fail, the person in whose favour the charge exists has control over that asset to the exclusion of the powers of the insolvency practitioner.

Borrowing on asset value

In certain circumstances the creation of a charge, or the acquisition of property on which a charge exists, entails the company registering details within a set time limit with the Registrar of Companies. The purpose of this is to *'put into the public arena'* details of the creation of the charge so that creditors dealing with the company are made aware that particular assets of the company appearing in the accounts, which might otherwise support their debt, have actually been taken out of the 'pool of assets' available for that purpose. The assets (wherever situated) over which the creation of a charge requires registration are:

- the securing of debentures;
- a charge on uncalled capital;
- a charge evidenced by an instrument which, if executed by an individual would require registration as a bill of sale;
- a charge on land or any interest in land;
- a floating charge on the undertaking of the business or its property;

- a charge on calls on share capital made but not paid;
- a charge on a ship (or a share in a ship) or aircraft;
- a charge on goodwill or intellectual property (including any patent or trade mark, registered design, unregistered design right, copyright or any licence in respect of any such rights);
- a charge on book debts.

Administration

In order to register a charge, a company must file with the Registrar:

- particulars of the charge;
- the instrument of charge;
- the appropriate form (MG01 – see s. 860 CA06, previously s. 395, s. 410 in Scotland, CA85);
- a £13 fee.

These items must be filed within 21 days of the creation of the charge. If the company attempts to file details after the 21-day period the documents will be returned by the Registrar stating that before the items can be registered the company will need to obtain clearance from the Company Court (which will require an explanation for the delay). When the documents are accepted by the Registrar, a certificate of filing can be issued which confirms that the charge has been entered on the records at CH and is therefore available to anyone inspecting the company's records. Those inspecting the Register of Charges are warned that they should not rely on the certificate in terms of the accuracy of the charge itself.

Legally it is the responsibility of an officer of the company to register the charge, and under CA06 the officers are liable if they do not do so. However very often, in practice it is the lender who files the charge as it is in their best interests to ensure the item is registered.

Effect of late and/or faulty registration

In the event of late registration (i.e. one that is filed more than 21 days after creation), the charge is voidable against a liquidator or a person who acquires an interest in the property subject to the charge until it is registered, although the charge remains valid between the company and the creditor. Late registration may be caused by documents needing execution and transmission from overseas.

If incorrect details have been registered, the company can submit a corrected version.

Register of charges

Every company must keep a register of charges (even a company that has no charges), and must keep that register at its registered address or SAIL and make it available to shareholders and creditors on request. If such a request is not granted within 14 days, the company and an officer are in default (s. 877(5) CA06).

Release of charge

Subject to receipt of a statutory declaration (for which there will be a charge of at least £5 per item by a commissioner of oaths) by an officer of the company on a form in accordance with s. 872 CA06 (formerly s. 403(a)), that the debt for which the charge was given has been paid or satisfied, and/or that the property charged has been released from the charge or has been sold or otherwise disposed of, the Registrar accepts the form and places the detail on the record. The charge itself however remains as part of the record – with the discharge effectively cancelling out the charge. However, under CA06 a charge will only be accepted as forming part of the register if, in addition to the above, there is confirmation from the lender that the money has been repaid and therefore that the charge can be lifted.

Discharging a charge in respect of a loan that has been repaid is often overlooked and it has been estimated that as many as a third of all the charges registered at CH are in respect of loans that have been repaid. Obviously, failing to notify CH that the money has been repaid and thus the charge is discharged could damage the company's perceived creditworthiness to anyone doing a search on the company.

Development of concept

Since 1989, there have been three consultation processes leading to recommendations for changes to the existing situation. The Law Commission's most recent set of proposals suggested:

- filing of details of charges with CH (which would not – as at present – issue a confirmation) would be carried out online by companies filing a 'financing statement' (this would include details of the debtor and the secured creditor, the security itself and whether the statement is for a set time or is to continue indefinitely);
- precedence would be decided by date order of filing;
- the online register would be called the Companies Security Register;
- filing could be carried out by either the company or the secured creditor (the legal obligation on the company to file being abolished by CA06);
- failure to file would result in the charge being ineffective against an administrator or liquidator of the company;

- a floating charge registered at certain times prior to the onset of insolvency proceedings would be void;
- the current rule whereby a fixed charge ranks before a floating charge would be changed so that the precedence would be in accordance with the dates of filing (meaning that floating charge holders could rank in precedence to preferential creditors);
- the list of assets which are covered by the existing registration rules would be replaced by an assumption that all security interests are registrable unless excepted;
- fixed charges over registered land which are required to be lodged with the Land Registry would not also need to be notified to CH;
- charges over unregistered land (regardless of whether they are lodged at the Land Registry) and all floating charges would need to be filed;
- factoring or invoice discounting facilities would need to be registered.

Case study	Curtailing the effectiveness of the charging process
	In the case of New Zealand construction company *Agnew v CIR (usually known as Brumark Investments)*, the Privy Council held that fixed charges are only effective on assets where the holder of the charge can control them. Thus the lender's fixed charge over Brumark's 'book debts' was ineffective (because the debts varied daily and so they could not control them) – and could only actually be a 'floating charge' (ranking behind preferential creditors). This ruling has recently been questioned in the Court of Appeal decision in the case of *Spectrum*, which followed the Court's own ruling in *Re New Bullas Trading Ltd* which said that 'book debts' and the 'proceeds from book debts' were separate assets capable of being secured by a fixed charge (over the debt) and a floating charge (over the proceeds).
	The effect is that banks could adopt a more restrictive attitude to lending and/or any extension of lending when a company requires short-term additional borrowing. In turn this could lead to a requirement for directors to provide personal guarantees of their company's debts (e.g. overdrafts). In any case this may be a requirement if the company takes advantage of the relaxation of accounts auditing requirements if its turnover is less than £6.5 million.

Note: At time of revising this edition it was unclear whether the Law Commission's suggestions were to be adopted. It may be that since the recommendations rely on computerisation this has been deferred pending the completion of the CA06 changes.

Classes of shares and class meetings

INTRODUCTION

The vast majority of shares issued by companies are 'ordinary' – the holders of which assume the greatest risk, should the company fail. However, companies can issue other types which, with the ordinary shares, comprise the issued share capital of the company. Issued share capital may only be a proportion of the total 'authorised' share capital. For existing companies their total authorised share capital is required to be specified in its memorandum and the share capital clause sets out all the classes of shares. Thus such a clause might read: *'The share capital of the company will be £1,000,000 divided into 500,000 ordinary shares of £1 and 500,000 preference shares of £1'*. However, for companies incorporated under CA06, the requirement to have a stated authorised share capital in the memorandum is abolished. Authority will be granted to the directors of a company formed under CA06 (unless the articles curtail this) to issue the number and value of shares that they feel is appropriate.

Ordinary shares

The first shareholders of companies formed under law are entrepreneurs (risk-takers) who take 'ordinary shares' in the companies. Ordinary shareholders are the real risk-takers in the company, since they have no right to any payment (dividend) in respect of their shareholding – or any repayment if the company fails and is insolvent. If the company is successful and profitable and yet the directors do not wish to pay a dividend, the only recourse of the ordinary shareholders would be to use their voting power to remove the directors by passing an ordinary resolution (subject to special notice, i.e. containing details of both sides of the proposal) or to make application to the court.

If the board of a listed PLC feels the market price of the company's shares is too high, subject to shareholder approval or to authority given to the board in the articles, it can increase the number of shares by issuing additional shares (making a *bonus issue*) in proportion to the shareholders' original holding, e.g. one bonus share for every five shares held. Thus, in that case the number of shares has been increased by 20 per cent, although the proportion held by each holder to the total number of shares in issue is unchanged (unless they sell some or all of the bonus shares or buy some bonus shares sold by other shareholders). Obviously the total value of the original plus the bonus shares should be the same as the total value of the existing shares before the bonus – although each individual share will be worth less.

If the board wishes to increase the number of shares in issue and, at the same time, raise more capital, provided it has or obtains authority from the existing shareholders, it can make a *rights issue*. This gives the existing shareholders the right to subscribe more capital for additional shares at a price which is often set at a discount to the market price to encourage subscription for the new shares. Those wishing to subscribe for the shares pay the price required and the new shares can be added to their original holding. Alternatively, the rights to subscribe for the new shares (or some of them) can be sold, since they may have a value of their own. Some large holders adopt the policy of selling sufficient of their rights to generate enough cash to subscribe for the remainder (a process known as 'swallowing the tail'), although this is only possible if the rights have a value of their own (usually only if the new shares are being issued at a discount to the market value).

Preference shares

As the name implies, holders of these shares take precedence (in terms of both annual dividend and repayment in a winding-up) over ordinary shareholders. Usually preference shares carry a stated rate of payment e.g. '7 per cent preference shares of £1', indicating that each year the holders must be paid a dividend of 7p in respect of each share held. Some company articles specify that if the dividend on the preference shares is in arrears, those shareholders have the right to attend the AGM and vote in accordance with the number of preference shares they own. They may have similar voting rights should there be a proposal to wind up the company.

Cumulative preference shares

If a year passes without payment of a dividend on their shares, ordinary shareholders have no right to recoup any 'missed dividend' later. Holders of cumulative shares, however, do have a right to recovery of any missed dividend(s). Thus, when there are no profits and insufficient cash to pay the dividend on their shares, their dividend is missed. However, in later, profitable, years these shareholders are entitled to the arrears of the missed dividends as well as the current year's dividend.

Convertible preference shares

Holders of such shares have the right (usually at specified times in the future and sometimes at specified rates of exchange) to convert their preference shares into ordinary shares.

Redeemable preference shares

Shares can be given a redemption date requiring the company to return the nominal value of the shares at some future date (or within a specified period). Thus someone holding 7 per cent Cumulative Redeemable Preference shares 2010/11 would have right to have the shares redeemed (or a pre-set proportion of them) between 2010 and 2011.

Non-redeemable preference shares

As their name implies, these shares cannot be redeemed. Neither (after issue) can they be converted into redeemable preference shares since this could be preferential treatment to the possible detriment of the creditors. They normally have a stated 'coupon rate' which must be paid, but only if they were also cumulative shares would holders be entitled to any missed dividends.

Deferred and/or founder shares

Usually, holders of such shares surrender immediate income from dividends on their shares in the hope or expectation that at some set or unspecific time in the future they will share in profits usually at a very advantageous rate – or see the value of their shares increase.

Debenture or loan stock

These are not shares at all (and do not form part of the issued share capital), but forms of guaranteed or secured borrowing. Debentures (with a set annual rate of payment) are issued under a trust deed which enables the trustee for the debenture holders, appointed under the deed, to protect their interests, to take action if the specified interest rate is not paid or there is a breach of any other covenants (i.e. legal promises) set out in the trust deed. The deed is usually backed by a CHARGE over all the assets and undertaking of the business (a floating charge) or some specified assets e.g. a freehold property (a fixed charge) of the company.

Pre-emption

Generally (unless the articles declare otherwise), if new shares are to be issued, they must first be offered to existing shareholders in the proportion that each holding bears to the total in issue. This is called a right of pre-emption (or 'first refusal') and may be pertinent if the proportions of shares held are important – e.g. a holder of 75 per cent of the ordinary shares has control of the contents of the articles, since with that proportion of votes they have power to change the provisions of the articles. If shares are not to be issued in accordance with this right, the members must first consent to waive their pre-emptive rights by resolution in general meeting (or by a WRITTEN resolution) and, if this varies the articles, it needs a special resolution (i.e. one requiring 75 per cent approval of those voting either in person or proxy or, if passed by written resolution, by 75 per cent of the total voting strength).

However, the following issues do not need a waiver of the pre-emption rights:

- shares for employee share schemes;
- non-participating preference and similar securities;
- any other non-equity securities;
- allotment of shares for a non-cash consideration; and
- allotment of shares under a renounceable letter of allotment.

Payment

The original subscribers to the memorandum of a PLC must pay for their shares in cash. But shares in LTDs are not always issued for cash – they can be issued in exchange for the rights to property or a patent or a new process, etc. If shares are issued for a consideration other than cash (i.e. assets), then such assets must be handed over within five years of the shares being issued. If this transfer does not take place, then the allottee is liable to pay cash for the shares (and any premium) plus interest for the period from the issue to the date of the transfer.

If shares are to be issued in exchange for an asset, the value of the asset must be assessed by an expert (i.e. a person qualified to act as an auditor).

A PLC cannot allot shares unless at least 25 per cent of the value of such shares (together with any premium) has been paid in cash.

Stamp duty

Entries related to a share transfer may only be made in the register of members following receipt of a signed and (if necessary) stamped stock transfer form and the surrender of the share certificate from the person selling the shares. Stamp duty must be paid according to the value of the shares (*ad valorem*) if the total exceeds £1,000. Since the value determines the duty, it is first necessary to establish the value, possibly asking the auditors to prepare such a valuation.

The following transactions are exempt from *ad valorem* stamp duty: namely share transfers resulting from

- property in the name of a trustee to a new trustee;
- security for a loan;
- a bequest to a beneficiary under a will and probate;
- a bequest to a beneficiary from an intestate's estate;
- a bequest to a residuary legatee;
- in consideration of marriage;
- a liquidator;
- no beneficial interest passing (e.g. from one nominee to another nominee);
- a gift.

A statement confirming that the transfer is exempt must be completed on the rear of the new stock transfer form. Formerly these transfers needed to be stamped with a nominal £5 (this was scrapped in March 2008).

Record and title

The issue of a share certificate acts as both receipt for the money subscribed and evidence of title to the shares. Many company articles state that share certificates are only valid as evidence of title if sealed, and if a company with such articles wishes to dispense with the use of the SEAL, either the articles need to be changed or a 'securities seal' purely for use on share certificates should be retained.

Each time new shares are allotted the secretary must:

- enter the register of members;
- issue a share certificate;
- send (within 28 days) notice of the allotment to the Registrar of Companies using Form SH01 in accordance with s. 555 CA06 (formerly s. 88(2) CA85).

Single member company

If a transfer of shares results in the company having only one shareholder or member (i.e. the transfer creates a SINGLE MEMBER COMPANY), this fact and the date of the event must be stated on the account for the remaining member (e.g. 'From [date] this is a single member company'). Conversely, should a single member transfer some of his shares to someone else, or (a) new share(s) be issued to a second shareholder, then the message 'From [date] this is no longer a single member company' must be written in the shareholder's account. The surviving shareholder of a company which becomes a single member company (e.g. one of two shareholders sells their shares to the remaining shareholder) after six months will have unlimited liability for the acts of the company.

Meetings

Normally only holders of ordinary shares have the right to attend general meetings of the company. However, when there are matters which may affect the interests of holders of various type of shares or loans, they may have the right to convene and attend a meeting of their own 'class' of shares. The articles will normally provide a protection to holders of such shares by stipulating that nothing can be done which could affect their interests without their agreement.

If agreement is needed to such a proposal the holders of the shares affected by the proposal have the right to meet to consider the matter. The detailed procedure for convening such a meeting will usually be set out in the articles but, if not, CA06 states that two or more holders owning 10 per cent or more of the shares of that class may convene a meeting. Legal advice should be taken to ensure the correct procedure and wording is followed so that there is no prejudicial effect.

Example	Notice of class meeting

To: The holders of the [specify] shares of [company name]

NOTICE OF CLASS MEETING

Notice is hereby given that a meeting of the holders of the [specify] shares in the company will be held at [time] on [date] at [place] for the purpose of considering and, if thought fit, passing the following resolution:

'THAT this class meeting of the holders of the [specify] of the [company] by this extraordinary resolution hereby consent to the variation of their rights by [specify]'

By order of the board.

Secretary   17th October 2XXX

A member entitled to attend and unable to do so may appoint a proxy to vote in his/her place. Such proxies should be sent to the registered office of the company to arrive not later than 48 hours before the commencement of the meeting.

The quorum for such a class meeting is, under s. 334 CA06, '*two persons ... holding at least one third ... of the issued shares ... in question*'. If 15 per cent or more of the affected members feel their interests have been prejudiced by the resolution or action they have the right to apply to the court and the resolution (if passed) cannot be implemented until the court sanctions it. Legal advice should be sought if class rights are to be varied.

The company secretary

INTRODUCTION

From 1856 until 2008, every company formed under company law was required to have a company secretary. In addition, PLCs must have two directors, but LTDs just one. Under CA06, the appointment of company secretary continues to be mandatory for PLCs (for which appointment specified levels of expertise are required), but since April 2008 the appointment has been made optional for LTDs (unless the articles of the company and/or the members specifically require there to be a company secretary). Whilst a director can also act as the company secretary (and this is often the case), should there be a requirement for two signatures, the same person cannot sign as both director and secretary.

The range of duties undertaken by company secretaries varies widely. Ironically CA06 requires greater attention to legal compliance, as well as creating dilutions available to LTDs which need to be checked out before they can be used – thus requiring the attention of exactly the appointee performing the role and undertaking the duties of a company secretary! If there is no company secretary, someone else must carry out these duties – ideally someone at board level. The company secretary is an officer of the company and the appointment is the responsibility of the board.

The role

The title 'secretary' is very old. Derived from the Latin word *secretarius*, it means 'a confidential aide', or 'a person in someone else's confidence sharing secret or private matters with them'. Unfortunately, being expected to be secretive and low key underplays the importance of the role – a misconception enhanced by the title often being confused with that of a 'senior typist'. This seriously, and dangerously, underestimates the importance of the role in terms of corporate compliance. As Sir John Harvey Jones (former chief executive of ICI, when that company was one of the largest UK companies) said: *'in many ways the appointment and role of the company secretary is key for the company – more vital than that of many directors – not least because of the increasing weight and scope of legislation and the increasing criminalisation of the activities of officers of the company … the company secretary needs to be dynamic'.*

Good company secretaryship, like good administration, tends not to be seen but plays its part with quiet efficiency. This also can have the effect of underplaying the vital and multi-faceted importance of the appointee, which can be defined as:

- *guardian*, ensuring fulfilment of the company's obligation to comply with legislation and protecting its books, registers, assets, reputation etc.;
- *facilitator*, easing communication between board and management;
- *recorder*, taking and protecting the legally required minutes of board meetings;
- *confidante*, supporting all members of the board and particularly the chairman; and
- *chief administrative officer* of the company (i.e. being a legal 'officer' of the company, with all the attendant responsibilities and liabilities that description entails).

The phrase *'chief administrative officer'* was coined in 1971 by the then Master of the Rolls, Lord Denning. He defined the secretary as *'the chief administrative officer of the company – he regularly makes representations on behalf of the company and enters into contracts on its behalf. He is entitled to sign contracts – all such matters come within the ostensible authority of the company secretary'*. Since then, the role has gained an increasing prominence – not least in the obligations under CORPORATE GOVERNANCE. In some companies the company secretary, like children in the Victorian age, is required to be *'seen but not heard'* – only supporting the board and its meetings administratively. However, using a person who is an officer of the company in this restricted role may be very short-sighted – not least since the secretary may have a more comprehensive view of the business under discussion than some of the members of the board – particularly non-executive directors. The secretary certainly has an obligation to be fully aware of all legal requirements affecting the company, its officers, its employees and its agents. To quote Sir John Harvey Jones again: *'I always work with a positive board system, by which I mean I don't allow silence. After discussing each subject I ask each member of the board what their opinion is and why – this includes the company secretary as I have always believed that his view should be heard.'*

To a large extent the importance of the role is determined by the fact that unlike directors, there are restrictions on those who are able to be appointed company secretary (at least in theory) for PLCs. Effectively, unless there are very strong reasons for the board ignoring the requirements, the company secretary of a PLC should hold one or more of several stated professional qualifications.

Indeed, the views of the company secretary may be more objective than that of directors, some of whom may, despite their board responsibilities, be more interested in *'fighting the corner'* for their own executive responsibilities.

The Cadbury Committee on Corporate Governance recognised the unique position of the company secretary, stating: *'the company secretary has a key role to play in ensuring that the board procedures are followed and regularly reviewed. The chairman and the board will look to the company secretary for guidance on what their responsibilities are'*.

The commentary went on: *'the company secretary must now more than ever show him or herself to be knowledgeable, reliable, discreet, an excellent communicator, a good listener and approachable. Directors and senior executives must have confidence in the company secretary and must consider him or her as their first port of call for advice and guidance. The company secretary must have the answers – or at least know where to find them'*.

The Cadbury Report also suggested that all directors (and this would apply particularly to non-executive directors which it regarded as having views that were independent from and potentially more objective than those of executive directors) should always have access to the company secretary and that any suggestion of the dismissal or removal of the company secretary should be considered by the whole board. (The thinking behind this is that the secretary was possibly the one person who could attempt to prevent wrongdoing and/or legal non-compliance on the part of the board – particularly a very dominant chairman – and if unable to do so, be prepared to WHISTLE-BLOW.)

It is one of the responsibilities of the board to appoint a suitable and capable company secretary and to ensure that the appointee maintains these attributes. In many ways this is his most onerous task, since the impact of legislation on companies from many areas is immense and continues to grow. Thus a prime responsibility of the postholder should be to 'keep the company legal' – and the directors out of jail. The company secretary has been described as *'the keeper of the company's conscience'* – a description with which in a recent survey, 85 per cent of respondents agreed. Although the ultimate responsibility for all the acts of the company rests with the directors, the company secretary under company law is an officer of the company and, under common law, he should never be in a position where he has a conflict of interests. Like the other officers he has a fiduciary duty to put the company's interests before his own.

The above encapsulates the challenge for those companies that decide not to appoint a company secretary. The role of the directors is to drive the company forward which is a markedly different requirement to the foregoing. Ideally companies need both *'risk taker and driver'* and *'keeper of the company's conscience and compliance officer'* (even if one person undertakes both roles).

Responsibilities

There are around three million UK companies, and no doubt around three million different job descriptions for their company secretaries. The following checklist sets out the main responsibilities of most company secretaries, but this should be individually customised. It is a prime responsibility of the board to ensure these duties are carried out.

CHECKLIST   Company secretary's duties

✓ Understand and interpret the requirements and obligations contained in the memorandum and articles and guide the board on these, recommending when the articles should be updated or revised.

✓ Maintain statutory registers. This entails keeping updated the various statutory books including the register of members which involves transferring shares, issuing new certificates etc. although many companies with large numbers of shareholders delegate such work to specialised divisions of, for example, the clearing banks.

✓ Update the company file with the Registrar of Companies. Although the board is ultimately responsible, it is the secretary who normally advises CH promptly (and within specified time limits) of all changes in directorate, of all charges over assets, of changes in shareholders etc., at least once a year, and of any other matters affecting the corporate nature of the company.

✓ Ensure compliance with company law. The company secretary must have a good working knowledge of the requirements placed upon the officers under company law and ensure that the company complies with such requirements and all changes and innovations.

✓ Liaise with shareholders. The extent of this responsibility will depend on the individual companies – in some, the directors take on this role, however in most the secretary is responsible for the documentary contact with shareholders – i.e. notice of general meetings, preparation and despatch of annual report etc.

✓ Ensure legally required documentation is prepared. This is a very wide-ranging responsibility, since much of what is required is derived from obligations under commercial, employment and other laws and familiarity with such laws and obligations is essential.

✓ Convene company and board meetings. The company secretary can only do this at the direction of the board, but to ensure the board fulfils its own duties he needs to ensure that board meetings are held regularly. He should ensure he attends board meetings.

✓ Compile minutes of board meetings and subcommittees. This is an onerous but essential part of his duties not simply to preserve the record of control, but also to have available documentary evidence which might be needed as a defence in any actions against directors (i.e. to be able to prove they exercised their duty of care and took account of the interests of the company stakeholders as required under CA06).

✓ File accounts and annual return. Increasingly the obligation to file such items within specified time limits is being backed by rigorously enforced fines. Repeated failure to file on time can lead to disqualification of the director(s) (since they have ultimate responsibility) from office under the Company Directors Disqualification Act.

✓ Carry out instructions of board. As the chief administrative officer of the company the secretary may have the prime role for interfacing with management.

Alternatively executive directors may take this role – whoever takes it needs to comply with the exact requirements of the board (as well as needing to be aware of legal compliance matters).

✓ (For listed PLCs only) liaise with the Stock Exchange and ensure the requirements of the Listing Agreement are complied with.

✓ Act as board/chairman's confidante. This is often one of the roles played by the secretary particularly where he is not also a director as he can bring an objective view to the work of the board. It is also often possible for the secretary to be aware of internal developments of which directors are not aware and thus provide a valuable communication conduit to the chairman/board.

✓ Act as chief administrative officer. The scope for this responsibility will vary from company to company, nevertheless the secretary is often the source from which management first learn of and are required to implement decisions.

✓ Protect the company's assets. It is the secretary's duty to protect the statutory books and records of the company and the confidentiality of the board's work. It may be logical to make him responsible for other aspects of corporate security.

✓ Ensure all proper returns are made (and in time). The officers of the company, of which the secretary is one, have an obligation to comply with the filing regulations of company law. If these items are not filed by the due date, fines can be levied, repetition of which could lead to disqualification as a company officer.

✓ Oversee legal matters. Often the secretary is legally qualified or will be the only executive with some experience of the law. Increasingly the law is intruding on all company activities and someone must assume this responsibility.

✓ Oversee the arrangements to allow shareholders and others to inspect certain records of the company and to provide access to statutory and other bodies to inspect other records.

✓ Ensure compliance generally – with all contractual and commercial law, health and safety law, environmental law, employment law, and so on.

Many company secretaries also take responsibility for insurance, pensions, property, security and employment and/or financial matters.

This is so vast an obligation (particularly legal compliance, given the amount of legislation – around 36,000 Acts of Parliament and Statutory Instruments etc. in 12 years – that the current Government has generated) that it is difficult to visualise how a working company secretary can hope to provide detailed and comprehensive advice and guidance on such matters. It may be that companies should be considering providing additional funding to enable this compliance obligation to be addressed adequately – unless this is available the secretary may be able to pass liability for acts or negligence to the board simply by arguing that he was unable to do the job properly due to insufficient resources.

Despite all the foregoing and the recognition of what a key player a company secretary is in the control of the corporate body, under CA06, LTDs are allowed to dispense with the appointment. This seems to evidence on the part of the lawmakers ignorance of the role and a lack of understanding of the responsibilities of the role particularly as companies where there is no company secretary are still required to comply with all the legislation but without the appointee who was the focal point for ensuring such compliance. During the consultation period for CA06 this proposal received almost unanimous criticism from people at the sharp end (not least on the basis that the proposal gained little but had much to lose). Despite this, those responsible ignored such expert advice and enacted the proposal – although the appointment was left optional. (Ironically the New Zealand (NZ) experience seems to have been overlooked. NZ company law made the appointment optional. However nine years later, only around 5 per cent of NZ companies did not have a company secretary.)

Board meeting duties

Much of the secretary's basic work may revolve around convening, servicing and providing the administrative support to board meetings. His responsibilities in this work are summarised below although inevitably individual companies will have different requirements. Directors have an obligation to ensure that this work is carried out appropriately, bearing in mind that board meetings and the legally required minutes thereof provide evidence of the reasons for and the decisions taken by the board – which could provide valuable evidence should there be a DERIVATIVE claim.

1   Ensuring the composition of the board is in accordance with the articles, that members have been properly appointed, have declared interests etc.
2   Generating an AGENDA and notice of meetings in liaison with the chairman.
3   Ensuring all data for consideration by the board accompanies the agenda or there is a date by which it will be ready and distributed. Accompanying data should be presented in the order in which it will be considered on the agenda.
4   Convening the meeting in good time. There is no legal requirement regarding the amount of notice due to be given of a board meeting but for commercial reasons and to allow the directors to be properly briefed at least seven days' notice with required data should be given. It would also be logical for the company secretary to take responsibility for compiling and updating a timetable of future meetings.
5   Ensuring, if a QUORUM is required to be present before the meeting can commence, that at least members satisfying that requirement will be present to avoid wasting the time of others attending. Checks

would also need to be made to ensure that, if required, there is a disinterested quorum, i.e. that any directors with interests in third parties are excluded from discussions affecting those third parties (see item 8).

6   Taking, reporting and recording any apologies for absence and noting any late arrivals or early departures so that it can be shown who was present when any decision was taken.

7   Having available any statutory and other registers that need to be inspected and/or signed (e.g. the registers of seals, director's interests, etc.).

8   Ensuring that any notifiable interests of directors are noted where these might affect the capacity of the director to vote (or even form part of the quorum for the meeting).

9   Checking members have all the documents required (and having available spare documents in case members have mislaid or forgotten them).

10   Ensuring the meeting's supports, provision of refreshments, note-taking aids, protection against interruption, and so on, are in operation.

11   Ensuring the chairman adheres to and does not overlook any item on the agenda.

12   Ensuring those who speak and vote are entitled to do so (see item 8 above regarding those with potential conflicts of interest).

13   Ensuring the meeting does take required decisions and that these are clear and clearly understood by all present.

14   Ensuring the appropriate voting power is reflected when votes are taken. In some joint venture companies, in the event of an equality of votes, directors nominated by one of the partners to the joint venture have enhanced voting rights.

15   Noting the sense of the meeting in notes that will become the draft minutes.

16   Preparing minutes, having them approved in draft by the chairman, distributed to the members and approved by them at their next following meeting.

17   Keeping the minutes secure. (The period of retention should be decided by the board. The legal limit is ten years, but many commentators feel it should be 'life of the company'.)

18   Making the minutes available to members of the board and the auditors.

19   Ensuring action is effected as required by the meeting and reported on at the appropriate time.

20   Anticipating the level of support available, and any antipathy or opposition to, matters due to be considered by the board and briefing the chairman accordingly.

21   Being proactive in all respects.

And so on.

Authority

The company secretary is an officer of the company and, in the event of culpable non-compliance, is liable with the directors for fines and other penalties. In the event of default, there is no way such responsibility can be evaded.

The secretary has several types of authority:

- *Actual* – by delegation from the board (via specific requirements set out in the board minutes etc.).
- *Ostensible* – since many documents require the signature of the person holding the post of company secretary at that time.
- *Derived* – from what has gone before and been accepted both internally and externally.
- *Express* – in that the secretary is appointed to hold office by law and the shareholders.

Unfortunately, it is not always the case that legislative and contractual requirements have been complied with and a newly appointed secretary should never assume that everything required to be done has been done. On appointment, checking the following may be advisable.

CHECKLIST   Appointment

✓ Check appointment. A note of the appointment should made in the board minutes, recorded in the Register of Secretaries and notified to the Registrar using form AP03 (under s. 276 CA06 (formerly s. 288(a) of CA85)) within 14 days of the operative date.

✓ Check memorandum and articles and any changes thereto and compliance therewith. Articles of LTDs should be reviewed at least every three years to ensure they reflect changed circumstances. With a group of companies it may be helpful to try to give all subsidiaries the same articles to aid ease of recall of requirements.

✓ Check statutory books entries (change of directors, secretary, shareholders, etc.). Buying a pro-forma combined register is advisable (alternatively a computer package can be utilised, although this may not be cost-effective for a group of less than, say, 15 companies).

✓ Locate the certificate of incorporation. This certificate records the exact name and number of the company which must be used where required as well as its date of incorporation. If the company's name (or its type of registration – e.g. LTD to PLC) is changed, a fresh certificate is issued by the Registrar confirming the new name – but the number remains unchanged. The certificate should be kept safely but no longer has to be displayed.

✓ Check disclosure of corporate details including NAME. A company's name is the embodiment of what it is and does – and may have a value in its own right. As such it needs to be protected and used. The way in which it is used is subject to controls and the secretary needs to be aware of these controls and requirements.

✓ ANNUAL RETURN. Check the Return's filing is up-to-date and note the due date of the next return.

✓ Ensure the accounts are filed within the time limits.

✓ Register of CHARGES. Every company must have a register of charges (whether it has a charge or not) and it should be checked that it is up-to-date.

✓ Locate and secure the minute books. Minutes of general meetings of the shareholders must be held at the registered office and made available for inspection and copying by such shareholders only. Minutes of board meetings can be kept anywhere and can be inspected by directors and auditors only (i.e. not by share-holders – unless they are also directors or the company secretary).

✓ Locate and secure the SEAL. The seal is the binding signature of the company. It should be kept safely and its use recorded.

✓ Ensure directors with interests with third parties have declared these and brought/ bring the declaration(s) up to date.

Maintaining a 'Registrar's file'

When filing items with the REGISTRAR OF COMPANIES, not only should a copy be kept of every form filed, but also an acknowledgement or receipt should be obtained for every document. With the (still relatively few) forms that can be filed electronically this is automatic, but for companies filing hard copy, a receipt can be obtained by sending in duplicate a covering letter referring to the item enclosed, as in the following example.

Alternatively a duplicate of the item itself or the Registrar's own form POST 31 could be sent. Provided a stamped return envelope is also enclosed, the Registrar will affix an adhesive bar code to the item as a receipt. Recently the Registrar acknowledged that over an 18-month period, around 200 accounts submitted had been lost internally in CH. A receipt may therefore become essential evidence that at least the item was received by CH.

Both a copy of the item sent and of the receipt should be added to the Registrar's file as a permanent record of what was sent and when.

Example	Covering letter to the Registrar
	Ref ABC/xyz
	7th February 2010
	Registrar of Companies
	Cardiff
	Sir,
	Any Company Ltd – Registered Number 01234567890
	I enclose a form AP01 evidencing the appointment of an additional director to the board of this company.
	Receipt
	Kindly acknowledge receipt for this document on the attached copy letter. I enclose a reply paid envelope.
	Yours faithfully,
	A B Bloggs
	Company Secretary
	[Added on duplicate to be returned…]
	I acknowledge receipt of the above document
	Registrar of Companies...

Joint and deputy company secretaries

It is possible to appoint joint company secretaries, each of whom will have joint responsibility and liability. Unless the company's articles allow, all so appointed will have to sign documents requiring the secretary's signature. Details of the appointees must be filed at CH in the normal way. A company's articles may also permit there to be a deputy or assistant secretary. In such a case, should the secretary be unable to act (or the position falls vacant) the role can be filled by a deputy or assistant.

Qualification

Anyone can be the company secretary of an LTD. For a PLC, CA06 requires the person appointed to hold one of several professional qualifications, although this requirement is somewhat negated by the last reference in the clause allowing the directors to appoint someone who *'appears to the directors to be capable of discharging [the] functions [of the company secretary]'*.

A corporate body can act as a company secretary – although this is not permitted if the sole director of a corporate body is also the sole director of the subject company. Similarly a partnership can be a company secretary:

- of an English or Welsh company, in which case all the partners are joint secretaries of the company;
- of a Scottish company, in which case the partnership itself is the secretary.

Corporate governance

INTRODUCTION

Until the 2008/9 'credit crunch', it was asserted that over 50 per cent of the 100 largest 'economic entities' in the world were corporations rather than countries. The rapid reduction of many leading international companies' 'size' and 'worth' has rendered such comparisons unreliable (although the 'size' of some of the countries being used as comparators has presumably also shrunk). In any event the comparison was between the companies' sales and the countries' gross domestic product, which was hardly comparing like with like. Nevertheless the development of the global market has led to the formation of mega-corporations. Whilst the economic rationale for such mergers and conglomerates may be unarguable, big business means big influence and big power – it also means, as recently experienced, when one part of the global market is adversely affected, there is little to stop this affecting the whole. This has led to widespread (and renewed) unease and to a number of activist-arranged demonstrations against globalisation, particularly against meetings of the government representatives of the largest economies (the G8 and G20 representatives' meetings), as well as criminal damage to the goods and premises of some high-profile organisations. The concern has been exacerbated by the fact that in some cases (particularly in companies featured in a number of recent scandals), those who control such organisations seem to be virtually unaccountable – and some of those in charge have even been caught with both hands deep in their company's till, whilst the level of incompetence at senior levels in some financial services organisations is breathtaking.

Size equates to power

Whilst the UK's mid-nineteenth-century innovation of LTD companies formed under legislation (now copied worldwide) encouraged investment in risk-based ventures with the protection that the liability was limited to an entrepreneur's actual investment, and most companies were operated properly, it also enabled unscrupulous directors to operate their companies knowing that if the company failed, they had no personal liability. Many unpaid creditors, in addition to numerous other commentators, maintained that the directors of such companies were being protected at the expense of the creditors, describing this innovative 'limited liability' protection as no more than a *'rogues' charter'* and *'a means of devising the encouragement of speculation, overtrading and swindling'*. This view permeated society to such an extent that Gilbert and Sullivan even wrote an operetta, 'Utopia Ltd', featuring a director/shareholder sheltering behind his limited liability protection! Widespread objections such as these ultimately led to the passing of the Insolvency Act 1986. This Act makes directors personally liable to repay the creditors if they knew or (the really pertinent words) *'should have known'* that their company was taking on credit which might not be paid on the due date, or within a reasonable time of that date.

Inevitably, in running large corporations with virtually unrestricted influence and power, legal obligations have been ignored, and/or corners have been cut by some. Scandals and abuses have proliferated – so much so that Prime Minister, Edward Heath commented that the somewhat dubious activities of one listed PLC (Lonhro) were the *'unacceptable face of capitalism'*. In the UK from the late 1980s running virtually to the end of the century and in the USA in the late 1990s running into the 21st century there were several scandals and high-profile collapses of companies and corporations. A common theme running through these was abuses of power by the (often dictatorial) chief executives in control. For example:

- in the Guinness affair there was an illegal price support system of its own shares when acting as a 'white knight' (i.e. a bidder preferred by the target of a hostile takeover bid) for Distillers Company;
- in the Bank of Credit and Commerce International scandal there was wholesale fraud and drug trafficking at a senior level which led to its collapse;
- Robert Maxwell's disappearance from his yacht followed his rifling of the Mirror Group pension fund. Ironically, a much earlier investigation of Maxwell, regarding his running of the failed Pergamon Press, had recommended that he should never again be allowed to be in charge of a company. Unfortunately there was no mechanism to stop him – a situation which led to the passing of the Company Directors Disqualification Act 1986. Had the CDDA96 already been available, Maxwell could have been disqualified for his activities at Pergamon and the later scandal and losses at the Daily Mirror might have been avoided.

Such scandals generated understandable concern on the part of creditors, the public and ultimately Government, although it must be said to some extent they pale into insignificance compared to the recent credit meltdown.

Paralleling the above there had also been for some time concern that many boards of these large (and thus powerful) boards were and are virtually self-perpetuating. A common theme was that shareholders should be encouraged to exercise in practice the control they had in theory. Although the principles and practice of the movement that became known as 'corporate governance' (CG) may be sound, they must have been called into question by the recently exposed activities – which in some cases it is not too extreme to describe as crass stupidity at the most senior level of management – of some banking and finance houses, albeit encouraged in the USA by governmental edicts and in the UK by apparently supine or ineffective regulators. The problem with the concept is that it assumes reasonable and responsible behaviour and decisions and a common sense (commercial 'nous') approach to business – if that base is lacking, then no amount of words and checklists and governance guidance that have been developed over nearly two decades can truly be effective.

Putting morality into capitalism – 'corporate governance'

In 1991 a Committee on the Financial Aspects of Corporate Governance was set up by the Stock Exchange, the Financial Reporting Council and the accounting profession. This committee, chaired by Sir Adrian Cadbury of Cadbury Schweppes, became known as the Cadbury Committee, and its conclusions as the 'Cadbury Code'. The aim was to make boards of companies more accountable. In the decade following the setting up of the Cadbury Committee (which published its report *A Code of Best Practice* in 1992), the Greenbury Committee (chaired by Sir Richard Greenbury of Marks & Spencer), and the Hampel Committee (chaired by Ronnie Hampel of ICI) enlarged the scope of the original CG principles. They were then followed by reports from committees chaired by Derek Higgs, Sir Robert Smith (Past President of the Institute of Chartered Accountants of Scotland) and Nigel Turnbull (from the Institute of Chartered Accountants of England).

The amalgamation of the advice of these committees is now encapsulated in a combined (and regularly updated) CG Code with which the Stock Exchange expects all listed PLCs to comply – or, if they do not, then they must explain why not. Although non-listed companies are not required to observe these requirements, this may be short-sighted, since increasingly most corporate entities will be forced by public and employee opinion to subscribe to many of the principles espoused, particularly the recommendations of the original committee chaired by Sir Adrian Cadbury. In terms of a constant examination of the way in which companies operate, relate to the environment, produce and sell goods, employ or cease to employ people, including their SOCIAL RESPONSIBILITY, CG is a matter of considerable and widespread concern which is unlikely to do anything other than grow.

a) The Cadbury Committee

The original CG Committee recommended the adoption of a code of best practice, with the manner of adoption of the principles being reported on in companies' annual reports.

CHECKLIST   The Cadbury Code of Best Practice

The board should:

✓ meet regularly, control the company and monitor management;

✓ make a clear distinction between the roles of chairman and chief executive to ensure a balance of power (if the roles are combined, there should be a strong independent, and non-executive, presence on the board);

✓ appoint non-executive directors capable of exerting power;

✓ prepare and adhere to a schedule of matters for consideration;

✓ arrange for directors to take independent professional advice, at the company's expense, and to have access to the company secretary;

✓ discuss as a body any question of the removal of the company secretary.

Non-executive directors should:

✓ Bring an independent judgement in board matters;

✓ include a majority who can act independently free from any relationship which might interfere with their judgement;

✓ be appointed for a set term without automatic reselection;

✓ be appointed formally by the whole board.

Executive directors should:

✓ not be granted service contracts in excess of three years' duration without shareholders' approval (currently there is pressure to limit service contracts to a duration of one year);

✓ ensure their pay is subject to the deliberations of a remuneration committee comprised wholly or partly of non-executive directors;

✓ disclose clearly and fully their total emoluments as well as the actual figures for the chairman and highest-paid director, providing separate figures for salary and performance-related elements.

Example	**Statement in accordance with the Cadbury Code requirements**
	1 *Frequency of board meetings* The board meets 10–12 times each year on a regular basis, and may meet on an ad hoc basis on any number of additional occasions.
	2 *Agenda* An agenda for each formal meeting is sent out at least a week in advance with all supporting data. A synopsis of ➝

Example	**Statement in accordance with the Cadbury Code requirements** – *continued*

any data to be tabled at the meeting (i.e. not sent with the agenda) should be provided.

Most meetings consist of:
- approval and signing of MINUTES of the previous meeting;
- reviewing financial criteria and results;
- considering corporate and statutory matters;
- consideration of reports on commercial operations;
- reviewing legislative and legal developments;
- considering planning and research requirements;
- safety report and considerations;
- updating contingency and crisis plans (see RISK).

Minutes of all board meetings are despatched within 48 (working) hours of the meeting to which they relate.

3 *Board composition and responsibilities (non-exhaustive)*

Chairman – shareholder relationships, strategy and planning, compliance, board operation, appraisal and succession, familiarisation of new directors, policy, etc.

Managing director – overall direct responsibility for all executive board members, operations and policies.

Finance – capital provision, collection and payments, funds flow control, investment monitoring, security, liaison with auditors.

Sales – ongoing development, marketing and selling of all products, market analysis, promotions etc.

Personnel – supply and training of adequate workforce at all levels, contracts, motivation and training, appraisal, social responsibility, environmental impact.

Development – new product control and implementation, assessment of and proposals for combating risk.

Non-executive directors (number) – compliance with strategy, independent view of all operations, directors' rewards, auditors' relationship. Non-executive directors are encouraged to visit all operations and facilities and talk to employees at all levels.

→

Example	Statement in accordance with the Cadbury Code requirements – *continued*

Company secretary – compliance, Stock Exchange and company registrar relationships, liaison with legal advisors, auditors, share registrar, patent agents, property advisors (as applicable).

4 *Roles for non-executive directors*
- audit, remuneration and compliance committees of board;
- reviewing new areas of business;
- appraising board performance.

5 *Library*
A reference section is kept updated continuously. This contains copies of all statutes, regulations, operating controls, Stock Exchange requirements (including guidance on insider dealing prohibitions) etc., with which the company is required to comply. Full data is kept on employment, safety, transport, consumer and trade marks issues, together with details on insurance and risk management developments.

6 *Authorities*
A comprehensive delegated authorities list, updated each six months, is in force. Regular policing is carried out to ensure compliance at all levels.

7 *Auditors*
The relationship with the auditors is as follows:
- Formal meetings are held at six-monthly intervals with the chairman, finance director and company secretary. Additional meetings are held as necessary.
- Following formulation of the interim and yearly results audit timetable, auditors are provided with every assistance to carry out their work.
- Compliance with recommendations of the management letter and any other audit requests is actioned within 28 days.
- The audit committee of the board meets representatives of the auditors at least every quarter.

8 *Internal auditing*
Under the control of the finance director, the internal audit department has a wide remit to visit and check on all

Example	Statement in accordance with the Cadbury Code requirements – *continued*

procedures and operations throughout the company, subject only to advising the executive responsible of their arrival. Those staffing this department are encouraged to 'walk the job' and to make spot checks at all levels.

The department oversees the content and compilation of the monthly management accounts package, including cash flow statements and debtor/creditor schedules, and monitors all deviations from budget.

9 *Going concern*
A solvency statement is prepared and submitted to all members of the board every month (whether or not a formal meeting is held).

Note: under recent changes to the Combined Code, a number of explanatory items (including an expansion of some of the above details) must be included in the annual report – see below.

The audit committee

A board's audit committee might examine the following:

- changes in accounting policies and the reasons for the changes, and assessing that such policies are appropriate for the company;
- reservations indicated by the auditors concerning the accounting policies or their implementation or interpretation;
- issues raised in the audit management letter;
- compliance by the accounts with latest standards;
- material changes from estimates included in previous accounts or statements;
- the effect of all known contingencies and material events being adequately reflected in the accounts;
- that disclosures have been made of all relevant party transactions;
- that the accounts disclose the effect of any and all acquisitions and disposals and any contingent liabilities including outstanding litigation;
- that interim accounts have been prepared in accordance with similar processes and policies as used at the year end, updated as necessary;
- compliance with changes in standards, law and/or Stock Exchange regulations;
- relationship between the company and professional advisers.

Note: the Financial Reporting Council in its latest Guidance on Audit Committees suggests audit committees should:

- consider the need to include in their risk evaluation, the possible withdrawal of their auditor from the market;
- consider the auditor's annual transparency report (if applicable);
- provide more information on the appointment, reappointment or removal of the auditor (e.g. the manner by which an auditor is selected and appointed);
- consider auditor independence (in line with the Auditing Practices Board's 'Ethical Standards for Auditors').

b) The Greenbury Committee

This committee concerned itself mainly with the rewards being paid to directors following a number of well-publicised instances of directors, particularly of the then recently privatised utility companies awarding themselves substantially enhanced reward packages for essentially doing the same jobs as they performed pre-privatisation. Although there are instances of abuse, those responsible for the media attention seemed to have overlooked the onerous responsibilities and liabilities assumed by directors – heavy potential burdens compared to, say, those in the entertainment or sporting disciplines who are in receipt of far larger sums whilst being subject to no equivalent responsibility or liabilities.

As a result of the Greenbury recommendations:

- Boards are required to set up remuneration committees of non-executive directors to determine the pay of executive directors, and to report directly to the shareholders on such matters (by including a report in the annual report and by the chairman of the remuneration committee attending the AGM and speaking at it).
- Only truly independent non-executive directors should sit on such remuneration committees. The committee should be charged with paying 'the right amount' (i.e. rates of pay should be related to comparable companies' rates).
- There should be a balanced approach to incentives and bonus schemes (e.g. executive share options should not be issued at a discount) which should always be subject to shareholder approval.
- Service contracts should ideally be limited to one year's duration, and a robust line should be taken when performance has been poor.

And so on.

The requirements for listed PLCs regarding the approval and disclosure of directors' pay were strengthened. Details of the following must now be published:

- details of individual salaries;
- the role of the remuneration committee;
- the company's remuneration policy;
- the policy which links pay to performance;
- any payments made to directors in charge of failed operations;
- details of performance requirements, monitoring etc.

In addition, shareholder approval must be obtained to remuneration packages.

Boards can proceed with proposals even if shareholders do not agree, although this could be unwise. (See DIRECTORS: PAYMENTS.)

c) The Hampel Committee

The main thrust of the Cadbury and Greenbury Committees had been to recommend changes in detailed control of boards etc. However, the Hampel Committee recommendations concerned what could be described as the *philosophy* of corporate governance rather than its practice (the practice having been, perhaps unfairly, classified as little more than 'box-ticking'). Hampel stressed that corporate governance was a force to aid business prosperity and required a change of approach – it could not and should not be accomplished by virtue of the mechanistic completion of a checklist. The report of the committee recommended that:

- companies should have an effective board, leading and controlling operations, and dependent upon the timely production of reliable information;
- the appointment of directors should be transparent, with pay and conditions sufficient to attract people of the calibre required;
- institutional shareholders should take a lead in exercising the power that their voting strength provides, and boards should enter into a dialogue with such shareholders;
- institutional shareholders – particularly pension funds – should be encouraged to take a longer-term view of performance;
- the AGM should be made a more meaningful meeting with a presentation particularly for the private shareholder;
- boards and companies are expected to comply with the law and these governance codes, with the company secretary given greater prominence in terms of ensuring such compliance. In turn the appointment/ removal of the company secretary should be a matter for the whole board (i.e. the company secretary should not be able to be removed merely on the authority of the chairman or managing director).

d) The Turnbull Committee

Some time after the conclusion of the above three committees, it was decided to address the board's responsibilities in terms of identifying and controlling risk; company law after all expects directors to take risk. Accordingly, the Turnbull Committee was charged with the task of making recommendations regarding directors' obligations in terms of the protection of the company assets. The practical effects of the recommendations of this committee are set out more fully in RISK MANAGEMENT.

e) The Higgs and Smith Committees' recommendations

These include:

- at least 50 per cent of the board should be non-executive;
- a list of potential non-executives drawn from the non-commercial area should be compiled;
- the positions of chairman and chief executive should not be held by the same person;
- there should be a senior independent director who should be the channel for shareholders to raise issues;
- non-executive directors should meet by themselves at least once a year;
- non-executive directors should normally serve for no more than two periods of three years each. Once in office for ten years they should no longer be considered 'independent';
- no-one should chair the board of more than one large company (this requirement has since been abandoned);
- a full-time executive should not take on more than one non-executive directorship;
- the auditors should be truly independent, objective and thorough (possibly restricting other non-audit work performed for the subject company);
- there should be at least three independent non-executives on the audit committee;
- the audit committee should be very forceful if poor or misleading information is being provided.

Evaluation

To assist with the process of checking the effectiveness of a company's commitment to the principles and practice of effective corporate governance, the ICSA (in conjunction with Kingfisher plc) developed an evaluation process which entails a three-year cycle, to assess the framework within which the board operates. The evaluation involves each board member, not only in identifying the procedures and processes of the board, but also in deciding the action to take where there is a need for improvement. The board can decide whether or not to publicise the review, but if progress on areas has not been made in the second and third years of the process, then the ICSA will not allow its name to be used in conjunction with the process. Such is the concern that boards should be made more accountable that it may be advisable for boards to prepare for the possibility of this being a requirement that could be imposed on them. Details of the ICSA process are available from the Corporate Services Policy Unit, ICSA, 16, Park Crescent, London W1B 1AH (tel 020 7612 7023).

Combined Code of Corporate Governance

The reports and recommendations whose individual details are set out above were reconstituted into a Combined Code to which listed PLCs must now subscribe (or explain why they have not done so). Included as one of the principles in the Combined Code were requirements that there should be sound controls to safeguard the company's assets and to protect the shareholders' interests. Virtually simultaneously the Law Commission recommended that it should be made easier for shareholders to take action against directors who do not act in their best interests: a recommendation which is now encapsulated in CA06 (see DERIVATIVE CLAIMS).

The combined code has the following main principles:

1 Every company should be headed by an effective board which is collectively responsible for the success of the company.
2 There should be a clear division at the top for the running of the board and the running of the business. No one individual should have unfettered powers.
3 The board should contain a balance of executives and (in particular) independent non-executives so that no one group can dominate.
4 The board must identify in the annual report those non-executives that it considers to be independent.
5 There should be a formal, rigorous and transparent procedure for appointing new directors.
6 The board should be provided with timely information in a form and of the quality necessary for it to do its job. All directors should receive induction upon appointment and should regularly update and refresh their skills and knowledge.
7 Each year, the board should review formally and rigorously its own performance, that of its committees and that of its individual directors.

8   Remuneration should be sufficient and adequate to attract, retain and motivate directors of the right quality, but not more than necessary. A significant proportion of remuneration should be linked to corporate and personal performance.

9   There should be a formal and transparent procedure for developing policy on executive pay and perks and for fixing the amounts for individual directors. No director should be involved in setting their own remuneration.

10 The board should present a balanced and understandable assessment of the company's position and prospects.

11 The board should maintain a sound system of internal control to safeguard shareholders' investments and the company's assets.

12 The board should establish formal and transparent arrangements for considering how they shall apply the financial and internal control principles and for maintaining appropriate auditor relations.

13 The board has a duty to ensure that a satisfactory dialogue takes place with shareholders, based upon a mutual understanding of objectives.

14 The AGM should be used to communicate with investors and encourage their participation.

15 Institutional shareholders should enter into a dialogue with companies based upon a mutual understanding of objectives.

16 All relevant factors (particularly board structure and composition) should be weighed and examined when evaluating governance disclosures.

17 Institutional shareholders have a duty to make considered use of their votes.

There are supporting principles for each of the above general principles, explaining how they are to be implemented.

Note: The combined code was altered in June 2008. See below.

Alternative Investment Market (AIM) company obligations

For companies quoted on AIM there is a streamlined version of the main market Combined Code. The recommendations include:

- a schedule of matters for board attention/decision should be compiled;
- the roles of chairman and chief executive should not be exercised by the same person;
- the company should have at least two independent non-executive directors;
- all directors should stand for re-election regularly;
- audit, remuneration and nomination committees should be established;

- there should be a regular supply of management information in a timely manner to enable the board to discharge its duties;
- the board should regularly review the effectiveness of the internal controls and report this fact to the shareholders;
- the board as whole has responsibility for ensuring that a satisfactory dialogue takes place with shareholders, based on a mutual understanding of objectives.

The 2008 changes

From June 2008, the Financial Reporting Council published a revised Code. The main changes are:

- removal of the restriction that an individual should be chairman of only one FTSE100 company; and
- permitting the chairman of a listed PLC (of companies below the FTSE 350) to be a member of (but not the chairman) of the audit committee as long as he was considered independent when appointed.

In addition companies are required to publish in their annual report statements:

- so that their shareholders can evaluate how the company has applied the main principles in the Code;
- showing whether the company has complied or not complied with the Code. If there is non-compliance, details of the provisions broken and reasons for such must be stated.

There are specific requirements for disclosures, as follows:

- how the board operates, the types of decisions taken by the board and those that are delegated to management;
- the names of the chairman, deputy chairman (if applicable), the chief executive, the senior independent director and the chairman and members of the various board committees (i.e. nomination, audit and remuneration);
- the number of board and board committees meetings; and individual attendance at both by directors;
- the names of non-executive directors who are independent (and the reasons for that assessment);
- any significant commitment(s) of the chairman outside the company;
- the manner in which the board, its committees and members are evaluated;
- the procedure by which the board (especially non-executive directors) understand the views of the company's major shareholders.

Companies are also required to state in their annual report:

- how the board's nomination committee carries out its work in finding new board appointees and explaining whether the advice of external advisers has been sought regarding the appointment of the chairman or deputy chairman;
- how the board's remuneration committee complies with the requirements of the Directors Remuneration Report Regulations 2002;
- whether any executive directors serve as non-executive directors of other companies and, if paid, whether the directors retain such earnings;
- statements explaining the directors' responsibility for preparing the accounts and (from the auditors) their reporting responsibilities;
- that, subject to any qualifications, and/or with assumptions used, the business is a going concern;
- that the board has conducted a review of the effectiveness of the internal controls used by the company;
- details of the work of the board's audit committee and, (if applicable) the reasons for not using an internal audit function;
- should the board have refused to accept a report and recommendations from the audit committee regarding the appointment/retention of the external auditors, the reasons for the rejection;
- details of any non-audit work the external auditor carries out for the company.

Further information required to be disclosed either in the annual report or on the company's website:

- the terms of reference of the board's committees (nomination, remuneration and audit), explaining their roles and authority;
- the terms and conditions of appointment of the non-executive directors;
- a statement, if any remuneration consultants were appointed, of whether they had any other connections with the company.

In addition, where there is a resolution regarding the re-election of directors/auditors, the company must provide:

- such biographical details that will enable shareholders to take an informed decision on their election or re-election;
- the reason(s) for someone being elected to a non-executive directorship;
- if the re-election of a non-executive director is to be considered, the chairman's confirmation that the performance of the person has been evaluated and has been found to be effective;
- if the re-election of an auditor is to be considered and the audit committee's recommendation is not accepted by the board, a statement showing both the recommendation and the reasons for the board opposing such recommendation.

Across the Atlantic

Attitudes to corporate governance in the USA were somewhat laid back, until it was beset by massive corporate scandals such as Enron and Worldcom. In Enron, with the apparent knowledge of its auditors, Arthur Anderson (in the USA, auditors are appointed by and report to the directors rather than the shareholders as in the UK), the company led by the chief executive, Ken Lay (who died just before he was due to commence a long term of imprisonment), used a number of 'special purpose entities' and other illegal off-balance-sheet companies to disguise the company's growing debts and obscure the financial realities. It has also been claimed that part of the company's head office featured a trading floor which was a complete sham – it was simply used to impress visitors, commentators and potential customers. The Enron Taskforce – a team of 34 government investigators – took four years to unpick what was little more than an elaborate fraud. At one time Enron shares were worth $90, but this value dropped to 26 cents and when the company collapsed it had debts of $65 billion. Americans who previously had regarded their industry leaders as heroes akin to movie stars and the like suddenly found some of their gods had feet of clay. The public and opinion formers were furious – 70 per cent later said that they no longer trusted what their brokers or corporations told them, and 60 per cent suspected that corporate wrongdoing was 'a widespread problem'.

In the aftermath of this and other collapses, the US Government rushed through the legislative response, the Sarbanes-Oxley Act (SOX). SOX parallels the UK corporate governance standards but goes well beyond those requirements. It stipulates significant changes to accounting procedures, disclosure, corporate governance principles and rules of business conduct. The Act however is not restricted to US companies, since if European and UK-registered companies have US listings, then they are also obliged to comply with its requirements. Conversely if they are subsidiaries of a US parent it is suggested that there could be 'trickle down' requirements as a result of the Act's application to their parent.

SOX applies to 'issuers' and 'public accounting firms'. Issuers are companies that have securities issued on the New York Stock Exchange or NASDAQ. Such companies have enhanced reporting requirements to the Securities Exchange Commission (SEC), which is the regulating body for publicly quoted US companies and others having US listings. Public accounting firms are those that engage in public accounting and auditing and included within this ambit are non-US audit firms, if they play a significant part in the audits of the Issuers. Such firms may not play a part in the management of client firms upon which they are performing audits (it was this formerly permitted close relationship between board and audit team which enabled the Enron scandal to be perpetuated). They may not audit their own work and they cannot act as advocates or advisers to their audit clients. A company's auditors can no longer provide:

- accounting and bookkeeping (otherwise they would be auditing work they themselves have done);
- financial information services;
- valuations and actuarial services;
- internal auditing;
- management or management consulting;
- human resource functions (including head-hunting);
- financial services;
- legal and other advice.

SOX was a draconian piece of legislation and some of its requirements have recently been diluted, for example, that there should be a new system of proportional securities regulation for smaller US companies, i.e. for 'Microcap' companies (those whose market capitalisation is the lowest 1 per cent of the US equity market) and 'Smallcap' companies (those whose market capitalisation is within the next 5 per cent of the US equity market).

The SOX audit committee

Companies affected must have audit committees comprised of directors of true independence. There are some dispensations for non-US issuers, particularly those that have two-tier boards. An audit committee must be given responsibility for the appointment and oversight of the auditors and for recommending their fees. In the USA (unlike the UK), auditors are appointed by the directors. The committee should comprise at least one member who has financial knowledge and experience and must report whether it is compliant with this requirement and if not, why. Non-US issuers committee members with financial knowledge can be specialists in Generally Accepted Accounting Principles (GAAP) that are relevant to their own territory, not necessarily the US GAAP.

The audit committee must:

- approve all audit and non-audit financial functions;
- ensure audit partners directly responsible for their audit rotate every five years (with a five-year gap);
- allow audit partners who play only a subsidiary role in the audit to serve for seven years without a gap and then rotate with at least a two-year gap;
- ensure the auditors report to them on matters involving critical accounting policies, alternative treatments of financial matters, and the whole question of communication with management (especially any constraints placed upon them during their audit);
- examine any conflicts of interests involving the auditors.

Chief executive's (CE) and chief financial executive's (CFE) duties

Companies must adopt a code of ethics to be observed by CEs and CFEs. If there is no code, then they must state why not. Waivers from the code must be reported immediately, although non-US issuers may report their waivers or non-compliance annually. There is a formalised process whereby CEs and CFEs must certify in prescribed terms that there have been non misstatements or omissions in published accounts or statements and that they have been made in a complete, timely and accurate manner. They must certify that the financial position of the entity has been fairly represented, including cash flows, and that full disclosures have been made to auditors and to the audit committee. Where non-GAAP figures are presented, their GAAP equivalents should be included.

All off-balance sheet transactions must be disclosed including the reasons for them, their nature, their effects upon the company and the effect if they were discontinued. There must be statements of effectiveness of controls, management responsibilities, and an auditors' attestation. There must be no improper influence on audits, no trading during 'blackouts' (these are periods similar to the 'no trading periods', usually of two months prior to the publication of price sensitive information in the UK, required by insider dealing prohibitions), and restrictions on loans to officers and directors.

EU Good Governance Code

The EU has put forward proposals for a new framework directive. It echoes the US attitude in general and the Sarbanes-Oxley legislation in particular and requires:

- the setting-up of supervisory boards to oversee the accountancy profession;
- independent audit committees for all publicly quoted companies (and public corporations);
- the group auditor to take full responsibility for group consolidated accounts;
- conflicts of interests to be revealed by auditors;
- lead auditor to be rotated after five years and whole audit firm after seven years;
- international accounting standards to be introduced throughout the EU.

WARNING

 Insurers have advised their clients that should they fail to comply with new accounting and corporate governance requirements, they may find that their liability insurance cover is withdrawn. Compliance with the requirements of the International Financial Reporting Standards, Corporate Governance, SOCIAL RESPONSIBILITY, and Operating and Financial Review (see ANNUAL REPORT) will rapidly become a necessity as well as a listing requirement. Multinational companies also have to comply with the Sarbane-Oxley Act if they are to retain liability cover in America.

Meaning for and effect on LTDs

The main thrust of the foregoing affects listed PLCs, which must either comply or explain why they have not complied. However, the principles of CG could be argued to be applicable to all companies, listed or not. Indeed many large charities have voluntarily adopted CG principles either in whole or part. Charities apart, many LTDs will feel that the full code is too complex for them, although some of the principles and practice could be useful. Particularly where there are shareholders not on the board, it could be argued that such boards could adopt a 'slimmed down' CG 'code', including (for example):

- recognition that the board is responsible for the success of the company and must organise itself to provide skills and experience suitable to achieving that end;
- board decisions as well as decisions of the owners should be transparent to all;
- board decisions must be taken in the best interests of the entity as a whole, recognising the interests of the various stakeholders in the company (see DIRECTORS: OBLIGATIONS), sublimating their personal interests if necessary;
- it is the board's direct responsibility for obtaining and providing accurate and reliable financial and supporting information.

These four items should form a base to which other aspects of the combined code could be added as required.

Postscript

One can only assume that the fall-out from the global credit crunch will generate still further corporate governance requirements. Indeed, the head of the Financial Reporting Council has already announced a 'new and improved code' (i.e. the Combined Code). Whilst any changes will provide an extra challenge and obligation for those who were already compliant, it must be questionable whether words can deal adequately with those who, because of managerial arrogance, do not consider themselves constrained by such strictures. American critics of the UK code argue that it is 'all about box ticking' and not so much about taking responsibility for the principles.

Further, it seems extremely unlikely that, however detailed and complex, legislation or codes will be unable to prevent imprudent decisions being made at very senior levels – particularly where large bonuses act both as massive incentives and suppressants of risk assessment. The exorbitant bonuses that banks, now bailed out by the UK taxpayer, wanted to pay post-collapse beggar belief and raise the question: 'Have they learned nothing?' Indeed, an onlooker can be excused for wondering what so-clever activities generated such payments? The senior staff anticipating such largesse are hardly likely to seek alternative employment elsewhere were the bonuses to be scrapped (the number of such jobs is decreasing) – although given their record this might be best, at least for the UK taxpayer. As the Under Secretary of State for Trade stated: '*[these] bonuses contributed to excessive risk taking*'. Ironically, this is virtually the same scenario that led 20 or so years ago to the misselling of private pensions. The salesmen employed by pension providers (with some notable exceptions) were mainly paid on commission – accordingly, simply selling the products became far more important for them than ensuring the customers were sold the best product for their needs.

Cupidity can easily lead to (and may even encourage) stupidity (and in some cases seems to have done just that) unless adequate controls and checks are in place – this is the real role of corporate governance, on an individual organisation basis. As the former head of risk at the (but for state and Lloyds Bank Plc intervention) failed HBOS bank said: '*I strongly believe that the real underlying cause of all the problems was ... a total failure of all key aspects of Corporate Governance.*' It was even more of a failure of corporate governance in his case, since having warned directors in the bank of the '*too high level of risk the Bank was taking on*', he was fired by the then chairman. HBOS was a listed PLC required to have a whistle-blowers policy and to protect people making comments such as these. It is all very well those formerly in charge apologising to their shareholders and employees later – talk is cheap but does nothing to repay the debts incurred. It seems that the kind of attitude of senior managers and directors referred to above is not an isolated incident. In early 2009 a City firm of headhunters surveyed 50 managers involved in compliance and internal audit working for FTSE 100 companies and discovered that half of them did not believe that they had sufficient influence to manage risk properly in their organisations; indeed 13 per cent stated that '*they were not influential at all*'. If this is so, it would seem that a substantial proportion of some of the UK's largest companies are paying little more than lip service to corporate governance, which was not the idea behind the movement at all. Indeed, as Hector Sands, head of the Financial Services Authority stated in 2009: '*Corporate governance activists may be able to hold their heads high – but they are few and far between.'* He went on to call for better surveillance (of directors and the company results) by investors, and a broader sense of responsibility.

Derivative claims

INTRODUCTION

Sections 260-269 of CA06 enhance shareholders' rights against directors where there is a belief that those to whom the shareholders have delegated the job of running their company have failed to act in their best interests. Thus a shareholder believing that the company has suffered loss because of a director's actions, or failure to act (defined as an *actual or proposed act or omission involving negligence, default, breach of duty or breach of trust*) can initiate legal action (a 'derivative' claim) against the director *on the company's behalf* (i.e. in the event of any compensation being determined to be payable by the director, the company will be the recipient, not the shareholder who has taken action on its behalf). One can only wonder whether shareholders in some of the failed companies involved in the credit crunch could initiate such actions.

Taking action

Shareholders have always been able to sue directors for failing to act in accordance with the provisions of their company's memorandum and/or articles. The articles lay down the rules under which the company is to be governed and directed, and any breach means that those responsible are acting *ultra vires* (beyond their powers) – and thus directors can be held liable for any losses incurred. If directors allowed the company to act outside its objects clauses (set out in the memorandum), this too is acting *ultra vires*. However the effect of this last 'offence' was diluted by CA89, which allowed the shareholders to authorise retrospectively the acts of a company that had been outside its objects clause – although directors who breached the requirements could still be held liable by the shareholders. Prosecuting an action against directors acting *ultra vires*, was not an easy process for shareholders. However, CA06 makes it easier for a shareholder to take such action on behalf of the company. Then, if their claim is successful, it is the company (not the shareholder initiating the action) that benefits, at the director's expense.

This right to initiate such claims has changed the previous situation, in which a director was not normally held liable for making a 'wrong' decision provided it was made in good faith, to one where a director can be held liable for an act (or omission) even if it is made in good faith and the person taking the decision does not benefit from that decision (i.e. there was no vested interest). With hindsight, everyone can make impeccable and correct judgements, but directors have to take decisions on what is known at the time – responding to many (and sometimes conflicting) pressures – not least the duty under the same Act to take account of the interests of a number of *'stakeholders'*. If it is easier for members to take legal action, making a contemporaneous record (i.e. detailed MINUTES) available as a defence may assume an even more important facet of company administration and record, showing the parameters within which the decision was made *at that time*.

Obviously in companies where all the members are directors, the possibility of facing a derivative claim may be minimised (although it must be said that dissent and enmity can arise even in family-owned companies). However, where there are 'outside' members (i.e. shareholders not on, or represented on, the board), the possibility of a derivative claim could be real, since the number of instances where a director could be accused of failing to act in the best interests of the shareholders is considerable.

Disgruntled shareholders

It is not impossible to imagine a scenario where an individual shareholder, angry at some action (or perceived action) or inaction of the director decides to initiate a claim; or simply a situation where a shareholder thinks they might benefit from a 'payment to desist' as a result of threatening such action. However, to bring a derivative action, a shareholder must first apply to the court for the right to bring such a claim. Only if the court sanctions the action, can it be allowed to proceed. Traditionally, courts have always been loath to interfere in the internal activities of companies, and if this precedent is followed perhaps the number of such actions may not be large as has been contemplated by some commentators.

Court control

The court cannot allow a member the right to prosecute such a claim if:

- the act (or omission) complained of has since been ratified by the company; or
- it is unreasonable (e.g. the act complained of is such that a person trying to promote the success of the company would not make such a claim).

The court has discretion in allowing a member to prosecute the claim, taking into account the views of independent shareholders and:

- whether the person bringing the claim is acting in good faith;
- the relevant importance of the claim to a person trying to promote the success of the company;

- whether the matter the subject of the claim is likely to be authorised by the company;
- whether the member could bring the claim in their own right and/or whether the company itself had already decided not to bring such a claim.

Notes

1   Unless they are charities, banks etc., companies whose turnover is less than £6.5 million do not need to have their accounts audited. Directors of such companies might find it prudent to consider whether retaining an independent view of their figures might help dissuade potential derivative claimants. Indeed the very fact that there are independent persons reviewing company and board actions may deter even disgruntled shareholders from taking some such actions.

2   Directors of companies whose turnover is less than €1,000,000, which the EU propose would not need to file accounts, might find such a suggestion dangerous if they have 'outside' shareholders.

3   Some PLCs have obtained shareholder agreement to alter their articles (burying these fundamental alterations amongst relatively unimportant changes), so that should the shareholders wish to challenge the directors, they are required (by the wording in the articles) to use arbitration. This means that publicity is denied to those wishing to challenge actions. This is hardly in the spirit of the transparency and accountability of CORPORATE GOVERNANCE requirements, and in theory might mean that even derivative claims might be transferred from the public arena of the courtroom to the private room of the arbitrator.

4   In the event of a claim being prosecuted and the court finding it to be unreasonable, costs can be awarded against the claimant. Conversely if the court feels it was a reasonable case, the court could award costs even to an unsuccessful claimant.

Directors: appointment and familiarisation

INTRODUCTION

One of the COMPANY SECRETARY'S prime responsibilities should be that of supporting directors and providing them, if required, with guidance to their legal duties, responsibilities and the obligations and expectations placed on them. On no occasion is this more essential than when asked to advise in anticipation of or following the appointment of a person who has not previously been a director. Most managers will understandably and appropriately fight their own corner to obtain investment and the best deal etc. for 'their' department. As a director, however, such vested interests must be sublimated to the collective responsibility concept of board work. This requires directors to take decisions which are in the best interests of the company as a whole (even if those decisions are diametrically opposed to the interests of a director's 'own' department – and even the director!) and to support such decisions when taken – even if they argued and voted against it.

Employees have a duty of fidelity but do not have a duty to put the company's interests before their own. Directors, however, do have a fiduciary duty, and must put the interests of the company itself before any other interest, including their own.

Numbers of directors

It is very common for the articles to state that there will be a minimum number of directors, for example, two – which is compulsory for PLCs. Some companies' articles also specify a maximum number, and care needs to be taken that either such a maximum is not exceeded or, before this should happen, that the articles are changed. Any directors appointed in excess of a specified maximum could find themselves personally liable for their actions on behalf of the company.

Eligibility for directorship

There are a number of guidelines which must be adhered to in order to determine who can (and cannot) be a director of a UK company:

- Both real and corporate persons can be directors of UK companies. However, since October 2008 there must be at least one real person on every board. (There is a transitional period for companies with two or more corporate directors, but no natural person director, allowing them until October 2010 to comply.)

- Since October 2008, the minimum age of a person acting as director in the UK has been 16. Persons registered as directors who were under 16 on 1 October 2008 were automatically removed by the Registrar, unless the Secretary of State had exempted them from this requirement.
- There is no upper legal age limit. Individual company articles may stipulate a maximum age, although this could be subject to challenge under age discrimination legislation.
- A person cannot be a director if they have been disqualified – either in the UK or in an overseas jurisdiction – for the period of the disqualification (see DIRECTORS: REMOVAL).
- A person cannot be a director if they are sectioned under the Mental Health Act (for the period of the sectioning) or are an undischarged bankrupt (unless the court specifically allows this).
- The auditor of the company cannot be a director (although he is an officer of the company).

Aspects of directorship

All directors are of equal status. There is no distinction between executive and non-executive directors, or between a director properly appointed in accordance with the articles and company law, and a SHADOW DIRECTOR. The board is usually given the right under the company's ARTICLES to make what is sometimes known as a 'casual' appointment to the board (i.e. the appointment by the board itself of an additional director). The articles will also usually specify that such a casual appointment can only be made at a properly constituted and convened board meeting. Since ultimately directors are appointed by shareholders, those appointed casually are normally required to retire at the next following meeting of the members, in order that they may seek confirmation of their appointment.

To effect the appointment correctly, the ARTICLES should be consulted to check what is required. Thus there should be a minuted board resolution, for example

'It was unanimously agreed that Mr J Bloggs be appointed a director of the Company with effect from [date]'

or, if the appointment is required to be made immediately,

'It was unanimously agreed that Mr J Bloggs be and he hereby is appointed a director of the Company.'

Registering the appointment

After the board resolution, full personal details should be entered in the various registers (see below), and within 14 days of the effective date, form AP01 (in accordance with s. 167 CA06, formerly s. 288(a)) must be sent to the Registrar of Companies. This form must be signed by a serving officer of the company, and the newly appointed director must sign the 'consent to act' section of the form. Personal details of the director must be recorded in the statutory books of the company as follows.

Register of directors

The director's name, date of birth, private address and (if they do not want their private address made public) a service address (for public disclosure) must be inserted in this register. Copies of this information are included on form AP01 to be sent to CH, where as well as signing to indicate their consent to act (to ensure that the director knows of the appointment), full details (including any former name) must be given. Failure to provide and file such personal data is an offence subject to both initial and daily fines. Whilst the director's private address must be disclosed to the Registrar in case official notice (e.g. for failure to file accounts, annual return, etc.) has to be served, a 'service address' can be supplied to be treated as the address available for public scrutiny. For some time, directors who regarded themselves as subject to serious personal threat (acknowledged as such by the police) have been able to conceal their personal addresses from public scrutiny at CH by using a 'service address' for the purposes of those inspecting the register. This exemption is extended to all directors by CA06 with effect from October 2009.

Any and all changes to the details (e.g. names, nationality, address, etc.) must be entered in the register and advised on form CH01. Although the residential address will not be available publicly, CH will be obliged to disclose residential addresses if required by the court, and to specified authorities and credit reference agencies.

Similarly, on termination of the appointment the effective date must be entered in the register and filed with the Registrar (using form TM01). Forms AP1, CH01 and TM01 must all be filed within 14 days.

Notes

1   The protection of personal addresses may prove limited, since the private address records at CH will only be 'screened' back to 2003. If someone asks for an annual return prior to that date the private address (unless a director has since moved) will be available.

2 Married female directors (and company secretaries) will be required to disclose their maiden name and any previous married surnames from 1 October 2009.

Register of directors' interests

For PLCs, details of each director's interests in the shares of the company and any subsidiary, fellow subsidiary or holding company must also be notified to the company within five days of the person's appointment and all changes thereafter must be separately notified within five days of their occurrence. This obligation not only relates to shares held personally by the director, but also to shares held by a director's spouse or partner and any infant children – who are known as 'connected persons' (see s. 809 CA06).

In addition, any share options (and changes, including their exercise) issued by the company to a director or his connected persons must also be recorded.

The only exceptions to this rule are:

- if the director holds the shares only as trustee (i.e. he has no personal interest in them);
- if the director is also a director of the company's holding company which already holds all such details; or
- if the holding is in a company incorporated overseas.

As dealt with in more detail in INTERESTS, should the director of a listed PLC wish to use his shares in the company as security (e.g. for a loan), that fact must be made known to the company, which in turn must make it known to the Stock Exchange, subject, in the event of non-compliance, to unlimited fines for both the director and the company.

A register of directors' share interests no longer has to be kept for LTDs, although it may be useful to retain it (deleting the word 'share' from its title), to serve as a record of any interests the director has in or with third parties etc., as follows.

Register of directors' interests in contracts

Under CA06 ss. 175-185, directors are obliged to notify their company of any interest they may have in contracts (or proposed contracts) being made by the company with a third party. Interests are defined are either general or specific.

- *General* – the director has an interest in all matters concerning a named third party. Such a statement could be made upon the director's appointment.

- *Specific* – a director has an interest in a particular contract. Such a declaration must be made at the first board meeting which considers the proposed contract, or on the director acquiring or becoming aware of the interest and/or of the contract.

There is no explicit requirement for the company to keep a register of such interests, but directors themselves may feel it prudent that such a register should be kept as evidence that they have informed the company, not least since failure to notify an interest is an offence punishable by initial and daily fines. (See DIRECTORS: PAYMENTS, LOANS AND INTERESTS.) As well as using this register as a document of record, it may be advisable for it to be brought to every board meeting so that the members of the board can see if any director has an interest in any matter under discussion. (See MINUTES.)

To compile such a register it might be appropriate to require directors to state on appointment as well as annually thereafter (whether or not there have been any changes) whether they have any interests in third parties that could conflict with those of the company. At the same time, directors could be asked to confirm that they have not been disqualified both in the UK and overseas (under CA06 no one disqualified in an overseas jurisdiction can be a director of a UK company). A form such as the following could be used.

Example	Confirmation of interests and non-disqualification

	To [Board of company – name]
	
	 Name [of director} .... Date ....
	
	 I confirm that
	
	   * I have no interests with third parties with which the company may do business
	
	   * I have the following interests in third parties with which the company does or may do business [give details]
	
	   * I am not disqualified from acting as a director under either UK law or the legislative process of another country.
	
	 * Delete as applicable
	
	 Signed ....

Appointment

Having gone through the process of finding a new appointee to the board, both company and subject appointee may find it advisable to consider a variety of matters as encapsulated in the following checklist.

CHECKLIST   Director's appointment

✓ Obtain a copy of latest accounts and management accounts (and any supplementary information) to enable appointee to consider the financial state of the company.

✓ Obtain a copy of the company's articles to determine the powers (and any restriction of powers) of directors and officers, and copy of the board minutes for the previous year and company for previous five years to check a) compliance and b) any alterations to articles. This check should also provide valuable background information on the tactics and strategy adopted by the board, disclose any authorities granted by the board on an individual or committee basis, which may require further investigation, etc.

✓ Check filing of documentation with Registrar of Companies and provision of statutorily required information, including that STATUTORY BOOKS are up-to-date.

✓ Obtain a copy of directors' and officers' liability insurance policy and renewal data. If there is no such cover and there are shareholders who are not on the board, raise the question of effecting such cover.

✓ Check if the articles grant an indemnity against personal costs and liabilities incurred as a result of acting as an officer of the company. Such an indemnity was given specifically by reg. 118 of Table A of CA85 and thus could still be part of the articles of a company registered under Acts preceding CA06. If not, it may be advisable to propose it is inserted in the articles (a SPECIAL RESOLUTION will be needed).

✓ Obtain copies of all loan notes, guarantees, charges, etc.

✓ Check if there is any requirement for a director to hold a number of the company's shares ('a qualification shareholding'), and, if so acquire such shares (avoiding any price-sensitive periods). If the articles require this and the director fails to subscribe for such shares within two months of the appointment, not only is the appointment invalid, but also the director can be held personally liable for acts undertaken until the share qualification requirement is satisfied.

✓ Prepare a list of companies and/or matters in which the appointee has an interest, and with which the company may be trading or negotiating and enter these in the register of Interests. These potential conflicts of interest must be disclosed within five days of appointment (and subsequently when they arise). Whether they are allowed to subsist, and/or the director can vote on any such matter (or even form part of the quorum during the discussion), and/or take any profit made from such interests should be checked with the articles.

✓ Check other board members' interests are noted and what they are.

✓ Establish whether any SHADOW DIRECTOR(s) exist, and, if so, attempt to ensure the position is rectified by their details being recorded in the various registers, etc.

✓ Obtain details of terms of appointment, service agreement, duties, reporting structure, etc. How is appointment evidenced – check authority. How are payments of fees, expenses, etc., made?

✓ Request a copy of any code of ethics or GIFTS or equivalent applicable to directors and/or senior members of the management of the company.

✓ Request schedule of board meetings and arrangements for obtaining information for discussion/decision at such meetings.

WARNING

 It can be embarrassing, to say the least, for a company to attempt to appoint to its board a person who has been disqualified from so acting. It may be prudent for the company secretary to check (discreetly of course) the Register of Disqualified Persons (maintained and updated by the Registrar of Companies). An appropriate question should be asked of foreign nationals required to be appointed to the board of a UK company (as required in the draft form above)

Not all directors involved in failed companies are disqualified, and to provide such 'track record' information, business information/credit agency Experian (www.experian.com/bi) maintains a database showing the names of directors who have previously been involved in such companies.

Familiarisation

Ideally there should be a structured process by which new directors are inducted into the company and the board activities. Part of the reason for the above checklist is to encourage them to ask questions and seek information; however the company should be proactive in this and should consider a programme by which they are provided with the information and support so that they can quickly become effective board members. This can be considered in two parts – first from the 'relationships' viewpoint, and secondly from the personal familiarisation viewpoint.

CHECKLIST   Relationships guidance

Preparation

✓ Set up a budget to cover board appointment familiarisation.

✓ Appoint a senior director to oversee the process.

✓ List shareholders and provide this to the new director, possibly arranging meetings with major holders.

✓ List all advisors and scope and areas of work.

Provide

✓ Details of any shareholders' agreement.

✓ Commentary to and copy of strategy of company.

✓ Copies of minutes and supporting papers.

✓ Copies of accounts (if not provided with appointment checklist).

✓ Summary of key factors and suggested methods of achieving.

✓ Current budget (and performance to date with commentary explaining variations).

✓ Banking arrangements, charges, covenants etc.

✓ Details of current products/services and developments.

✓ Promotional and advertising plans.

✓ Details of all locations and status (freehold, leasehold etc.).

✓ Details of any outstanding legal actions.

✓ Staff details, newsletters, works council minutes etc.

✓ Organisation chart(s).

✓ Ethical and/or corporate social responsibility statement.

✓ Relationship with non-executives/executives/company secretary.

✓ Personal details of such directors and guidance to areas of operation.

✓ Monitoring of the performance of both the board and individual members.

✓ Name and personal details of board member appointed to mentor the newcomer.

Many directors are appointed 'from within' – that is, promoted from management. However, accepting the role of a director requires a quantum leap from operating as a manager, and it is important that those undertaking the job realise what is required of them. Boards are increasingly put under pressure to ensure directors are adequately trained. Companies should discover the range of knowledge of their directors – and supply means by which gaps in that knowledge are filled.

Directors have personal legal liability for their companies' activities. Clearly, the boardroom is where the buck stops, and those in the boardroom need to know for what they have responsibility. If any answers to the questions in the following checklist are 'no', coaching and/or reading may be necessary to fill the knowledge gap thereby disclosed. Almost certainly this will be on-going, since many aspects are constantly changing – it might be helpful for a brief précis of legislative and other changes to be presented at each board meeting.

CHECKLIST   Directors' induction

Legal obligations

Does the director understand the legislative environment under which the company operates, e.g.:

✓ the basis and outline of company law?

✓ the latest commercial legislation, including competition law?

✓ outline requirements of employment law?

✓ general requirements of other legislation specifically affecting the company?

✓ the internal operating rules of the company (e.g. the articles of association)?

✓ has the chairman checked the scope of such knowledge?

✓ that the board are responsible for the information required to be regularly filed at CH?

✓ (if a listed PLC) the latest requirements under CORPORATE GOVERNANCE?

Finance

Does the director understand:

✓ the management and published accounts and ancillary data?

✓ that he has personal responsibility for the figures?

✓ the method by which queries should be raised?

✓ that since he must always be confident of the future solvency of the company, he should not allow credit to be taken on when it might not be paid on the due date or within a reasonable time thereof?

✓ that commitment to expenditure on behalf of the company should only be in accordance with the regularly reviewed authority/risk chart?

Board work

Does the director realise:

✓ that he has a fiduciary duty to the company and must always put its interests first and foremost (sublimating his own and, if applicable, his departments' interests)?

✓ that for the company's success, its aims and the means to attain those aims must be delineated (and updated regularly)?

✓ that he has an implied obligation to attend board meetings and to contribute to the discussion (which infers that he is satisfactorily briefed on all matters)?

✓ that he should always declare an interest in any third party with which the company is dealing?

✓ that he should always reach his decisions independently of other directors (even if this means he is in a minority of one)?

✓ that minutes should be read and agreed (or objected to and corrected), and not passed without consideration?

✓ that his role is proactive not reactive – he must make things happen?

✓ that the performance of every board member should be regularly and formally assessed?

✓ that he should insist (except in emergency) that at least two working days are allowed between the receipt of items (other than routine matters) and a decision?

✓ that he should insist decisions are properly minuted and that any requested dissent is included?

✓ that if there are matters of which he is unaware (both in and outside the board room) this should be made clear and he must take steps to obtain the information?

Morality

Has the director:

✓ been given a copy of the code of ethics, corporate governance and/or any other similar requirements?

✓ shown that his knowledge of such items is adequate?

✓ been told that bribes, inducements etc. must not be offered or made by any person on behalf of the company (and that he could be personally criminally liable if this occurs)?

✓ if he becomes aware of wrongdoing, been told that he should take immediate steps to ensure it ceases and the errors are, if at all possible, rectified?

Accountability

Does the director realise:

✓ that he is answerable to the shareholders for the activities and actions of the company and its results?

✓ that he is expected to take risks but only after a proper assessment of those risks and their potential outcome? (Note: This requires alteration for charitable companies since, under charity law, risks must not be taken.)

✓ that contingency and disaster recovery plans should be prepared and updated covering all major eventualities?

✓ that he is answerable to the various regulatory authorities for the activities of the company and its employees?

Employees

Does the director appreciate:

✓ that the true value and worth of employees can only be gained if they are properly and continuously trained and/or coached in their work and any changes?

✓ that the board should regularly audit personnel practice and interfacing – to generate real communication between the parties?

The value of this kind of checklist (and of the appraisal checklist below) is that unless the director can truthfully answer 'yes' to each question, it demonstrates an area where knowledge is incomplete.

Listed PLCs are required to ensure those appointed to the board undergo a process of familiarisation. The above checklist is a non-authoritative (and non-exhaustive) checklist which can act as a base to try to comply with this requirement. Whilst it may be tempting for directors of non-listed PLCs and LTDs to feel they can ignore the above, under company law there is no differentiation between the types of companies – and the obligations of their directors. Ignorance of the law is no excuse, regardless of size.

Responsibility and appraisal

A board of directors acts as an entity with shared (collective) responsibility for all the company activities – even if a director is implacably opposed to a course of action supported by his colleagues. Irrespective of his executive responsibilities for a particular discipline, a director must take decisions, and share in the overall decision-making process. This could mean he must support a board decision which is detrimental to the interests of the discipline he heads. Once the decision has been made, even a dissenting director must accept the decision and work to it. If he finds this impossible, and he cannot influence his colleagues to change their views, his only recourse is to resign.

Listed PLCs are required to review their directors' performance annually and the following (again non-authoritative and not necessarily exhaustive) checklist could be a base for effecting this requirement.

CHECKLIST Appraisal

In the past year has the director:

✓ accepted and worked towards the decisions arrived at by the board?
✓ contributed effectively to the corporate strategy decision making?
✓ formulated the current and immediate future aims and purposes of the company and worked to their implementation?
✓ ensured tactical decisions and actions have taken the same general direction as the strategy of the company (i.e. ensured that no short-term decisions have been taken which impede the long-term strategy)?

✓ helped formulate/update, promulgate and ensure adherence to an internal code of ethics?

✓ ensured the company complies with its own constitution (i.e. the memorandum and articles) and, if a listed PLC, the listing agreement, and custom and practice for the industry?

✓ acted effectively as company spokesperson, promoting the corporate entity and its products/services at all times?

✓ kept up to date his skills and knowledge and made it available at board level (and through board members and management at all levels)?

✓ ensured his own staff are motivated to perform well, and warned and disciplined (in accordance with pre-set rules) when performance or actions have not been in accordance with requirements?

✓ complied with controls over the commitment of the company to contracts, etc., and adequate authority control over all purchases and ensured those under his control have also complied?

✓ displayed understanding of the financial records and reports of the company?

✓ worked towards ensuring the products and services of the company are developed, so that continuity of earning power of the organisation is maintained?

✓ assisted effectively in the expansion of the company based on well-researched, well-prepared and well-considered plans?

✓ updated or initiated contingency plans to protect it's the company's earning capacity in the event of a downturn or change in demand, and the effects of possible disasters affecting operations?

✓ helped protect the corporate entity and the products/services from criticism, attack and loss as far as possible?

✓ displayed comprehension of all new legislative enactments affecting the organisation?

✓ attended formal and informal meetings of the board and made effective contributions?

✓ performed in a proactive manner to meet the challenges affecting the company and/or his department?

✓ taken a properly independent attitude to board decisions?

✓ applied the corporate governance principles and ensured such principles (as applicable) have been adopted by the board?

And so on.

Directors: employment status

INTRODUCTION

Although it is one of the most widely used terms in business, the term 'director' is not precisely defined anywhere – s. 250 CA06 echoes previous legislation by stating that a director is *'any person occupying the position of director by whatever name called'*. In fact company and ancilliary legislation tends not to refer to directors but more often to 'officers' (a collective term which includes the directors and the company secretary as well as senior managers). Generally, anyone who controls (directs) or contributes to such control of a company will be regarded as a director (and as having a fiduciary duty and obligation to the company, i.e. they must act in the utmost good faith, putting the interests of the company first and foremost) – even if not known by that description and if they do not use the description 'director'.

'Officers' of the company have a considerable number of obligations and responsibilities. They may even be required, should they be found guilty of WRONGFUL or FRAUDULENT TRADING, to contribute to the assets of a failed company from their own personal resources – the effects of which potential liability they will not normally be able to insure. However, what is often unclear is whether directors are also employees.

Employment test

Although directors' personal details may be recorded as if they were employees, and payments to them may appear as part of the company's employment payroll, even to the extent that PAYE and NI contributions are deducted, no assumption can be made regarding them being employees as well as officers. To ascertain whether directors are employees, the facts of each individual case need to be reviewed.

The Employment Appeal Tribunal (EAT) suggested companies should ask the following questions:

- Is the employment salary determined by the board?
- Is the salary commensurate with responsibilities?
- How much remuneration does the director receive via dividends (i.e. do they draw the bulk of remuneration via dividends or salary)?
- Are they listed as employees in the company's 'wages book'?
- Have their earnings increased in the last three years? (If so, it could suggest employment.)
- How are directors' salaries assessed?

Case study	Judged to be an employee/director
	In *Pemberton v Claimstart t/a Parkin Westbury & Co*, Mrs Pemberton owned a third of the shares of the company of which she was a director and company secretary. The company was put into receivership, and following her dismissal by the receiver, she claimed unfair dismissal. The tribunal decided she was not an employee and thus they had no jurisdiction to hear her claim. This was perhaps unsurprising as the decisions in the *Fleming* and *Bottrill* cases (see below) had not been promulgated at the time the tribunal made its decision. However, the Employment Appeal Tribunal (EAT) held that being a shareholder did not preclude her from also being an employee.

■ Did the board meet in the ordinary course of business or not? If not, then that would suggest there was no genuine employment relationship between the parties.

Ideally, to avoid disputes, the dual or triple (i.e. shareholder, director and employee) relationship with the company should be clearly evidenced in writing. If an executive director has virtually the same relationship with their company as that of an ordinary employee (and this is probably the case for the vast majority of LTDs), then this should be evidenced.

Keeping separate records of the decisions of what could be loosely said to be those exercising strategical control (shareholders), tactical control and fiduciary duty (directors and other officers) and administrative control and duty of fidelity (employees) might aid the identification of the true (and possibly multi-faceted) relationship.

Service contract

The duties to be undertaken by directors for the company are customarily controlled by and set out in a document termed a service contract negotiated between the director and the company on an individual basis. Whilst this will specify most of the normal details to be enjoyed by the average employee – pay, holiday, title and duties, sickness benefit, notice and termination and so on – it will not necessarily contain all the items required to be included in a contract of employment. It will often contain restrictions on the work that can be undertaken immediately after its termination which may be more restrictive than those for an ordinary employee and even a 'garden leave' (i.e. enforced idleness) clause. The service contract is itself governed by company law, in that it must be made available for inspection by shareholders for two hours each working day. If it is required that the director should also be regarded as an employee, then the service contract must also address the requirements to be stated under employment law.

Clarify the relationship

Ideally, a contract seeking to evidence a dual relationship of officer and employee should specify

- that the subject of the contract is an employee as well as a director; and
- that it is the 'principal statement' required under the Employment Rights Act 1996 as well as being the service contract required to be displayed under company law.

An example of wording is given below, but legal advice should be taken to ensure proper drafting of the appropriate clauses – and their relationship to the subject company and director.

Many articles require a proportion (very often, a third) of the board to retire, 'by rotation', at the company's ANNUAL GENERAL MEETING and to offer themselves for re-election. If rotation is required, directors who have been in office longest must put themselves forward for re-election. Should the shareholders either refuse to re-elect or simply dismiss the director, this will almost certainly entail an action for breach of the director's service contract, but the situation regarding their employment rights may remain unclear. Indeed, if the person has duties other than those as a director, it could be argued that these (and thus the person's employment by the company) continue, regardless of the cessation of the appointment as a director. Conversely, although perhaps somewhat unlikely, a director with other responsibilities could 'resign' from those employment obligations one day, and insist on attending a board meeting the following day.

Legal precedents

Although there have been a number of tribunal cases which have found that in specific circumstances shareholding directors were not also employees, this is not always so.

Case studies	Deemed to be an employee (and determination of status)
	In *Secretary of State for Trade & Industry v Bottrill*, and *Fleming v Secretary of State* (Bottrill and Fleming were both directors and majority shareholders of their respective companies) the court commented that *'the fact of majority shareholding was no more than a relevant factor in determining whether the director was also an employee and there was no rule of law which said that a majority (controlling) director could not be an employee'*.

Similarly, in *Heffer v Secretary of State for Trade & Industry* the Employment Appeal Tribunal made the following findings:

- a limited company is a distinct legal entity from its shareholders and directors;

- a director of a limited company may enter into and work under a contract of employment with that company;

- a shareholder of a limited company may enter into and work under a contract of employment with that company.

The Court of Appeal held in *Nesbitt & Nesbitt v Secretary of State for Trade and Industry* that even though the Nesbitts between them held 99.9 per cent of the shares, they were also employees of their failed company, and thus could claim redundancy payments from the state. Neither of the Nesbitts had received dividends or directors' fees.

In *Clark v Clark Const. Initiative Ltd* the EAT set out further guidelines regarding decisions about the twin relationship, as follows:

- if there is an ostensible contract of employment, the onus is on the other party to prove that it is not what it appears to be (for example, if such a contract has not been set out in writing, that could be an argument against employment);

- whether the director works in accordance with what would normally be expected of an employee (if so, that could be a strong argument in favour of them being employed);

- the mere fact that the director has a controlling shareholding does not prevent him also having a contract of employment (although it may raises doubts about it);

→

Case studies	Deemed to be an employee (and determination of status) – *continued*

- taking a salary rather than dividends might be an argument in favour of employment;

- the fact that the person founded and built the company will not prevent there also being an employment relationship;

- the fact that the person had financial arrangements with the company (e.g. had loans from it or made loans to it, or gives guarantees) will not normally be of assistance in determining whether there is an employment relationship.

In *Neufeld v A&N Communications in Print Ltd (in Liquidation)* Neufeld was originally an employee. He started work in 1982 but became a shareholder and a director in 1988. He was made managing director with 90 per cent of the shares and in addition he gave guarantees in respect of the company's liabilities. Although there were no written contracts between the three directors and the company, Neufeld, despite his large shareholding, continued as part of the sales team – literally working as a salesman. When the company went into liquidation, the EAT found that he was an employee and entitled to redundancy and other payments in the same way as other employees. This was recently confirmed by the Court of Appeal.

Administration

Some companies not only set out the relationships in a joint service/employment contract, as mentioned above, but also insert a clause which, in the event of its termination, grants to the company a power of attorney giving it the right to act as if it were the director. Thus, the company would then be able to sign a resignation letter and any other documents which, in the event of a dispute, the director would no doubt refuse to sign, to retain greater bargaining power (see NOMINEE SHAREHOLDINGS). Granting such power could not restrict the right of the director to take action under the service contract, for breach, and possibly, under the 'contract of employment', for unfair dismissal. Alternatively the situation could be clarified in the articles, with authority by which directorships can be 'resigned' being included. Again, legal advice should be taken.

Example	Draft contract

This Agreement is made this day of 2XXX, between [the company] and .... (the executive).

It is hereby agreed that:

1 The company shall employ the executive as [title, list of duties, etc.] and the executive shall serve the company commencing the day of 2XXX (the commencement date) for a rolling period of a maximum of three years so that (unless either party shall have given written notice of termination of this contract) the period shall be extended by a further one year on each anniversary of the commencement date.

The appointment of the executive as director and employment of the executive shall otherwise continue until the occurrence of:

a) three months from the date on which either party shall give to the other three months' notice of termination in writing. For the purposes of employment legislation the date continuous employment commenced was [date],

or

b) the passing by the shareholders of a resolution removing the executive as a director,

or

c) summary dismissal as a result of gross misconduct committed either as a director or as an employee. The executive hereby grants a power of attorney in favour of the company authorising it to sign the required forms evidencing such removal as resignation from the post of director, and all ancillary matters, notwithstanding any rights the director may have under this agreement.

2 The executive shall during the continuance of this agreement well and faithfully serve the company and use his utmost endeavours to promote the interests of the company and its shareholders, giving it at all times the full benefit of his knowledge, skill and ingenuity, and shall perform all his duties as may from time to time be assigned or vested in him/her by the board of directors of the company (the board).

3 The executive shall during the continuance of this agreement devote the whole of his time and attention to the duties of

➡

Example	Draft contract – *continued*

the appointment (unless prevented from so doing by illness). He shall not, and shall cause his spouse and immediate family not to, directly or indirectly enter into, or be concerned in any manner (other than with the consent in writing of the board or as a minority shareholder in a company quoted on a public stock exchange or bourse) with any company or organisation deemed to be (at the discretion of the board) a competitor of the company.

4 The duties covered by this agreement shall be mainly carried out at the head office for the time being of the company, but the director will be expected to travel to all company locations and elsewhere on company business and may be required to relocate within a [250 mile] radius of [London].

5 During the continuance of this agreement the company shall pay the executive (monthly) at the rate of £XXXXXXX per annum or such other rate as may from time to time be agreed by the Board and will provide (at the cost of the company) a private motor car to the equivalent of [exact terms of allocation and use could be inserted here].

6 In addition to remuneration, the director will be entitled to reimbursement of all travelling, hotel and other expenses properly and reasonably incurred in the exercise of these duties and supported, as far as possible, by VAT receipts (if possible made out in the name of the employer) and invoices.

7 The director will be entitled to [ ] paid days' holiday in each year (plus public or Bank holidays) at such times as may be agreed by the board. At least 20 days each year must be taken within the holiday year.

8 In the event of the director falling sick and being unable to perform the duties, the company will continue to pay the normal salary (for the time being) for a maximum of [ ] days in any one year. Should incapacity exceed such a period, further payment(s) will be at the discretion of the board. *[It may be advisable to specify the relationship between Statutory Sick Pay and salary – e.g. whether the company will pay only SSP or top it up to the normal pay.]*

Example	**Draft contract** – *continued*

9 Should the director become unable (by reason of ill-health, imprisonment) to perform the duties adequately, or fail or neglect to perform the duties, or breach any of the provisions of this Agreement, then the company may forthwith determine this Agreement without notice as previously stipulated.

10 The director shall not, without the consent in writing of the company, divulge to any other person, firm or company, and shall use his best endeavours to prevent the publication to any other person, firm or company of any information concerning the business or its finances or any of the secrets, dealings, transactions or affairs of or relating to the company.

11 The director acknowledges receipt of the company's code of ethics and undertakes to abide by the requirements thereof.

12 The director undertakes to notify the company immediately of interest he may have in a third party with which the company does business, and of any change to such interest(s) and to advise the company immediately of any disqualification order made against him either in the UK or elsewhere.

[13 The director acknowledges receipt of the company's Stock Exchange listing agreement and undertakes to abide by the requirements thereof.]

14 The whole interest of the director in any inventions emanating as a result of his employment shall become the absolute property of the company without any payment being due to him.

15 Upon the termination of this Agreement (whether by effluxion of time or otherwise) the director shall not (without the express written permission of the company) for a period of six months thereafter be connected with, or take part in the management of, or advise or direct, another business whose activities could conflict with the activities of the company. In addition the director will not for a period of six months from such termination, solicit or take away any staff, custom, or business under the control of the company at the time of the termination.

➔

Example	Draft contract – *continued*

16 If the director resigns in order to join a competitor or to set up in competition with the company, the company stipulates (and it is specifically agreed by the executive) that for a period of six months from the date of such resignation he will not work for that competitor and will remain on 'garden leave'.

For the purposes of clarity it is stipulated that the principle behind this clause is to provide protection for the company in respect of up-to-date knowledge gained by the executive during employment. As such the company requires that, should a period of 'garden leave' be implemented it is expressly understood that during such leave, the director will:

- take any accrued holiday to which he is entitled;
- have no right to carry out any work for the employer;
- not approach or enter the premises of the employer (other than at the specific and previous request of the employer);
- not contact any employee or customer of the employer by any means whatever;
- during the whole duration of the contract and during any period of garden leave, not work for or advise a competitor, or set up as a competitor of, this organisation;
- not represent himself to any third party as being or still being an employee of the employer.

The provisions of the Contracts (Rights of Third Parties) Act 1999 are specifically excluded from this clause.

17 Any notice or other document required to be given under this agreement shall be deemed to be served if it is sent by recorded delivery:

- by the company to the director at their last recorded home address; or
- by the director to the company via the chairman or company secretary at their last recorded home address.

Signatures of parties

Witness

Notes

1 Such a document grants rights and responsibilities. It is provided as a draft, needs to be customised and legal advice should be taken.

2 It should be treated as a deed and sealed (or signed as a deed), rather than simply signed.

3 Unless there is no alternative, it would be preferable that the subject director was not a signatory on behalf of the company.

4 The requirement for the subject not to work for a competitor for a set period after termination of employment (so that personal knowledge and/or contacts become outdated and of less relevance) will almost certainly mean the company has to continue payment for the term of this so-called 'garden leave' (i.e. enforced inactivity) period.

5 'Payment' in respect of garden leave periods must include all non-cash benefits in respect of the period (e.g. car, health cover, etc.) whilst holiday entitlement should be taken. Only the cash equivalent of holiday that it is impossible to be taken should be paid.

6 The exclusion of the Contracts (Rights of Third Parties) Act attempts to prevent someone not immediately involved in the contract being able to circumvent its clauses.

Case study	Third party negates garden leave
	In a case where a husband who had a contract with a six-month 'garden leave' clause, resigned to join a competitor, his employer enforced the garden leave clause. However his wife exercised her rights under the Contract (Rights of Third Parties) Act to insist that his employer gave him work to do (thus at least in part negating the effect of the garden leave clause), because she didn't want him 'getting under her feet' with nothing to do at home! She won her case.

Implied 'garden leave' clause

In a recent employment case, two employees on three months' notice resigned. The employer put them on garden leave even though it had no right to do so under the employees' contracts. The employees claimed constructive dismissal, stating they were entitled to receive work during the notice period. However the employer had evidence that they were stealing confidential information and planning to join a competitor and to poach the employer's employees. The High Court granted the employer a 'garden leave injunction' preventing the employees joining the competitor during the notice period because they had fundamentally breached their contractual and implied duties to the employer.

Directors: obligations, expectations and liabilities

INTRODUCTION

Directors are officers of the company with a fiduciary duty to their company. This fiduciary duty was spelt out in the judgment in the *Selangor* case in 1968, i.e. directors must act with the *'utmost good faith'*, putting the company's interests first, and, if necessary, sublimating their own interests. Directors hold the company's assets in trust, giving account of their stewardship of those assets each year through the annual report and AGM. Such an appointment not only carries prestige but also considerable personal legal liabilities. Those taking up a directorship should be briefed to ensure they fully understand all their obligations and responsibilities, as well as the expectations indicated by courts as they have interpreted the law. The filing and compliance requirements of CA06 and other Acts are extensive. Failing to adhere to the law, or breaching it (even in ignorance), can lead to fines, disqualification, personal liability and even imprisonment for up to ten years.

Fiduciary duties

A director owes a fiduciary duty to his company. If as well as being a director he is an employee then he also has a duty of fidelity. Directors are required:

- *To act at all times in the best interests of the company.* Defining what are a company's 'best interests' can be a matter of opinion, but nevertheless this is an obligation and a balance or choice may need to be made between the short term and long term. As well as the interests of the company (i.e. those of the members or shareholders), under CA06 directors must also consider the interests of the employees (a continuing obligation under company law, since this was first imposed under CA85), the creditors (another continuing obligation first required by the Insolvency Act 1986), its customers (originally under various trading laws, particularly the Sale of Goods Acts as well as the Competition and Enterprise Acts), its visitors and trespassers (under the Occupiers' Liability Act and various health and safety regulations), and the environment (now under company law as well as environment protection legislation).

    Directors must act fairly between members of the company and must not unfairly prejudice the interests of a minority shareholder.

Their decisions must be for the benefit of the company and in the interests of the shareholders as a whole (from the decision in *Re Smith & Fawcett*).

■ *To act as a trustee in respect of the company's assets.* Directors are stewards looking after the assets for the owners of the business and required to give account of their stewardship to those owners each year. Accordingly a director must act without any additional purpose which would affect the main and overriding interests of the company (even if this means acting against his own best interests). Directors have powers under the company's constitution but must use those powers for the proper purposes of the company (guidance also derived from the decision in *Re Smith & Fawcett*). Obviously a director should not make a secret profit without the consent or permission of the company members under the company's constitution (as stated in the *Regal Hastings Ltd v Gulliver* case, although now overtaken by CA06, see below).

■ *To exercise the best degree of skill and care depending upon his personal knowledge and experience.* Historically a director could not be made liable for a judgemental error. He was expected to 'give of his best' and be judged in this respect on his level of experience. Obviously he could be penalised if he was found to have acted negligently. However, under CA06, it is possible for a shareholder who believes that the company has suffered loss because of the activity(ies) of a director (defined as *'an actual or proposed act or omission involving negligence, default, breach of duty or breach of trust'*) to initiate legal action (a DERIVATIVE CLAIM) against the director on the company's behalf. If the claim is successful it is the company (not the shareholder initiating the action) that benefits. This could have the effect of changing the previous assumption that a director could not be liable for making a 'wrong' decision, provided it was made in good faith, to one where the director can be held liable for an act (or omission) even if it was made in good faith and the person taking the decision does not benefit from that decision (i.e. he had no vested interest).

■ *To declare all and any interests and to act honestly and reasonably, particularly where his own interests may be in conflict with the interests of the company.* Only if not proscribed by the articles and agreed by a disinterested quorum of the board (for LTDs), and only if specifically permitted by the articles and agreed by a disinterested quorum of the board (for PLCs) may any personal profit made by a director by virtue of the appointment be retained. On appointment and on occurrence, when later, a director must immediately declare any and all interests to the board. Failure to disclose an interest can result in personal penalties – on summary trial to a £5,000 fine, whilst on trial on indictment the fine is unlimited. In addition the Court could find the director in breach of his fiduciary duty which could in turn lead to further penalties. (Note: see the suggested form of declaration of interests in DIRECTORS: APPOINTMENT.)

Case studies	Act with propriety

In *Item Software (UK) Ltd v Fassihi & ors,* a director sabotaged negotiations between the company of which he was a director and a third party, so that he could divert the contract (and the business) to himself (in a new company he was setting up). The director was held to have breached his duties by:

- sabotaging the negotiations for his own purposes (which was a breach of his fiduciary duty): and

- failing to tell the company of that breach.

Obviously employees should not defraud their employing company (if they do, they breach their duty of fidelity) but they are not under an obligation to tell their employer of their wrongdoing. However, because they have a fiduciary duty, officers must tell the company of their wrongdoing.

The court described the director's actions as *fraudulent concealment* and stated that if a director appropriates business for himself, then he has a duty to account to the company for any profit. The director was ordered to pay damages for his failure to disclose the breach.

In *Tesco Stores Ltd v Pook,* a senior manager fraudulently arranged for payments on false invoices and received a 'bribe' for doing so from the 'supplier'. The court held that directors and senior managers (who are company officers), because of their fiduciary duty, have an obligation to disclose their breach to the employer and advise them of secret profits. Pook was in breach of this requirement and therefore had to pass the 'bribe' to Tesco as well as the fraudulent receipts. Since he had a fiduciary duty to the company he also had a duty to tell the company what he was doing. This case provides some clarity regarding the term 'officer' which is used in company legislation – the term includes directors, the company secretary and senior managers.

In *Continental Assurance Co of London,* a director described himself as a 'corporate financier' but was unable to understand the statutory accounts of his company. He was disqualified under the Company Directors Disqualification Act, since it would be reasonable for all those dealing with him to expect a person calling themselves a 'corporate financier' to be able to understand financial statements.

Case studies	Act with propriety
	In *Scottish Co-op Wholesale Society v Meyer*, the court said a director must maintain independence of judgement and not fetter his decision, whilst in *Blaikie Brothers v Aberdeen Railway Co*, it was said that directors must not have a conflict of interests without the members' consent (now overtaken by CA06 – see below).

■ *To ensure the company acts in accordance with the requirements of laws affecting the company.* Some time ago the Accounting Practices Board suggested that boards should compile a register of all the laws and regulations with which their companies are required to comply. Compiling such a register is of course merely an administrative chore – the underlying purpose of the suggestion is for a complete set of the company's obligations to be generated, promulgated (to encourage compliance) and policed (to ensure compliance). Indeed the act of recording the legislation is virtually an impossibility for the average company, since the UK Government is passing over 3,000 new laws each year at present – and few, if any, are repealed.

Directors' fraudulent activities

Corporate fraud is on the increase. It has been stated that 60 per cent of all UK companies are losing as much as 5 per cent of their turnover to fraud and theft. The impact is of course felt directly on the bottom line. For a company earning 10 per cent profit, sales of ten times any amount lost to thieves will have to be generated simply in order to regain the pre-theft 'profit-position'. Fraud is specifically outlawed (oddly enough for the first time in English law) under the Fraud Act. A person can commit fraud by:

■ making a false representation;
■ failing to disclose information where there is a legal duty to do so; and
■ abusing their position.

Since a director must by virtue of his position safeguard and protect the shareholders' assets, any dereliction of this duty means he commits fraud. Similarly, if he abuses his position or makes a gain by abusing his position (or causes the company loss by so doing), that is also fraudulent. CA06, s. 176 allows a director to seek authorisation from the board to exploit personally some property or opportunity even though there is or may be a conflict between his interests and those of the company. In an LTD, this can be done, provided there is nothing in its constitution (the articles) banning it. However, directors of PLCs can only do this if there is specific authorisation in the constitution that allows it.

A director's 'Ten Commandments'

The comments made by courts in the judgments in the following cases can help us understand what is currently expected of directors – forming what colloquially we could term their 'Ten Commandments'. Interestingly, some of the key words used by judges in the following cases can now be found as part of the terminology used in CA06.

1   A director must be *diligent*

Case study	Act diligently
	In the *D'Jan* case, where a director signed an insurance proposal form that contained an erroneous statement, the court stated that directors must be:
	'diligent person[s] having … the general knowledge, skill and experience that may reasonably expected of a person carrying out the same functions as are carried out by that director in relation to the company'.
	The court held that although the director could be excused some liability as the mistake was *'not gross. It was the kind of thing that could happen to a busy man, although that is not enough to excuse it'*, he would still be required to contribute £20,000 to the loss suffered by the creditors of his failed company, since he had not shown the degree of care expected of him.
	The judge stated that it was unrealistic to expect a director to read everything presented to him for signature, but he had to exercise some judgement; here the proposal consisted of only a few sentences. (One must wonder how many directors read everything that is presented to them for signature?)

2   A director must not be *reckless*

Case study	Investigation required before decision
	In *Gwyer & Associates v London Wharf (Limehouse) Ltd*, a director made no effort to ascertain what were the interests of his company (which was approaching insolvency) before voting on a board resolution.
	The court held he was not only negligent but also in breach of his fiduciary duty to exercise his discretion independently and *bona fides* in the interests of the company. It went on to state that where a company was on the brink of insolvency, the directors owed a duty *'to consider as paramount'* the interests of the creditors.

3   A director has a *duty of care*

Case study	Duties cannot be delegated
	In *Dorchester Finance Co Ltd v Stebbing*, there were three directors of the company, of whom two, X and Y, were effectively non-executive and left the running of the company to Z. X and Y often signed blank cheques for use by Z, and made no enquiry as to how funds were obtained or used. The company failed, owing creditors considerable sums.
	The court found that both X and Y had failed to apply the necessary skill and care in the performance of their duties (and indeed that they had failed to perform any duties in their positions as directors). In addition, Z (who, like X was a qualified accountant) had failed to exercise any skill or care as a director and had misapplied the assets. All three directors were held to be liable for damages.
	In the judgment the court ruled:
	• Each director must exercise in his duties *'the degree of skill that may reasonably be expected'* from a person of his knowledge and experience. Thus in considering liability for wrongful trading, a court might consider a director who is a qualified accountant to be more culpable than (say) a

Case study	Duties cannot be delegated – *continued*
	personnel director, because of the former's professional training and expected knowledge in the corporate field.
	● A director must in the exercise of his duties take such care that a man might be expected to take on his own account. The question that could be asked is: *'Would I be so cavalier concerning these funds, were this my own cash/bank account rather than it being that of my company?'*
	● A director must exercise the powers granted to him in good faith and in the interests of the company of which he is a director.

4 A director must maintain his *knowledge of the business*

Case study	Keep updated
	In the investigation following the collapse of Barings Bank after the devastating losses caused by illegal trading in its Singapore office, the court stated: *'directors, collectively and individually [have] a duty to acquire and maintain a sufficient knowledge of the company's business to enable them to discharge their responsibilities'.*

Case study	The liabilities of executive and non-executive directors are identical
	The imminent collapse of hotel group Queens Moat Houses was avoided by the creditor banks providing ongoing (and very long-term) essential financial support to avoid liquidation, mainly since they could not let the company fail (because the massive bad debts would have affected their own balance sheets). Board members (who included three qualified accountants) were disqualified as directors for a variety of periods – ten, eight and seven years – whilst the former deputy chairman, Martin Marcus, was also fined £250,000. Finally the chairman, John $\rightarrow$

Case study	The liabilities of executive and non-executive directors are identical – *continued*

Bairstow, who founded the company and originally built it into a major hotel chain, was disqualified for six years.

The judge stated: *'Had Mr Bairstow performed his duty as director and chairman of QMH properly he would have been aware from the information available to him that the profit figures given to the banks were seriously unrealistic.'*

John Bairstow commented: *'It seems that all directors, including non-executives, are deemed liable for any accounts whether they had any involvement or not.'*

Well that's what the law states Mr B – and it is surely reasonable to expect the chairman of a listed PLC to be familiar with the law – or be advised concerning it!

5 A director should *promote the company* (and must not act against its interests)

Case study	'A house divided among itself must fail'

In *British Midland Tools v Midland International Tooling,* four directors of the original company secretly decided to leave their company and set up another in competition. Three remained in office, but their colleague resigned and set up the new company to compete with the old. The three who remained in office enticed employees to join the new company and poached customers for it. The court held that the three directors who remained in office had a duty to the original company to stop the enticement and poaching and were thus liable for not taking such action.

Perhaps the most well-known breach of this guideline was that made by Gerald Ratner when in a presentation to the Institute of Directors (and as a 'joke' to enliven his presentation) he compared some of the products his company sold in its shops to human waste and having a value not much in excess of 'a Marks and Spencer sandwich'. In the aftermath he had to resign as chairman and then as a director, the company had to sell nearly 200 shops and nearly failed, whilst the share price plummeted from approaching £4 to a few pence per share.

6 A director is expected to *lead* the company

In the 21st century there is increasing pressure for directors to lead rather than manage or direct. Leadership (probably in somewhat short supply) is a more dynamic undertaking than management.

> *'Management is about doing things right but leadership is about doing the right things'* and
> *'Management without leadership is like arranging the deckchairs on the Titanic.'*
> (Stephen Covey)

Interestingly, the Hampel Committee (one of the six committees whose deliberations eventually led to the combined code of corporate governance) in its report uses the word 'leadership' to the complete exclusion of the word 'management'.

7 A director must ensure the company *complies with legal requirements*

The maxim *'ignorance of the law is no defence'* poses a considerable challenge to directors, particularly in the current legalistic environment. This is a major problem for the board, possibly requiring considerable investment of resources not only to *'keep the company legal'* and avoid its resources being consumed as a result of liability claims, but also in order to protect their personal position. Increasingly, directors can be held personally liable. Often prosecutions (for example for a safety breach) may be linked to the Company Directors Disqualification Act where, if found guilty, the director can be disqualified from acting as a director for up to 15 years.

8 A director must *act within his powers*

The powers of directors are set out in the articles and memorandum (i.e. the company's constitution). Failing to act in accordance with these requirements can render the director personally liable for his actions.

Case study	Twin breaches
	In *Smith v Henniker-Major* a director acting on his own purported to pass a board resolution at a board meeting of which he had deliberately not given his colleagues notice. That was a breach of CA85 – since all directors have a right to receive notice of all board meetings unless they are outside the UK at the time. In addition, however, the company articles stipulated that the ➡

Case study	Twin breaches – *continued*
	quorum for valid board meetings was two directors, whereas he was on his own. The court stated that his 'resolution' was a worthless piece of paper.
	The director here put himself in a dangerous position. Since he had acted *ultra vires* under the articles which required a quorum of two, if he acted on the 'resolution' and the company had lost money as a result, the shareholders could have held him personally liable for those losses.

9 A director must comply with the seven explicit duties set out in CA06

See detailed guidance below.

10 A director must *take action if the company is in financial trouble*

Under both company law and insolvency law, responsibilities are placed on directors that at all times they will be aware of the state of solvency of their company.

If they are not so aware, continue to trade and take on credit when there is no reasonable prospect of the creditors being paid on, or within a reasonable time of, the due date for payment of their debt, then directors can become personally liable to contribute to the shortfall to reimburse the creditors of a failed company.

(See WRONGFUL AND FRAUDULENT TRADING.)

General aims/responsibilities of the board

Collective

A board must act as an entity with shared responsibility for all the activities of the company. Thus, irrespective of whether a director 'heads up' a particular discipline, he must take decisions, and share in the decision-making process, in respect of all matters concerning the company, even if that means supporting a board decision which is in fact detrimental to the interests of the discipline he heads – or even to him. Once the decision is taken – even if by majority vote – any director not in favour of the proposal must sublimate his personal preferences and work to implement the decision with his best endeavours. If he simply cannot accept the decision, he should resign.

Individual

The items of a corporate nature expected of a director could include:

- ensuring company strategy is formulated, known widely and adhered to;
- formulating the aims and purposes of the company and ensuring that these are both known and borne in mind internally at all times, and that at appropriate times they are promulgated, with the strategic direction of the company, outside the company (e.g. to the media, shareholders, advisers, etc.);
- ensuring tactical decisions and actions take the same general direction as the strategy of the company (i.e. ensuring that short-term decisions do not hamper or impede the progress of the long-term strategy);
- formulating, promulgating and ensuring adherence to an internal code of ethics covering GIFTS etc.;
- ensuring the company complies with its own constitution (i.e. the articles) and, if a listed PLC, the listing agreement, and custom and practice for the industry;
- acting as company spokesperson, promoting the corporate entity and its products/ services at all times;
- ensuring the appropriate blend of skills is available at board level (and through board members and management at all other levels), that people at all levels know what is expected of them, are motivated to perform well, and warned and disciplined (in accordance with pre-set rules) when performance or actions are not in accordance with requirements;
- ensuring there are adequate controls over the commitment of the company to contracts, etc., and adequate authority control over all other purchases;
- ensuring the financial records and reports of the company are prepared in accordance with legal and other accounting requirements, and that such reports are filed with the requisite authorities within the set time limits;
- ensuring the products and services of the company are developed so that continuity of earning power of the organisation is ongoing;
- expanding the company based on well-researched, well-prepared, and well-considered planning;
- ensuring the company has formulated contingency (disaster recovery) plans to protect its earning capacity in the event of a downturn or change in demand, and the effects of possible disasters affecting operations (see RISK);
- protecting the corporate entity and the products/services from criticism, attack and loss as far as possible.

Personal liability

The range of instances in which a director can find himself liable to fines, compensation, even imprisonment, etc. is considerable and ever-increasing.

Specifically (but not exhaustively) a director could be held liable for:

- generally failing to comply with company law, employment law, safety law, environmental law, competition law, and data protection law, etc.;
- acting as a director whilst disqualified;
- 20 years, as a director of a dissolved company (for liabilities discovered subsequently, but occurring prior to the dissolution, for which he can be held responsible);
- acting in contempt of court;
- making a misleading representation (particularly when raising capital);
- abusing the interests of minority shareholders;
- making negligent comments or statements;
- acting outside his authority.

In addition to the above, directors may be placed under pressure, in the interests of the company, to accept personal liabilities. For example, bankers may be unwilling to allow the company to borrow money unless the directors give personal guarantees. This may become increasingly prevalent with companies formed under CA06 which do not have the restriction of the traditional objects clause in a memorandum (although there is nothing to stop a company adopting an objects clause and inserting it in its articles). Since the bank has no evidence of the purposes of the company for which the finance is sought, they may seek undertakings from the directors that they will use the money only for specific and detailed purposes – and will be personally liable should the funds be used in other enterprises.

Explicit legal duties

CA06 contains explicit requirements of directors – certain key terms of which have been derived from the language used in judgments in some of the cases referred to above. This is the first time the law has laid down explicit duties expected of directors, although it can be argued that these duties had previously been implied. In themselves the duties should not pose too many challenges to directors. The concern may be more that they set criteria against which directors can be judged, particularly by shareholders who may wish to bring DERIVATIVE claims where the directors are alleged not to have acted in the best interests of the shareholders. Thus directors must:

I   Act within their powers (s. 171)

Many directors (particularly in smaller companies, which form the majority of UK companies) have not read (and sometimes do not even know about) their company's articles, which set out the company's owners' stipulations concerning the powers and requirements of the directors. For companies formed under CA06 the articles will be the company's constitution and thus all actions must be in accordance with the content, whilst for an existing company its 'constitution' will be formed by their articles, to which their objects clauses will be deemed to be transferred. Directors of LTDs that decide to operate without a company secretary must ensure one of their number – if not all of them – know(s) the contents of the articles (including the 'objects' clauses deemed transferred from the memorandum) to ensure they do not breach these requirements.

2   Promote the success of the company (s. 172)

Directors must act in good faith and in a way which would be most likely to promote the success of the company for the benefit of and in the interests of the company's members whilst taking into account the interests of employees, customers, the environment and suppliers. The directors need to be aware of the long-term consequences of decisions and the desirability of the company maintaining a reputation for high standards of business conduct. Thus the interests of those considered to be the 'stakeholders' must be considered. The difficulty may be that some of the interests to be taken into account may be diametrically opposed to others.

   Thus directors need to consider (as CA06 states):

- the long-term consequences of all decisions;
- the interests of employees as a result of the decisions;
- the need to foster business relationships with suppliers, customers and others;
- the impact of the company's operations (and thus their decisions concerning those operations) on the community and the environment;
- the desirability of the company maintaining a reputation for high standards of business conduct; and
- the need to act fairly as between members of the company.

3   Exercise independent judgement (s. 173)

A director must vote according to his own personal views – even if this results in him being in a minority of one. If a director finds himself in such a minority, it might be advisable to require that the fact (his dissent) is noted in the minutes in case it is ever challenged in future. If including his objection in the minutes is resisted the director should write a note to the chairman (and keep a copy).

4 Exercise reasonable care skill and diligence (s. 174)

The test here is that the director should act with the degree of care, skill and diligence that would be exercised by a reasonably diligent person with the general knowledge, skill and experience reasonably expected of a person carrying out the functions carried out by the director.

5 Avoid conflicts of interest (s. 175)

A director will not breach this requirement if:

- the conflict has been authorised by the directors (at a meeting where there is a disinterested quorum); and
- for an LTD, it is not specifically prohibited by the articles; or
- for a PLC, the directors are given specific power to allow it.

Section 182 requires, additionally to s. 175, that a director must declare an interest (direct or indirect) which is already in existence.

Obviously in allowing a colleague to retain an interest which could be a conflict, the other directors would have to take the decision, bearing in mind their own fiduciary duty to the company.

Since under s. 184 interests are required to be brought to the attention of the directors, it might be as well for a company to maintain a 'register of directors' interests', to be available for inspection on every occasion when board decisions are made.

WARNING

 The Companies Act 2006 (Commencement No. 5, Transitional Provisions and Savings) Order 2007, stipulates that all companies formed before 1 October 2008 must obtain shareholders' consent giving the directors permission to authorise such conflicts. Although it is not stipulated that this needs to be a special resolution (thus amending the articles), such a course might be safest.

6 Not accept benefits from third parties (s. 176)

However, if the benefit cannot reasonably be regarded as giving rise to a conflict of interest, it can be allowed to subsist. It might be prudent to request that any benefit received from a third party – even if not giving rise to a conflict – should be entered into a 'register of directors' interests' which could be available at each board meeting and thus available so that all other directors are advised of the interest.

7 Declare any interest in proposed transactions with the company (s. 177)

Such declaration can be either a specific (s. 184) or general (s. 185) notice, but a director does not have to make a declaration if the interest cannot reasonably be regarded as likely to give rise to a conflict.

Note

The challenge for directors may be to be able to *prove* that they did take account of these statutory duties when taking decisions. Inherent is the need to take account of the interests of a number of interested parties – some of whose interests could be diametrically opposed to those of others, as the following chart demonstrates.

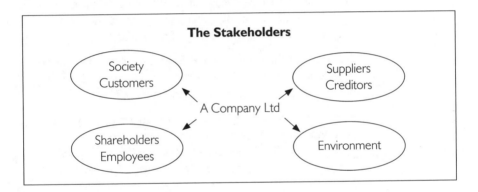

It may be that (perhaps at the first board meeting after the start of every financial year, and the first meeting after a new appointment to the board) there should be a minute to the effect:

'The board reminded themselves of the seven duties of directors set out in the Companies Act 2006 and confirmed that in taking all decisions they would continue to take account of these duties and bear in mind the disparate interests of the company's stakeholders.'

Under CA06, it is possible for a shareholder who believes that the company has suffered loss because of the activities of a director (defined as *'an actual or proposed act or omission involving negligence, default, breach of duty or breach of trust'*) to initiate legal action (a 'DERIVATIVE' CLAIM) against the director on the company's behalf. If the claim is successful it will be the company (not the shareholder initiating the action) that will benefit.

Liability to employees

Directors can be held responsible for everything that goes on in the workplace.

Case studies	Employer held liable – I
	A director and his company were both found guilty of a breach of safety law by using an unguarded machine, which resulted in an employee losing an arm. *Rainham Waste Recycling Ltd* was fined £25,000 plus £4,000 costs, whilst the director was fined £5,000. In addition, under the Company Directors Disqualification Act he was disqualified from acting as a director for five years.
	In the *Lyme Bay* canoe tragedy case, both company and director were found guilty of manslaughter – the director was jailed for three years whilst the company was fined £60,000.
	In a case brought by the Health & Safety Executive regarding the illegal employment of children, a company was fined £2,000, a director £4,500 and the manager responsible £7,500.
	In *R v F Howe & Son (Engineers) Ltd*, where the company was held responsible for the electrocution of an employee and initially fined £48,000 plus £7,500 costs, the Court of Appeal stated: *'some safety offences could be so serious that they could lead to fines being levied at a rate that would bankrupt the company'.*
	The Court stated that the fines for health and safety offences were too low and, where death was involved, this should be reflected in the fine. It urged lower courts to judge how far defendants fell short of the *'reasonably practicable'* test. In doing so, courts should ignore the size of employers – the standard of care expected is the same irrespective of size.

It is perhaps surprising that CA06 does not specifically require the board to consider their obligations regarding 'safety' – although it could be argued that it is covered by the requirement to take account of the *'interests of employees'* when taking every decision. In a recent survey, 63 per cent of company secretaries felt *'a duty to consider safety'* should be a specific requirement. The Health and Safety Executive has recommended that safety should be a regular item on the board agenda and obviously any decisions regarding safety matters should be properly minuted.

Case studies	Employer (and employee) held liable – 2

In *Bryans v Northumberland College of Arts & Technology* a total of £29,901 (including costs) was awarded to Mr Bryans who, amongst other things, had been called *'an Irish prat'*. Of the total, the College had to pay £13,000, his line manager had to pay £6,500, the curriculum director £1,500 and the colleague who actually said the words £5,000.

In *Yeboah v London Borough of Hackney* the employer was required to pay £380,000 compensation, but in addition the director responsible for acts of racial discrimination against Yeboah was required to pay £45,000 plus £14,000 interest.

In *Jones v Tower Boot* the Court of Appeal held that the company was responsible for employees who branded, taunted and harassed a young black employee, even though they were not *'acting in the course of their employment'* (a defence which previously had enabled employers to escape liability for the personal acts of their employees).

In *National Rivers Authority v Alfred McAlpine Homes East Ltd* a company was held liable for pollution caused by its employees washing cement into a stream. The court regarded the employees who actioned the pollution as acting within the course and scope of their employment.

In a long-running court case regarding the supply of ready mixed concrete (*Re Smith's Concrete Ltd*), the company stated (and could prove in court) that they had tried to ensure at all times that their employees complied with the law and trading guidelines. Whilst the Court of Appeal held that the company could not be liable for the action of its employees when they wilfully broke such rules and regulations and disobeyed instructions, this ruling was overturned by the House of Lords. Their Lordships held that a company *was* liable for the acts of its employees (even though the company had forbidden such acts), and also commented that the original fines imposed were too low. This was followed by the imposition of £8,000,000 fines against 17 ready-mixed concrete companies and individual fines of up to £20,000 against individual employees. The presiding judge commented that future cases would result in jail sentences.

If discriminating against or harassing other employees, in the course of their employment, in a situation where the company has laid down rules regarding acceptable behaviour and has drawn the rules to the attention of the employees and regularly polices such rules, the employees may find that they are either joined in an action with their employer, or action is taken against them in their personal capacity.

The ever-increasing dimension of directors' liabilities

So if the corporate environment is becoming more and more dangerous for those charged with running corporate bodies, an obvious question is: *'how can we remove our liability?'* The short answer is that company directors cannot, but they may be able to minimise or restrict their exposure by taking action.

1 By keeping aware

The whole area of liability is fast-moving and constantly developing, as our society becomes progressively more litigious. Boards need to be aware of the liabilities they have and how this scenario is changed. Company secretaries need to make themselves aware of the developments, and a prime responsibility is to keep up to date on the law, its interpretation, the range of liability – and the level of compensation awards being made.

2 By formulating rules and procedures

Adequate and effective rules, procedures etc. can provide some measure of defence, in that the company can be shown to have recognised the problem and to have taken steps to try and eradicate it. Thus the company should try to ensure that:

- All rules regarding trading, outlawing price-fixing, safety, recruitment and relationships as well as attitudes and actions towards employees during employment are clear regarding fair treatment and complete observance at all times. These 'pieces of paper' must work, be seen to work and be policed.
- All employees have read and understood the rules, and all procedures etc., are regularly checked and policed and always adhered to (without exception) and everyone is regularly reminded of the requirements.
- Immediate action is taken once there is any question of an accusation or suspicion that there is a breach of such rules, and sanctions are applied against everyone in breach. (The Law Commission has recently proposed two new laws concerning bribery – one prohibiting the giving of bribes and another prohibiting the taking of bribes. In addition there would be new laws prohibiting the bribing of a foreign

official residing or doing business in the UK, and negligently failing to prevent bribery by an employee or agent. The latter is particularly relevant to companies, which would need to ensure that their internal rules outlaw such practices – and that such rules are stringently policed – see AUTHORITY CONTROL.)

- All safety rules are adhered to, specifications regarding maintenance are compiled and inspections carried out in accordance therewith. Adequate protective measures are in place and observed. Risk assessments are prepared and updated.
- All reports of problems potentially affecting safety, concerning bullying, discrimination, harassment, stress etc. are dealt with immediately, effectively and responsibly.
- All employees are advised of their responsibilities for their own safety and for the safety of their colleagues and of their employer's assets.
- Everyone is constantly reminded of the need to adhere to rules, procedures etc., to think before acting or speaking and to consider the implications of liability claims, etc.

3   By obtaining an indemnity

Many directors already have an indemnity – even though probably few know it. If a company has used Table A of CA85 as part, or the whole, of its articles, it almost certainly will have retained reg. 118. This provides a standard indemnity clause. Inevitably, such indemnity can only be utilised by persons acting legally, and only has value if the company is solvent.

4   By effecting insurance cover

Directors and officers (D&O) insurance cover could be effected. Care must be taken to check the extent of such cover – i.e. to read the small print. It is against public interest to be able to insure against the commission of an illegal act, so if the matter is illegal, even with D&O cover there may be no payout. In addition, a board deciding to effect D&O cover should check they have authority in the company's articles. Is there, for example, a disinterested quorum at the meeting at which the decision is made?

Further guidance to the expectations of directors can be found on the website of the Institute of Chartered Secretaries website (http://www.icsa.org.uk/).

The penalties?

Obviously some of the potential breaches referred to above are fraudulent, in which case the offenders could be prosecuted under the Fraud Acts and those found guilty could receive a prison sentence of up to seven years, or ten years where there is FRAUDULENT TRADING. Almost certainly in addition to such a prosecution a breach of the Company Directors Disqualification Act will also be alleged. As well as disqualifying the person from acting as a director of a UK company for up to 15 years, this could lead to a fine.

Case study	Disqualified and fined
	In *R v Owide*, a director was disqualified for seven years in 2000. However he continued to run a number of businesses. In January 2004 he was disqualified for a further five years and fined £200,000. The court also stated that unless the fine was paid within 18 months, he faced an 18-month prison sentence.

It is not only UK law that directors need to observe. Should the conduct breach the laws of other countries, directors could find themselves subject to extradition requests, not only from the USA (concerning which there is a high awareness of the possibility, due to the case of the 'NatWest three' who were unable to prevent their extradition to face charges connected with the failure of Enron) but also from the EU. Many EU member countries have laws which outlaw certain activities that are not illegal in the UK. The Extradition Act 2003 introduced the European arrest warrant, which enables EU member countries to extradite inhabitants of other member states to face criminal charges in their courts. There were expected to be around 1,000 such orders against UK nationals in 2009.

Directors: payments, loans and interests

INTRODUCTION

Directors occupy positions of considerable power, controlling the assets of the company on behalf of their shareholders. As such their personal transactions with their company must be, and are legally required to be, highly transparent. Directors also subject themselves on appointment and thereafter to potentially considerable personal liabilities, and would be prudent to consider whether there are ways in which these liabilities can be minimised – it being unlikely that such liabilities can be insured against or indemnified. All legal obligations apply equally to all directors, including SHADOW DIRECTORS.

Payments

Generally full disclosure of all value given to directors must be made in the company's ANNUAL REPORT each year. Such value includes all benefits in kind as well as cash. In addition, all payments made to (or value given by) persons connected to the director (see below) must also be disclosed. The requirement covers all payments, goods or services in kind and benefits. It also includes any sums etc. paid to a person as an inducement to their becoming a director, as well as any such items paid to them following their ceasing to be a director. Provision of any sums to a third party for the benefit of the director (or to any person being a 'connected person' to the director) must also be disclosed.

Connected persons

Any interests of persons deemed to be 'connected' to a director are subject to the same controls and disclosure as above. Connected persons include:

- husband, wife or civil partner of a director;
- a partner in an enduring family relationship with a director;
- a director's children or step-children up to the age of 18 from the relationships set out above;
- the parents of a director;
- bodies in which the director has a holding of 20 per cent or more.

In addition, any payments to a body to which any director has been seconded must be disclosed.

New requirements concerning pay

New disclosure rules (see CORPORATE GOVERNANCE) regarding directors' pay require listed PLCs to provide:

Explanations of:

- performance criteria for long-term incentive and share-option schemes;
- comparator groups of companies used to determine 'appropriate' pay levels;
- the balance between the elements of a package that are/are not related to performance;
- the company's policy on contracts and notice periods.

Details of:

- membership of the remuneration committee;
- whether the recommendations of that committee were accepted without amendment;
- any remuneration consultants that advised the committee.

Companies are required to disclose the details in a set tabular format, so that inter-company comparisons can be facilitated. In addition, performance graphs must be provided, again to facilitate comparison of reward with individuals' pay. Boards should seek to obtain shareholder approval of directors' pay, although they can implement their recommendations even if the shareholders do not agree.

Although the Institute of Directors welcomed the transparency that the requirements entail, the reaction of many corporate investors has been one of disappointment, since although they will have more (and comparable) information, their ability to influence rates etc. is unchanged. The 'Big 8' investors, who between them hold 5 per cent of the UK Stock Market, have combined to request a vote on pay policy at the AGMs of the largest 750 companies. In the light of recent company failures despite massive salaries and bonuses being paid to directors, greater attention is likely to be paid to this subject by institutional shareholders (and private shareholders) in the future.

There have been some high-profile comments on this matter:

- There was considerable criticism of the Royal Bank of Scotland paying bonuses to its directors and staff following the takeover of National

Westminster Bank on the basis that it is the management of the business that should generate additional earnings and value, and the act of taking over another company does not necessarily create additional earnings. (In the light of later developments regarding this company, such criticism seems both prescient and well-founded.)

■ Whilst there is no doubt that some directors do abuse their positions it is doubtful if this is true of the majority, whilst seldom is the point made during such discussions that in accepting a directorship, an individual also accepts considerable responsibilities and, at least in theory, extensive personal liabilities (which have been substantially increased in recent years).

■ In 'Having their cake … how the City and big bosses are consuming UK business' (Young and Scott, Kogan Page) the authors pointed out (some years ago) that the highest-paid FTSE 100 directors were receiving around 70 times the pay of the average employee – a bigger differential than in any other country apart from the USA, and commented: 'top managers tend to be rewarded for creating a high share price, not a good company'.

This assumes that managers do actually create a 'high share price', which is surely an over-simplification and/or exaggeration of the effect. Directors' efforts (and thus the company's results) are just one of a number of factors that can affect the share price, and simply basing rewards on increases in share price can be over-generous. Some of the movement of share prices is a simple reflection of general market trends as well as trends specific to the sector in which the company operates. Further, if reward is to be linked to share price, should it not be reduced if the share price dips? An interesting concept, given the recent steep falls in share prices of so many companies (directly or indirectly attributable in part to the policies adopted by directors and senior management).

■ The Government criticised senior directors of insurance companies for awarding themselves valuable packages at a time when their industry was allegedly failing most of those whom it sought to serve. In addition pressure was put on boards of banks bailed out by public money to curb excessive salaries and bonuses. One of the strands of criticism that led to the Combined Code of Corporate Governance (CG) was that the directors of many companies were paying themselves too much – the 'fat cat' syndrome. That this was the case in certain instances was indefensible, particularly when considering the rewards of directors in the newly privatised state monopolies where little had changed, there was restricted exposure to market forces or competition, and there was little risk. To many onlookers it must be galling that in many of the companies now asking to be bailed out by public money, boards were overpaying themselves whilst taking decisions which were inherently dubious – and ultimately very costly. Perhaps one benefit of the 'credit crunch' may be more realism in the matter of boardroom pay – a link to a realistic multiple of the average shop floor wage should be considered. After all, when the board get it wrong, as many have spectacularly recently, it is very often those on the shop floor that suffer most, whilst those actually taking the faulty decisions are protected.

Loans

CA06 changes the requirements regarding loans being made to directors. The wording is complex – as indeed it was in CA85. Reference should be made to ss. 197-214 for the full details. Subject to a £50,000 limit, a company can make a loan to a director:

- to carry out the work of the company; and/or
- to incur costs in defending himself in civil or criminal proceedings or in an investigation into negligence etc. (if he is found guilty the loan must be repaid, and if he is innocent presumably the loan should become a grant).

Other than loans for the above purposes, a company is only allowed to make loans to its directors and/or connected persons up to the following limits (larger amounts need the permission of the members):

- a loan or quasi-loan up to £10,000 (previously £5,000);
- a credit transaction £15,000 (previously £10,000);
- a loan in the ordinary course of the company's business (e.g. part of the company's business is to lend money to allow the purchase of an individual's main residence) – no limit (previously £100,000).

If it is proposed that loans should be made to directors, advice should be taken to ensure there is compliance with the detailed requirements of the Act. If a director does borrow money in circumstances that are in breach of the Act (e.g. to the detriment of the creditors), he can be required to repay the amount. Thus in *Currencies Direct Ltd v Ellis*, a former director of a company was required to repay a loan made to him whilst he was a director.

Indemnities

A company may not indemnify its directors (or anyone else) against an illegal act. Subject to that overriding prohibition, under CA06 ss. 232, 237 and 238, indemnities can be granted but these must be recorded and kept in a register at the registered or other 'designated' office. Any such indemnity must be retained for at least one year from termination or expiry of contract (although many commentators feel this is too short a period). Companies must make the records available for free inspection by its members within seven days of a request. In addition, directors and officers liability insurance can be effected, provided this is disclosed in the directors' report (s. 236).

If director(s) have been negligent, or have defaulted on required actions or breached their duties, such acts can be ratified by the members provided that a majority (disregarding any votes cast by the director who is the subject of the matter) is in favour of such ratification (s. 239). (See DERIVATIVE CLAIMS.)

Interests

Under CA06, the obligations of directors regarding matters concerning their company in which they have a personal interest are considerably expanded.

Section 175 states that directors (and their connected persons) must avoid conflicts of interest. However a director will not breach this requirement if:

- the conflict has been authorised by the directors (at a meeting where there was a disinterested quorum); and
- for an LTD, it is not specifically prohibited by the articles; or
- for a PLC, the directors are given specific power to allow it.

When a disinterested quorum are asked to permit an interest to subsist, they should ensure in agreeing that they do not breach their own fiduciary duty to the company.

Section 182 requires that a director must declare an interest (direct or indirect) which is already in existence.

Since, under s. 184, interests are required to be brought to the attention of the directors, it might be as well for a company to maintain a 'register of directors' interests' to be available for inspection on every occasion when board decisions are made. Obviously there should be an element of realism concerning interests – being entertained at this level is very commonplace, the difficulty may be in deciding what is 'run of the mill' entertaining, as an opportunity to discuss business, and a situation where the value of the benefit is such that to a reasonable outsider it could suggest that a 'bribe' is being offered. (See the examples in GIFTS and also the draft form for declaring interests in DIRECTORS: APPOINTMENT.)

WARNING

 The Companies Act 2006 (Commencement No. 5, Transitional Provisions and Savings) Order 2007 stipulates that all companies formed before 1 October 2008 must obtain shareholders' consent giving the directors permission to authorise such conflicts. Although it is not stipulated that this needs to be a special resolution (thus amending the articles), this course might be safest.

Under s. 176 a director must not accept benefits from third parties. However, if the benefit cannot reasonably be regarded as giving rise to a conflict of interest, it can be allowed to subsist. It might be prudent to request that any benefit received from a third party – even if not giving rise to a conflict – should be entered into a 'register of directors' interests'.

Under s. 177 a director must declare any interest in proposed transactions with the company. Such declaration can be either a specific (s. 184) or general (s. 185) notice, but a director does not have to make a declaration if the interest cannot reasonably be regarded as likely to give rise to a conflict.

Reference should be made to the articles as to action to be taken if and when a director notifies an interest. There is no general rule and the articles might stipulate any, or any combination of the following:

- the interest (or the directorship) cannot continue;
- the director cannot take part in any vote concerned with the third party;
- the director cannot be counted as part of the quorum for that part of the meeting;
- the director can vote providing the interest has been previously declared (or is of a stated minority size);
- any profit made by him as a result of such interest must be given to the company;
- any profit made by him must be declared and the board can decide the outcome;
- any profit made can be kept by him.

Note: the General Counsel of the London Stock Exchange FTSE 100 Companies (GC100) has published a guidance paper for those companies that wish to amend their articles by way of a general power for directors to authorise conflicts of interests. The paper gives guidance to the wording of an amendment, best practice on directors authorising conflicts, and how to review previous authorisations.

Directors: removal

INTRODUCTION

Other than by their death, directors can cease to hold office by resignation, removal or disqualification. Resignation should hold no real problem, since it infers a mutual agreement, often with goodwill on both sides. Any administrative requirements are likely to be completed swiftly, i.e. signed letter of resignation, entry made in the register of directors, filing of form TM01 as required under s. 167 CA06 (formerly s. 288(b)) within 14 days with the REGISTRAR. However, difficulties are likely to arise when the removal is involuntary. See NOMINEE SHAREHOLDINGS, SINGLE MEMBER COMPANIES.

Disqualification

A person will be disqualified from acting as a director, if he:

- has been declared bankrupt (although eligibility can be regained by permission of the court). Under the Enterprise Act 2002, directors of companies who become bankrupt through no fault of their own (i.e. they are not classified as having been irresponsible) can be permitted to retain some personal assets (up to £20,000) and to regain eligibility to act as directors in one rather than three years;
- has been convicted of WRONGFUL or FRAUDULENT TRADING under the Insolvency Act 1986 (numbers of directors potentially liable under these laws are almost certain to increase, since company failures are currently increasing by around 50 per cent);
- is insane. For example, if a director is sectioned under the Mental Health Act he must be removed from the board (at least for the period of the sectioning). For companies using the model articles accompanying CA06, a director can be removed if a registered medical practitioner gives a written opinion stating that the director has become physically or mentally incapable of acting as a director and that condition is likely to last for at least three months;
- has been disqualified under the Company Directors Disqualification Act 1986;
- has been responsible for the persistent late filing of documents at CH, or because other conduct makes the director unfit to act, and the court has made a disqualification order.

Being disqualified as a director of any UK company, means that the director is simultaneously disqualified from the boards of *all* UK companies of which he is a director – and may not become a director during the period of disqualification. To effect this, following the making of a disqualification order, the Registrar sends to the director form(s) TM01 (under s. 167 CA06 (formerly s. 288b CA85)) for each of the affected companies, requesting him to resign his directorship(s). If the director does not act then the Registrar may seek the aid of the other directors of those companies (who may not know of his disqualification) to effect his resignation(s).

Disqualification is not the only sanction for wrongdoing – the court can also levy fines.

Case study	Acting whilst disqualified
	In *R v Owide*, the director was disqualified for seven years in 2000. However, he continued to run a number of businesses. In January 2004 he was disqualified for a further five years and fined £200,000. The judge also stipulated that unless the fine was paid within 18 months Owide faced an 18-month prison sentence.

Neither a beneficed clergyman nor a convict can be a director. Although companies can act as directors of other companies (i.e. hold corporate directorships), since October 2008 there must be at least one real person on every board (although companies which do not have a real person as a director can take advantage of a transitional relaxation of this new rule until 2010).

Forcible removal

Whereas under the various disqualification provisions the director will cease to hold office by the action of external requirements, removal in this context covers instances where the company is taking the initiative. The removal of a director in this way can result in high-profile publicity, which the company may wish to avoid. It is normal for there to be a negotiated settlement contingent on the director tendering his resignation. If not, the process of compulsory removal must be followed.

CHECKLIST   Compulsory removal of a director

✓ Check the articles for any powers of removal granted to the board. (In certain circumstances, some articles grant the remainder of the board powers to remove a director without recourse to the shareholders.)

✓ Check the director's attendance record. If a company has adopted reg. 81 of Table A of CA85 as its articles, then a director can be removed if, without the permission of the rest of the board, he is absent for six months from board meetings held in that period, and the directors resolve to remove him.

✓ Check the provisions of the director's service contract; some of the more recent contracts cover this point (see below and DIRECTORS: EMPLOYMENT STATUS).

✓ If the director is due to retire by rotation at a forthcoming annual general meeting, voting against his re-election may be arranged. In this case the director would probably have a right of action for breach of contract, whilst the legality of such a move needs to be checked in each individual case.

If none of the above is available, the removal will need to be effected under the following company law provisions:

▓ Give notice to the director of the intention to remove him at a general meeting at least seven days before the date on which notice of the meeting must be despatched.

▓ The director may within those seven days lodge with the company any representations (i.e. arguments against his removal) regarding such a proposal.

▓ Both the intention to remove (with reasons) and the director's representations for not removing him must be given to all shareholders entitled to attend the (extraordinary) general meeting (or AGM if it is timely) with the notice convening the meeting. This is termed 'special notice'.

▓ At the meeting, the director must be allowed to put any representations to the meeting (even if he is not a shareholder) before any vote is taken.

▓ The resolution to remove is an ordinary resolution, requiring only a simple majority of those casting their votes in person or by proxy.

▓ Removing a director in this way does not necessarily prejudice any subsequent action for breach of contract.

For whatever reason, once a director ceases to hold office, under s. 167 of CA06 the Registrar must be advised on form TM01, and suitable entries must be made in the register of directors. Listed PLCs must also advise the stock exchange(s) on which their securities are listed. The written resolution process cannot be used to remove a director – it can only be effected at a meeting.

Removal powers

The device of retaining to the company a power of attorney in directors' service contracts, with the sole purpose of enabling the company to 'resign' the director in the event of a disagreement, is increasingly used. The legality of such a power should be checked individually and the articles' requirements reviewed. Such a device – even though it may be quite legitimate – would not prejudice any action the director may have for breach of contract.

Note: since October 2008, no one under 16 has been allowed to be a director of a UK company unless the Secretary of State issues permission for an exception. Anyone attempting to avoid this prohibition can be removed from the board by order of the Secretary of State.

INTRODUCTION

Although there are many descriptive and/or colloquial names given to directors, virtually none of these widely used descriptions are referred to in the laws that control their activities. In fact, in company legislation the word 'director' itself is hardly used at all – in most cases the reference is to 'officers' (an all-embracing term which includes the company secretary and senior managers as well as the board members). The legal definition of a director is *'any person acting as a director by whatever name called'*, which is not particularly helpful. Since, in addition, the word 'director' is very often linked with a description and used colloquially it may be helpful to identify what is normally expected of those using such descriptive terms.

Executive

All directors are either executive or non-executive, not that there is any distinction under company law between them. An executive director is a member of the board who is authorised to carry out certain day-to-day functions, including entering into contracts, managing staff and assets and generally executing the decisions of the board made collectively by both executive and (if any) non-executive directors. An executive director may be an employee as well as an officer and, if this is what the company wishes, the paperwork concerning their appointment should reflect this (see DIRECTORS: EMPLOYMENT STATUS).

Non-executive

Most company boards consist predominantly – sometimes exclusively – of persons working full-time in the company, i.e. executive directors. Since it can be difficult for such executives to retain an objective view of the company, it has become increasingly common to appoint additional directors who do not work in the company. Drawn from senior management (and often retired former directors) from the same or different industries as the subject company, these directors have no executive responsibilities. Their purpose is to provide executive directors with advice and input drawn from their experience. Since they do not depend for their living on any payment made by the company, as do most executive directors, the theory is that such non-executive directors can be (and should be) far more objective regarding the progress (or lack of progress) of the company, and, in essence, require answers to questions the executive directors may least want asked. It may also be easier for non-executive directors to question the appropriateness of certain actions. For example, in the Guinness affair, the '*wrongdoing*' of certain of the executive directors, was eventually challenged by the non-executive directors (albeit prompted by the Bank of England). Should the actions complained of persist, non-executive directors should find it easier to resign in protest, with possible attendant publicity (the so-called '*noisy exit*'). However, non-executive directors rank equally with (and have exactly the same responsibilities – and liabilities – as) their executive director colleagues in all respects. Both the Institute of Directors and the Stock Exchange are very much in favour of the extension of the non-executive director concept, whilst draft legislation from the European Union would require there to be a majority of non-executive directors on the boards of all listed PLCs. The Non-Executive Directors Association (NEDA) was launched in late 2007 – details available at www.nedaglobal.com.uk.

Any marked extension of the numbers of non-executive directors (for example as required by proposed new EU directives and/or envisaged by the corporate governance movement) seems unlikely in the light of recent cases where prosecutors have attempted to make non-executive directors liable for actions or inactions of the board. For example, the former non-executive directors of Equitable Life (who were each being paid on average less than £20,000 a year) were to be sued personally for £3.2 billion, because it was alleged they had failed to exercise due care concerning their company granting over-generous guarantees to policy holders. Ultimately the action was dropped, but its initiation epitomises the potential liability of directors, whether executive or non-executive. It would hardly be surprising if, in future, few were willing to risk personal liability for such relatively low rewards – particularly as a non-executive director is likely to know far less of the detail of what is going on in the company than his executive colleagues.

A recent survey by the Audit Committee Institute disclosed that:

- only one company (out of more than 700 in the FTSE All-share index) did not have a non-executive director;
- six had fewer than three non-executives (including a FTSE 100 company).

Note

Company law is often in conflict with charity law. In running a charity, non-executive trustees often form the entire board. Since someone must execute the decisions of the board, this would seem to pose a dilemma. If the person ultimately executing the board's decisions is not a director, they may be so regarded under company law (in any event that person is almost certainly an 'officer'). Very often of course it is the general manager or chief executive of the charity who acts in this way, and almost certainly recommends actions to the (non-executive) board who, by following his recommendations, so resolve. This can put such persons in a position of power vis-à-vis the board such that they could be described either as a 'de facto' or 'shadow' directors. Concerned that chief executives of charities could be so regarded, the Association of Chief Executives of Voluntary Organisations (ACEVO) took legal advice on these positions. The advice was that if such persons acted in this way they were almost certainly de facto or shadow directors.

Such charities may wish to reconstitute themselves as a charitable incorporated organisation (CIO) (see TYPES), when the terms of that new entity are finalised.

Chairman

Most boards can only operate if there is a person who is 'first among equals', and thus articles usually require members of a board to elect one of their number to be a chairman and to lead both board and board meetings. Although often described as such in the media, the chairman is not chairman of the 'company' (such an appointment does not exist), but simply of the 'board' and, indeed, depending on the wording of the ARTICLES OF ASSOCIATION, may be appointed only *'for the time being'*. In addition the board chairman may not necessarily be the person that takes the chair at members' meetings. This point should be checked before convening an AGM or (E)GM – it is somewhat embarrassing if the board chairman goes to take the chair at a members' meeting, only to be required to vacate since the rules state that the members present may elect one of their number as chairman.

The question, in the event of an equality of votes on a board decision, of whether the chairman has a second or casting vote needs to be determined. In the draft articles for an LTD company accompanying CA06, it is stipulated that before any person is given a casting vote, all the directors must approve the suggestion – i.e. it should be decided at the first board meeting.

Managing director

In many organisations the functions of chairman and managing director are combined and vested in one person. There has been criticism of this practice being used by listed PLCs, critics inferring that the concentration of power in one person's hands is detrimental to the overall control of the company. Companies operating under the Stock Exchange listing agreement are put under pressure to subscribe to CORPORATE GOVERNANCE requirements which argue against combining the two roles. However, research seems to suggest that in many companies where the two roles are performed by one person, the financial results are better than in companies where the functions are split. Where there is a separate managing director function, it may be more usual for the chairman to be non-executive and to interface with external parties, leaving the managing director to ensure other board members and management who report to him carry out the requirements of the board and their own responsibilities – that is, essentially an internal role. However, it is difficult to be precise about this since companies operate in different ways – e.g. some letting the managing director assume a greater external role, whilst the chairman adopts a lower profile. To a certain extent this is inevitable, since the personalities and talents of the persons themselves may well affect their division of their duties.

Legally the managing director may be in a different position to every other director and his powers, responsibilities and the provisions of his re-election need to be checked in the ARTICLES OF ASSOCIATION. Under some articles, a proportion (often a third) of the directors must retire at each annual general meeting of the company shareholders and seek re-election by those shareholders at that meeting. A managing director, however, is often excluded from this requirement – indeed under reg. 84 of Table A CA85 (which many companies registered under that Act will have as part of their articles) it is only the non-executive directors who are required to retire by rotation. Since under CA06, LTDs are not obliged to hold AGMs (unless their articles stipulate they must or their directors or members wish it), the transitional arrangements suggest that where the articles require retirement of directors by rotation at the AGM, and there is no AGM, the directors simply continue in office unless and until the articles are changed or an AGM is held.

Alternate

A director is allowed under company law, provided their company's articles also permit, to appoint an alternate to act on his behalf. Alternate directors act as a full representative for the appointee and have the right to receive all data and items sent to other directors. Such an appointment is usually made subject to the agreement of the rest of the board. Historically there have been relatively few alternate directors. This situation could change quite dramatically, however, as a result of the recent extension of maternity leave to 52 weeks. If, during a director's maternity leave, she is not present in the workplace, does not attend board meetings etc., she could be accused of abrogating or not complying with her duty of care as a director. It is hardly constructive (albeit perhaps safer) for her to resign, and it may be preferable for her to appoint an alternate to act on her behalf during her maternity leave. If the articles do not allow for the appointment of an alternate director, they will have to be altered first. However, the most recent changes to maternity leave allow a new mother to work for her employer for up to ten 'in touch' days during her maternity leave, which may negate this problem.

Associate, local, regional, divisional

It is quite common for companies to allow senior employees (not on the board and not registered at CH) to use as a kind of courtesy title, a description which incorporates the word 'director'. This indicates that the company is granting to the person a high level of authority – possibly commensurate to that of a director. Although executives using such titles are not legal or statutory directors, if they use the title in such a way as to suggest that they are, they could be held liable as if they were directors – particularly if the company fails. They could be deemed to have 'held themselves out to be directors to third parties,' and be judged accordingly. In any event, almost certainly persons using such titles (by virtue of their senior positions) would be regarded as 'officers' of the company – and potentially liable as such.

Courtesy titles

Titles such as 'Director of ....', again neither legal nor statutory directorships, may be similarly used to grant a level of authority to a person who is not a board member and who may not even be an employee.

Case study	Called a 'director', hence a director
	In *SMC Electronic Ltd v Akhter Computers Ltd*, an employee used the title 'Director of Power Supplies Unit Sales', and signed a contract as such on behalf of the company. The court held that the company could not repudiate the contract, as it was reasonable for the other party to assume in dealing with a person with that title that they were dealing with someone with power to bind his company.
	(Note: An AUTHORITY chart, made available to suppliers, might have avoided this problem – at least the supplier would have been put on alert to enquire whether the person had the necessary authority to bind their company.)

Use of the description 'director' by a non-legally appointed director may result in that person sharing in the responsibilities and personal liabilities of a director without necessarily having any say in decisions impacting such responsibilities. (See WRONGFUL trading.)

'De facto'

Courtesy titles such as those outlined above, are used by persons wishing to indicate to the outside world that they have a senior level of authority. At the opposite end of the spectrum are those who wish to direct the activities of a company but have no wish to advertise that reality to the outside world; indeed wishing to conceal their input altogether (possibly sheltering behind their *'front men'* appointees). However the fact of the matter (i.e. the Latin *'de facto'*) is that they are the people who are directing operations. It is to

Case study	Catchall

In *Secretary of State for Trade & Industry v Holler*, the company had become insolvent and the husband/father had been disqualified. However his wife and son acted as if they were directors, taking decisions and requiring actions as directors. They were found to be *de facto* directors and both were disqualified. A second son also acted in the company but was not found to have been part of its corporate governance and therefore was not a *de facto* director – and hence not disqualified.

The judge offered some guidance to determining whether a person was a *de facto* director:

- Was the person part of the corporate governing structure? (If so, he was probably a *de facto* director.)

- A distinction must be made between someone who participates in collective decision making at board level (who would be a *de facto* director) and someone who participates in management (who would not be).

- The decision is to be determined objectively on the basis of all relevant facts. A person may be a *de facto* director even though there is no day-to-day control of the company's affairs and/or he is involved in only part of its activities.

- Factors such as a family relationship may be relevant.

ensure such persons can be held liable for their actions that the definition of a director in the Companies Act is *'any person occupying the position of director by whatever name called'* (s. 250 CA06, formerly s. 741 CA85).

Nominee

Major shareholders who wish to exercise some control over the board and/or shareholders of joint venture companies often appoint their own nominees to the board. Directors nominated in this way owe obligations to two separate bodies and may need to take care to avoid a conflict of interests (i.e. the interests of the company of which they are a director must always be put first since they owe it a fiduciary duty). A nominee director may have enhanced voting rights (e.g. a vote exercised by a nominee may rank greater than the combined votes of all other members). In such a case the company may be regarded as a subsidiary of the shareholder appointing the nominee director, with all the accounting and taxation implications that such a relationship entails.

If a nominee regularly acts in accordance with the wishes of his principal this probably makes the principal a shadow director. Since the nominee is acting in accordance with the instructions of a 'shadow', he too can be held liable if action is taken against the 'shadow'. (See SHADOW DIRECTORS, particularly the case study 'The Sark Lark'.)

Shadow directors

See separate section.

Sole shareholder

CA89 allowed companies to have just one shareholder. Previously all companies had to have two shareholders. LTDs have always been allowed to have just one director. It is also perfectly legal for the sole shareholder to appoint himself sole director. Thus since 1989 it has been possible for a company to have the same person as shareholder and director. However, there is an inherent practical danger in such a situation, since if the sole director is killed or unable to act in some other way, so too is the shareholder. Thus there is no one in a position to appoint someone to replace the director. The company will be unable to continue to trade until the ownership of the share(s) is determined – a process which could take several weeks (or a much longer time), during which time the company could fail.

This is to some extent overcome (at least for companies registered under CA06) by provisions in the articles accompanying CA06 which allow for the personal representatives of the deceased shareholder or guarantor to appoint a new director (presumably without awaiting grant of probate or letters of administration). Those needing to deal with such 'personal representatives' would need to check carefully their right to act if seeking to do so prior to the grant of probate or letters of administration and might want them to sign an undertaking to 'hold the company harmless' for any liability incurred as a result of acting in accordance with their instructions. The whole situation becomes even more difficult if the company has opted not to have a company secretary. If there is a company secretary at least there is an officer (and signatory) who can act.

Silent or sleeping directors

Directors have a duty of care from which they cannot be absolved. If a person accepts the appointment as director, they accept full legal liability for the actions of the company. If they fail to attend board meetings or to find out on an ongoing basis what is going on in their company, they still have liability. Basically it is impossible for a director to delegate their responsibility (and liability) for operating the company. Ignorance of what is going on (as of the law) is no excuse.

Case study	Sleeping danger
	In *Dorchester Finance Co Ltd v Stebbing* there were three directors (all qualified accountants), two of whom left the running of the company entirely to their colleague. The former often signed blank cheques for use by their colleague and made no enquiry of how the funds were used by him. When the company failed, owing substantial sums to its creditors, all three directors were prosecuted. The court found that the two 'sleeping directors' had failed to apply the necessary skill and care in the performance of their duties (and indeed that they had failed to perform any duties in their positions as directors).
	In the judgment the court stated that a director must in the exercise of his duties:
	● exercise the degree of skill and care reasonably to be expected from a person of his knowledge and experience (hence the expectations of directors who were qualified accountants – as was the case here – would be high in view of their professional training);

→

Case study	Sleeping danger – *continued*

- take such care that a person might be expected to take on his own account. Would you be reckless with your own personal bank account? If not, why be reckless with the company bank account?

- use the powers granted to him in good faith and in the interests of the company of which he is a director.

Directors must be proactive in the exercise of their responsibilities (inactivity is not an option, if personal liability is to be to be limited).

Collective responsibility

Once a board decision has been taken, a director, even if he was fundamentally against the agreed course of action (and may well have voted against it, and may also – as is his right – have required his dissent to be noted in the MINUTES) nevertheless must now support it – this is the collective responsibility principle. If he finds himself unable to do so, he really needs to consider his position on the board. Resignation may be the only sensible solution.

Dividends

INTRODUCTION

Members of companies limited by shares can be rewarded for, or gain value from, their investment by capital growth and/or dividends which can, if profits and/or reserves allow, be paid each year. However, the decision for the recommendation of a dividend rests entirely with the directors, who have complete control – the shareholders cannot force the directors to pay a dividend, although they could, subject to gaining a simple majority of votes, initiate the REMOVAL of the directors if they refuse to do so. Conversely, even though it is usual for only one interim dividend to be paid, there is actually nothing to stop the directors authorising and paying several interim dividends in respect of the same financial year. Control over dividends only passes to the shareholders when a final dividend for that financial year is proposed, since their authority is required to authorise such a dividend. Even here their power is circumscribed in that they can only approve, reduce or reject the figure proposed by the board – they cannot increase the dividend beyond the rate proposed by the board.

Taxation

Corporation tax is a complex subject and the advice of the auditors or other tax advisers should be sought when considering the payment of a dividend so that the full effects of the payment and the allied corporation tax payment are appreciated.

Dividends are received by shareholders as a net amount but are 'accompanied' by a tax credit (currently 10 per cent of the grossed-up dividend). Thus in paying a dividend on 800 shares in Bloggs Products Ltd at a rate of 5.6p a share, a net payment of £44.80 is due to a shareholder. The shareholder would receive a dividend voucher showing this amount as the net payment, but with an accompanying tax credit of £4.97 (the difference between the net dividend and its grossed-up equivalent i.e. £49.77). The accumulation of the tax credits on dividends paid must be accounted for by the company under its corporation tax calculation and is usually paid quarterly. The shareholder can use the tax credit to offset their personal tax liability.

Ability to pay

Companies can only pay dividends from earnings – they cannot be paid out of capital. Should current profits be insufficient to pay the amount recommended, previously undistributed profits (that is, the balance of revenue reserves arising from the accumulation of previously undistributed profits) can be used for this purpose. Listed PLCs cannot pay a dividend unless the net assets (as defined) of the company exceed the aggregate amount of their paid-up share capital and undistributable reserves by at least the amount of the proposed dividend (in other words after the payment of the dividend there would still be a surplus).

Striking date

An effective date for payment of the dividend must be set together with a date as at which members will be entitled to it – the dividend striking date. Shares in listed PLCs can be bought and sold at any time, but only members on the register as at the striking date will be entitled to the dividend. Whether, when share ownership changes around the time of the striking date, the previous holder or new purchaser of shares is entitled to the dividend is a matter for them, rather than the company, to determine. Listed PLCs are quoted 'ex div' or 'without the dividend' in the market once the striking date has passed. Since the previous owner may still be sent the dividend, they may need to account for it to the new member. (If the share is quoted 'cum div' it means that if it is sold the purchaser will get the benefit of the dividend. Obviously whether a share is 'ex div' or 'cum div' will affect its price.)

Tax voucher

In paying a dividend, the company has to prepare both a dividend voucher (a cheque or account credit) and a tax voucher such as the drafts set out below.

Example	Dividend payment

Dividend No 4 Bloggs Products Ltd 3rd July 2XXX

The attached cheque is in payment of the FINAL DIVIDEND for the financial year ended 31st March 2XXX at the rate of 5.6p per share on the 800 Ordinary shares of £1 registered in your name on 15th June 2XXX and payable on 3rd July 2XXX.

J Bloggs, Company Secretary

Name and address of shareholder

Reference	Holding	Tax credit	Net dividend
oyup12/g	800	£4.97	£44.80

(Dividend cheque)

Bloggs Products Ltd 3rd July 2XXX

(Valid 12 months)

Ordinary shares dividend warrant

PAY A. Shareholder £44.80 Account payee only

For and on behalf of Bloggs Products Ltd

(Autographical signature)

Dividend payment No. 4. Signed : J Bloggs

This voucher should be preserved safely. It will be accepted by HM Revenue & Customs as evidence of a tax credit.

Notes

1 The form of the dividend cheque should comply with the latest requirements of the Association for Payment Clearing Services.

2 The cheque is stated to be valid for 12 months, as many shareholders fail to present dividend cheques for a considerable time. Although cheques are usually said to be 'stale' after six months, discretion remains with a bank whether to accept or refuse a cheque which is older than six months.

3 Understandably, most companies prefer dividends to be paid by bank transfer direct to the accounts of their shareholders (i.e. via BACS), since it is less expensive than sending the dividend and tax voucher to the shareholder's address. However, since the process by which

the tax voucher is passed to the shareholder by their banks is often less than satisfactory when BACS is used, many private shareholders prefer to receive the dividend cheque and tax voucher direct.

Share accumulations

To encourage the extension, particularly, of private investor shareholdings, some listed PLCs offer their shareholders the option of taking new shares in place of the dividend or allowing the shareholder to invest the dividend in additional shares (a process which the company carries out for the shareholder). Under this 'dividend reinvestment' concept, the value of the existing shares in the market is used as the basis on which new shares are valued. This value is then applied to the dividend, generating a number of new shares that can be 'purchased' by surrendering the dividend payment.

Members can simply nominate to receive up to that number of shares in place of part or the whole of the dividend with any excess dividend either being paid to them or carried forward to the next dividend payment and added to the amount then available for the same purpose.

In the 1990s, when research indicated that 35 per cent of shareholders took new shares in place of a dividend, several companies (in order to reduce cash flow) offered 'enhanced' schemes whereby the number of shares offered for exchange was greater than that which would be 'purchased' by the dividend. The 'enhanced' custom has since been abandoned.

Other information

In sending dividends to members twice a year there is an opportunity to encourage communication between company and member. Thus, details of discounts available on company products or services can be included, as can vouchers redeemable in the outlets of the company, notification of changes of address and even requests to be placed on the company's internal mailing list. These links can aid communication and shareholder loyalty, which may be invaluable should there be a hostile takeover bid.

The London Stock Exchange sends listed PLCs a Dividend Procedure Timetable each year. If it follows the LSE's dividend timetable, a company does not have to notify the LSE in advance provided the company secretary sends an announcement to the Exchange containing the amount of the dividend, the striking and payment dates (which should not be more than 30 days apart) and a note of whether there is any 'share/dividend' exchange.

Elective regime

INTRODUCTION

In an effort to relieve LTDs from administrative obligations (particularly companies where all the shares were held by board members), CA89 (amending CA85) introduced the 'elective regime' which allowed the shareholders (but only if acting unanimously, i.e. every entitled vote had to be in favour) to 'elect' to allow their company to take certain actions, otherwise required by company law. Whilst such resolutions could be passed at a meeting, they could also be passed by a WRITTEN RESOLUTION (which also originally required 100 per cent unanimity) where the members did not even have to meet. Originally there were five items of business in respect to which this relaxation could be applied. However, since CA06 allows LTDs not to hold AGMs, elective resolutions (which mainly relate to the administration of and business at AGMs) have been largely rendered superfluous.

Authority

The elective regime could be used by LTDs irrespective of the provisions in their articles – although this may seem undemocratic, since 100 per cent agreement of every single one of the votes was needed, the rights of the owners were preserved. Authority to adopt an elective resolution was obtained by gaining unanimous agreement from everyone entitled to attend and vote at a general meeting of which 21 days' notice had been given. At the meeting the elective resolution(s) was/were proposed, and providing unanimous support was obtained, became effective. However, under the Companies (Resolutions of Private Companies) Order 1995, provided all the members agreed, the requirement to give 21 days' notice was waived. In fact using the WRITTEN RESOLUTION procedure the need to hold a meeting to pass the elective resolution could be completely avoided. A written resolution originally entailed obtaining 100 per cent support – which is also the level of support required to pass an elective resolution.

CA06 reduces the level of support for a written resolution depending on the type of resolution. Thus to be passed as a written resolution an ordinary resolution requires a simple majority (i.e. 50 per cent plus one) and a special resolution a 75 per cent majority of the total voting strength.

Uses

The elective regime was originally used to:

- Give, renew or extend the directors' five-year authority to ALLOT shares. The effect of this resolution was that the directors could allot shares within a limitation either in time or number of shares, which of course would have had to be within the limits in the memorandum unless these requirements were first changed, without convening a meeting and seeking such permission from the shareholders at the time. Companies registered under CA06 will not be required to have an authorised share capital and the directors can issue shares they feel are warranted. If required, control over shares to be issued etc. could be inserted by shareholders in the articles.
- Dispense with laying the accounts before the ANNUAL GENERAL MEETING. When such a resolution was adopted the accounts were still required to be sent to each member. CA06 abolishes the need for LTDs to hold AGMs unless the articles state one must be held (or the directors or shareholders want such a meeting), although of course the accounts must still be sent to the owners.
- Dispense with holding an AGM. The business normally undertaken at the AGM is fairly routine. In any event, under CA06, LTDs do not need to hold AGMs unless their articles state they must have one, or their shareholders or directors state that they want one.
- Reduce the percentage required for sanctioning short notice of an EGM from 95 per cent to 90 per cent (a relaxation which is rarely used). This has also been overtaken by CA06 which allows short notice providing 90 per cent of the voting rights agree (although a company's articles can stipulate a higher threshold up to 95 per cent).
- Dispense with annual reappointment of auditors (in which case the auditors are deemed to be re-elected automatically). If an LTD does not hold AGMs the auditors simply continue in office.

Recording

All elective resolutions were required to be filed with the Registrar within 15 days of being passed. If passed at a meeting, the minutes evidencing the adoption of the elective resolution(s) must be prepared and filed in the ordinary way. If passed using a written resolution, the requirements relating to recording of such resolutions apply.

Revocation

If an LTD re-registered as a PLC, elective resolutions ceased to be effective. An elective resolution was also able to be revoked by the members passing an ORDINARY RESOLUTION (which itself had to be filed with the Registrar). Of course the effect of this was that a shareholder who acquired shares after an elective resolution had been passed was subject to it unless and until he could muster sufficient support to pass an ordinary resolution of revocation.

Postscript

CA06 is silent concerning elective resolutions, and effectively abolishes the concept (unless of course the principle has been written into a company's articles), although if all the members are in agreement, obviously they can still resolve all legal business. If unanimity is not possible, either the WRITTEN resolution process could be used – the level of support for which has been reduced (see above), or a meeting could be convened (a process that the elective resolution regime was aimed at avoiding).

Electronic communications

INTRODUCTION

Technological advances have resulted in instant and comprehensive information transfer being made available to virtually everyone – even throughout the world. Some refer to this as 'perfect communication'. This is erroneous since it is certainly not perfect, and it is questionable if it is communication at all. Simply passing information from A to B (however speedily and accurately this can be effected) does not even approach the concept of communication. As the word itself suggests, communication is a two-way process and for it to be achieved requires input and/or feedback from the target to ensure that whatever message was required to be transferred has been received by the target and understood by them in the way that was intended by the sender. Increasingly companies have rights to use electronic means to pass information to their shareholders. However, companies also have a challenge in controlling use and (more pertinently) abuse of electronic information transfer (particularly the downloading and distribution of material from the Internet) by their employees some of which is of an unacceptable type and which can have the result of creating a situation where the company can be held liable. Both aspects of information transfer need to be addressed by companies.

Shareholder information

The Electronic Communications Act 2000 repealed s. 707 CA85 and replaced it with a section which provided the authority under which companies could pass information to their shareholders in ways other than the traditional printed page, e.g. by fax, phone, e-mail and website publication. These relaxations have been overtaken by CA06, which entitles companies to communicate with their shareholders (e.g. sending reports etc.) by electronic means (e-mail, fax, disk in post etc.).

Website communication is also allowed, and unless a shareholder specifically opts out of 'using the website' they will be regarded as having 'received' the document if it is posted there. If they opt out then they will need to be sent the information in some other way. However, when a document is posted on the website, companies have to notify their shareholders of such posting (using hard copy, unless the shareholders have agreed that such notification itself can be transmitted by electronic means).

Since January 2007 under the Companies Registrar, Languages and Trading Disclosures Regulations 2006, companies using a website must include their name and registered number and office, country of registration and VAT number (if appropriate) on the display. The details do not have to appear on every page and there is no stipulation as to where the data appears. Similar information has always been required to be displayed on external e-mails under s. 349/351 of CA85, although this was a requirement far more noted in the breach than the observance!

Wherever electronic communication is used a shareholder still has the right to a hard copy version (even if he has agreed to receive documents in electronic form) within 21 days of such a request.

Case study	Faxed notices of AGM
	In *PNC Telecom plc v Thomas* the court held that it was valid to serve notice of a meeting by fax. This was the first occasion on which this matter was challenged in court.

Companies can:

- publish their annual reports and accounts on their website and simply advise shareholders that they are so available. However a shareholder who wants to receive a hard copy must be given the opportunity to obtain this;
- allow shareholders to use fax and e-mail to appoint proxies and give their proxies voting instructions;
- publish other information on their website. (It should be made clear whether such information has been subject to audit or not.)

The ICSA has published a guide to electronic communications, and companies wishing to use this option would be wise to follow the practical steps laid down there to minimise any challenge to their methods – it can be downloaded from the ICSA website at www.icsa.org.uk.

CA06 requires PLCs to publish their annual reports on their websites as soon as they are available and immediately after:

- they have been approved by the board and auditors; and
- the report is available to the market.

It is recommended that this should happen within 120 days (roughly four months) of the year end.

In the United States well over 80 per cent of the Fortune 500 companies publish financial information on the Internet; whilst in the UK, a recent survey by accountants Deloitte's indicated that around 70 per cent of the UK's FTSE 100 are doing so. Companies wishing to adopt this option will need to liaise with their auditors, since they may wish to check that it is made clear what information is subject to their audit – and what is not.

Suitable security of the website needs to be installed to prevent unauthorised changes being made.

If the shareholders of a listed PLC have agreed and the company offers to all its shareholders the *'facility for shareholders to vote by electronic means'*, then it need only give 14 days' notice of its AGM.

Electronic filing

The Registrar of Companies is progressively working towards a situation where all filing can be carried out electronically. Powers are granted to the Registrar under CA06 to insist not only that all filing be carried out electronically, but also that all company formations use this format, although there are no proposals at present to stipulate this. Those wishing to file electronically must first apply to the Registrar for a password and a reference number. In addition, many of the forms needed for filing at CH can be downloaded on-line.

Internal use of electronic systems

The main challenges regarding electronic communication and Internet access requiring board attention and control if the company and its employees personally are to avoid penalty, are as follows.

CHECKLIST Avoiding breaching legislation and incurring financial penalties

✓ Company legislation requires companies to state certain data (i.e. full name, registered country, number and office) on their notepaper etc. Failure to do so is punishable by fine. If a message is sent by e-mail it is considered to equate to a message sent on a letterhead (i.e. to be a business letter), and as such the required data must appear.

✓ The ability to generate an instant response, rather than waiting for a letter/memo to be typed, has led to numerous instances where ill-considered, overhasty and even rude messages have been generated and sent – and later regretted since they tend to lead to confrontations which more thought could have avoided.

✓ When negotiating electronically it is possible unintentionally to create a binding contract where none was intended. It is advisable to require all such correspondence to carry an automatically generated disclaimer to attempt to indemnify the originating company against improper use of electronic messages and/or to stipulate that a contractual relationship will only exist when confirmed in hard copy. (The legally required information referred to in the first item in this checklist, could also be inserted in such a disclaimer.)

✓ It is possible to commit libel via e-mail which, once sent, is treated as a written document, and the persons responsible can be sued.

✓ All e-mails can be reconstituted in hard copy for up to two years. Such messages can be made subject to disclosure requirements – thus a third party with whom the company is in dispute can require details of such messages. The commitment to sourcing the relevant information should not be underestimated.

✓ E-mail and intranets are used widely for the dissemination of personal material. In addition, third parties can 'dump' unwanted messages. As a result valuable messages may be buried in unwanted electronic communications, resulting in considerable time being wasted in sorting the essential from the trivial.

✓ External e-mails can contain viruses capable of affecting the recipient's computer system, and virus shields should be installed.

✓ In a number of instances companies' websites have been either tampered with or copied (with unauthorised additions/deletions). The format of the website should if possible be protected by copyright, whilst employees must be advised that such actions are regarded as gross misconduct.

✓ An EU survey found that most employees use their employer's access to the Internet for private purposes – often to source pornography (70 per cent of which is stated to be downloaded from the Internet during normal office hours). As a further development, in a number of instances such material has then been circulated to other employees via an employer's intranet, leading to claims of harassment and discrimination.

✓ E-mail and intranets are increasingly being used by employees for harassment, discrimination and bullying of their colleagues, which could mean potential liability for the company and possibly its officers as well as those generating such illegal acts. A recent survey indicated that 50 per cent of those questioned had received obscene, sexist or otherwise inappropriate e-mails within the previous year. In addition, access to the Internet enables 'electronic stalking' to take place.

✓ Where paedophilic images are found on a computer system, the owner of the system (even if not responsible for the generation of such images) potentially could be held liable for severe penalties.

Many companies have developed a policy to ensure that all aspects of the problems posed by new technology are addressed. Often the policy is included as part of the terms and conditions of employment – including a right to eavesdrop on all communications to try to ensure compliance.

Only if there are rules and guidelines as to what is and is not permissible, and the procedures are regularly policed and those who offend are made subject to sanctions, can employers hope to avoid this responsibility and liability – and having to pay what can be substantial sums of compensation.

Environmental considerations

INTRODUCTION

All companies operate in – and thus have an impact on – the environment within which they exist. Until relatively recently, only a minority of organisations were concerned about the effect their processes might have on the environment, unless these created noticeable nuisance or were subject to the formerly very limited legal obligations. Increasingly since those perhaps naive days, society – indeed a worldwide movement – has been and is continuing to attempt to force all users of resources and energy to consider more carefully such use, and to minimise any adverse effect that their operations might have on the environment. Under CA06, directors, in running their businesses and taking decisions, are (for the first time under company law) specifically required to take into account the interests of the environment which, together with society as a whole, employees, creditors and shareholders, is now regarded as one of the 'stakeholders' in the business. In addition, within their business review (See OPERATING and FINANCIAL REVIEW), boards must provide information regarding the effect of their companies' operations on the environment.

Saving the world

Supporters of the 'Gaia Capitalism' movement contend that the planet is an entity, and all aspects of life and existence on earth interrelate. Careless treatment of the environment can have a domino effect on apparently unrelated matters – an effect that increases exponentially. For some time scientists and others have warned of 'climate change'. Whether this results from human beings and their activities generating too much CO_2, thereby creating 'the greenhouse effect', or from cyclical fluctuations in solar energy or other natural disturbances, it seems certain that climate change is upon us. The activities of commercial organisations must be presumed to be having an effect on climate change, and thus companies all have a part to play in minimising their environmental impact. The Gaia (from the Greek for the Earth goddess – *Ge*, or *Gaia*) Capitalism movement seeks to enlighten everyone:

- to the dangers of climate change (regardless of source);
- of the need to take positive (and urgent) steps to reduce harmful emissions and pollution (and/or to replace the sources of such effects with non-harmful alternatives); and

■ that every organisation (and everyone concerned with the activities of every organisation) has a part to play, and that small savings by a large number of people can create a very large contribution in global terms.

This is too wide a subject to deal with in any detail here and it may be more appropriate to highlight some obvious areas of attention, and some practical and relatively unsophisticated means whereby even the commitment of employees in very small organisations could be harnessed to help play a part in this world-wide movement. Increasingly, companies will not only be required but also expected (by employees and others) to report on the steps they are taking in this endeavour. Thus a board would be prudent to commence consideration of the impact of their company's activities so that they can report positively – as well as helping the planet.

Examples	Environmental effects
	(a) Until the mid-1950s most UK organisations were virtually self-sufficient. That is they tended to make most (some as much as 90 per cent) of what they needed to create their end product. Nowadays such self-sufficiency in the UK seems a thing of the past and most internal self-generation has been 'outsourced'. With the considerable reduction of the UK's manufacturing industry (although it still contributes in excess of 25 per cent of the gross domestic product), many of these items are now sourced overseas, meaning that they have to be shipped in from (for example) China or India etc. In turn this has led to an explosion of demand in China (where two power stations were – at least until the credit crunch – being opened every week), which is exporting its products throughout the world. Both activities play a part in raising the earth's temperature – not least since the coal used by the Chinese power stations, and the diesel used by the ships carrying the goods, creates far more global warming than, for instance, the emissions of the fuel used by aircraft (around 2 per cent of the whole), on which so much media attention seems to be focused. (In fact cows and sheep produce produce five times as much greenhouse gas (methane, in their case) as that produced by aircraft.) One of the major sources of CO_2 (and thus, many argue, the chief cause of global warming) is vehicle exhaust generated by the consumption of fossil $\rightarrow$

Examples	Environmental considerations

fuels, yet neither Henry Ford nor Rudolf Diesel, two of the great combustion engine pioneers, originally meant them to use such fuels. In a 1925 interview with the *New York Times*, Henry Ford stated that he thought the *'fuel of the future is going to come from fruit like apples [as well as] weeds and sawdust'*. Ironically, 80 years later fossil fuels are slowly being replaced by fuel derived from exactly those sources. Ford's first car ran on fuel made from hemp, (see *'Screw it, let's do it'*, Branson), whilst some of the other early cars were electric-powered – a century later, the wheel seems to be coming full circle!

(b) Until the mid-1950s, the UK created relatively little waste, since most surplus materials were re-used or recycled (either automatically or as a result of government initiatives). Nowadays a massive amount of waste is created each year and only a small (but increasing) percentage is recycled. The UK government has published strategies to reduce the production of waste and the risk of pollution or harm to human health from waste disposal or recovery, with the twin aims of encouraging everyone to generate less waste and recycle more. The Secretary of State is empowered to make regulations concerning 'producer responsibility' in order to increase the re-use, recovery and/or recycling of products or material, for which initiatives there is increasing pressure from the European Community. A considerable amount of waste is created by packaging, and in this respect the EU's Packaging (Essential Requirements) Regulations 2003 will bite increasingly. Indeed, given the UK government's announced commitment to requiring householders to both reduce and recyle their rubbish (although the market for recycled rubbish has all but disappeared as a result of the recession), there could be a dual pressure (from government and consumer) on companies and boards to reduce packaging inherent in the presentation of their products etc.

Reducing packaging

The packaging regulations published by BERR stipulate that packaging shall be manufactured so that:

- volume and weight are limited to the minimum adequate to maintain the necessary levels of safety, hygiene and acceptability;
- the presence of noxious and other hazardous substances and materials is minimised with regard to their presence in emissions, ash or leachate when packaging or residues from management operations or packaging waste are incinerated or used as landfill; and
- it shall be designed, produced and commercialised in such a way as to permit its recovery, including recycling, and to minimise its impact on the environment when packaging waste or residues from packaging waste management operations are disposed of.

Case studies	Waste into energy

1 A company producing pine furniture had high wastage. Whilst steps were taken to reduce the wastage itself (by designing products which could utilise offcuts), it was realised that instead of paying waste collectors to take it away, the surplus could be utilised as fuel. A wood-burning boiler was installed and as a result the costs of heating the factory and ancillary offices were reduced by around 20 per cent, whilst the relatively costly procedure of bagging and transporting away substantial quantities of pine was avoided.

2 A similar approach was adopted by Swinton Park – an ancestral home – which switched its heating source to a woodchip burning boiler using the fallen wood and surplus timber from its 20,000 acres of woodlands. The annual saving was £18,000.

3 The Bank of England printing works in Essex constantly withdraws old and damaged notes from circulation. These notes must be burned, and, somewhat understandably, the bank uses its own incinerators. These however are linked to the printing works' internal heating system.

4 There are now a number of experimental processes whereby the contents of landfill can be converted to alcohol, which can in turn substitute for motor fuel. Currently the process is uneconomic, but no doubt progress will be made in this regard.

Companies with over 200 employees are required to publish environmental policies covering waste, and to devise and implement systems to give effect to them. The Business Resource Efficiency & Waste (BREW) programme (launched in 2005) has public money available to assist businesses in:

- minimising waste;
- diverting waste from landfill; and
- improving resource efficiency.

Targets for recovered or recycled paper packaging were required to increase by 1 per cent per year, from 65 per cent in 2004 to 70 per cent by 2008. Not all waste may need to be disposed of however – some may have a potential for re-use.

Waste

In our current society, a 'throw away' attitude has been endemic, not least since, until recently, there were so many consecutive years of boom. The effects of the current credit crunch may have one benefit – that of forcing a revision of such attitudes. Everything that is discarded first had to be produced, and almost certainly in the production of those items, emissions were created and energy was used. Many businesses are capable of saving between 4 per cent and 5 per cent of their turnover by employing waste-minimisation techniques – which, in some cases, would mean they could double their profits. However that reflects an acceptance of waste-creation, whereas ideally it should be prevented. It has been estimated that implementing cost-effective energy efficiency measures could save UK industry as a whole nearly £2 billion a year. Energy costs will inevitably rise and affect all energy users – worldwide demand alone is expected to double or triple by 2050. Energy demands from the BRIC countries (Brazil, Russia, India and China, the world's four fastest growing economies which – at least until recently – were expected to overtake the existing top five world economies) are increasing rapidly. Greater demand inevitably leads to greater cost.

The Carbon Trust (an independent organisation established by the UK Government with the task of cutting carbon emissions, which are partly responsible for damage to the environment, global warming etc.) estimates that most organisations fritter away 20 per cent and some waste as much as 50 per cent of the energy they use. As the need to reduce energy consumption becomes more widely understood, those perceived to be economical energy users may be able to steal a march on their competitors – not least in increasing profits and recruiting the most responsible employees.

Example	Waste reduction

1 Boards could require annual reports of the costs of all energy being used, reflecting not only the current year's cost but also comparative costs over the previous five years. Expressing these costs as a percentage of the sale price of goods or services may help concentrate attention.

2 Such reports could also focus on any progress to self-sufficiency and for outsourced items, their country of origin and the environmental cost of transportation.

3 All bills and readings should be checked for accuracy. Charges should be departmentalised, so that the cost to each department/process can be identified. Communicate the results to those using the energy. It might even be feasible to share any savings achieved with the users.

4 Many employees leave computers on standby, believing there is no cost. All items left on standby use electricity, and the slight extra cost of starting up will usually be more than saved by switching off. Some computers now have energy-saving devices.

5 Leaving a photocopier on overnight means using energy sufficient to generate 1,500 copies – which in many operations is more than a day's use. Since copiers create heat, if they are sited in a separate office there may not be a need to heat it. Alternatively, siting equipment within a general office might help reduce the cost of heating that area.

6 Implement a process whereby each time light bulbs, strip lights and appliances need to be changed, consumption figures are considered so that energy-efficient replacements are installed. It is claimed that although energy-saving light bulbs are slightly more expensive than standard bulbs, they consume over 70 per cent less electricity and last up to 10 times as long. Modern slimline fluorescent tubes are not only cheaper than thicker tubes, they also consume 10 per cent less power. The EU has already taken the decision that the new energy-saving bulbs will effectively be compulsory from 2011 (the traditional 100 watt bulb being phased out by the end of 2010).

→

Example	Waste reduction – *continued*

7   Photoelectric cells can be used to ensure lights are only on when someone needs them to be on (for example in toilets, cloakrooms, infrequently used passageways etc.). Similar devices can be used for toilet hand driers – and for the use of water in the urinals.

8   When refitting large offices or other areas, consider installing separate switching systems to break the overall area into smaller sections, so that not all lights have to be on simultaneously.

9   Check heating/air conditioning systems. The situation where the central heating is fully on, all the radiators are hot, but windows immediately above some of them are open, is very common. Reducing the level of a thermostat of a heating system by 1 degree centigrade can save around 8 per cent of the cost. In addition, the effectiveness of radiators is often impaired by placing desks, cupboards etc. against them.

10 Water may be heated to too high a temperature. It is common to find that the hot water supplied must first be cooled by adding cold water (e.g. before washing hands). Unless there are hygiene requirements, this is extremely wasteful – apart from being dangerous to the unwary (and creating more waste by requiring the posting of warning notices).

11 Motors use energy, and a badly adjusted motor uses energy inefficiently. Variable speed drives fitted to pumps to reduce speed of operation (if this is not essential) can considerably reduce running costs. All equipment, regardless of energy source, should be checked for efficiency.

12 Compressed air facilities are often subject to leakages which means the compressor is working inefficiently.

13 The question 'do we really need to heat the whole facility?' should be posed. Remove heating from areas where employees do not work – or provide localised heating only where necessary. Providing materials stored in such areas will not deteriorate, why heat such areas?

Case study	Only heat the real workplace

The Zodiac toy chain acquired a new purpose-built warehouse in Bedford. At 40,000 sq ft and with an eaves height of 25 ft, the projected cost of heating it was considerable. Since most products were not temperature-sensitive, rather than the whole area being heated, picking areas operated by employees were surrounded by plastic sheeting. Employees working in the unheated areas (mainly using fork lift trucks to feed the picking areas) were issued with appropriate clothing – and high-quality vending machines were on hand so hot drinks were always freely available.

Example	Waste reduction – *continued*

14 Warehouses need to open their main doors for deliveries and issues. The cost of opening main doors as well as the loss of heat whilst they are open can be considerable. Using plastic strip curtains can insulate the interior whilst still providing access to the exterior – particularly if a double 'air-lock' system is used.

15 For added security, many organisations use exterior lighting, although much of the time it is simply consuming energy. Increasingly, powerful solar-powered lights are available. Most operate on an 'activity-generated' basis – that is they light up when there is any activity. With lights like these it means that some of their security effect may be offset. However if half the lights could be supplied on a traditional basis with the other half solar, at least some savings of both energy and cost might be made.

16 Solar panels can also be installed on roofs to generate an additional energy source – mainly as a supplement to traditional sources.

17 Check with suppliers regarding their own commitment to energy-saving and environmental concepts

18 Involve employees in energy-saving and environment-saving ideas, providing prizes to motivate innovation.

Example	Waste reduction – *continued*
	19 Encourage homeworking – not only does productivity tend to rise, but also occupation costs as well as energy consumption tend to fall. 20 Include the results of all the initiatives in the annual report to shareholders.

The *Sunday Times*/Business in the Community *'Companies that Count'* initiative seeks to highlight companies that have taken the initiative to help reduce global warming, cut wasteful use of resources and to have a true sense of corporate responsibility. The citations for the top 100 companies in the survey provide a fruitful source of suggestions for those who have not already accepted this challenge.

The need to challenge existing procedures – and attitudes

Refusing to accept what has always been done in the past, as cast in stone for the future (i.e. challenging – or slaughtering – sacred cows) is essential. The twenty-first century is and will be a very different century from the

Case study	Why?
	The newcomer was bemused on entering a factory office to see a bucket hanging from an overhead pipe. From the base of the bucket a hose led to a small broken window, through which the hose had been poked, discharging its contents onto the waste ground outside. A cold draught was blowing through the broken window so the radiator was on full to keep the office temperature reasonable. On questioning this bizarre set-up, the newcomer was told that there was a leak in the process being conducted on the next floor up, so the bucket had been installed to catch the leak. Since the bucket swiftly filled, the hose had been installed in the bucket to prevent it overflowing – and the window had been broken so that the contents of the hose didn't need to be constantly emptied. The obvious question: *'Why not mend the leak on the upper floor?'* did not really elicit a proper answer.

twentieth – flexibility of approach is essential. Boards may find it valuable to pose the question 'Why?' to existing processes and procedures.

Adopting a 'save it' mentality and attitude may be a question of speculating in order to accumulate. Marks & Spencer adopted their '*Plan A (because there is no plan B)*' initiative for waste reclamation and recycling, and started charging for plastic bags. In a poll of 'ethical clothing retailers', Marks & Spencer came top, scoring 10 per cent more than their closest rival in customers' perception of them as a responsible retailer.

Financial year end

INTRODUCTION

Within nine months of its date of INCORPORATION, a company must notify the REGISTRAR at CH of the date to which its first accounts will be made up, i.e. its financial year end. This date is known as the company's accounting reference date (ARD). If the company does not notify the Registrar of the date, then the Registrar allocates an ARD to the company, which will be the end of the month in which the anniversary of its incorporation falls. The accounts of a newly incorporated company must be filed not more than nine (or six if it is a PLC) months after the anniversary of its incorporation, or not more than three months after its first ARD, whichever is the later.

Significance

LTDs are required to file accounts with the Registrar within nine months of their ARD. PLCs must file their accounts within six months of their ARD, although listed PLCs must publish their accounts on their websites within four months of their year end, so presumably would file them with the Registrar simultaneously. Any company filing late is subject to a fine. Since the preparation and auditing of the accounts can be an onerous task, due regard should be given to selecting a year end date which is convenient for this work, and is also appropriate for the business. A date just after the end of the busiest (and/or most profitable) period may be applicable (e.g. in retailing, with a preponderance of pre-Christmas sales, choosing 31 December or 31 January), although a great many companies use 31 March, thus making their financial year coterminous with the tax and fiscal year.

Traditionally the word 'month', in terms of the time from the ARD by which a company's accounts must be filed, has been strictly interpreted as the actual day x months later. Thus when an LTD with an ARD of 28 February was required to file its accounts within ten months of its year end, then the accounts were required to be filed by 28 (not 31) December.

However, with the shortening of the time limits under CA06 as set out above, 'end of the month' will now mean the last day of the calendar month six or nine months later.

Change

During an accounting reference period (that is before the anniversary of the previous ARD) a company can change its accounting reference date (provided this would not mean an accounting period in excess of 18 months). The accounting period can only be lengthened once in five years, although the period can be shortened without limitation (indeed an accounting period that has been lengthened could subsequently be shortened). However, a change of the reference date of the current period cannot be made after the end of that period.

Notification

Once the ARD has been notified, any subsequent change in the date requires the use of form AA01 (under s. 392 CA06 (previously s. 225(1))) to notify CH. For companies formed under CA06, their first accounting reference period must last not less than six but not more than 18 months from the date of incorporation, and the accounts must be filed no later than 21 months after incorporation (i.e. no later than nine months after the anniversary of the company's incorporation).

Forms

INTRODUCTION

Until CA06, the forms to be filed at CH, providing the public record of all items concerning the company, bore (and tended to be referred to by) the number of the section in the Act to which the filing requirement referred. The forms required as a result of CA06 break with this tradition and use letters derived from the words in the title of the form, and listed below. These forms cannot be used until October 2009. Forms that can be filed electronically are indicated by *E* – the position as at July 2009. The intention of CH is that all the forms progressively will be adapted so that they can be be filed electronically. Electronic filing is available at CH from 7.00am until midnight, seven days a week.

Incorporation and updating

- Application to register a company IN01
- Change of registered office AD01 *(E)*
- Notification of Single Alternative Inspection Location (SAIL) AD02
- Annual return AR01 *(E)*

Name

- Exemption of use of 'limited' from name NE01
- Change of name by resolution NM01
- Change of name by conditional resolution NM02
- Notification confirming satisfaction of conditional resolution NM03
- Change of name by authority in articles NM04
- Change of name by directors' resolution NM05 (where required by Secretary of State or on company being restored to the register)
- Seeking comments from bodies on change of name NM06

Shares

- Return of allotment of shares SH01 *(E)*
- Notice of consolidation, subdivision, etc. of shares SH02
- Return of purchase of own shares SH03
- Notice of sale or transfer to treasury of shares by a PLC SH04
- Notice of cancellation of treasury shares SH05
- Notice of cancellation of shares SH06

- Notice of cancellation of shares held by or for a PLC SH07
- Notice of name or other designation of class of shares SH08
- Return of allotment of new class of share by unlimited company SH09
- Notice of particulars of variation of share rights SH10
- Notice of new class of members SH11
- Notice of particulars of variation of class rights SH12
- Notice of name or other designation of class of members SH13
- Notice of redenomination SH14
- Notice of reduction of capital following redenomination SH15
- Notice by court applicants for cancellation of resolution re redemption or purchase of shares out of capital SH16
- Notice by company for cancellation of resolution re redemption or purchase of shares out of capital SH17
- Statement of capital SH19
- Application for trading certificate for PLC SH50

Directors

- Appointment AP01 *(E)*
- Appointment of corporate director AP02 *(E)*
- Change of details CH01 *(E)*
- Change of corporate director's details CH02 *(E)*
- Termination of appointment TM01 *(E)*

Secretary

- Appointment AP03 *(E)*
- Appointment of corporate secretary AP04 *(E)*
- Change of details CH03 *(E)*
- Change of corporate secretary's details CH04 *(E)*
- Termination of appointment TM02 *(E)*

Manager appointed re Companies (Audit, Investigations & Community Enterprise) Act 2004

- Appointment of manager AP05
- Change of service address of manager CH05
- Termination of appointment TM03

Filing

- Consent form for paper filing of PROOF filing member PR03

Accounting

- Accounting reference date – change AA01 *(E)*
- Dormant company accounts AA02

Mortgage/charge

- Particulars of charge MG01

Striking off

- Application to strike off DS01

Oversea company (OC)

- OC establishing a place of business in UK BR1

General meetings

INTRODUCTION

PLCs must still hold an AGM, but under CA06 LTDs no longer need to, unless the articles stipulate it must (or its shareholders or directors require it to). This means for companies which do not hold an AGM, those running such companies would not formally meet those owning it (who are not on the board), even to discuss routine business. Whether such a development (i.e. those owning the company not meeting those running it for them) is appropriate, is for each company and board to decide. Non-routine business has always been able to be conducted at the AGM provided the appropriate required notice has been given and the timing of the meeting was appropriate. Should there be no obligation to hold an AGM and/or the timing of that meeting is inappropriate for the consideration of business requiring shareholder decision, an extraordinary general meeting (EGM) can be convened. For a company formed under CA06, however, all meetings other than the AGM are called 'general meetings' (GM), the 'extraordinary' being dropped. However 'extraordinary general meetings' are referred to in the articles of the majority of the 3,000,000 existing companies on the Register which were formed under earlier legislation, particularly CA85, which means that until all these companies change their articles or become defunct, the term will continue in use. The method of convening and running EGMs and GMs is identical – which rather begs the question 'why the change?', which gains nothing and simply creates confusion.

Convening

An (E)GM can be convened by:

- the board;
- the members in accordance with the ARTICLES;
- for an LTD, those holding 10 per cent of the members' voting strength (unless there has not been a general meeting for at least 12 months, in which case the required percentage is only 5 per cent);
- for a listed PLC, those holding 5 per cent of the voting strength (the previous requirement of 10 per cent having been altered as a result of the EU Shareholder Rights Directive);
- the AUDITORS, should they resign and/or feel there are matters which should be brought to the attention of the members; and
- the court.

Members' request

If the board receive a members' request to convene an (E)GM then it must do so within 21 days of receiving the request and the meeting itself must be convened for a date within a further 28 days (that is, the meeting must be held within a total of 49 days from the date of the original request). Minutes of the meeting must be taken and made available to the members (should they wish to inspect them) for two hours every business day.

Notice

An (E)GM normally only requires 14 days' notice. Traditionally, some resolutions relating to specific business have required longer notice in their own right. For example, until the introduction of CA06, special resolutions required 21 days' notice. Notice periods for all resolutions and meetings (other than PLC's AGMs, which still require 21 days' notice) have been rationalised at 14 days under CA06. However this relaxation is subject to an individual company's articles and, if the articles specifically require a special resolution to be subject to 21 days' notice that amount of notice must be given unless and until the articles themselves are changed. An (E)GM of an LTD can be held with shorter or no notice, provided 90 per cent (or any higher percentage stipulated in the articles) of the voting rights agree. A shareholder unable to attend a general meeting has a right to lodge a PROXY with company stipulating how he wishes his votes to be cast.

If the board becomes aware of member concerns which could lead to a request for a meeting, it may be advisable to try and discuss requirements in advance of or instead of such a request, since requisitioning a meeting can be expensive. A shareholder holding more than 10 per cent of the shares in Millwall Football Club's parent company requisitioned a meeting regarding development plans for the club. His proposals were rejected, but convening and running the meeting cost the club over £50,000.

Administration

The various aspects concerning the preparation for the meeting, provision of proxies, taking of minutes, etc., as set out in the sections on ANNUAL GENERAL MEETING, MINUTES and PROXIES, apply equally to an (E)GM.

Gifts, ethics and interests

INTRODUCTION

Although under CORPORATE GOVERNANCE requirements, directors of listed PLCs have been required to subscribe to what could be described as something akin to a moral code, until October 2008 there were no such obligations on directors of other companies, except where such or similar requirements were incorporated in their articles. CA06 imposes controls regarding conflicts of interests, disclosure of benefits provided for a director or obtained by virtue of the directorship of all companies. It may be advisable for companies to adopt an internal code dealing with such matters – and the inclusion within its ambit of those dealing with suppliers and/or customers should be considered. Of course the impact of such a code may not necessarily be restricted to directors. In the event of an investigation, the fact that a code had been adopted might at least provide some basis for a defence. The legal maxim, *'in litigation the person with the best paperwork stands a better chance of winning'*, may be apposite.

Codes of Ethics

The chairman of the first corporate governance committee – Sir Adrian Cadbury – once stated: *'from a company's point of view, codes of conduct are a form of safeguard for their reputation'*. Loss of, or damage to, its reputation was placed top of a list of risks that could affect a company detrimentally in a recent survey. Increasingly, public opinion expects those who control organisations to act in a responsible manner, and to ensure that all those whom they employ act similarly. Companies produce wealth and, as a result, become powerful; the danger with such a situation being, as economist J K Galbraith once said: *'the greater the wealth, the thicker will be the dirt'* – perhaps somewhat pertinent, given the recent failures of formerly highly regarded financial undertakings headed by people paying themselves extremely large amounts of money. Earlier scandals like Guinness and Enron also bear witness to this and of course, any code can only be as effective as:

- the clarity with which it is promulgated;
- the willingness of those affected to comply with its requirements; and
- the effectiveness of the policing of its requirements.

This responsibility to try to keep the company legal, and for it to operate within the confines of the law, could be linked with any general requirement to comply with legislation under an organisation's SOCIAL RESPONSIBILITY commitment.

The Law Commission has proposed two entirely new bribery laws – one prohibiting the giving of bribes and another prohibiting the taking of bribes. In addition there would be new laws prohibiting the bribing of a foreign official residing or doing business in the UK and negligently failing to prevent bribery by an employee or agent. The latter is particularly relevant to companies who would need to ensure that their internal rules outlaw such practices – and that such rules are stringently policed.

Boardroom compliance

If for no other reason than to bring the expectation of ethical attitudes and actions, a board could adopt and promulgate a code of ethics.

Example	Code of Ethics
	1 Standards
	This [organisation] operates under high quality standards – of products, of services and of customer care, and requires these standards to be adhered to at all times in all its dealings.
	2 Morality
	The organisation will not:
	• trade with any regime or organisation that is regarded as oppressive and/or which does not recognise human rights,
	• trade with any producer of weapons,
	• speculate against the currency of its own country,
	and will endeavour to prevent its activities being used for any illegal purposes, including money laundering and/or drug trafficking.
	(Adopting such a code will not necessarily impair business competitiveness and profitability. When the Co-operative Bank adopted ethical investment and supply policies, it subsequently reported a large increase in profits. Conversely, Primark was recently voted the least ethical clothing retailer in a survey conducted by Populous, after a BBC *Panorama* programme revealed that some of Primark's suppliers in ➡

Example	Code of Ethics – *continued*

India were contracting out embroidery work to firms using child labour.)

3   Personal obligations

All employees are expected to:
- be loyal to the organisation in all their endeavours on its behalf
- be honest and diligent, and maintain high standards of dignity in undertaking their duties and responsibilities

and should not:
- act in any manner that will or could affect the reputation of the organisation
- accept any bribe or inducement [see below] from anyone or anybody (or any person or organisation acting on their behalf) involved in any way with the organisation
- permit any activity which might result in a conflict of interests with this organisation, or use any organisational information or material for personal gain.

4   Inducements

Other than properly authorised trade and retail promotions, no inducement may be offered to or given to any customer or outlet whereby they will be induced or encouraged to place an order for or take any product or service offered by the [organisation], or to any supplier or creditor to obtain improved terms of trade.

Under the Anti-Terrorism, Crime and Security Act 2001, any act involving a tip, inducement or bribery conducted by UK companies overseas is subject to the same criminal penalties as if the act were conducted in the UK.

5   Entertainment
i.   Whilst it is acceptable to entertain a customer or supplier to lunch or dinner to discuss normal contractual matters, this must be at places and to the limits laid down in the [organisation's] gifts/entertainment guide. On no account must the limits and guidelines included in that guide be broken without prior written approval of [name].
ii.   In the event of any person considering that he needs to entertain or provide a gift for a customer and that the

→

Example	Code of Ethics – *continued*

limits are inappropriate (for example the matter concerns an attempt to compensate for previous poor service, quality etc.) the written authority of a member of the board should be obtained and indication of any limitation agreed and this authority referred to in the subsequent expenses claim.

6   Hospitality

Employees are allowed to accept hospitality from major customers and suppliers in terms of lunches and/or dinners or other similar value entertainment, to a maximum of [number of occasions] per third party organisation per year. In the event that the value obtained is in excess of that laid down in the company entertainment guide, this fact must be made known to a board member as soon as possible. If the entertainment provided is considered to be in excess of that warranted by the circumstances, the director responsible may need to contact the third party to explain the policy.

(See also GIFT POLICY.)

7   Anti-competitive practices

This [organisation] operates in a competitive industry and welcomes healthy competition. On no account may any employee or person acting on behalf of the organisation enter into or agree to enter into an arrangement whereby the effect is to price fix, arrange collusive tendering, split or allocate markets or customers with a competitor, abuse a dominant market position or act in any way which constitutes a breach of the anti-competition legislation and/or is to the detriment of a consumer. Any suggestion of such activity from a third party should be reported immediately to [name].

8   Legal compliance

The [organisation] operates within the [specify] industry and is required to and wishes to comply with all laws, regulations and codes of practice etc. It seeks to trade legally, fairly, openly and honestly with all third parties and to give value for money in all its dealings. It requires and expects its employees to carry out their work and responsibilities

→

Example	Code of Ethics – *continued*
	and to conduct their relationships and dealings with third parties in accordance with these precepts. All dealings must be conducted openly and fairly in such a way that should every aspect of the transaction become widely known (for example in the media) this would not cause any embarrassment, injury or damage to the reputation of the [organisation] whatever. 9 Respect All employees are required to act responsibly, decently and with due regard for the dignity and rights of others in both business and personal dealings. In many instances personnel (particularly senior personnel) will be seen as acting on behalf of, or by virtue of their position in the [organisation], in place of the [organisation], the reputation of which must be protected at all times. 10 Whistle-blowing All employees at whatever level in the [organisation] are encouraged to report any activities which seem to them to be in breach of this code to [director]. Such reports will be treated as confidential and provided they are made in good faith and not be made with the aim of personal gain, the person making the report should not fear reprisals or detriment (see WHISTLE-BLOWING POLICY).

To try to ensure adherence to required ethical conduct some companies require their employees to sign the code, some even requiring this to be an annual undertaking. It may be advisable to point out that failing to comply with items 7 and 8 above could not only result in the application of disciplinary sanctions but also in criminal penalties – including imprisonment.

An increasing trend

The Institute of Business Ethics monitors the growing adherence to Codes of Ethics and reports that 90 per cent of the FTSE 100 companies have one, whilst 80 per cent of employees believe their employer is ethically sound. Simon Webley (the Institute's Director) commented: '*[The failure of] Enron happened because greed was the predominant culture in that company. You can only do that for a short period before the company collapses.*' In the light of recent events, it seems regrettable more senior people in financial institutions did not take this message to heart.

The 'Fraud Barometer', updated annually by accountants KPMG, shows that a third of the cases brought to trial involves management or employees defrauding their employers – totalling in excess of £100 million each year. Fraud is rising in the UK by around 14 per cent per year. PriceWaterhouseCoopers' own report on the same matter disclosed that 70 per cent of large employers suffer from fraud, and that an average of £4 million per employer is lost each year. Their survey involved interviewing executives of 3,000 companies, statutory bodies and charities across Europe. Nine of these had lost over £60 million. Little is ever recovered – only 15 per cent of those surveyed claimed to have recovered over half their losses. Over 60 per cent of these losses were discovered purely by accident, which could infer that the actual figures for losses are very much higher than those stated here, which would hardly be surprising as the figures reported can only be of known frauds. Company fraud is perpetrated mainly by employees (the figure quoted by accountants Ernst & Young is 89 per cent), the previous records or references of many of whom had not been checked.

BDO Stoy Hayward's 'Fraudtrack' showed that the value of employee fraud against businesses increased from £43 million to £78 million in a three-year period. In fact the situation must be far worse than this, since their survey only covered frauds in excess of £50,000 (and only known frauds, of course). Rules and procedures – and regular policing of both – is essential.

The use of an AUTHORITY chart may assist, but in truth the phrase *'the best manure is the farmer's boot'* is apposite. Directors walking the job, preferably unannounced, can help keep people on their toes, as well as being beneficial for morale and motivation. However, this can only work if the directors themselves are above suspicion. If senior people act in a way that negates the intent of these rules, so too will at least some of their subordinates.

Legislation has now created the general offence of 'fraud' which would, if the act is conducted with the intent of making a gain or causing loss, include:

- making a false representation; and/or
- wrongfully failing to disclose information; and/or
- secretly abusing a position of trust.

Of course, directors who fail to take reasonable steps to ensure compliance with internal rules etc. could be held to be failing in their duty to the owners of their companies to *'act in their best interests'*. If the owners suffer loss, then the directors acting in breach could be held liable for such losses (see DERIVATIVE CLAIMS). Surely, as demonstrated by the above two case studies, simple checking of references is essential?

Note: the International Federation of Accountants publishes 'Defining and developing an effective Code of Conduct for organisations' available free of charge from http://www.ifac.org.

Case studies	Checking the record

Following an accountant defrauding his employer of £4 million, the employer adopted a 'stable door' policy and checked the accountant's previous working record. During a gap of 18 months in his employment record he claimed that he had been studying for an accountancy qualification. He may well have been doing so, since he had time on his hands serving an 18-month sentence in Strangeways jail for defrauding a previous employer.

No professional accounting body would allow a person already convicted of fraud to qualify. Any claim to professional status can easily be either verified or refuted. Whilst the Rehabilitation of Offenders Act permits details of some previous offences to be 'wiped clean' after set periods, there are some occupations (including that of accountancy) where previous offences are not wiped clean, and thus a check via the Criminal Records Bureau (CRB) would also have disclosed the conviction. In view of this, it may be advisable to include on all application forms for employment a statement such as *All claims and/or statements of skills, experience and employment will be checked. In the event of false claims being made, any offer of employment will be terminated. [The organisation] also reserves the right to recover any costs incurred as the result of the employment of an applicant who has submitted an application form containing false claims.'*

Sharon Bridgewater, the finance director of a radio station, was known to own several properties as well as several Porsche 911s, and loved eating in expensive restaurants and drinking fine wines – a lifestyle that was inconsistent with her relatively low salary. How did she afford it? Simple – she stole from her employer! That was unfortunate, but who in the radio station from which she defrauded £2 million had put her in such a position of trust (and opportunity) without first checking her out with a previous employer? Had they done so they would have discovered that she had also defrauded them – and been convicted for the fraud. Is not failure to check the record of a person being put into such a position of trust negligence on the part of the directors – potentially generating a DERIVATIVE claim?

Gift policy

Many employees and directors experience a situation where a customer, adviser or supplier wishes to personally reward them for good service etc., and in principle and moderation there should be nothing wrong with this. However, it is all too easy, if the gift is substantial, for it to become not so much a 'thank you' for past service but a latent or explicit bribe to obtain advantage in the future. Adoption of a gift policy may be helpful, both as a guide as to what can be accepted, and a way of tactfully refusing larger items.

Example	Gift policy
	i Other than at Christmas [and/or other religious/national celebrations where there is a custom that presents are exchanged], employees are not allowed to accept or retain gifts made by any customer or supplier or other third parties, generated as a result of the business relationship. In the event that such gifts are delivered and it seems potentially damaging to the relationship to return them, then, subject to the approval of [director] the gifts may be retained and will be handed to [the Social Club] for use as raffle prizes or disposed of in a similar way. The director will contact the donor and explain what has occurred and why (i.e. it is in accordance with internal rules). *Practical guidance: a bottle of wine or spirits once a year can be accepted – a bottle every week should not.* ii At Christmas [or other religious/national celebrations], employees are allowed to accept the normal gifts to a maximum of [amount] per donor. If gifts above this level are received then, subject to the approval of the [director] they may be retained. *Practical guidance: a gift of value £20 may be acceptable once a year – a gift of £200 might not, other than in very exceptional circumstances.* iii If multiple gifts are received to mark good service which has been provided by a number of employees, these may be retained and distributed to the employees concerned provided the value per employee does not exceed the guidance laid down in the entertainment policy. →

Example	Gift policy – *continued*

Practical guidance: a case of wine at Christmas is acceptable, but should be distributed between the team. A case of wine every week/month would not be acceptable.

iv   The attention of all employees is drawn to the danger of a customer or third party using the previous or anticipated delivery of gifts or inducements as a bribe or to exert pressure (either overt or latent) to obtain concessions (e.g. orders, better terms, preferential treatment) or any other consideration; or such persons using the threat of or actual publicity concerning the previous acceptance of a gift or lavish entertainment as pressure to obtain such concessions etc. In all circumstances the response: *'I cannot comment further – I must contact [director] to discuss this matter'* should be made.

Practical guidance: being entertained at a sporting or social activity once a year is acceptable. Accepting such invitations more often/ regularly would not be acceptable. Thus an all expenses paid trip to see the Beijing Olympics would have been unacceptable, although a trip (on the same basis) to see one day at the forthcoming London Olympics would probably be acceptable.

v   Any suggestion of using facilities owned, occupied or made available to a third party (for example, a holiday villa or other property, concessionary travel, etc.) either on a free basis or for any consideration which seems or is less than the market price, should be communicated to the [director], at whose discretion the matter can proceed or be concluded.

Practical guidance: such a scenario is unacceptable, but a short, expenses paid visit, made because it is genuinely necessary to check facilities that might be used by the organisation, could be acceptable.

vi   Any employee feeling unsure about any of the foregoing, or that they are being placed in an 'awkward' position by a third party, should report the matter to [named person]. This guidance is best summarised as *'if in doubt, shout'*.

Although this is a policy drafted to provide internal guidance, there is no reason why it could not also be distributed to suppliers, customers etc., so that the incidence of them making a gesture that would breach the rules can be avoided, thus preventing embarrassment. It is also a method of advertising the subject organisation's wish to act and be seen to act ethically at all times.

Interests

Directors' conflicts of interests are now strictly controlled by CA06. The detailed obligations are set out in DIRECTORS: PAYMENTS, LOANS AND INTERESTS. However, many companies may wish to restrict executives other than the board from having such interests and thus potential conflicts. Accordingly publication of guidance regarding the company's attitude to such matters may be advisable – for example in the employee handbook or similar procedure manual.

Inevitably, since directors are effectively in control of their company's assets, the possibility of them (or their connected persons) acquiring such

Example	Control of conflicting interests clause
	1 No one working for or employed by, or providing services for the [organisation] is to make, or encourage another to make any personal gain out of its activities in any way whatsoever without this being agreed to by [named person/ board].
	2 Any person becoming aware of a personal gain or interest (or potential gain or interest) as a result of which they would benefit is required to notify [name]. Only if it is agreed by [person/board] will such a matter be allowed to subsist.
	3 Anyone being in a situation such as is outlined in 2. who does not report the matter will be regarded as having committed an act of gross misconduct for which the usual penalty is dismissal.
	4 Anyone reporting a matter which could involve a benefit being made by or given to another and/or which could conflict with that person's obligations, provided there are reasonable grounds for such suspicion, will be protected.
	5 All employees are expected to report any suspicion or knowledge of wrongdoing to [named person].

assets when they are no longer required within the company (or selling personal assets to the company) is likely to arise. Whilst assuming that an 'arm's-length' valuation is obtained, and that since there is nothing in the articles to prevent such a transfer, such a transaction could proceed, it would be prudent:

- for a disinterested quorum of the board to resolve that the transfer goes ahead;
- for details to be entered in the Register of Directors' Interests (see STATUTORY BOOKS);
- for the matter to be disclosed to the auditors.

Prior approval of the members is required if the value of the asset exceeds £100,000 or is 10 per cent or more of the company's net assets (and exceeds £5,000).

Incorporation

INTRODUCTION

Other than buying the shares of an existing company, a company can be acquired 'off the shelf' from a company formation agent, solicitors, etc. for a cost of less than £200, or by a promoter taking the steps set out in the checklist set out below. The REGISTRAR offers both a 'same day' incorporation service as well as an electronic incorporation service. However the latter is probably only usable by company formation agents, since their software systems need to be compatible with and approved by the Registrar for this service to work effectively.

CHECKLIST   Incorporation

✓ Decide on NAME, with alternative choices (see Registrar's guidance note on choice and use of name).

✓ Apply to Registrar for clearance of name. If it is required to change a company's name, and the date of change is critical it may be safer to form a shell company with the required name and then for both existing and new companies to pass SPECIAL RESOLUTIONS exchanging names on the same subsequent date. If an original name has been invented, it may be advisable to try and incorporate the company with that name without checking (possibly using the Registrar's 'same day' incorporation service). If the application goes through, then the name is protected immediately. If it is rejected, then little, other than the attempted filing fee, has been lost. Even checking a name out may allow someone else to slip in first — although this possibility is, to some extent, prevented by the new company names tribunal. Alternatively, a preferred name can be checked for availability/usage using the Registrar's Webcheck service.

✓ Describe activities or objects. Traditionally these details have been set out in the MEMORANDUM and it was usual for them to cover virtually every conceivable activity the company could ever enter into. CA89 made it possible to use an abbreviated objects clause simply stating that a company would be a *general commercial company*. The option was used infrequently mainly since banks approached to lend money to a company which such a wide objects clause preferred to know for what purpose the funds they were asked to supply would be used. Lacking delineated objects clauses, which would limit the variety of uses of the funds, they were loath to advance funds. However, for companies formed under CA06, objects clauses (other than for charities) no longer limit the company's activities and the sometimes lengthy objects clauses will not be part of the memorandum – if they are required at all they must form part of the articles. Existing companies' objects clauses are now deemed to be part of their articles, although it might be preferable for the articles to be changed so that the objects clauses (updated as necessary) are recited there.

✓ Decide location of the company's registered office which, pending ratification of European Union proposals allowing freedom of relocation within the EU must be within the country of the company's incorporation.

✓ Purchase STATUTORY BOOKS in hard copy or set up electronic versions. These are registers of:

- members (shareholders or guarantors);
- directors and company secretary (the latter being an optional appointment for LTDs);
- directors' shareholdings (PLCs only);
- substantial interests in shares (i.e. those held by other shareholders);
- debenture and/or loan holders (if any); and
- CHARGES.

The register of directors' previous directorships (held within the previous five years) is no longer needed for any company; the register of directors' interests (in the shares of their company) is no longer required for LTDs. Since, however, companies must be advised of third parties etc. in which their directors may have an interest – and thus a potential or actual conflict – it would be best if the company kept a record of such information. This register (with the word 'share' deleted from its title) could suffice for that requirement.

- In addition, a new company will also need:

✓ minute books for meetings of both members and directors

and may need:

- a seal and sealing register (and/or register of items signed as deeds).

✓ Determine share capital (or for a guarantee company the amount of each guarantee). There is no lower limit on the amount of an LTD's share capital, but for a company to be a PLC, a minimum of £50,000 issued share capital, of which 25 per cent or more is paid up in cash, must be subscribed. A company formed under CA06 will not need to have an 'authorised' share capital. The amount of share capital of such a company will be decided by the directors (subject to any limitations imposed by the shareholders).

✓ Determine any rights of shares other than the ordinary shares.

✓ Arrange initial subscribers. Until CA89, every company had to have two shareholders, but that Act made it legal to operate a company with only one shareholder – a SINGLE MEMBER COMPANY.

✓ Draft MEMORANDUM and ARTICLES OF ASSOCIATION of which the final versions need to be signed by the subscriber(s) (and dated and witnessed). Under

CA06 the memorandum will need little drafting as it will only contain the name and type of company (PLC, LTD – limited either by shares or guarantee), country and date of registration (with the copy sent to CH also stating the subscriber(s) name(s)).

✓ Although traditionally there had to be two subscribers for a PLC, only one is required under CA06. The company's articles can be originated, using the drafts accompanying the Act, or by using a draft as a base and customising additional clauses.

✓ Appoint initial directors of whom full personal details (name, address, date of birth, occupation) will be required both for the register of directors and formation publicity (although a service address rather than a director's private address can be used for public disclosure from October 2009).

✓ Complete and submit form IN01 (in compliance with s. 9 and s. 14 CA06, formerly forms 10 and 12) to Registrar with fee and a statement of compliance (see s. 1068 CA06) with contents (to be determined by the Registrar of Companies) This is an original requirement. The Registrar has been given powers to:
  ● stipulate in which form it must be lodged. This could mean that such documents must be lodged electronically (see s. 1069);
  ● require standard contents;
  ● require it to be authenticated by a particular person.

✓ A PLC must obtain a *certificate to commence trading* from the Registrar, before trading. If a PLC trades before it has this certificate, the directors can be held liable for its debts, etc.

✓ Open bank accounts, appoint auditors, solicitors, obtain a VAT number, notify HM Revenue and Customs, although the Revenue is automatically notified of the formation of every company and writes to companies requiring information etc.

Certificate of incorporation

Evidencing the formation and existence of the company, the Registrar issues a certificate of incorporation (the equivalent of a birth certificate for a real person). This certificate states:

1 The company's name. Since October 2008 the name is shown in upper case although this does not prevent it being used with other configurations (i.e. with upper and lower case letters), as long as the name itself is identical.

2 The registered number. This entirely distinct (and never re-used) number remains unchanged with the company throughout its life (no matter how often the company's name is changed). There are proposals (no date yet set) to add computer check digits to all company numbers to aid filing at CH.

3   The date of incorporation.
4   That the company is limited by shares or guarantee or is unlimited.
5   Whether it is an LTD or a PLC.
6   The country of registration (England and Wales, Scotland or Northern Ireland).

The certificate is either signed by the Registrar or bears the Registrar's seal and is conclusive evidence that the legislative requirements have been met and the company is registered under the Act. Since this is virtually the same information as is required to be included in the MEMORANDUM for a company formed under CA06, the question arises as to why CA06 did not simply abolish the memorandum for such companies and put all this information on the certificate. A similar certificate is issued if a company changes its name.

Name

The name of the company, as shown on the certificate of incorporation, must be used (but no longer on the outside of the buildings):

- at every place of business. In default of the requirements every director and the company secretary are liable to an initial fine plus an additional fine for every day the company is in default;
- on all business letters, purchase orders, notices, website and official publications (see ELECTRONIC COMMUNICATIONS);
- on the common SEAL (and any securities seal) of the company;
- on all invoices, bills of exchange, purchase orders, orders for money etc.

Failure to comply with this requirement could render those at fault liable to initial plus daily fines. (Previously if an individual signed a cheque (or equivalent) which did not bear the full company name, they could become personally liable for the amount involved if it was not met by the company, however this liability was abolished in late 2008.)

Date of incorporation

This date (D) is used as the start point for various time limits regarding items to be filed.

- D: Incorporation – company is formed, liability of the members is limited, etc.
- D plus nine months: Notify Registrar of accounting reference date (i.e. FINANCIAL YEAR END).
- D plus 12 months: Latest date for making up first ANNUAL RETURN.

- ▣ D plus a year plus nine months (if LTD) or six months (if PLC) – file accounts.

Preservation

A replica of the certificate of incorporation is often inserted as the first page of the printed memorandum and articles. On any change of company's name, the Registrar issues a certificate of change of name which then stands in place of the original certificate of incorporation. The certificate of incorporation (or certificate on change of name) should be kept safely and permanently – it does not have to be displayed (as was previously the case).

Interests in shares

INTRODUCTION

The fact that someone holds (or adds to or disposes of a holding of) shares (particularly if it is a substantial number or percentage) in a listed PLC can sometimes have a marked effect on the market value of such shares, as well as being of considerable interest to those dealing with the company or preparing to buy or sell such shares. In the interests of creating a *'level playing field'* of knowledge for all investors, those whose share interests exceed certain levels are required to advise the company which must, having recorded the information, then advise the Stock Exchange. Obviously changes in shareholdings of directors of the company can have an even greater impact on the perceived values of a company's shares.

Major interests

Members whose shareholding reaches or exceeds 3 per cent of the issued shares of a listed or quoted PLC must, as part of the Listing Agreement requirements, notify the company of the total of their interest. In addition, whenever their holding above this level increases or decreases so that a whole percentage point is altered (that is it goes from (say) 3 per cent to 4 per cent or 5 per cent, or down from (say) 7 per cent to 6 per cent), that change must also be notified, as must any development which takes their interest below 3 per cent. All such notifications must take place within two days.

In addition, the company is legally required within three days of receipt of such information to record in its Register of Substantial Interests in Shares, the date, the name of the shareholder and the data itself – and, under the Listing Agreement, to inform the Stock Exchange.

Non-material holdings

Non-material holdings of 10 per cent or more must also be notified. A non-material interest exists where the named holder acts (for example as a trustee) and has no personal interest in the shares. If both material and non-material holdings are in existence then it is necessary to disclose the aggregate if this reaches or exceeds 10 per cent, even though the constituent parts separately need not be declared. For example, if the material interest was less than 3 per cent and the non-material interest was just over 7 per cent, but their total is less than 10 per cent, there is no obligation to disclose either interest under the individual notification requirements. However, if in aggregate they exceed 10 per cent both interests must be disclosed. This situation needs to be watched carefully since if (in the above example) there was an increase in the non-material holding this could push the total of the two interests over the 10 per cent disclosure threshold. The effect of a sudden disclosure of an interest of 10 per cent when none was formerly recorded could have a material effect on the share price – even though there may have been very little actual change in the overall share ownership.

There is now an additional requirement to notify non-material interests at a 5 per cent level but not at the intervening percentage points between this level and the original 10 per cent level.

Discovering the true ownership

Companies who believe that the owner of the shares (by the name noti-fied) is not the actual owner are permitted to serve a notice on the disclosed owner (who it suspects is a nominee) requiring disclosure of the person who has beneficial ownership. The notice, permitted under s. 793 CA06 (for-merly s. 212 CA85) is required to be complied with within two days of being served. It is not unusual to find one nominee holds it for another nominee and so on, and to find that the true owner is not disclosed until after several notices have been served in respect of the same holding.

Failure to provide adequate answers to such questions or even to obtain a reply to the request can lead to the company having the right to disen-franchise the shares, although the Stock Exchange requires a 'cooling off' period for further negotiations before this can be implemented since it pre-fers not to have franchised and disenfranchised shares circulating simulta-neously in the market.

Example	Section 793 notice (*based on a draft of a notice under the former s. 212 of CA85 and made available by BERR (formerly the DTI)*
	Name of Company
	Address Date Reference Person dealing
	Name of shareholder
	Address →

Example	**Section 793 notice** (*based on a draft of a notice under the former s. 212 of CA85 and made available by BERR (formerly the DTI) – continued*
	Companies Act 2006, s. 793. (Description of type, classification, etc. of shares) We have registered a holding of (number and description) of our shares in your name. As authorised by section 793 of the Companies Act 2006, we require you, within two days by letter, fax or telex, to provide us with the answers to the following questions: 1 In how many shares of the above description do you currently have an interest? 2 What is your interest in such shares? 3 If you have disposed of the shares, on which date(s) was your interest disposed of, and, if you are aware, who now has that interest? 4 Please state the full details of any agreement or arrangement of which you are aware regarding the exercise of any voting rights in respect of such shares Yours, etc.

Directors' holdings

Having been informed of a director's interest in the shares of the company (or of any change) details should be placed in the register of directors' share interests within three days (this is no longer necessary for directors of LTDs). For a listed PLC, the holdings (and any changes thereto) of directors in their company's shares must also be advised to the Stock Exchange within five days of the transaction. There is also a requirement that for a period (usually two months) before the announcement by the company of what could be 'price-sensitive' information (e.g. the announcement of results) that directors should not trade in their company's shares.

Should a director of a listed PLC use his shares as security for a loan or similar then that fact must also be advised to the company (and he should gain clearance for his action from the board prior to implementation). The company must then disclose the fact to the Stock Exchange. This is a requirement under the rules of the Financial Services Authority (FSA) and in compliance with the Disclosure and Transparency Rules.

However, following the case in late 2008 of David Ross (former deputy chairman of Carphones Warehouse), who used shares in that company as security for a large loan, the FSA admitted that although its rules regarding disclosure were as set out above, there was no sanction should a director fail to comply! The fallout from this high-profile breach prompted the FSA to announce a two-week amnesty in January 2009 for companies that had failed to disclose such actions by their directors. Many were somewhat surprised that during the amnesty, over 50 companies *'came clean'* and made such a disclosure.

The FSA has now clarified the rules and as a result, directors must now disclose to the company if and when they pledged shares for a loan. Such disclosure must be made within four days of the event, and the company must then inform the Stock Exchange. Failure to do so renders both company and director to an unlimited fine.

Memorandum of association

INTRODUCTION

Disclosure of information (to the public in general and their creditors in particular) is the price that limited liability companies pay for the restriction of the liability of their shareholders to the amount of their shareholding. An important part of this disclosure has involved the company stating to everyone interested or involved in or with the company, the nature of the business it wishes to conduct (i.e. the objects for which it is formed), what share capital has been invested and who promoted (formed) the company. These items, required for over 150 years, have been set out in a company's memorandum of association. For a company formed under CA06, although there is still an obligation for it to have a memorandum, it is reduced to just a few lines – and virtually duplicates the content of the certificate of incorporation.

Content

For a company formed under CA06, its memorandum must state:

1. Who promoted the company (the subscriber(s)), although once INCORPORATION is completed this is of purely academic interest. Formerly at least two members were needed to sign the memorandum, although the memorandum of a SINGLE MEMBER COMPANY needed only to be signed by one person. Under CA06 a single person can form any type of company.

2. For a company limited by shares, the number of shares taken by each subscriber, although this is of interest only on formation since thereafter additional shares can be issued. In the memorandum of a company limited by guarantee, the maximum amount of the guarantee(s) must be stated.

3. The name of the country (England and Wales, Scotland or Northern Ireland) in which the REGISTERED OFFICE is to be situated. Pending the implementation of current EU proposals to relax this restriction, a company registered in England and Wales, or in Scotland or in Northern Ireland can have its registered office only in its country of registration. Although the actual address (within the country of registration) of the registered office need not be stated in the memorandum, under s. 9 CA06, on INCOPORATION a note of this address

must be filed with CH using form IN01. Any alteration in the address of the registered office of the company must be filed with the Registrar on form AD01 (in accordance with s. 87 CA06, formerly form 287). On the change of a registered office, a 14-day period is allowed during which both old and new offices are valid for the service of notices.

For a company formed under CA06 its memorandum is unalterable, however this is of little import considering the minimum amount of information included – all of which is historical.

Former contents

Memorandums of companies formed under Acts prior to CA06 were also required to contain:

- A statement of the total number of shares (and their various categories if applicable) that the company was authorised to issue. Whilst this is valuable information to creditors, since (at least in theory) it shows some of the funds available as security for their debts, the amount and type of share capital has always been subject to alteration. If the company is to be formed as (or re-registered as) a PLC, the share issued capital must be at least £50,000 of which 25 per cent (i.e. at least £12,500) must be paid up. A company formed under CA06 does not need to state its 'authorised share capital' since it will be permitted to have the share capital its directors from time to time determine, possibly governed by the shareholders by limitations inserted in the articles.
- The objects of the company. These, often extremely numerous, clauses are a public statement of the business the company was formed to undertake, and effectively act as a limitation on its directors' authority to conduct business and as a contract between the company and the outside world. Under CA89, companies were instead permitted to have a short form 'objects clause', e.g. *'the company will be a general commercial company'*. Effectively this would mean that it would be very unlikely that the company could ever act beyond its powers. Such a clause was rarely used mainly since it was criticised by the banking profession which is averse to lending money to a company if the aims or objects of the company are unrestricted. Such concerns over using an abbreviated objects clause reflect the original purpose of stating the objects – to protect those dealing with the company by confirming the nature of its business. It may be feasible to use the abbreviated clause for a subsidiary, or joint venture company where lenders' concerns could be overcome by the parent(s) giving guarantees. Section 39 CA06 states that (other than for charitable companies) the validity of an act done by a company cannot be questioned on grounds of 'lack

of capacity'. Companies that wish to (or must, if they are charities) preserve their objects clauses will need to recite them as part of the articles. The objects clauses of existing companies that do not change or rewrite their articles, will be deemed to be part of the company's articles (then referred to as its constitution).

Minutes

INTRODUCTION

A prime responsibility of most company secretaries is preparation for and administration of meetings and the composing/editing the record of proceedings at those meetings – both members' meetings (AGM and (E)GM, which in many companies will be fairly formal) and the (usually far less formal) board meetings. The clear recording and promulgation of decisions made both by the members of the company and the board are essential for the good and proper administration of the company – as well as being a legal requirement under s. 248 CA06. This requirement is effected by compiling minutes detailing the decisions taken at board meetings. However, in addition to providing a record of board decisions, minutes can also provide contemporaneous and written evidence that the directors were conscious of and complying with their duty of care; grant authority for directors or others to carry out acts on behalf of the company, and can act as a means of progress-chasing decided business. In addition, since CA06 sets out explicit duties of directors, the minutes that address the manner of compliance with these requirements may also help in convincing any investigator that the board was aware of and complied with such obligations. Minutes should, therefore, be compiled with care, read by the board with similar care and corrected/approved appropriately. However experience indicates that there is seldom any training provided for minute taking and the format and content differs widely from company to company. Minutes do not have to be handwritten and may be best kept in loose-leaf folders so that minutes of subsequent meetings can easily be added to create an ongoing record. Such folders should be kept securely.

Content

Generally minutes should record:

I *The constitution*: the auspices under which the meeting is taking place. This may be fairly obvious for a board meeting since the directors are meeting with the authority of their appointment (and in accordance with their duty under company law and to the members) to take decisions to operate the company on behalf of and for the benefit of the owners, whilst taking into account in reaching those decisions the interests of the other company 'stakeholders' (employees, creditors, consumers and the environment).

Where there is a meeting of, for example, a sub-committee of the board, the terms of reference of that committee might usefully be set out in the minutes of its first meeting (as well as in the minutes of the appointing body, of course).

2   *The administration*: when and where the meeting took place and who was there. Minutes should record the board members 'present', as well as advisers (usually referred to as being 'in attendance') as well as any comings and goings of members during the meeting (and the points of the meeting at which such entrances and exits occurred).

3   *The information:* data (e.g. reports) on which decisions were taken (including a note of whether these were tabled or distributed previously). The information that was provided demonstrates the basis on which decisions were taken, and, by exception, what information was not available to the board (which might be of considerable importance should the company get into difficulties – see WRONGFUL AND FRAUDULENT TRADING).

4   *The official back-up*: details of which registers were sealed, initialled, etc. and which reports were considered.

5   *The decisions*: whilst the content will differ according to individual company requirements, it is usually considered preferable for minutes to record decisions (and any dissent therefrom, if applicable) rather than discussion and arguments for and against the matter and reasons for arriving at it. Most of those experienced in taking and using minutes agree that the briefer the minutes the better – although, ideally, they should contain sufficient information to enable a third party to comprehend the reasons for decisions taken, which may mean at times that some limited (and occasionally even detailed) commentary should be included to explain the basis for decisions.

6   *The authority:* minutes should be signed as a true record of the preceding meeting at the next following meeting (with minutes of AGMs and (E)GMs being approved and signed at the next following board meeting). Under s. 249 CA06, signing the minutes grants them status as evidence (in Scotland, sufficient evidence) of the proceedings. They may then be produced as such in court. In addition, some articles stipulate that if the minutes are approved and signed then they will be conclusive evidence of the proceedings, meaning that it will be virtually impossible to challenge them later.

7   *The record*: once the minutes have been drafted they should be approved in principle by the chairman, with drafts sent out to all members. Ideally this should happen within three to four working days of the meeting. If (a) board member(s) object to the wording proposed, and the objection has general support, the minutes should be changed. Although this can be done by alteration, it may be preferable for a fresh version, incorporating the required change(s), to be prepared.

If members wish to make more substantial amendments this may require further drafts until there is a consensus that the record is an accurate reflection of what was (or more likely is now) agreed. It must be said that when directors see decisions in a written format they sometimes wish to change the record. If all are in agreement that a revision is necessary, it is probably preferable for a fresh draft of the minutes to be prepared even if this means that the latest record is now at variance with the original 'decision'. But if that is what is now agreed to be the decision – then that is the decision. This scenario is reminiscent of the wry (but accurate) comment contained in the last stanza of a nineteenth-century rhyme (source unknown):

> *'So whilst the great ones repair to their dinner*
> *The Secretary stays getting thinner and thinner*
> *Racking his brains to record and report*
> *What he thinks, they will think that they ought to have thought!'*

Sending the minutes out as soon as possible after the meeting means they may be able to act not just as a record of the board decisions, but also as prompts to those required to effect the decisions, not least since some members' recollection of what they agreed and/or were required to do may be hazy. Those in receipt of such copies may also need to be reminded of the need for adequate security. Minutes should be a true fair and accurate record which is of particular importance should the company need to produce a certified copy of a minute to a third party, for example to evidence a member's authority to sign a contract, ratify a bank mandate etc.

Different approaches have been used in the following examples to illustrate alternative methods of compiling minutes. These should be regarded as guidance only, since the style may not suit every company. Under each version, references to explanatory notes have been included – indicated by the numbers in brackets shown on the right hand side of the page – and the notes are set out at the end of each draft.

Example	Draft minutes – 1
	ANY COMPANY LIMITED 182(1)
	MINUTES of a BOARD MEETING held on 30th March [year]
	At [address] at 10.00 a.m.
	Present: XYZ (in the chair)
	ABC
	DEF
	GHI

Example	Draft minutes – I – *continued*

In attendance : JKL (company secretary)

(Mr TSS, auditor was in attendance for items covered by Minute 3 i and ii) (2)

An apology for absence due to illness was received from UVW and this was accepted. Those present signed the attendance book. (3)

The board reminded themselves of the seven duties of directors set out in the Companies Act 2006 and confirmed that in taking all decisions they would continue to take account of these duties and bear in mind the disparate interests of the company's stakeholders. (4)

I   MINUTES

The minutes of the board meeting held on 29th February [year] previously distributed were taken as read, approved and signed. (5)

2   DIRECTORS' INTERESTS

The register recording interests of board members as advised to the company was laid on the table. (6)

3   SHAREHOLDER MATTERS

It was resolved that a share transfer covering 500 Ordinary shares in the company from Mrs MNO to Mr PQR be and it hereby is approved and that a share certificate in the name of Mr PQR be issued and the required entries be made in the register of members. The secretary was asked to write to Mr PQR welcoming him as a shareholder.   Action: JKL (7)

A report from the company secretary recommending that responsibility for the share registration work of the company be placed with Share Registrars Ltd was accepted and the terms of the contract approved. The company secretary was requested to make the necessary arrangements in liaison with the chairman. Action: JKL

(Mr DEF, having previously notified the company that he had a consultancy agreement with Share Registrars Ltd did not take any part in this discussion or decision.) (8)

→

Example	Draft minutes – I – *continued*

4 FINANCE

i) Management accounts.
The accounts for the month of February and the cumulative 11 months were tabled and discussed in detail. The favourable comparison with budget was welcomed, as was the managing director's opinion that the trading and financial situation would continue to show improvement, both in real terms and against budget. It was noted that the situation regarding discounts and promotional payments was still being clarified and additional controls would be introduced from the commencement of the new financial year. A number of estimated provisions were listed for possible incorporation in the year end accounts.

Action: ABC

ii) Depreciation. It was agreed to change the company's accounting policies so that depreciation would be charged on vehicles, office equipment and computers at 33.3 per cent p.a. straightline. It was noted that this change would have to be recorded in the published Accounting Policies.

iii) Capital expenditure.

a) It was agreed that a further five production units at a cost of around £4,000 each could be purchased in stages over the remainder of 2XXX to allow the sale of [detail]. Mr UVW (whom failing, the company secretary) would authorise each item bearing in mind the effect on cash flow.

Action: UVW/JKL (9)

b) The chairman referred to Capital Expenditure Project form number 13/2XXX for the investment in [detail] which projected a first year return of 14 per cent rising to 17 per cent in year 2 on a fully absorbed basis. The project was approved for implementation no earlier than 31st December [year]

Action: ABC

iv) Cash flow. The latest projection for the period ending 31st December [year] was tabled, discussed and approved

v) Investigations for the replacement of the company vehicles allocated to six area managers would be carried

Example	Draft minutes – 1 – *continued*

out. The guidance of the auditors as to the company's and individual's tax situation would be sought.

Action: GHI

vi) Bank Mandate. The secretary reported that the company's bankers had requested that a new mandate on the main drawing account be completed. It was resolved that the company operate the No 1 Main Drawing account in its name with the Finance Bank Plc on the terms and subject to the restrictions set out in a new mandate a copy of which initialled by the chairman for the purposes of identification is attached to these minutes, and that the secretary be and he hereby is empowered to take such actions as might be necessary to give effect to this resolution. Action: JKL (10)

vii) Borrowings. The secretary reported that in the absence of Mr UVW he had negotiated an additional £100,000 overdraft facility with the Finance Bank on the same terms as the existing facility. This additional borrowing was available for the eight weeks until end of August [year]. Although he had expected to receive documentation requiring board approval to evidence this borrowing this had not arrived before the meeting. It was resolved that the chairman, ABC and UVW (whom failing the company secretary) be and they hereby are empowered to sign such documents and take such actions to provide the company's bankers with the documentation they required in order to facilitate the advance of this additional borrowing requirement.

The secretary was instructed to let each board member have copies of the relevant items and documentation when these were to hand.

The secretary confirmed that even with this additional borrowing the limits in the articles had not been breached. Action: XYZ, ABC, UVW, JKL (11)

5   CURRENT TRADING

The managing director reported that [synopsis of report …]. An analysis showing the deterioration over a five year period of sales of the main product was tabled and it was agreed that the deadline for delivery of supplies of Project

Example	Draft minutes – 1 – *continued*

X needed to be brought forward to compensate for the expected shortfall in sales in the latter part of the calendar year. Action: ABC

DEF requested that his dissent from this course of action be noted in the minutes with the note that in his opinion not enough was being done to incentivise the sales force and he had serious doubts concerning the effectiveness of the recently appointed sales manager. (12)

6 PERSONNEL

A report from the divisional director (Personnel) had been sent to all members and the contents were accepted. It was agreed that negotiations should commence with employee representatives to try to agree the wage increase with effect from 1st July [year] along the lines outlined in the report.

7 PROPERTY The following items were noted: (13)

[Facility address]: Little progress had been made on any of the pending rent reviews which would update the list accompanying the agenda for the meeting other than the following:

[Facility]: Approval was granted to a letter of response to the landlords requesting that an extension to the user be agreed.

[Facility]: Evidence thought to be misleading had been submitted by the landlord's agents.

[Facility]: The landlord's agents had reduced their figure for the reviewed rent to £13,500. Negotiations continued.

The sale of [facility] was proceeding with exchange of contracts expected for mid-July and completion by 1st August. It was noted that receipt of the sale monies had not been built into the cash flow forecast and that if this sale completed as anticipated the additional overdraft facility would not be needed.

The possibility of selling the business and licensing or underletting the lease at [facility] was being pursued urgently.

Insurance: The secretary would draft a letter to be sent to all landlords of leased premises requesting that the interest of

Example	Draft minutes – 1 – *continued*

the company be noted on the insurance policies to ensure any liability in the event of loss was minimised.   Action: JKL

(Mr DEF apologised and with the permission of the chairman left the meeting.)   (14)

8   SAFETY MATTERS
  i)   The monthly report was accepted, no actions being required.
  ii) The secretary reported:
       (a) that he had investigated the requirements of the current health and safety legislation regarding fire precautions in the workplace and tabled a brief synopsis of the action he felt it was necessary for the company to take in order to comply with the requirements. The board requested him to obtain detailed cost estimates for the various requirements with, in each case, an indication of the proposed timetable for implementation of the recommendations;
       (b) that he had commissioned reports to determine whether there were any asbestos-containing materials in the company's properties.
                                                           Action: JKL (15)

9   SEALING

The secretary produced the Register of Sealing (and documents signed as deeds) to the board and approval was granted to the affixing of the company seal to items numbered 345 to 357 and 359 to 361, and approval granted to the signing as a deed of item 358. The chairman was authorised to sign the register in evidence of this approval.   (16)

10 BOARD MEETING TIMETABLE

The dates of future meetings of the board were confirmed as 28th April, 30th May, 30th June, 28th July, 31st August, 29th September, 25th October, 23rd November, and 21st December.

→

Example	Draft minutes – I – *continued*

The secretary was requested to inform Messrs DEF and UVW of these dates as soon as possible. (17)

Chairman .... 28th April [year] (18)

Action points: (19)

Welcoming shareholder	JKL [Completion date]
New Share Registrars	JKL [Completion date]
Provisions in accounts	ABC [Completion date]
Capex products purchase	UVW(JKL) [Ongoing]

and so on.

Explanatory notes

1   Ideally pages of minutes should be consecutively numbered (particularly if a looseleaf binder is used), to try to prevent fraudulent alterations. The subject of each minute (where applicable) should be indexed and a degree of cross-referencing provided.

2   Stating the exact period of attendance of advisors, and even of members if not present for the whole meeting, is advisable.

3   It is arguable that only if an apology for absence is accepted that the absence is permissible. Indeed in some boards if an apology is not received (or accepted) that fact is stated in the minutes (i.e. *'No apology was received from....'* which underlines the implied obligation that directors should be present at board meetings). Under Regulation 81 of Table A of CA85, if a director does not attend board meetings for six months or more, he can be removed from the board by his colleagues.

It may also be advisable for directors to sign an attendance book (although it would not normally be necessary to minute this if done as a routine).

4   CA06 places explicit duties on directors and to be able to demonstrate that they were aware of these duties wording such as this could be inserted in the minutes once a year as a reminder (and in the minutes of any board which a director is attending for the first time so that newcomers have the point brought to their attention).

5   Ideally the chairman should initial each page of the minutes except for the last which should be signed. See 18 below.

6 Under CA06 there is an implied requirement to record items in which directors have an interest – e.g. indemnities, loans, potential and/or actual conflicts of interest etc. It may be prudent to maintain a 'Register of Directors' Interests' into which details of such items are entered and to have this available at each board meeting so that all members are aware of each of their interests. This may also assist the secretary should an item of business require a 'disinterested quorum'. This register can be updated regularly if the concept of requiring directors to complete a statement of their interests each year is adopted. (See APPOINTMENT.)

7 Directors of many LTDs have the right to refuse to allow transfer of shares to a person of whom they do not approve. It is probably unlikely that an LTD would need to retain external registrars to deal with its share registration work as is suggested here – although this is often used by listed PLCs.

In addition placing the initials of the person due to deal with the item enables the minutes (already a document of record and reference) to act also as a means of encouraging prompt action.

8 Depending on articles requirements, it is important that any director with an interest in the subject matter should declare that interest and that the point be noted. DEF's interest with Share Registrars should have been entered in the Register of Directors' Interests – see 6 above.

9 Framing a decision in this way leaves some leeway for delay should the circumstances at the time warrant such delay and also covers the situation should UVW not return.

10 Where a lengthy document is required to be approved, rather than repeating the whole item in the minutes, it could be copied and attached to the minutes. It should then be numbered either consecutively after the last page number for that meeting's minutes, or take the number of the past page and 'a', 'b', 'c' etc., added with a designatory letter for each page of the item. Banks may wish to have a set form of resolution adopted for the approval of their mandate and similar forms.

11 Reference should be made to the articles to ensure the board are acting in accordance with them. They often set out the requirements and restrictions on board activities, particularly constraints on the maximum amount the board is allowed to borrow. If such pre-set figures need to be exceeded the articles should be changed otherwise the directors will be acting *ultra vires* and could be held personally liable to repay the excess borrowed.

12 In the event that any director wishes his dissent to be recorded this must occur – it is a common law right – although often the chairman will seek to avoid the inclusion of such a comment.

13 To save the time of the meeting, it may be possible to distribute a report (as here) with the agenda and simply report on any update since the date of the agenda.

14 Ideally all directors should be present for the whole meeting – and there is a presumption that this is the case. If it is not possible, the time that a director left (or arrived, if late) should be noted in the minutes.

15 The Health and Safety Executive has recommended that safety should be a regular item for discussion by the board. This is sound advice not least since it may be valuable evidence that the company took and takes safety considerations seriously. It might be best if there were a regular safety report – at the very least the board could review the results of the regular Responsible Person's inspections regarding fire safety required to be carried out at every place of work.

16 Although not a statutory requirement, the use of a Register of Seals or Sealing (and/or of documents signed as deeds) and subsequent board approval of all entries provides board authority for the items. It also enables details to be noted of items signed as deeds where the use of the seal has been dispensed with. The chairman should sign under the last number authorised at the meeting and should add the date. Ideally the number of each seal entry in the Register should appear on the item sealed as a further cross-reference of authority.

17 Meetings arranged in the absence of a colleague can clash with other commitments already entered into, hence early advice of meeting dates is essential. The dates of board meetings may best be arranged on a rolling 18-month basis, with the immediate six months dates firm, the following six months subject to some leeway and the third six months indicative only. Progressively, of course, the six-month sections become firmer with additional outline indications tacked on.

18 Inserting a place for the chairman to sign and adding the date (of the next planned meeting) emphasises the importance of signing as well as improving the presentation of the minutes themselves

19 Some companies that utilise the actions points concept (see 7 above), additionally list these at the end of the minutes and insert a required 'completion date' by each.

These Minutes are put forward only as an example. However they are based upon the minutes successfully provided for the boards of actual companies so the style and format can be said to be an effective way of drafting minutes. This is not to say that there cannot be other ways of recording decisions etc., which are equally effective. It is up to a company's board to decide the way it wishes to record its deliberations and to adopt a suitable style.

Example	Draft minutes – 2

ANY OTHER COMPANY LTD   431(1)

MINUTES of the [x]th ANNUAL GENERAL MEETING

held on Thursday, 24 October 2XXX at [address] at 10.00 a.m.

Present: ABC (in the Chair)

HIJ

KLM

NOP

12 shareholders

In attendance: AAA (Secretary) and BBB (Auditor)

1   NOTICE

The secretary read the notice of the meeting.   (2)

2   DIRECTORS' REPORT for the year ended 30 June 2XXX

The chairman referred members to the Report and
Accounts for the year ended 30th June 2XXX and the
balance sheet as at that date. He requested BBB (of
accountants – name) to read the audit report which he
did.   (3)

The chairman proposed, NOP seconded and it was
resolved unanimously that the report and accounts of
the company for the year ended 30th June 2XXX and
the balance sheet as at that date be and they are hereby
received.   (4)

3   DECLARATION OF DIVIDEND

The chairman referred to the payment of an interim
dividend in January 2XXX and to the fact that the board
were recommending payment of a final dividend of 2p per
ordinary share. He proposed, KLM seconded and it was
resolved unanimously that the company should pay a final
dividend on 27th October 2XXX in respect of the year
ended 30th June 2XXX of 2p per ordinary share to the
holders of ordinary shares registered on the books as at
1st October 2XXX.   (5)

→

Example	Draft minutes – 2 – *continued*

4 RETIREMENT BY ROTATION OF DIRECTORS

The chairman stated that in accordance with the articles of association and as set out in the notice of the meeting, Mrs EFG and Mr KLM were retiring by rotation and each being eligible, had submitted themselves for re-election. The chairman proposed, Mr HIJ seconded and it was resolved unanimously that the re-election of both retiring directors could be put to the meeting as one motion.   (6)

The chairman proposed, Mr K Jones, a shareholder seconded, and it was resolved unanimously that Mrs EFG and Mr KLM be and they hereby are re-elected directors of the company.

5 AUDITORS

It was proposed by Mrs EFG, seconded by the chairman and resolved *nemo contendare* that Messrs [Name] be and they are hereby reappointed auditors of the company until the conclusion of the next following AGM on terms to be agreed by the directors.   (7)

The meeting terminated at 10.25 a.m.

Chairman .... 29th November 2XXX   (8)

Explanatory notes

General: under CA06, LTD companies no longer need to hold AGMs unless their members (or the company's articles or the directors) so require. If AGMs are held then minutes must be taken and preserved for ten years (although many people might feel this is too short a period and may prefer them preserved in perpetuity).

I The pages should be numbered consecutively. Often minutes of general and board meetings are kept in the same folder and numbered consecutively as one complete record. This can pose a problem should a member wish to inspect them, since although members have a right to see the minutes of general meetings, they have no right to see the minutes of board meetings. Thus the minutes would have to be separated and the page numbering might look somewhat odd. Minutes of meetings of shareholders must be kept at the registered office. There is no restriction regarding the location of minutes of board meetings, although in view of their content they should be kept securely.

2   There is no requirement to read the notice of the meeting but it can be helpful (if only to cover the arrival of latecomers).

3   Similarly there is no requirement for the auditors to read the audit report (which they will already have had to sign) but again it does little harm and, at the very least, helps identify the auditor to the members.

4   The members only have a right to receive accounts already approved by the directors – they have no right of approval or rejection. Under common law, when the chairman proposes a resolution a seconder is unnecessary. However, since few members may know this it may be better to arrange seconders and for them to be shareholders who are not directors. This gives, at least, the appearance of democracy at work.

5   The members can either approve, reduce or reject a proposed final dividend: they cannot increase it. Using a 'striking date' of some time before the meeting should enable all the calculations to be carried out, and even cheques drawn, on the assumption that the dividend will be approved. Once this happens, the cheques can be signed and despatched (or the amounts transferred via the banking credit system) so that members receive them on the due date. Listed PLCs have also to notify the Stock Exchange once a dividend is approved (and indeed to give notice of a board meeting at which there will be consideration of dividend declaration).

6   The re-election of directors *en masse* can only take place if the meeting has previously approved (as here) that the re-election can take place in this way.

7   *'Nemo contendare'* is Latin and means that no one objected to the proposal. Thus, although everyone voted in favour of all the previous proposals, in this instance, whilst no-one voted against, one or more members abstained. (Generally Latin tags should be avoided – it has been included in case readers ever see it.)

8   Best practice suggests that the minutes of AGMs and (E)GMs should be approved and then signed by the chairman at the next following board meeting.

Names and name changes

INTRODUCTION

A company's name, registered number and office and country of incorporation are the fundamental facts evidencing its existence as a 'legal' person. These details are confirmed within its certificate of incorporation and evidence its incorporation, in the same way that a birth certificate evidences the existence of a real person. These details are constantly required to be used and advertised by the company as a legal person to ensure those dealing with it know where to contact it. This satisfies the basic principle that everyone has a right to know the identity of the person with whom they are dealing. There are strict rules regarding the name a company can use – see the REGISTRAR's guidance note GBF/2 and the brief outline below. For active companies the corporate name must be displayed at every location at which a company's business is carried on – although not if this is essentially a domestic residence. Whilst some companies use their corporate name as a well-marketed and well-known trading name, others have high-profile product names but virtually unknown corporate names. Choosing and changing the corporate name can thus involve work ranging from a relatively simple administrative exercise to a major undertaking – with costs to match.

Publication

The corporate name, registered number and office, and the country of incorporation are required to be shown:

- at the registered office (and any Single Alternative Inspection Location (SAIL) used for inspection of records);
- at all places where business is transacted (although no longer, as previously required, on the 'outside' of such places);
- on all business letters and purchase orders;
- on all official publications and notices;
- on any website operated by the company (where the VAT number, if applicable, must also be stated);
- on all bills of exchange, promissory notes, cheques, money orders, etc.;
- on all invoices, receipts and letters of credit.

These rules apply to all communications with third parties. Thus a communication sent by fax or e-mail to a third party must also comply with the disclosure requirements. It is not necessary for a business card or compliment slip to bear these details, although if such a slip was used to handwrite an offer or confirm a contractual commitment this could create 'a business letter' and could be caught by the requirements.

Business names

Formerly where any business traded under a name which is not its corporate name, under the Business Names Act 1985 (BNA85) it was required to state this fact and, if it was a company, it was required to state the corporate name, registered number and office and country of registration on all business letters, orders, invoices, purchase orders and demands for payment of debts. Although BNA85 has been repealed, its requirements are repeated in ss. 1192-1199 of CA06. This is curious, since the legislation is binding on all organisations trading under a name which is not that of a real or legal person. This means that organisations that are not companies are also bound by it, although it is extremely doubtful if a sole trader, partnership, etc., would think of checking company law for obligations on him if he uses a 'trading' or 'business' name!

Example	Statement of corporate name and registration
	BLOGGS PEGS is a business name of BLOGGS LTD [Registered in England, No.111222333, registered office address]

A company must also display at all premises where business is carried on, its corporate name and an address where official documents can be sent or served, and, should anyone request that information, it must be supplied in writing within five days (failing to do so rendering the company liable to a fine). Thus a company with many outlets (for example, a retail chain) must in each outlet display a notice stating the corporate name and address for service of documents, again complying with the basic rule, even where the transactions are of tiny worth, that everyone has a right to know the legal identity and address of the 'person' with whom they are trading, and to know to what address any formal communication (e.g. regarding a dispute) must be sent. It must be said that this *'declare the person using the business name requirement'* is more noted for its breach than its observance. However, in *Department of Trade & Industry v Cedenio* it was held that a sole trader did not breach BNA85 where, in a business letter, although he stated that he was the author of the letter he did not state that he was the proprietor of the business. Further he was not obliged, having given an address for the business, to state that this was an address on which legal notices could be served. This decision seems to rather undermine the whole principle behind the business names' legislation.

Choosing and changing its name

I   A company can choose and change its name to another provided the proposed name itself does not offend certain rules.

2   The name must not:
  ▪ duplicate an existing name (on the Registrar's index, including any name of an insolvent company);
  ▪ be misleadingly similar to an existing company's name;
  ▪ be offensive or criminal (both in accordance with criteria as laid down by the Secretary of State);
  ▪ infer a local or central government connection;
  and must contain:
  ▪ certain words as required by the Secretary of State (e.g. Limited, Ltd or LTD, Public Limited Company, Plc or PLC, etc., as applicable);
  ▪ other restricted words provided the permission of bodies controlling such use has been obtained and not withdrawn.
  It is also wise to check whether any company is already using the name as a registered trade mark, since attempting to use a protected name may generate an infringement or 'passing off' action. This can be effected using the Companies House Webcheck service.
  Increasingly there has been a trend to use combinations of letters and symbols to form 'original' company names. Since some of these symbols have caused problems at CH there are restrictions regarding their use.

3   Assuming the new name has been cleared for use, the company needs to pass a SPECIAL RESOLUTION. The resolution could be authorised at the AGM, or, if the timing is inappropriate, at an extraordinary general meeting, or, for companies formed under CA06, a general meeting. Alternatively it could be passed by written resolution provided 75 per cent of the total voting strength is in favour. If the articles specify that being a special resolution it requires 21 days' notice, the resolution would need to be given that amount of notice unless notice was waived in whole or in part. (See example of notice below.)

4   Within 15 days of the passing of the resolution, a printed copy of it, certified as such by the secretary or a director, together with the current fee, must be filed with the Registrar of Companies. There is a specified format – see example below.

Example	Meeting notice and draft resolution

Any Company Ltd

Notice is hereby given that a(n)

(Extraordinary) General Meeting of the company

will be held on Monday, 18th December 2XXX

for the purpose of considering, and if thought fit passing the following resolution as a SPECIAL RESOLUTION

'THAT the name of the company be changed from Any Company Ltd to Another Company Ltd'

By order of the board

Name, Secretary 16th November 2XXX

Example	Wording for CH notification

SPECIAL RESOLUTION ON CHANGE OF NAME

Companies Act [1985–1989]

Company, 0009876543 ANY COMPANY LTD

At a(n) (Extraordinary) General Meeting of members of the above-named Company, duly convened and held on 18th December 2XXX the following SPECIAL RESOLUTION was duly passed:

THAT the name of the company be changed to

Another Company Ltd

Signed..........................Secretary 30th December 2XXX

Accompanying the resolution must be form NM01 (Notice of change of name by resolution under s. 78 CA06).

5 The Registrar then issues a Certificate of Incorporation on Change of Name.

If the date of the name change is critical, or the company wishes to ensure that no one else can use the new name before the change can be effected, it may be safer to form a shell company with the new name and then for old and new companies to exchange names subsequently and simultaneously.

Control

For many years, companies have been required to change their names if:

- the name is too like that of another company;
- information provided to support the use of the name was misleading;
- any description of activities in the name is misleading;
- the name of an oversea company is such that it could not have been approved for use in the United Kingdom.

There is detailed guidance on 'sensitive' words in the Registrar's Guidance Note. However, since October 2008, control over company names has been exercised by the Company Names adjudicator's office and additionally, if a company wishes to use, and thus objects regarding, a name already registered, it can challenge the existing name. The person owning the existing name will only be able to resist the challenge if it can show:

(a) the name was registered before the objector obtained any value or goodwill in it;

(b) the company using that name has already operated under the name and/or has incurred costs preparing and/or using the name;

(c) the company was registered in the ordinary course of company formation and is available to the objector on commercial terms of company formation;

(d) the company was formed in good faith;

(e) the objector's interests are not adversely affected to any significant extent.

However, if the objector can prove that the purpose in registering the name was purely to obtain value from the objector, the tribunal can order the original company to change its name. If it does not comply the tribunal will effectively change it for it, i.e. allocating a name of its own choosing! The company can appeal a decision to the High Court. This legislation is retrospective so even companies formed speculatively before October 2008 could be affected.

This process was deemed necessary since there had been instances of people (on a purely speculative basis) forming dormant companies with names they felt (often correctly) might wish to be used by (mainly) much larger organisations in the development of their products and services. The owners of the dormant companies with 'valuable' names then sold them to the trading companies that wished to use them!

'Too similar' name objection and monitoring

Although the Registrar is not permitted to allow the registration of a company name which is the same as or *too like* an existing company name, there have been instances where this has (at least in the view of the original companies) taken place. Companies have 12 months within which to object to the registration of a new name which they feel is too like their own. Once the 12-month period has expired, there is no right to require a change. Companies concerned to protect their name may wish to monitor the list of proposed company names regularly so that any objections can be lodged before the time limit expires. There are a number of formation agents etc., who, for an annual fee of around £50 per name being protected, offer a 'company name watch service'. Alternatively, using the CH website, anyone can check the current register and therefore see whether there is a new company which has been registered with a 'too similar' name.

Unfortunately this *'too same a name'* protection does not extend to companies registered in the Isle of Man, Jersey, Guernsey etc. which, if they trade in Great Britain through a third party (i.e. they do not have a place of business in Great Britain which would classify them as an oversea company – see TYPES) cannot be prevented from using the same name as a company registered in Great Britain.

Although registering a company name at CH should protect that name, in terms of preventing another company using it as their corporate name, this does not necessarily prevent others using it commercially. Trade marks are distinct from company names and action to protect such assets may be necessary.

Case study	Need to protect name
	In 1998, IBM registered 'Websphere' for software products as a Community Trade Mark (CTM). In 1999, a competitor company, Publiweb Ltd, changed its company name to Web-Sphere Ltd and registered three domain names using their new corporate name. A CTM owner is entitled to prevent other parties using an identical mark in relation to identical products (and may be able to prevent use in relation to similar goods). IBM sued Web-Sphere Ltd for passing off their products as if they were IBM's. Web-Sphere tried to use the argument that this could not be so since it was merely using its 'company' name, but this failed and the company was held to have infringed IBM's CTM. The High Court also held that it was entitled to require Web-Sphere to change its name and to cease using the domain names.

Larger companies and those with valuable trading names or trade marks regularly check the CH register. To avoid wasting money a company wishing to change its name should attempt to check that a desired name will not infringe someone else's rights. Conversely, not all companies command good reputations, the possibility of a company name being similar to that of a company with a poor reputation should not be overlooked.

A new website (www.businesslink.gov.uk/nameandtrademark) has been launched by Business Link (incorporating data from both CH and the Intellectual Property Office) which enables users to check registers of company names and trade marks simultaneously, thus trying to avoid unnecessary applications or subsequent challenges.

Postscript: If a company has permission to omit 'Limited' (or 'cyfyngedig' for Welsh companies) from its name and the Secretary of State has determined that this permission to omit should be rescinded, or where a company has been restored to the register having previously been removed from it, the directors can resolve to change its name and then lodge form NM05 with CH. (Dropping 'Limited' from the name under s. 60 of CA06 is carried out by submitting form NE01 to CH.)

- If the articles of the company permit a name change other than by special resolution, form NM04 can be used to notify CH.
- If a company wishes to change its name to one which requires permission from a third party, form NM02 can be used to notify CH (thus presumably preventing others using the name); with form NM03 used if and when the required permission is granted.

Nominee shareholdings

INTRODUCTION

Although rendered unnecessary by the Companies (Single Member Private Limited Companies) Regulations 1992, which allow UK companies to be formed with (or subsequently to have) only one member, there still exist a number of companies, mainly subsidiaries, where their holding (parent) company owns (say) 99 shares and another party (very often one of the directors) holds the single remaining share. This single share is usually held by the person as a nominee for the holding company. This was (and still is) a perfectly legitimate device (although now rendered entirely unnecessary), to comply with the previous requirement that every company should have at least two members.

Directors as nominees

As stated, there is no reason to continue with the device of a director (or anyone else) holding an additional share, as companies can have just one member – thereby becoming a 'SINGLE MEMBER COMPANY' (SMC) – the nominee shareholding being transferred to the main shareholder. Thus, if the company originally had two shareholders and the single share is transferred to the parent, the required entries are made in the register of members, and the Registrar is informed, the company becomes an SMC. In such an instance, in the entry providing details of the sole member in the register of members the phrase 'On [date] this company became a single member company' must be entered. If an SMC subsequently acquires additional member(s), the note 'On [date] this company ceased to be a single member company' – and the effective date of change – must be added to the former sole member's account and the Registrar must be informed.

A difficulty may arise where a director (or some other appointee) is the nominee holding the single share and a disagreement arises and they leave, or are told to leave, the company. In order to register the transfer, either to another nominee or to the parent company, the nominee's signature is required on a stock transfer form, which, if relationships are strained, may be difficult to obtain. Alternatively, the request to sign a stock transfer form can be used by the nominee as a lever to try to obtain an enhanced settlement.

Administration

If it is decided to maintain or create such nominee holdings or to appoint a new nominee, a declaration of trust together with an undated stock transfer form relating to the share(s) and signed by the nominee should be obtained. Provided the nominee has previously signed a stock transfer form, then all that is required to be done, should the majority owner ever wish to change their nominee (or simply to transfer the share into its own name), is to insert the name of a new holder, date the form, and lodge it with the share certificate so that the transfer can take place. Obviously such a signed stock transfer form should be preserved safely. Since March 2008 such a transfer no longer attracts stamp duty.

Example	Draft declaration of trust for nominee shareholder
	This Declaration of Trust is made by me (NAME) of (ADDRESS) on this (DATE) concerning the ONE share of (NOMINAL VALUE) held by me in (COMPANY).
	I confirm that I hold the above share on behalf of, and as Trustee for (NAME and ADDRESS OF BENEFICIAL OWNER) who is the legal owner of the share. I confirm that any dividends received by me in respect of my holding this share on behalf of the said (OWNER) will be immediately remitted by me to (OWNER), or immediately disposed of in accordance with any instructions issued by (OWNER).
	I also confirm that on receipt of instructions from (OWNER) I will immediately transfer the share as directed, in anticipation of which instructions I have today signed a stock transfer form which has the identity of the transferee left blank.
	Signed .... Witness............................

Operating and financial business review

INTRODUCTION

For several years prior to late 2005, listed PLCs and large LTDs were to be required to produce an operating and financial review (OFR) which, it was intended, should extend the scope of information to be made available to interested parties and give a discursive and balanced overview of the company's trading and financial position. This document was stated to be required *'because it is felt that readers of annual reports have gleaned little information from them'*. The then Secretary of State commented (somewhat optimistically, many thought) that *'the OFR will improve the quality of the reporting and complete the corporate jigsaw to give investors a clearer picture'*. Whether this would ever have been the case is academic, since in the 2005 Pre-Budget review the requirement was scrapped, without any advance warning. There was an outcry from various City bodies and others, not least because of the time and money already invested in preparing for the requirement. Indeed some companies had already produced their first OFRs. Since many had welcomed the new reporting requirements, a requirement was inserted in CA06 requiring all companies above the audit threshold, to provide a business review. This means of course that many additional thousands of companies are caught by the requirement than had formerly been intended.

Content

The OFRs that had already been produced contained discussion on corporate objectives and strategy (more in outline than detail for understandable reasons), as well as analyses of past performance and future prospects – all items the average shareholder would expect to find in the annual report (and which are in essence part of that document's main purpose). Additional items which were to be included were details of a company's relationship with its suppliers, and its social and environmental policies – again all items which could be included in the annual report. In a recent survey, directors of 33 per cent of PLCs and 75 per cent of LTDs stated they would not discuss strategy – hardly surprising, given that such information could be extremely valuable to competitors and thus potentially detrimental to the owners of the company, particularly in the current highly competitive and restricted economic environment with business confidence badly shaken. The new requirement has roused the anger of many shareholders, since their companies are required to incur additional costs to produce and distribute such a report for little apparent benefit. Centrica plc, for example, estimated it would cost them an additional £300,000.

However some of those involved in listed PLCs welcomed the additional requirement. Indeed on hearing the news of the abandonment of the OFR, one non-executive director commented *'What's he done that for? Not only have we been gearing up to producing it, we found the reporting standard rigorous enough that it gave us non-executive directors a hook on which to ask searching questions of management – and to get them [the executive directors] to back their answers up with solid data'* – which is after all exactly the role required of non-executive directors under the precepts of CORPORATE GOVERNANCE.

A recent report from the Institute of Chartered Accountants indicated that whilst many annual reports do give some general information about the market place within which the company operates, most of it is valueless for comparison purpose. The report stated that companies should:

- report on brand equity and market performance;
- give quantitative and consistent statistics and information;
- include core data such as market definition, size, market share and marketing investment.

(Contact : www.icaew.co.uk.)

Business review

All companies (other than those designated as 'small' see 'Using this book') must now provide a 'business review'. The purpose of the review is stated as being *'to inform members and help them assess how the directors have performed their duty to promote the success of the company having regard to employees, community and the environment'.*

Section 417 of CA06 states that the review must contain:

- a fair review of the company's business;
- a description of the principal risks and uncertainties facing the company;

and be a fair analysis of:

- the development and performance of the company's business; and
- the position of the company's business at the end of the financial year.

The review must contain, for the purpose of understanding the performance, development or position of business:

- analysis using financial key performance indicators; and
- where appropriate, analysis using other key performance indicators, including information relating to environmental and employment matters.

The last item – non-financial information – is optional for medium-sized companies.

Quoted PLCs must also state:

- trends and factors likely to affect the company's future development;
- principal risks and uncertainties;
- information re environmental matters:
  - employees;
  - social and community issues;
- details re key contracts (that is, 'significant relationships with major suppliers which are likely to affect (directly or indirectly) the value and performance of the business').

Directors are personally liable for the content of the report and could be held liable to compensate the company for any loss it suffers as a result of any untrue or misleading statement in, or any omission from, the report, if they knew (or were reckless as to whether) the statement was true – or knew the statement to be a dishonest concealment of a material fact.

Note: There is considerable antipathy regarding the obligations on quoted companies and inclusion of some of the items may be left on a voluntary basis. After all, highlighting risks, unless there is also guidance on how these risks are being controlled or guarded against, undermines confidence – and business is all about confidence sadly lacking at present. Further, disclosure of key contracts could be prejudicial to companies obtaining advantageous terms – and the suppliers would not want such disclosure. There are exceptions – thus where the disclosure would *'be seriously prejudicial to the interests of the company'* the information does not need to be disclosed. One must wonder how often that would be used to avoid disclosing the information required.

INTRODUCTION

In relation to companies, the word 'proxy' has three separate but interrelated meanings. It is:

(a) the right given to a member of a company to authorise another person to vote in their place in respect of their shareholding (or part of it);

(b) the form evidencing that appointment; and

(c) the means by which the person who is appointed as a member's proxy exercises that member's voting rights to the extent of and in accordance with the authority granted to them.

Authority

Most ARTICLES confer an authority on the members of the company to appoint another person to act on their behalf (i.e. to act as their proxy), and may stipulate the requirements re drafting and submitting the proxy forms. It is usual for a company to send out a form of proxy with the notice of the meeting and to state that it must be lodged (usually at the registered office or office of the share registrar of the company) by a set time before the meeting. Under reg. 62 of Table A of CA85, the time for lodging cannot exceed 48 hours before the meeting (or 24 hours where the poll is taken after the meeting). In the articles for an LTD accompanying CA06, any time limit can be set by the company within its articles, so companies adopting these articles would need to add specific requirements in this regard. Although it is administratively preferable for members to use the standard printed form, the use of an alternative is usually allowed, provided the wording gives clear instructions.

Form

Proxies can be either general or specific. A general proxy simply appoints another person to act and vote on behalf of the member in accordance with their (the proxy's) own views – which may of course have been dictated to them by the member previously. Specific proxies, or two-way proxies, allow the member to indicate, for each resolution to be considered by the meeting, how the votes must be cast.

Example	**General proxy**

GENERAL PROXY Bloggs Manufacturing Ltd

I, [name] of [address] being a member of Bloggs Manufacturing Ltd hereby appoint [name of proxy], or failing him/her, [name], as my proxy to vote in my name and on my behalf at the [type of meeting] GENERAL MEETING of the company to be held on [date] and at any adjournment thereof [as he/she thinks fit].

Signed................ Date................

Example	**Specific proxy**

SPECIFIC PROXY Bloggs Manufacturing Plc

I, [name] of [address] being a member of Bloggs Manufacturing Plc hereby appoint [name of proxy], or failing him/her, [name], as my proxy to vote in my name and on my behalf at the ANNUAL GENERAL MEETING of the company to be held on [date] and at any adjournment thereof as is stated below :

Resolution 1 Adoption of accounts for the year ended

30th June 2XXX and Balance sheet as at
that date   FOR/AGAINST*

Resolution 2 Payment of dividend   FOR/AGAINST*

Resolution 3 Re-election of directors

J Bloggs   FOR/AGAINST*

A N Other   FOR/AGAINST*

Resolution 4 Re-election of Auditors   FOR/AGAINST*

Resolution 5 Authority for directors to agree

the auditors' remuneration   FOR/AGAINST*

Signed.................................... Date................

* Delete as appropriate. Unless the way a vote is to be cast is indicated, the proxy will vote as they think fit.

Proxy administration

1 It is usual to insert 'the Chairman of the meeting' as the first choice proxy with space to allow the member to delete this and insert an alternative.
2 A proxy need not be a member of the company.
3 Listed PLCs must use the specific or two-way proxy, not the general proxy (so that the voting intention of the member in respect of each resolution is clear and can be counted in advance of the meeting).
4 Where there are large numbers of members it may be helpful to suggest that members give the person acting as their proxy, a copy of the form of proxy to aid identification when attending the meeting.
5 Proxies should be date and time stamped on receipt. It is possible for a member to file a subsequent proxy (before the final time limit) in which case the later proxy revokes the earlier.
6 An analysis of the proxy forms should be made as soon as the required time of deposit has passed so that voting strength both for and against (where specific proxies are used) is known in advance.
7 The ARTICLES should be checked for clarification of whether or not a proxy is to be counted towards meeting QUORUM requirements.
8 Under the Electronic Communications Act, companies are allowed to let their members submit proxies by electronic means.
9 Under CA06 members are allowed to appoint more than one proxy – each representing part of their holding.

Revocation

Proxies are revoked by:

- the submission of a later proxy in place of one filed previously;
- the death of the member, provided this is known before the expiry of the time limit for filing proxies;
- the attendance by the member in person at the meeting, although it would be safer to check the position (i.e. who is going to vote), if both member and proxy are present.

Operation

The use of the authority vested in a proxy (person) by the proxy (form) depends on the ARTICLES:

- in an LTD it is usual for the proxy to have the right to speak as well as vote, but not to be able to vote on a show of hands (although the proxy can request or join in the request for a poll);

■ in a PLC, usually the proxy can vote on a show of hands but does not have the right to speak except to request or join in the request for a poll.

Calling for a poll

The full power of shareholding can usually only be felt when a poll is called, since then all votes eligible (rather than one 'hand' per shareholder, regardless of whether they have ten shares or 10,000) can be counted. A poll can usually be demanded or called by:

■ the chairman;
■ any two members (which includes representatives of corporate shareholders); or
■ any member(s) holding 10 per cent or more of the share capital.

In addition, the proforma articles for an LTD accompanying CA06 allow 'the directors' to demand a poll.

Thus an individual proxy, unless speaking for member(s) holding 10 per cent or more of the share capital, can only join in the request for a poll.

Some listed PLCs have changed their articles and abolished voting by show of hands. All votes are thus conducted by poll and thus business can only be resolved by (potentially) the full voting strength.

Representatives

Institutional members should not complete a form of proxy, but instead should appoint a representative. This requires a resolution of the board of the member institution which appoints a named individual to act on its behalf. Such a representative acts in all respects as an individual member with all the rights of a member.

Electronic proxies

The EU Shareholder Rights directive was implemented with effect from August 2009 and stipulates that listed PLCs must give their members at least 21 days' notice of a general meeting, but this can be reduced to 14 days, provided:

■ the shareholders have firstly approved (by special resolution), every year, the shortening of such notice; and
■ shareholders are able to cast their votes by electronic means available to all shareholders.

The wording for such a resolution could run:

'That any meeting other than the Annual General Meeting of the company be properly convened providing 14 days' notice is given to members entitled to attend and vote'.

Quorum

INTRODUCTION

As a precaution against major decisions being taken by a minority of the members of a meeting (whether this be at a directors' board meeting or a members' general meeting) during the absence of the majority, for whatever reason, the concept of there needing to be a quorum (that is, a minimum number) of members present, is widespread.

Board meetings

The ARTICLES should be consulted to check any provision regarding any quorum requirements. The pro forma articles for an LTD accompanying CA06 state that the quorum can be fixed from time to time by the directors themselves, but it must never be less than two (and if it is not fixed, it will be two) – virtually the same provisions as those in Table A of CA85.

However reference should also be made to any article governing directors' interests, since in some articles it is stated that if a director has an interest in an item for discussion then they may not be counted as part of the quorum for that item – that is there must be what is called a *'disinterested quorum'* considering the item. If so, at least the required minimum number who are not interested in the matter must be present. If the number of directors is small and the quorum requirements are high, a director being disqualified from being counted in the quorum could mean there is delay in gaining proper authority for decisions. Failing to abide by the requirements of the articles renders those responsible personally liable for any losses occasioned thereby, since they are stated to be acting *ultra vires* (beyond the powers given them by) the articles.

General meetings

Other than in a SINGLE MEMBER COMPANY where the sole member is the quorum (in which case all decisions taken by such sole member should be recorded either by means of a written resolution or by minutes of that person's 'meeting') normally, unless the articles make separate provision, a quorum is two persons personally present. Thus, in such circumstances, the attendance of a proxy may be insufficient to generate a quorum if only one other member is present in person.

Case study	Ignorance is no excuse
	In *Smith v Henniker-Major* a director had deliberately failed to notify his colleagues that he was convening a board meeting. Acting on his own on the date he had set, he then purported to pass a board resolution. However he failed to check the articles, which stipulated that the quorum for a valid board meeting was two directors. Not only was the failure to give notice of the board meeting to his colleagues a breach of company law, he was also acting *ultra vires* his company's articles. The Court of Appeal stated that the 'resolution' he purported to pass was a worthless piece of paper. In addition, since the director had acted in breach of the articles, he was personally liable for any loss occasioned as a result of his action. (Nowadays, if the company had suffered loss as a result of actioning the 'resolution' he had 'passed', he could be held to be liable under the new 'derivative claims' legislation.)

Conducting business

Normally, if within 30 minutes of the time set by the notice of the meeting, a quorum is not present, the meeting cannot proceed and must be adjourned. However, Table A of CA85 stipulates that if a quorum was present at the commencement of the meeting but then the meeting ceased to be 'quorate' (i.e. to have a quorum, the minimum required not being present) because a person forming part of the quorum left (or was disqualified, for example because of a conflict of interests), then, providing there were still at least two members present, the meeting can continue.

Single member quorum

Other than for a SINGLE MEMBER COMPANY, where obviously a general meeting can be validly held by the single shareholder, where more than one person is entitled to attend, the court has power to authorise the holding of a meeting even though it is known in advance that only one person will be present (either in person or by proxy). Thus in a case where the minority shareholder refused to attend meetings at which the business to be conducted was his dismissal by the majority shareholder, the court allowed the majority shareholder to be present and to act alone to conduct the business.

If there is only one holder of a class of shares (for example, preference shares) the decision of that person on behalf of the whole class (see CLASSES OF SHARES AND CLASS MEETINGS) will be binding even though no 'meeting' as such has taken (or ever could take) place.

INTRODUCTION

A company is a legal person that can trade, take on credit, contract with its employees, suppliers, customers etc., in exactly the same way as a real person (a human being) can. The company has obligations to make the details contained in certain of its statutory records available to numerous persons, organisations and regulatory bodies. This includes those with 'internal' rights (shareholders, creditors, and auditors), as well as those with 'external' rights (regulatory bodies, whose numbers have doubled during the past two decades, according to surveys conducted by the Federation of Small Businesses). In addition there are many other records which need to be preserved for various lengths of time. (Guidance to these can be found in *The ICSA Guide to Document Retention* and in the author's section of the LexisNexis publication, *Company Secretary's Link*). Alternatively, auditors and solicitors can provide guidance.

Policy for document and records preservation

To ensure that the documents required to be made available are protected and able to be displayed, companies may be well advised to adopt a policy.

Example	Company policy for document protection
	Document and records preservation [Company] PLC/LTD
	1 Responsibility for preserving the various books, registers and records of the company, in order to comply with legislation and business practice is devolved to [the company secretary or person responsible for secretarial matters if there is no company secretary].
	2 Such responsibility includes: ■ ensuring safe storage with reasonable accessibility whilst the items are current;
	→

Example	Company policy for document protection
	<ul><li>provision of adequate back-up systems capable of providing current record data, should the original be lost for any reason;</li><li>preserving records in accordance with a procedure and timetable to be devised, and in those archives.</li></ul> 3. The various terms of retention, as set out in *The ICSA Guide to Document Retention* or LexisNexis' *Company Secretary's Link*, (subject to any extension, but not contraction, of the suggested time limits for reasons particular to the company) are to be adhered to at all times. 4 Suitably secure premises/facilities will be utilised for this purpose. Such premises etc. need to be protected from rodents, fire and flood, intruders etc. 5 Checks will be made that all records held electronically will still be able to be accessed before any change of system/ software is implemented. 6 [The company secretary] will monitor changes in requirements and effect appropriate alterations. 7 [The company secretary] will be required to report annually to the board on compliance with the requirements of this procedure.

Promulgation

It is not simply a case of the board and the company secretary knowing the company's obligations, but also ensuring that those responsible for admitting visitors to the company know how to deal with their enquiries, quickly and efficiently. A well-rehearsed procedure is advisable. Until the introduction of CA06, those wishing to inspect the register of members were able to do so for *'two hours every business day'*. CA06 changed that right to one where those wishing to inspect that record must apply to the board who, if they do not feel the request is for a legitimate purpose, can reject the request and apply to the court for powers to resist the inspection (anyone can inspect the company's latest annual return filed at CH, although admittedly it could be as much as a year out of date).

The remaining records are available as before – for example, members have a right of access to all registers, and creditors have a right of access to the register of charges. In fact personal inspections are rare and most people wishing to check such data will prefer to access the company data filed at CH electronically even though it may be somewhat out of date (i.e. the list of shareholders will be that disclosed by the most recent annual return which will now only give their names).

Suggested procedure

1 Identify all those having a right of access and the records to which such rights apply.

2 The credentials of the person requesting access to the records (i.e. their relationship) should be checked in order to ensure that they have the right to access (or make a request to access) the record requested. (Shareholders' names should be checked against the latest members' register printout, creditors against the purchase ledger printout, debenture/loan holders against their register, and so on.)

3 They should be conducted to the interview room. Those with an immediate right of inspection (members and creditors) will be interviewed by the company secretary, failing whom the assistant company secretary, failing whom the chief accountant.

Should the visitor require copies of the documentation, charges as laid down may be levied. An invoice should be raised and payment obtained before the visitor leaves [or before inspection]. A company representative should remain in the interview room during the inspection/copying to ensure the protection of the record. A note of the inspection should be made in the visitors book and the fact reported at the next following board meeting.

Those without an immediate right of inspection will be advised that their request will be passed to the board for decision and they will be advised of the decision within 48 hours.

Notes

The charges for inspection and copying are as follows:

(a) Register of members:
Inspection: £3.50 each hour or part thereof.
Copies: £3.50 for first 50 entries, £31.50 for next 950 entries or part thereof, £20 for next 4,000 entries or part thereof and £25 for every subsequent 5,000 entries or part thereof.

(b) Directors' service contracts and/or indemnity provisions, resolutions and meetings, report under s. 805: 20p per 1,000 words or part thereof.

(c) There is no obligation for the company to provide photocopying facilities.

'Internal' bodies' access

The records covered are shown below, with notes of those with rights of access. Unless otherwise stated the records should be held at the registered office or, under CA06, at a single alternative inspection location (SAIL). If such records are held in a non-legible form, the records should be held at the registered office and the Registrar of Companies informed. If a SAIL is used, all the records must be held there.

A

Register of members must be held at the registered office (RO) or SAIL
Access: on application to the directors
The board must within five days allow the inspection or apply to the court (telling the person wishing to inspect that it has done so) for permission to resist the inspection because they feel it is 'not a fit purpose'.

The reasons for resisting an inspection could include purposes that:

- are unlawful;
- would breach the Data Protection Act;
- are to enable a third party to check credit or identities of shareholders;
- are to market investments or commercial products;
- might result in the threatening, harassment or intimidation of shareholders;
- seek to market securities, and so on.

When wishing to resist an inspection, taking legal advice may be appropriate.

Note: There is further guidance as to *'proper purpose'* tests on the ICSA website (http://www.icsa.org.uk).

B

Register of directors and secretary (RO or SAIL)
Register of directors' shareholdings (RO or SAIL) – PLCs only
Register of significant shareholdings/substantial interests (RO or SAIL) – listed PLCs only
Overseas branch register (with register of members)
Reports on disclosures under s. 793 CA06 (formerly s. 212 CA85) notices (listed PLCs only) (RO or SAIL)
Contract/statutory declaration for purchase by company of own shares
Access: by members – every working day. By others – on application to the directors

C

Minutes of general meetings

Directors' service contracts (RO or SAIL with register of members) (must also be available for inspection at AGM.)

Access: by members only (who must also be sent a copy if requested – see note above re charges)

D

Register of charges (RO or SAIL)

Access : by members and creditors

E

Register of debenture/loan holders (RO or SAIL in place where register of members is held)

Access: by members, and debenture stock/loan holders

F

Statutory declaration of payment out of capital for redemption or purchase by company of own shares (RO or SAIL)

Access: by members and creditors

Additional requirements

The notes in the first part of this section cover only those corporate records where there is a requirement to preserve them and to make them available for inspection. The preservation of a considerable number of other records is required – to comply with legislation, for commercial reasons and since they form part of the history of the company. The time limits applicable to preservation for legislative demands vary widely, which adds complexity to the obligation – for example, evidence which supports a recruit's claim that he has the right to work in the UK have, since February 2008, been required to be held by employers to the date the employee leaves plus two years.

Detailed consideration is essential for the safe protection and accessibility of such records. In view of any space limitations, the possibility of record preservation via microfilming or recording on disk might be examined, although great care should be taken and reference should be made to the British Standard BS6498 on the 'Preparation of microfilm for use in evidence' and their 'Code of practice on the legal admissibility of information stored on electronic document management systems'. Under the Civil Evidence Act 1995, computer-generated records are admissible as evidence.

Retention periods

Generally records such as those stated above must be held for at least the life of the company. However since a company is a legal rather than a real person, not only can it 'die' (be dissolved, wound up, struck off, etc.) but, by order of the court, it can also be resuscitated (see RESURRECTION) for the purpose of facing a liability claim. It may be safest (other than for companies which have never traded) to retain such records for at least (say) 12 years beyond the life of the company. Since resuscitation or resurrection is effected to enable a company to respond to a liability claim, it would be prudent to keep liability insurers' records for the same length of time. The time limit on resuscitation is now six (formerly two) years after removal from the register. Records other than those stated above may be held for shorter periods and guidance should be sought in each case.

'External bodies' access

As well as those persons connected with the company that have rights to the corporate records, a considerable number of other bodies have rights of access to the company premises, records, etc., and it is essential to be prepared for such visits and to brief those responsible in the company to deal with them.

Procedure

1   Representatives of organisations on the following list have a right of access to company premises, may have a right to inspect records and interview employees and may also have a right to remove records, data and registers, etc. Denial of access to some of these regulatory bodies can be a criminal offence.

2   The receptionist/gate keeper on duty should establish the agency the visitor(s) represent and inspect their credentials to ensure their bona fides. They should be conducted to the waiting room and the company representative stated should be contacted. The contact will then be responsible for dealing with the enquiry.

(a) Government and statutory regulatory agencies

Department of Business, Enterprise and Regulatory Reform (BERR), Financial Services Authority (FSA), Serious Fraud Office (SFO), Office of Fair Trading (OFT)/Competition Commission (CC), European Union inspectors (EU).

Scope

- *BERR*: under company legislation, BERR has power to investigate company affairs, ownership, dealings in shares, including insider dealing. Exact nature of investigation must be ascertained.
- *FSA*: under the Financial Services Act 1986 the FSA has powers to investigate the affairs of all companies operating under its aegis. In addition, the FSA has authority under the Financial Services and Markets Act 2000 to regulate all financial business in the UK and investigate instances of market abuse and manipulation including insider dealing. It has a wide range of disciplinary and enforcement powers.
- *SFO* has powers, wider in many cases than those available to the police or FSA, under the Criminal Justice Act 1987, to investigate matters of fraud likely to total in excess of £2 million and to be of public concern.
- *OFT* has an obligation to investigate whether supplies of goods or services breach the principles of the Fair Trading Act 1973 and is now the policing arm of the Competition Commission.
- *CC:* the Competition Commission (acting under the Competition Act 1998 and the Enterprise Act 2002) can investigate (and gain access to inspect records etc.) any company which is suspected of infringing the prohibitions set out in those Acts.
- *EU* inspectors have rights (without notice) to enter the premises of organisations of member states under the Communities Act 1972. It is on record that, in doing so, the inspectors should act in accordance with the laws of the member state (and in concert with the domestic regulatory agency) concerned, although this does not always happen and there have been inspections by EU staff unaccompanied by representatives from domestic agencies.

Persons dealing

Company secretary (whom failing assistant company secretary, whom failing chief accountant).

Actions

- Telephone chairman and board, corporate lawyers, and public relations staff (in case media require information).
- Meet representatives and endeavour to ascertain requirements.
- Check requirements with corporate lawyers.
- Endeavour to assist investigators whilst minimising the potential damage to the company name and reputation.
- Write report of visit, requirements, action carried out, records inspected/removed.

WARNING

 The need to obtain legal advice in view of the lack of the right to silence that can be threatened by these agencies (that is refusing to answer questions and remaining silent can bring about sanctions including imprisonment) cannot be emphasised too strongly. It is also essential to try to obtain and keep copies of everything seized during such a search although some agencies will not allow this, stating they will provide copies of the documents seized within a week.

(b) Statutory reporting agencies

HM Revenue and Customs (HMRC), Health and Safety Executive/local authority (HSE/LA), Trading Standards Officers (TSO), Pensions Regulator (PR), rating authorities (RA).

Scope

- *HMRC*: powers of access tend to be exercised by the Audit Department of the Inland Revenue, or the Compliance units of the Department of Work and Pensions, which are charged with the duty of checking the validity of the way an employer has paid and deducted tax from employees and workers. The DWP has a right under the National Minimum Wage legislation to check that employers are paying at least the wage rates specified to those entitled (and to sponsor criminal prosecution if not) – which may be extended to investigations regarding payments made to apprentices.
- *Customs and Excise* has wide powers of access in respect of its VAT collection duties which emanate from their previous and existing role as Excise officers. The penalties for errors, in VAT collection and payment, even where they are totally accidental, are severe, despite recent amelioration.
- *HSE and/or LAs* have rights under the Working Time Regulations 1998 to inspect records of hours worked by those opting out of the maximum 48 hours worked per week rule.
- *TSOs* have rights under the Consumer Protection Act 1987 to ensure compliance with such legislation.
- *PR* has rights under various Pensions Acts to check compliance, in particular that pension contribution deductions made from employees wages have been paid to the appropriate trustees and that, where necessary, access to the provider of a stakeholder pensions is provided and the deductions made are being paid over.
- *RA* have a right of access for the purpose of checking the valuation for the purposes of the Uniform Business rate (or any appeal in respect thereof).

Persons dealing

Chief accountant/personnel director (failing whom finance director, failing whom company secretary).

Actions

- Meet representatives and establish nature of enquiry.
- Provide information required.
- Advise chairman and board and corporate lawyers (via company secretary).
- Ensure if errors are found that systems are changed to avoid a repetition, whilst those responsible should be disciplined if procedures have not been followed correctly. Inland Revenue have a right to pursue an employee if through their actions – rather than those of the employer – tax has been underpaid in respect of payroll liabilities.
- Write report of visit, action required and effected.

(c) Emergency and utilities services

Fire, police, Health and Safety Executive, Factory Inspectorate, Environmental Health Officers, gas, water and electricity utilities.

Scope

- *Fire*: right of access to premises mainly for the purposes of checking compliance with the Regulatory Reform (Fire Safety) Order 2005 (i.e. that there is a Responsible Person appointed for every location and that they regularly conduct inspections of the premises).
- *Police:* unless in the belief, or in connection with such belief, that a crime has been, is being or is about to be committed, or in hot pursuit of a suspected person, or accompanying Government and Statutory Regulatory Agencies (see above), the police have no immediate right of access to premises other than with the permission of the owner/occupier.
- *Health & Safety Executive (HSE), Environmental Health Officers (EHOs) and Factory Inspectors* have a range of powers which vary from industry to industry. Operators of large (and potentially hazardous) facilities are obliged (under the Control of Industrial Major Accident Regulations 1988) to file and keep up to date details of plans and emergency evacuations etc., which will require contact with the appropriate department, which may well wish to check the site. EHOs also have rights of access under the Food Safety Act 1992 to check that food preparation and serving areas are suitable. HSE inspectors have a right of inspection of certificates of employers' liability (although since these are no longer required to be kept for 40 years, as was the case from 1999 until October 2008, presumably this right is now only to inspect the current certificate).

- *Utilities* have rights of access to read meters and, if leaks/breaks are suspected, to rectify on an emergency basis, which could even entail forced entry.

Persons dealing

Personnel director (failing whom company secretary, failing whom personnel manager).

Actions

- Meet representative and establish problem.
- Rectify, if required and possible.
- Update procedures, if required.
- Write report of visit and action effected.

(d) Others

- *Border & Immigration Agency*: to check that all employees (and ex-employees for up to two years after they have left) have/had the right to work in the UK (and the documentation evidencing that right), and, if using immigrants from outside the EU, that the employer has a licence.

Persons dealing

Personnel/HR manager (failing whom company secretary).

Action

Be prepared to produce copies of relevant evidence (in a form which cannot be altered) and, if applicable, the licence.

- *Department of Transport*: to inspect transport (fleet) operators licence and administration.

Persons dealing

Transport manager (failing whom, company secretary).

Action

Be prepared to produce operator's licence and back-up records etc.

- *Local Authorities:* have an increasing range of obligations – see above. In addition they are responsible for ensuring compliance with environment protection legislation.

Persons dealing

Personnel/HR manager, failing whom company secretary.

- *Landlords and agents*: to inspect condition and use of premises, assess value for insurance, prepare dilapidations ('wants of repair') reports, under the provisions of leases and licences.

Persons dealing

Company secretary (failing whom assistant company secretary, failing whom chief accountant).

Action

- Meet representatives – since most leases state that (say) 48 hours' notice of such an inspection must be given, there should be no need to allow immediate access unless it is an emergency. Good landlord/tenant relations may require a positive and helpful approach.
- If a dilapidations notice and schedule of 'wants of repair' (a requirement to put the premises into good order and repair, since the tenant has not complied with the repairing/decoration covenants in the lease) is to be served, refer to the lease for the procedure to be followed.

There may be other bodies with rights of access for particular industries (e.g. Charities Commission for charitable companies, etc.) These should be identified, and with guidance re appropriate action, added to the list which may also need customising to fit individual companies' requirements.

Registered number and office

INTRODUCTION

To facilitate the identification of companies, at INCORPORATION each is allocated an individual number by the Registrar of Companies. A company's registered number is never changed (and never reissued even if the company is removed from the active company register). It is sometimes possible to obtain a 'cherished' or preferred number if it is not already in use, and reference should be made to the Registrar on this point. In addition, companies must nominate a registered office – which must be within their country of registration – and advise CH should the company at any time wish to change this (again, within the company's country of registration). The number cannot be changed.

Consistent identification

Although a company can change its name (by special resolution), business (by changing its objects clause), type of registration (e.g. an LTD can RE-REGISTER as a PLC, and vice versa, an unlimited company can re-register as an LTD and so on), ownership, etc., the one consistent aspect of its existence is its registered number, which remains unaltered for ever and is never reused by the Registrar even if the company is dissolved, wound up etc. However, under s. 1066 CA06, the Registrar has been given powers to add check digits to a company's registered number for the purpose of facilitating electronic filing and access. There are no plans for this at present, and if it were implemented, a three-year period (during which both old and new numbers would be acceptable) would be allowed whilst letterheads and other stationery stocks could be exhausted and new equivalents printed.

For the purposes of the official lodgement of papers (matters concerning the corporate entity, legal actions, notices, etc.) and to comply with the principle that all those dealing with the company have a right to know with whom they are dealing, every company must have a registered office. The registered office can only be situated within the country in which the company is incorporated (although there are EU proposals that would allow a company to move its registered office anywhere within the EU – in which case it would be bound by the corporate laws of the country to which its principal office relocated). On registration, the registered office must be advised to the Registrar (as part of the application to register a company on form IN01), and all subsequent changes of address must be notified to the Registrar on form AD01 (under s. 87 CA06 formerly s. 287 CA85). The country of registration (but not necessarily the address within that country) must be stated in the memorandum. Around 50 per cent of companies registered in England and Wales have their registered office in London or the south-east of England.

Promulgation

In the same way that the company name is required to be displayed at every place at which the company undertakes business (but no longer, as was formerly the case, on the exterior of those places), the fact than an address is the registered office of the company must be displayed on the exterior of that location (although not if the address is a domestic residence). In addition, details of the registered office must be shown on all invoices, order forms, letterheads, websites and monetary documentation. This includes fax and e-mail communications where software should be changed to incorporate these legal requirements as standard on every item sent outside the company. There is no requirement to put the name, registered office or number on business cards or compliment slips. Under CA06 the Secretary of State is given powers to stipulate where the company name must be displayed.

Changing the location of the registered office

Any alteration in location of the registered office must be filed with the Registrar using form AD01. Registering the change is not simply a question of legal compliance, there is a practical aspect. All communications from the Registrar are sent to the registered office. If there is no postal redirection, the ANNUAL RETURN and other communications may go astray. This could result in the company failing to file within the required time limit, in turn leading to prosecution and fines for the directors – and even to the company being struck off the register (thereby incurring potential cost to be reinstated to the register).

On notifying CH of a change of registered office, a 14-day period during which both old and new offices are valid for the service of notices is allowed. If a company is required to move in an emergency (for example because of a fire, flood or other disaster, or the unexpected action of a landlord), the penalties for failing to notify the change of registered office to the Registrar are waived, provided notification of the new office is made within 14 days of the enforced move being known.

'Company hi-jacking'

There have been a number of instances of unauthorised persons filing a change of registered address form with the Registrar, thereby changing a company's registered office to a location under their own control. From that new location such persons have carried on business as if they were the original company. Anyone suspicious of the situation, on checking the company's file at CH would find the change of address filed, as they might think, correctly. Having taken on credit as if they were the company, the fraudsters then abscond, owing substantial sums to unpaid creditors who would understandably think they were owed the money by the original company. Since the Registrar does not take action to prevent this situation (e.g. by acknowledging all changes of registered offices to the private address of an officer of the company), regular checking of the company's details on file (via the CH website) should be undertaken. Alternatively the company could either add its own name (with a stated address) to the Registrar's Monitor service, so that all changes to CH records are notified to a stated address (i.e. other than the registered office), or use the Registrar's PROOF service under which the company agrees to file all items electronically which (needing both an authorisation code and a password) should provide greater protection than the paper system. Having signed up to this system, any subsequent hard copy notification would be rejected by the Registrar. (Until it is possible to file all the forms electronically, this could create problems if the company, after subscribing to PROOF, then needed to file a form which cannot yet be filed electronically.)

Administration

Companies must have a registered office so that third parties in dispute with it know where official or legal notices can be served. The means by which such documents are processed after delivery should be given due attention. There have been instances where documents requiring instant action have been filed rather than actioned.

Case study	Expensive inactivity
	In a case concerning an unpaid claim made on a leading UK insurance company, documents giving notice to the company of a legal hearing for a winding-up order against it, legitimately served by the creditor in north-east England, were filed rather than actioned. Because there was no response, the winding-up petition was listed for a court hearing, to the considerable embarrassment of the company, whose bankers then indicated that unless there was immediate clarification they might have to refuse to honour the company's cheques. The judge refused to accept the company's explanation and promise to pay, in order to allow delisting of the application, unless they produced the ➡

Case study	Expensive inactivity – continued
	creditor in court to confirm personally that he had been paid. The company had to transport him to London and accommodate him in a hotel prior to the hearing – all at their expense!

A responsible person should oversee the receipt of post and ensure such notices are brought to the prompt attention of someone in authority and that appropriate (and timely) action ensues.

Disclosure

As the registered number helps identification of the legal person and the registered office confirms the location of the legal person, both must appear on all business letters and communications, invoices, websites, statements and order forms etc. In view of the requirement also to state the country of incorporation, it is normal to use a form of words such as the following, and to instruct printers to incorporate them on all such business stationery.

Example	Wording for incorporation on company letterheads, etc.
	Bloggs Manufacturing Co. Ltd. Registered in England No 123456789
	Registered office: Bloggs House, 1, Bloggs Rd, Bloggsville, Bloggshire, BL1 5H1.

Notes

1 The names of directors are not required to be shown on letterheads, unless one is named, in which case all must be named. However where the printing of a name merely indicates a personalisation of corporate notepaper (e.g. 'from the office of [name of director])', BERR has stated that this is not normally regarded as being a breach of this requirement.
2 Fines can be levied against both company and officers for failure to comply with the requirements set out above.

Registrar of Companies

INTRODUCTION

The UK Registrar of Companies was set up in 1844 and was the first such organisation in the world to act as a repository of data on limited liability companies and to provide a facility by which those trading with a company, particularly if advancing it credit, as well as members of the public, could source and check a company's corporate details. Thus the *quid pro quo* for the valuable limiting of the liability of shareholders was disclosure of information. This remains the purpose of lodging data with the Registrar to this day, and explains the increasingly strict attitude to time limits on filing data with the Registrar and thus making the data public – particularly the annual financial records and the contents of the annual return of each company. CH is an executive agency of the Department of Business, Enterprise and Regulatory Reform (BERR). CH maintains records on around 3,000,000 'current' companies, (including up to 600,000 that are dormant), and over 2,000,000 dissolved companies. Approximately 25,000 new companies are registered each month and over 100,000 companies are deleted from the active register each year.

Locations

The main company registry for English and Welsh companies is in Cardiff:

- address: Companies House, Crown Way, Maindy, Cardiff CF4 3UZ;
- website: www.companieshouse.gov.uk;
- telephone (which reaches all departments in all offices): 0303 1234 500.

There is a single satellite office in London at 21 Bloomsbury Street, WC1B 3XD.

The records of companies registered in Scotland are located at 37 Castle Terrace, Edinburgh, EH1 2RB, and the records of companies registered in Northern Ireland are located at IDB House, 64 Chichester St, Belfast, BT1 4JX.

It has been proposed that the three UK Registers should be combined, which is now feasible since CA06 applies throughout the UK whereas previous company legislation did not – companies in Northern Ireland being required to comply with separate, although very similar, 'derived' legislation.

At each location, inspection and search facilities are available for all callers usually between the hours of 9.30am and 4.00pm, Monday to Friday excluding Bank Holidays. Copies of documents can be obtained. There are charges for both searching and copying.

CH offices have letterboxes which are cleared at midnight each day. Items placed in these boxes, even if posted there after normal office hours, provided it is before midnight, are regarded as being filed on that day – a useful facility should a company find it has insufficient time otherwise to comply with the filing requirements to avoid being fined.

The service

Information on CH requirements and data available is freely available and includes:

I   Guidance notes: user-friendly booklets are available on the following topics:

Formation
Company Formation (GBF1)
Company Names (GBF2)
Business Names (GBF3)

Administration and Management
Directors and Secretaries Guide (GBA1)
Annual Return (GBA2)
Accounts and Accounting Reference Date (GBA3)
Auditors (GBA4)
Late Filing Penalties (GBA5)
Share Capital and Prospectuses (GBA6)
Resolutions (GBA7)
Company Charges and Mortgages (GBA8)
Company Charges (Scotland) (GBA8(S))
Flat Management Companies (GBA9)
Dormant Accounts (GBA10)
Late Filing Penalties: Appeals (GBA11)

Winding up
Liquidation and Insolvency (GBW1)
Liquidation and Insolvency (Scotland) (GBW1(S))
Strike-off, Dissolution and Restoration (GBW2) and
Strike-off, Dissolution and Restoration (Scotland) (GBW2(S)).

2   CH's *Monitor* is a subscription service which enables subscribers to nominate certain companies in which they are interested so that each time an item is filed in respect of such companies, they are automatically sent a copy. As added security, a company could include its own

name on the list to act as a check that only items that it files update the record.

3 CH's *Direct* is another subscription service which enables subscribers who wish to obtain information on any company on a regular basis to do so at any time by direct access. The charges are deducted from a float paid in advance to the Registrar.

4 *WebCHeck* is a web-based service which enables those paying by credit card to access information on companies electronically and virtually instantaneously. It differs from CH *Direct* in that it is provided for those who require such information on an occasional basis.

5 *'Scan on demand'*. Since 1995 all company data has been reconstituted in virtual format by CH and is available on demand. Earlier records are progressively being reconstituted in virtual format. Where this has not taken place records are available on microfiche. Until all files are available electronically (which is currently an ongoing undertaking), CH operates a service whereby copies of data not available in virtual format can be requested electronically, accessed and scanned and then made available (on an individual basis) electronically.

6 *Register* is a journal for CH customers which is available free to those wishing to add their names to the mailing list. It is normally published two or three times a year (although on a somewhat irregular basis), and features the latest comment on and guidance to changes, as well as new and proposed legislation, notification of fees, etc. By going to the CH website and to the mailing list for *Register,* readers can add their names to the list to receive a copy of future issues. Except in special circumstances *Register* will now only be supplied in electronic format.

7 CH *PROOF,* which stands for PROtected Online Filing facility. Companies which sign up to this service commit themselves to file all documents electronically (although of course only around 20 forms can be filed electronically at present) and thus any paper documents (if, for example, filed by fraudsters to try and 'hijack' the company) would be rejected. Details of the *PROOF* system can be found on the CH website.

8 CD-rom. Every month CH produces a CD-rom (available on application to CH) containing details of all the active companies on the register, as well as those in liquidation, in receivership. In addition, details of all companies dissolved, struck off, etc., in the previous 12 months are included. The information includes the name, number and address of the company and its type, its year end or accounting reference date (ARD), dates of the latest annual return and accounts.

9 General information, which normally includes information on most of the foregoing plus (when appropriate) a copy of the CH annual report, promotional material etc. This is available either by phone or through the CH website.

Filing requirements

All data (ultimately held by CH in a computerised format) is subject to two requirements, to be filed:

- on or before time; and
- in an appropriate format.

Documents must be submitted:

- showing the company's registered number;
- on plain white paper between 80 and 100 gsm weight (or else of a background density not greater than 0.3);
- on matt paper;
- using size A4;
- using black ink;
- with clear legible writing of uniform density or in printed format (but not on a dot matrix printer);
- letters must not be smaller than 1.8 mm, with a line width of not less than 0.25 mm;
- with a margin all round not less than 10 mm wide.

Documents submitted other than in the above formats will be rejected. Thus listed PLCs which normally produce a glossy promotionally orientated annual report must also produce an alternative black and white document for filing – the glossy version is not acceptable.

Filing

Before a company can be entered on the Register, form IN01 plus certain information and data (see INCORPORATION) must be filed with the Registrar who, assuming all is in order, will issue a certificate of incorporation bearing the company number (a number which is never changed and never reused, even after the company to which it was allocated has been wound up etc.). Hard copy forms, returns etc., can be sent by post or delivered by hand to each office. The majority of items are still submitted to CH via post or via the British Document Exchange service. However, companies can file an increasing number of forms electronically. Those wishing to file electronically must apply to CH to obtain an authorisation code and a user password which must be used for each filing. Hitherto the forms have been referred to by numbers corresponding to the sections in the Act to which they refer, but during the implementation period of CA06 all the forms have been redesigned. In future they will be referred to by their subject matter rather than by number (although the Act's section number will still appear on each). See FORMS.

Although the intent of CH is to have all forms capable of being filed electronically, currently fewer than 20 can be so filed, namely:

- return of allotment of shares (88(2) – new form SH01);
- change of accounting reference period (225 – AA01);
- change of registered office (287 – AD01);
- appointment, change and termination of director (288a, b, c – AP01, AP02, CH01, CH02, TM01);
- appointment, change and termination of secretary (288a, b, c – AP03, AP04, CH03, CH04, TM02); and
- annual return (363 – AR01).

In addition it is possible to electronically file audit-exempt accounts and dormant company accounts (using form DCA).

Receipt

If filing by posting or delivering hard copy documents (i.e. not using the electronic process where there is an automatic receipt via e-mail), apart from the company registry in Belfast, CH no longer issues a receipt for every document received. Since it is advisable to be able to evidence receipt (in case of later challenge regarding late or non-filing), either the name of the subject company should be added to the Monitoring service referred to above, or a covering letter in duplicate should be sent with each item filed. The original letter should request that the Registrar receipts the copy letter and returns it. The Registrar is prepared to do this (by affixing a bar code sticker to the copy letter) provided a stamped return envelope is provided. Alternatively the Registrar can provide blank forms POST 31 for similar processing or can simply affix the bar code to a duplicate copy of the form itself.

Much of the data required to be filed is subject to time limits, with fines for breaching such limits and/or non-compliance. There are at least four separate filing time limits:

- most forms must be filed within 14 days;
- certain ordinary resolutions (i.e. increasing the share capital, authorising the directors to allot shares, authorising a voluntarily winding-up and revoking an elective resolution) as well as all special and extraordinary RESOLUTIONS must be filed within 15 days;
- details of charges must be filed within 21 days (if not, the charge cannot be filed and the company will have to apply to the court to explain the reason for the delay);
- details of new shares issued (but not existing shares being transferred or transmitted), and the annual return must be filed within 28 days.

It was suggested during the consultation process that led to CA06, that these differing limits be rationalised, but this was not done. It may be simpler to

Example	Letter to Registrar requesting receipt for item filed

LETTERHEAD

Registrar of Companies

Crown Way, Maindy

Cardiff CF4 3UZ

Dear Sir

A Bloggs & Co. Ltd Reg. Number 12345678987

I enclose form [number, in the following case AP01] relating to [specify subject, e.g. in this case, 'the appointment of an additional director to this company's board of directors'].

Kindly acknowledge receipt by signing and returning the attached copy letter. A stamped addressed return envelope is attached.

Yours faithfully

J. Bloggs

Secretary

Enc. Copy letter

Form [number]

Reply paid return envelope

[On copy in addition to the above wording]

I acknowledge receipt of the document referred to above.

Signed ....

Registrar of Companies

assume that all items require 14 days filing which is the shortest period and saves needing to remember the others.

Although such fines for late filing often comprise both an initial fine and an additional daily default fine, fines for late filing most of the forms are rarely applied. However careful attention is needed to ensure that the accounts and the annual return (see below) are filed on time, since any breach will normally generate a fine. Directors and company secretaries responsible can also be subject to personal fines for late filing, whilst under s. 3 of the Company Directors Disqualification Act 1986, those responsible for (amongst other offences) *'persistent late filing'* at CH can be disqualified from office and from acting as a company officer (of all companies, not just the one in respect of which there has been a breach).

Accounts

Although smaller and dormant companies can claim exemption from having their accounts audited, they in common with all other companies are required to file their accounts with the Registrar. For accounts in respect of all accounting periods commencing after April 2008, LTDs must file within nine months of their accounting reference date (ARD – see FINANCIAL YEAR END) and PLCs within six months of their ARD. A late filing penalty is applied to the company if accounts are filed late – and CH simply issues an invoice for payment to the registered office of the company. If the delay is:

- between one day and one month late for LTDs the penalty is £150 (PLCs, £750);
- more than one but less than three months late, the penalty is £375 (PLCs £1,500);
- more than three but less than six months late, the penalty is £750 (PLCs £3,000);
- more than six months late the penalty is £1,500 (PLCs £7,500).

It is understood that these figures are to be doubled in 2010 if the late filing is repeated.

The Registrar adopts a very strict approach to the time limits. However, if it is the first time a company has late-filed and the delay is not more than three days, the penalty may be waived. If the accounts were filed in time but had to be returned for amendment, then provided the corrected accounts are returned within 14 days the penalty may be waived. In addition to the late filing penalty on the company, individuals responsible may be made subject to personal fines in the criminal court (i.e. resulting in them having a criminal record) and the Registrar may take action to strike the company off the Register. If the company is subsequently restored to the Register, penalties may be required in respect of the late (or non-) filing of data during the period the company was 'off the register'.

If there are exceptional difficulties in filing the accounts by the due date, providing CH is contacted before the deadline for filing, it may be possible to obtain an extension. If this is carried out by telephone it would be advisable to record all the details including the date and time of the call in a letter or e-mail to CH. All calls to CH are recorded and kept for a year.

Appeal

If a company feels that a fine has been misapplied (or has any other complaint against a CH procedure – or member of staff etc.) it can lodge details with the resident CH adjudicator at the CH office. A report on the previous year's appeals and complaints is provided by the Adjudicator in *Register*.

Dormant companies accounts

A company which has not traded (i.e. has had *'no significant accounting trans-actions'*) within the year being reported on, can claim exemption from audit (by passing a special resolution exempting itself from appointing auditors) and need only file with CH an abbreviated balance sheet and notes (i.e. there is no requirement to file a profit and loss account or a directors' report, although the latter must be sent to the members). If the dormant company does not wish to prepare a set of accounts there is a simplified process for filing account details with CH. Thus form DCA can be completed, although the Registrar recommends that this form should only be used where the company has never traded and should not be used for companies which have become dormant having previously traded.

Filing requirements re other organisations

In addition to the requirements set out above mainly relating to LTDs (including companies limited by guarantee which, subject to certain conditions, can apply to be excused the requirement to include the word 'limited' in their name) and PLCs, a number of other organisations are required to file data with the Registrar.

(a) *Unlimited liability companies.* The main reason for limited liability companies being required to file their accounts is (or at least the theory is) to permit those who have advanced credit to the company access to its financial details to check, for example, the likelihood of their invoices being paid. Unlimited companies do not limit the liability of their members or shareholders and thus, since the creditors would be able to sue the members personally for payment of outstanding accounts, they are relieved from filing accounts, although they are still required to make all other returns. If however an unlimited company is part of a group or has associated companies, it is still obliged to file its accounts.

(b) *Oversea companies.* If a company, incorporated outside Great Britain, establishes a place of business within Great Britain it comes under the provisions of ss. 1046 to 1059 of CA06 (formerly ss. 691-703 CA85) and is required to file similar information to that set out above for LTDs and PLCs and to provide translations if the accounts have been prepared in a foreign language.

(c) *European Economic Interest Groupings* (EEIGs). Since 1985 mainly smaller operations within the European Community have been able to form EEIGs to develop their activities and increase profits by combining resources and services. EEIGs must be based within a member country of the EU but can be formed without a share capital. They are thus regarded in terms of trading vehicles as partnerships. EEIGs must register with the member state within which they operate and thus, in the UK, come under the jurisdiction of the Registrar of Companies which provides customised filing forms.

(d) *Limited liability partnerships* (LLP*)*. Under the Limited Liability Partnerships Act, partnerships have since 2001 been able to incorporate and gain the benefit of limiting the liability of the partners. An LLP is a hybrid – it is neither a true partnership (where the partners have unlimited liability) nor a company. It is not required to have a secretary, although someone will need to undertake the compliance work which is similar to that required of a company. CH acts as the repository for required filing on behalf of these organisations and there are various standard forms for use by them. The fines for late filing of accounts of LLPs are the same as those set out above for companies. There are similar guidance booklets for LLPs regarding the interface with CH to those referred to above for companies.

(e) *Societas Europaea* (SE). EU legislation created a legal framework for a new form of company – an SE – which is available to commercial companies with operations in more than one EU country. It must have a minimum share capital of €120,000. The forms applicable to this type of company are available from the Registrar.

Form provision

All the FORMS used for filing data are freely available from CH and many can be downloaded from the CH website. Care needs to be taken if keeping stocks of forms since (if a form has been updated), although the Registrar will accept an old version for a year after its replacement, any old forms submitted after that anniversary will be returned with a request to use the latest version. This of course is a particularly apposite warning as a result of CA06 being introduced, since the forms (used since 1985) have been/are being changed. In addition the 'titles' of the forms (or the number by which historically they are known) are no longer used: the forms now have an abbreviation of the substance of the form as their titles.

Routine filing matters

A company is required to prepare an ANNUAL RETURN made up to the anniversary of its incorporation and to file it within 28 days of that 'return date'. Thereafter the company must make subsequent returns to dates no later than the anniversaries of previous 'return dates', and file such returns within 28 days of those dates. The return date can be brought forward before the anniversary of the previous return – but not deferred.

For companies filing electronically, the procedure is that the Registrar generates an annual return (form AR01) in accordance with s. 854 CA06 (formerly s. 363 CA85) from the data in the records and transmits it to the company with a covering letter indicating the date to which it must be made up and by which it must be filed. The company can simply amend any out-of-date data and send the return back. In amending the data in the return the company may be indicating to the Registrar that it has failed to advise such changes previously.

However companies wishing to file hard copy have to request a blank return form and complete all the details themselves. The aim is to encourage companies to file electronically.

The filing fee is £15 (or £30 if filing hard copy). Around a third of all hard copy annual returns have to be rejected and returned because they are unsigned and/or are not accompanied by a cheque or contain incorrect information. In around 3,000 cases each year the Registrar claims to receive cheques without the return and, in some cases, completely empty envelopes. Cheques should bear the company registration number of the subject company on their reverse. This is particularly important where the cheque is drawn on an account other than one in the company's name. There is no longer a requirement to insert the names of other companies of which directors of the subject company have been directors during the previous five years. This information is available to the Registrar from CH's own records.

The arrangement to obtain a receipt (see above) should be followed, although in this case the paid cheque will itself be evidence of receipt. Alternatively (for example when it wishes to bring forward the date of the next return and did not notify this on the previous return) the company can obtain a blank form from the Registrar and complete it. If this occurs, then as well as the points made above, companies should ensure that the directors' names are inserted in alphabetical order and that the correct years of birth are inserted (some compilers insert the current year!).

Failure to file the annual return can involve those responsible being fined, being given a criminal record and can even involve the company being struck off the register – all as is stated in the Registrar's covering letter sent with the return.

Non-form filing

As well as the forms referred to above which must be filed, companies are also required to file:

- details of their constitution (the memorandum and articles) and any changes thereto. Such changes will normally require Special Resolutions which will also need to be filed. It will not be possible to alter the memorandum of a company formed under CA06.

- certain ordinary RESOLUTIONS. The following resolutions must be filed within 15 days: those that authorise:
  - an increase in the authorised share capital;
  - the directors to allot shares; and
  - a voluntary winding-up of the company; or
  - revoke an elective resolution (although to a large extent such resolutions are effectively rendered unnecessary by CA06);
- special resolutions and extraordinary resolutions (although again the latter are effectively rendered obsolete).

Format of resolution for filing

The following is a draft of the format that would be acceptable to the Registrar.

Example	Wording of resolution for filing at Companies House
	Company Name Registered number [12345678987] Ordinary/Special/[Extraordinary] Resolution(s)* of [Company Name] At a general meeting of the members of the above-named company duly convened and held on [date] at [time] at the registered office of the company [address], the following resolution(s) was/were* duly Passed: THAT....[detail] Signed................. Director/Secretary * Date.................... * delete as applicable

Penalties

In 2008 CH imposed just under £55 million in fines and filing penalties for late filing, and states that each year:

- 40 per cent of companies file their annual returns late;
- 28 per cent of returns contain incorrect information; and
- 70 per cent of accounts are rejected.

Re-registration

INTRODUCTION

There are just under three million LTDs but only around 25,000 PLCs (of which fewer than 3,000 in total are listed on either the main market or the Alternative Investment Market of the Stock Exchange). Most companies retain their original status throughout their life. A small proportion of LTDs, however, become PLCs and an even smaller proportion gain access to the capital market and 'go public' by applying for a Stock Exchange listing or quotation, which is achieved by making at least 30 per cent of their shares available to the public. In floating its shares on the Stock Exchange, a company makes itself liable to the additional rules and requirements of the Exchange listing agreement, as well as to tighter requirements regarding disclosure of information etc. A tiny number of listed or unlisted PLCs 'go private' (i.e. revert to being an LTD). Many LTDs re-register as unlisted or unquoted PLCs simply to gain increased prestige, the letters PLC at the end of the company's name being perceived as indicative of greater size, strength and reliability (although the credit crunch which has brought many household name PLCs to their knees – or worse – may have done something to erode this concept).

Private to public

To re-register an LTD as an unlisted PLC (see ss. 90–96 CA06), the following steps must be taken:

1   The company must have an issued share capital of £50,000, of which 25 per cent or more must be paid up in cash. If there is insufficient capital then the members must first pass an ordinary resolution (which must be lodged with CH within 15 days) increasing the authorised and issued capital.
2   The company must pass a special RESOLUTION, which could be a WRITTEN resolution, stating that it wishes to re-register as a PLC.
3   It must alter its MEMORANDUM and ARTICLES accordingly. To do this it must change its NAME so that it ends 'public limited company' (or 'plc', 'Plc', or 'PLC' (or, if it is a Welsh plc, the initials, in similar variant forms, are CCC, standing for Cwmni Cyfyngedig Cyhoeddus), instead of 'limited' (or 'Ltd' or LTD'), insert a statement that it is to be a PLC, and remove any restrictions (e.g. on the directors' right to refuse a share transfer) that are incompatible with PLC status.

4 If it does not have a company secretary it must appoint one.
5 A copy of the change of name Resolution must be filed with the Registrar within 15 days of it being passed, together with:
   - a printed copy of the amended memorandum and articles;
   - an auditors' statement regarding an accompanying balance sheet which must not be more than six months old, reflecting the tighter timetable for filing of PLCs' accounts, and must bear an unqualified auditors' report and show that net assets exceed the paid-up share capital and reserves;
   - if part of the paid-up capital is represented by a consideration other than cash, the company must obtain and submit an expert's opinion on its value;
   - the appropriate fee.
6 The Registrar will then issue a certificate of re-registration in the name of the company as a PLC.

Public to private

To re-register a PLC as an LTD (see CA06 ss. 97-101), the following steps must be taken:

1 Pass a special resolution (which could be written), resolving that the company is to be an LTD, thus changing the name from ending PLC to LTD.
2 Alter the name stated in the memorandum and articles of association.
3 Send to CH (within 15 days) a copy of the change of name special resolution and the altered memorandum and articles.

There follows a 28-day delay to allow time for any minority shareholder who wishes to apply for cancellation of the resolution. However if all members of the company endorse the special resolution, the 28-day period can be waived. The Registrar then issues a certificate of re-registration in the new LTD status and name.

Unlimited companies

An LTD can re-register as an unlimited company (see CA06 ss. 102-104), an unlimited company can be re-registered as an LTD (see CA06 ss. 105-108), and a PLC can become an unlimited company (see CA06 ss. 109-111).

Resolutions

INTRODUCTION

Control of companies is exercised ultimately by its members in general meetings, or by means of WRITTEN RESOLUTIONS if it is more convenient and/or economic to obtain their agreement without convening a meeting. There are several types of resolutions: ordinary, ordinary with special notice (i.e. additional requirements and details required if proposing the removal of a director or auditor), extraordinary (which have to some extent been rendered obsolete under CA06), and special. Whilst normally resolutions are initiated by the directors, it is possible for an (extraordinary) GENERAL MEETING to be required to be convened by the members to consider a resolution that they wish to propose.

Ordinary

Any resolution which is not special (or extraordinary) is 'ordinary'. Ordinary resolutions are used to obtain approval by members in general meeting by means of a simple majority of the votes that are actually cast. The votes that are not cast either in person or by proxy are effectively disenfranchised – but that is the choice of the holder in deciding not to make their views known. The following ordinary resolutions are required to be filed with the Registrar of Companies within 15 days of being passed:

- for a company with a share capital, any resolution increasing it (since the effect of increasing the share capital means a change to the MEMORANDUM of the company – although for companies formed under CA06 this will cease to be a requirement as there is no necessity for them to state an 'authorised share capital');
- a resolution authorising the directors to allot shares (this too will become unnecessary for companies formed under CA06, although the directors may need to gain permission from the members if that is required in the company's articles);
- a resolution voluntarily winding up the company; and
- a resolution revoking an elective resolution (again effectively rendered unnecessary under CA06).

'Simple majority' means a majority of the votes that are actually cast either in person or by proxy. Hence if only some of the votes are cast then an ordinary resolution is passed if 50 per cent plus one of those cast, are in favour.

Special notice (of an ordinary resolution)

Certain ordinary resolutions require special notice being given to the members. Special notice (that is at least 21 days' notice with full details of the proposal and any objections or representations of the other party(ies)) is required for:

- any resolution relating to an auditor other than for his re-election or to settle his remuneration; and
- the removal of a director (see DIRECTORS: REMOVAL).

Special

Special resolutions are required:

- to alter the objects clause;
- to alter the articles;
- to change the name of the company;
- to RE-REGISTER an LTD as a PLC, an unlimited company as an LTD or a PLC as an LTD;
- to disapply any pre-emption rights of shareholders (i.e. a right of pre-emption means that if additional shares are issued existing shareholders have the right of first refusal on subscribing for those shares in proportion that their shares bear to the total);
- to authorise the purchase by the company of its own shares or the provision of assistance to allow purchase of its own shares. The Companies (Acquisition of Own Shares) (Treasury Shares) Regulations 2003 (which is only applicable to PLCs) relaxed the former rules regarding a company purchasing its own shares. A company can purchase (out of distributable profits) a maximum of 10 per cent of its issued share capital. The shares purchased are held 'in treasury', not cancelled (since this would lead to a reduction of capital which is subject to separate rules – see below) but held in the company's own name. No voting or dividend rights attach to shares held in treasury. This may be a simple method of acquiring shares for later use (for example in an employee share scheme) rather than needing to issue more shares.
- to reduce the company's share capital. For a PLC, a resolution to reduce share capital can normally only be effected with the approval of the court, and provided the articles allow for it (if they do not the articles must be changed first). The reduction is only effective when the

Registrar of Companies has issued a certificate to this effect. However, under CA06 (s. 943) an LTD can reduce its share capital by special resolution and either going to court or the directors swearing a solvency certificate (stating under all the directors' names and the date) that each of the directors has formed the opinion that there are no grounds on which the company could be found to be unable to pay its debts for the year ahead, or, if the winding up of the company is expected to commence within a year, that the company will be able to pay its debts. (Bearing in mind the current economic situation, it would not be surprising if in such circumstances directors would prefer to go to court, bearing in mind that a great deal – which might be virtually impossible to foresee – can happen in the year following them swearing such a certificate);

- for any resolution relating to business stated in the articles to require a special resolution.

Under CA06, the notice required for special resolutions can be reduced from 21 to 14 days' notice (unless a company's articles specify the longer period). The approval of 75 per cent of the votes cast in person or by proxy is required.

Copies of all special resolutions must be filed with the Registrar within 15 days of the date of the resolution.

Extraordinary

An extraordinary resolution is needed to resolve:

- any matter stated by the company's articles to require an extraordinary resolution;
- that a company cannot continue in business by reason of its liabilities and should be wound up;
- to grant certain powers to the liquidator in a members' voluntary winding up;
- that assets of the company in a winding up can be distributed to the members *in specie*.

Extraordinary resolutions require 14 days' notice and the approval of at least 75 per cent of the votes cast by members present in person or by proxy. However, since all resolutions now require 14 days' notice there is no longer any difference between the requirements for special and extraordinary resolutions, both of which must be filed with the Registrar within 15 days.

Somewhat confusingly, CA06 ignores extraordinary resolutions, assuming that in their place special resolutions will be used. However a company should refer to its articles since if they stipulate certain business must be passed *'by an extraordinary resolution'*, this should be the manner of resolving the matter. Legal advice might usefully be taken. (Actually it might have been better to lose the description 'special resolutions', thus leaving ordinary resolutions, ordinary resolutions with special notice and extraordinary resolutions, and avoiding the understandable confusion between ordinary resolutions needing special notice, and special resolutions, which have nothing to do with each other!)

Wording

Where it is necessary to frame the wording for a resolution relating to non-routine items, legal advice may best be sought. Generally, however, the wording is straightforward although care should be taken to ensure the operative date of the resolution is made clear. Thus it may be better, rather than resolving:

> *'That the report of the directors and the annual accounts for the year ended 30th June 2XXX, together with the Balance sheet as at that date are accepted',*

to word the resolution:

> *'That the report of the directors and the annual accounts for the year ended 30th June 2XXX, together with the Balance sheet as at that date be and they are hereby accepted'.*

The word *'hereby'* indicates that the resolution was passed on and became effective on that date. However with resolutions where the operative date is dependent on the actions of some third party (for example, the change of the company name is not effective until the date of the certificate of incorporation on change of name issued by the Registrar), the wording might be:

> *'That the name of the company be changed from ANY COMPANY LTD to ANY OTHER COMPANY LIMITED and that the new name be operative from the date stipulated by the Registrar of Companies'.*

Filing with the Registrar

As noted above, several ordinary resolutions as well as all special and extraordinary resolutions must be filed with the Registrar. In addition the following must also be filed:

- any resolution passed unanimously which would otherwise have been a special resolution;
- any resolution passed unanimously by a class of shareholder which would have required a specified majority; and
- any resolution directed by the Secretary of State requiring the directors to change the company name to include the word 'limited'.

The following format should be acceptable at CH. All items filed at CH must be 'black on white paper'.

Example	Suggested wording for filing at CH
	SPECIAL RESOLUTION ON CHANGE OF NAME
	Companies Act [1985] or (2006]
	Company 00123456789 ANY COMPANY LTD
	At an [Extraordinary] General Meeting of members of the above-named company, duly convened and held at [address, usually the registered office] on [date] the following SPECIAL RESOLUTION was passed:
	THAT the name of the company be changed to ANY OTHER COMPANY LTD
	Signed.............................Secretary [Date...............]

Resurrection of companies

INTRODUCTION

If a claimant wishes to lodge a liability claim against a company that is no longer on the active register at CH, it is possible, so that the action can be defended, for a defunct company to be resurrected by authority of the court. The previous time limit was two years (although the court could extend this), but ss. 1024 and 1030 extend this to six years. However, companies that were defunct before 16th November 1969 (i.e. 20 years before the date when the original rule regarding resurrection came into force) cannot be resurrected.

Action

The actions that could generate application to the court for resurrection are those concerned with claims for damages in respect of personal injuries or claims under the Fatal Injuries Act 1976 or Damages (Scotland) Act 1976, and would mainly be generated by application from or on behalf of former employees who, for example, have become subject to a condition which surfaced after the company was removed from the register but which it is alleged can be proved to have originated prior to that date. For example, it can take many years for diseases caused by industrial activity (e.g. mesothelioma, caused by inhaling asbestos fibres) to manifest themselves. If it is alleged that the condition was caused by the company whilst it was active but is now defunct, the company can be resurrected to face the claim brought by the injured party.

Administration

Shareholders or guarantors allowing their companies, or parent companies allowing their subsidiaries, to be struck off should ensure they keep details of insurers, as well as the various records of the defunct company in case such an action is brought in accordance with this relaxation. It may be prudent to keep (securely) company statutory books, etc., for 'life of the company' plus (say) 20 years (since the court has powers to extend the period during which resuscitation can take place). There are now a number of commercial organisations providing safekeeping facilities.

Certificates of employers' liability insurance

The principle of allowing company resurrection to face liability claims flows from the realisation (as above) that some claims for liability may not arise for some time after they originated. From 1999 the annual certificates of employers' liability insurance were required to be kept for 40 years, and had to be displayed at every place of work. In October 2008, however, the requirement on a company to keep these certificates (somewhat oddly) was abandoned, whilst the obligation to display the annual certificates was relaxed provided the details were kept electronically on a system to which every employee had access. Employers who have not kept such certificates may be best advised to apply to their insurers over the period since January 1999 (when the requirement first came into operation) and to ask for copies of the certificates or other evidence of cover to complete their records until October 2008, and it might be prudent, despite the relaxation, to continue to keep a copy of each future certificate – possibly with the statutory books.

Risk management

INTRODUCTION

As a part of the continuing move to improve CORPORATE GOVERNANCE of listed PLCs, the Turnbull Committee (the last of six committees whose recommendations eventually led to the creation of the Combined Code of Corporate Governance) was commissioned to consider ways in which directors should take action to protect their company's assets and business. Although there is a presumption under company law that directors (other than directors of charities) should take risks in order to drive the company forward, they must always act (and be seen to act) in the best interests of the members or shareholders. This should include taking adequate steps to preserve and protect the assets of the business, e.g. the creation of contingency and crisis plans. Inevitably, many companies will suffer loss as a result of incidents affecting their businesses and the generation of plans to assist them in coping with such events seems entirely sensible – even though a recent report by accountants Deloitte and Touche found that 30 per cent of UK companies had no formal disaster plan. Directors of LTDs are of course responsible to their members or shareholders for the protection of their assets in exactly the same way as directors of listed PLCs and thus (even though they are not subject to corporate governance requirements) they too need to be proactive to protect their companies from risk – particularly if they have shareholders who are not board members.

The Turnbull recommendations

The report of the Turnbull Committee states that:

- internal risk control should be embedded in the company processes. It should not be seen as a separate exercise and for this reason the board should regularly review contingency and disaster plans;
- risk control should be responsive to changing circumstances in particular related to new risk areas;
- companies should customise their own plans and regularly update them.

Although only listed PLCs are required to comply (or state why they have not complied) with the Turnbull principles (as part of their adherence to the Combined Code of Corporate Governance), they have a validity which applies to all companies. This is particularly so in companies where there are shareholders who are not directors, since they have every right to expect the directors (i.e. their appointees) to protect the assets they jointly own – and to hold them responsible if they fail to do so because of their alleged negligence. The requirements can be summarised as:

- allocating responsibility to a board member;
- giving the requirement a priority;
- involving management at all levels;
- identifying clear objectives and satisfying them;
- identifying all risk areas and prioritising the risks so identified;
- establishing risk management and reduction programmes and procedures;
- regularly updating the detail (considering as part of this process all new risks and threats).

Full details of the report (which concludes with a 'Twenty Questions'-type checklist) are available from the Institute of Chartered Accountants in England and Wales, PO Box 433, Moorgate Place, London, EC2P 2BJ, or via their website www.icaew.co.uk/internalcontrol.

Turnbull updated

The recommendations of the Turnbull Committee have been revised, and now require boards to:

- review on a continuing basis their application of the guidance and regard and treat the internal control statement as an opportunity to inform their shareholders how they manage risk and internal control;
- apply the same standard of care when reviewing the effectiveness of internal control, as when exercising the directors' general duties;
- confirm in the annual report that necessary action has been or is being taken to remedy any significant failings or weaknesses identified from their review of the effectiveness of the internal control system;
- include within the annual report such information as considered necessary to help shareholders understand the main features of the risk management processes and system of internal control.

Given the recent failure (or prevention of failure only by an influx of public monies) of a number of PLC banks and financial institutions, one has to wonder where were the people applying the Turnbull guidelines? We know now that at least one risk manager was trying to flag up problems, and the reaction of his superiors was to dismiss him. It is exactly that kind of attitude that the corporate governance movement has been trying to eradicate. Presumably more than one shareholder who lost out must have wondered whether there is a case for a derivative claim against the directors who failed to listen to such warnings?

Media interest

Many disasters generate media interest and the company must be prepared to provide some information should the media require updating. In BRIEFING THE CHAIRMAN: GENERAL AND MEDIA, the question of relationships with the media is examined on the assumption that normally the chairman will be the spokesperson for the company. It may be, however, that in the event of a crisis, because the chairman is not available, someone else, perhaps the company secretary, has to deal with the initial enquiry.

Whilst briefing the media on the more mundane aspects of company performance may be relatively easy, dealing with such interest in the aftermath of a calamity or disaster (particularly if there has been a personal injury or death) may pose considerable problems. These can be tackled most effectively and efficiently if reactions are based on contingency planning. Plans, resulting from an anticipation of a disaster, have the advantage that lengthy, calm advance thought can be given to alternative tactics and reactions, without the massive time pressure for reaction and action that the incidence of disaster causes. In addition, consideration of alternative actions in the event of disaster may suggest beneficial changes in current operations. Obviously if it is to be of value, such planning must be both initially comprehensive and regularly updated.

Reaction planning

The following checklist assumes a major and unexpected disaster has befallen the company and that the media are pressing for comment, and that the chairman is not available.

CHECKLIST   Reaction planning

Background: Initial contact will usually be by telephone. A person should be nominated, possibly the company secretary, though there should always be one or two back-up personnel to handle initial queries if the spokesperson is not available.

✓ Keep calm and listen to exactly what the inquirer is asking.

✓ Make notes of, or record (in which case the caller should be told that the call is being recorded), the call content, time, the caller's name, position and media represented, the caller's telephone number and location.

✓ Do not respond to questions, comments, observations – simply make notes as set out above and state that by a (stated) time someone will respond either in a press release or by telephone, and so on.

✓ Do not allow yourself to become flustered by (or comment on) indications of deadlines, insistence on immediate response, outrageous accusations, or innuendo.

✓ By the time promised, except in extreme cases not more than an hour later ensure someone does ring the caller back with comments.

✓ Keep responses, press statements, and so on, short. Embroidery can both offset the 'punch effect' and provide other 'angles' from which the reporter can come back at the author.

✓ Provide a contact name/number.

✓ Should such contact be used then the above guidelines should be applied. If necessary the spokesperson should ring back after time for thought.

✓ If media releases are used, these need to be drafted carefully so that:

- the essential features of the news to be reported are set out in the first (relatively brief) paragraph;
- the news is of substance and presented concisely and clearly;
- the content provides quotable quotes from named authorities; and
- the data specifies a realistic release date and gives an in-house contact and telephone number.

Shareholder action

Failing to devise disaster or contingency plans can be costly. Ultimately, shareholders could sue the directors for a breach of the requirement to act in their best interests. Under CA06, it has been made easier for a shareholder who believes that the company has suffered loss because of the activity(ies) (defined as *an actual or proposed act or omission involving negligence, default, breach of duty or breach of trust*) of a director, to initiate legal action (a 'DERIVATIVE' claim) against the director on the company's behalf. If such a claim is successful, it is the company (not the shareholder initiating the action) that benefits. This is a worrying development, since it changes the previous situation whereby a director could not be liable for making a 'wrong' decision, provided it was made in good faith, to one where the director could be held liable for an act (or omission) even if it was made in good faith and the person taking the decision does not benefit from that decision (i.e. there was no vested interest). CA06 places obligations on directors, not only to act in the best interests of the shareholders and to take account of the interests of their employees (as at present), but also to consider the impact of the company's operations on the environment and the community at large, and the desirability of the company maintaining a reputation for high standards of business conduct.

Insurers are increasingly enquiring about individual insureds' disaster recovery planning, the answers to which enquiries could well be a factor in calculating premium costs. Many organisations – particularly those operating in the financial services sector – in London and other major centres now keep 'ghost offices' available for activation in the event that their main office is subject to an event such as terrorist activity or simply being denied access to the site.

An example of the approach may be helpful. The following case study is based upon a genuine company and the potential problems that it identified.

Case study	Being prepared pays dividends

Gee Publishing formerly occupied a five-storey building next to Canary Wharf in part of London's rejuvenated docklands. One Thursday in February 1996, I delivered the final manuscript of my (then) latest employment law loose-leaf manual to Gee's offices. 24 hours later I saw on television, the same office devastated by one of the largest IRA bombs ever exploded on the mainland. Since the previously blue glass-fronted but now wrecked building was designated a crime scene by the police, Gee were not allowed back into the building (even if only to collect files and papers) for six months. Yet early the following Monday morning I received a phone call from my editor checking that I had another copy of everything passed to her the previous Thursday.

Because of the lessons learned from the bomb which was exploded in Bishopsgate, London, some time earlier, Gee, having realised that being located immediately next to a very recognisable landmark (Canary Wharf) they were vulnerable, had developed a detailed contingency plan. During the weekend the plan had been activated. They had sourced, and relocated to, temporary (now permanent) offices. Whilst inevitably there was disruption and losses of some records etc., a substantial part of the business was up and running without missing a single working day – indeed within one working hour of the bomb. Such instant reaction is only possible if there is a detailed recovery plan – and suitable stand-by facilities, whether that be an office, hard copy records, back-up computer records etc.

Of course the parent company shareholders could not have held Gee's directors responsible for the bomb – but they could have held them responsible for failing to plan on a 'what if' basis so that the business could recover swiftly from just such an event.

Example	Disaster recovery planning

You are the company secretary/administrator of a company producing widgets. Widgets are a high-value product which need careful handling and storage and have a relatively short shelf life. They are sold throughout the UK and there is a growing export market to immediately adjacent European countries. The company occupies three factories (two freehold and one leasehold; one large, two small) as well as a main warehouse (leasehold), plus a number of satellite warehouses supplying retail customers within 24 hours of order.

The production process is partly mechanised but entails a certain amount of manual work, which, since it requires dexterity, means a large proportion of the workforce is female. A shrinking product market has led to a lengthening list of debtors, despite constant chasing by the credit control department and, in addition, the banks are pressurising the organisation to reduce its overdraft. Meanwhile there has been a constant rise in raw material costs and it is proving impossible to pass these on in the form of price increases to the customer – conversely, many are looking for discounts. Formerly a small amount of raw material was derived as a by-product of animal experimentation, but this has not been the case for several years.

Certain anonymous terrorist threats have been made against the company and a number of small incendiary devices have been received via the post at both head office, factory and warehouse.

The board is concerned that its operations could become a target for some serious large-scale terrorist activity and has asked you to prepare a report highlighting areas of weakness and vulnerability, suggesting initiatives that could be taken to defuse the situation and, should such activity occur, to recover the status quo.

Suggested areas of attention (these are not exhaustive but provided only as examples):

Establish the 'worst case' scenario

In this instance, probably the worst case that could occur would be for all productive units to be wiped out simultaneously. This

Example	Disaster recovery planning – *continued*

may be regarded as so unlikely that it can be safely ignored, although animal activists have been able to incapacitate several facilities simultaneously so perhaps increased security at each should be considered. The next worst instance could envisage the main factory being wiped out, followed possibly by the head office being lost, and so on. What do we do?

Research the enemy

Establishing who is likely to be the enemy (whether animate – the activists – or inanimate, in terms of a fire, water, or loss of funds, etc.) and what they need and what their aims are will help establish ways of dealing with the likely threat. For example, if the Animal Liberation Front were suspected, it might be possible to contact them to explain the cessation of the work which seems to be the source of their complaints. If fire is thought to be a serious hazard, it should be remembered that fire needs three factors before if can cause damage – a source of ignition/ heat, raw material and time. If any of these are absent, there should be little threat from such a source – this may be little comfort, bearing in mind that a considerable proportion of fires are started deliberately. Cash flow might be able to be increased if any surplus assets can be identified and liquidated or new customers might only be accepted on a 'pro-forma' (cash up front) basis. Approach landlords of leased premises to see if they would accept rent monthly in advance rather than quarterly; don't agree to 'upwards only' rent reviews; only agree to the length of a lease equivalent to the organisation being able to plan ahead with some degree of confidence, and so on.

Use any advantages

The way this particular group is geographically spread provides an advantage. It has a number of sites and it is extremely unlikely, though not impossible, that all could be hit simultaneously. Assuming there is a multiplicity of sites, the development of flexibility of roles could be addressed, so that if one site is disabled, another can cover, at least temporarily. Conversely, any inter-dependability of sites could be reduced.

Example	Disaster recovery planning – *continued*

Take advice

No one can be expert in all areas. There are experts specialising in this field and their input could be sought. Even though the plan developed may never be used, the examination of procedures and practices may almost amount to a minor process re-engineering survey, generating benefits of immediate use and value.

Examine vulnerability

- Post – institute controls and examination. Arrange for delivery elsewhere than own premises – passing to premises only when opened safely.

- Access – examine security generally (entrances and exits, control, etc.).

- Deliveries – institute letters of authority to ensure access provided only to genuine suppliers.

- Publicity – promote 'clean hands' image, termination of links with animal experimentation.

- Screen employees – check references, institute right of search, control internal access to sensitive areas, maintain records of unsatisfactory employees.

- Increase internal security precautions – fire, explosion, etc. (creation of 'safe' areas).

- Increase anonymity of units.

Consider means of recovery

- Relocation of workforce – difficult in view of nature of employment – consider 'bussing'.

- Possibility of production at warehouses.

- Need to check/circumvent lease restrictions.

- Keep watch on local property market for knowledge of what is available.

Example	Disaster recovery planning – *continued*
	<ul><li>Buy in product/assembly.</li><li>Home working (check security and quality control).</li><li>Media messages and spokesperson.</li><li>Parallel working particularly of computer system (credit control seems especially vulnerable).</li><li>Ghost facilities (i.e. a back-up facility containing regularly updated computer access, tables and chairs, telephones etc., ready at a few minutes notice) for emergency use.</li></ul>And so on.

Employers are required to compile assessments of risks in all aspects of their operations and to make these available (thus they should be both easily accessible and essentially user-friendly) to all those who might be at risk from all activities they undertake. Whilst there is no obligation to remove all risk (which in many cases would probably be impossible), employers must take 'appropriate steps' to reduce the risk to the lowest level that is reasonably practicable. In doing so they need to consider the task, and particularly the employee (and thus their expertise or competency – or lack of same) who is to carry out the task. It has been said that when considering risk assessment, there is an obligation to assume that common sense is entirely lacking.

Case study	Make it idiot-proof
	In *O'Neill v DSG Retail Ltd*, the court stated that when assessing the risk the employer must also take into account that employees might not act with full and proper consideration for their own safety. Risk assessments should therefore be comprehensive and, as far as possible, 'idiot-proof'.

The safety 'buck' stops in the boardroom

Imprudent lending apart, for most companies, risks to the person are likely to generate the greatest potential financial exposure. Increasingly, boards are being held liable where there has been carelessness or negligence. The Health and Safety Executive has suggested that:

- boards should nominate one of their number to be a safety director;
- safety should be a regular item for board discussion (and decision) and, by implication,
- safety considerations should be examined regularly (and every time new systems, procedures etc. are commissioned or are changed);
- the items discussed and the decisions taken should be minuted (if only so that should there be a prosecution this could act as the basis for a defence).

Case studies	Holding the officers and the company responsible
1	In *Rainham Waste Recycling Ltd* a director and his company were both found guilty of a breach of safety law by using an unguarded machine, which resulted in an employee's arm being amputated. The company was fined £25,000 plus £4,000 costs, whilst the director was fined £5,000. In addition, under the Company Directors Disqualification Act, the court disqualified him from acting as a director for five years.
2	In the *Lyme Bay* canoe tragedy case, both company and director were found guilty of manslaughter – the director was jailed for three years whilst the company was fined £60,000.
3	Following an accident in Germany in which a bricklayer fell to his death, a British property developer was fined £6,500, given a five-month suspended jail sentence, and instructed to pay £4,500 to the widow.
4	In a case brought by the Health and Safety Executive regarding the illegal employment of children, a manager was fined £7,500 whilst in addition the employing company was fined £2,000, and its director £4,500, even though they could demonstrate that they had told the manager not to employ under-age children.

→

Case studies	Holding the officers and the company responsible – *continued*

5. In *R v F Howe & Son (Engineers) Ltd,* where the company was held responsible for the electrocution of an employee and was initially fined £48,000 plus £7,500, the Court of Appeal stated: *'some safety offences could be so serious that they could lead to fines being levied at a rate that would bankrupt the company.'* The Court went on to comment that generally the fines for health and safety offences were too low and, where death was involved, this should be reflected in the fine, and urged lower courts to judge how far defendants fell short of the 'reasonably practicable' test and told them they should ignore the size of employers.

6. *Balfour Beatty Civil Engineering* was found responsible for the collapse of tunnels at Heathrow Airport in the mid-1990s. Despite the fact that no one was hurt, the court found that the incident was 'a disgrace' and the company were fined £1.2 million (plus the HSE's £200,000 legal costs) under ss. 2(1) and 3(1) of the Health and Safety at Work Act 1974. In addition a subcontractor, Geoconsult, was fined £500,000 in respect of the same incident.

Increasingly, in various branches of the law, courts are holding employers responsible for the acts of their employees, even where those employees may have broken the rules laid down by the employer.

Case studies	Responsible even when rules are breached

1. In *Jones v Tower Boot* the Court of Appeal held that the company was responsible for employees who branded, taunted and harassed a young black employee, even though they were not 'acting in the course of their employment' (the employer's attempted defence, which previously could be used to escape liability).

2. In *National Rivers Authority v Alfred McAlpine Homes East Ltd* a company was held liable for pollution caused by its employees washing cement into a stream. The court

Case studies	Responsible even when rules are breached – *continued*

regarded the employees who actioned the pollution as acting within the course and scope of their employment, even though they were clearly in breach of instructions issued by their employer.

3 In the long-running court case regarding the supply of ready-mixed concrete (*Re Smith's Concrete Ltd*), the company stated (and proved in court) that they tried to ensure at all times that their employees complied with the law and trading guidelines. The Court of Appeal held that the company could not be liable for the actions of its employees when they wilfully broke such rules and regulations and disobeyed instructions, but this decision was overturned by the House of Lords, which held that a company *was* liable for the acts of its employees even if it had forbidden such acts. The House of Lords also commented that the original fines were too low and imposed fines of £8,000,000 against 17 ready-mixed concrete companies and individual fines of up to £20,000 against individual employees. The judges went on to state that future cases would result in jail sentences.

4 In *R v Rhone Poulenc Rorer*, an engineer went on to the roof of an industrial building. Like many such roofs it was not designed to bear the weight of a human being, and a notice stating the roof was fragile and that 'crawling boards should be used' was displayed. Ignoring this advice he stepped onto the roof, plunged through and was killed. His widow sued the company, whose defence was that because he was an engineer and thus competent and could read, he must have known the risks and therefore they could rely on the notice as their defence. The court stated that they could not rely on a sign – there needed to be practical preventative measures.

Many may think that the courts are asking an impossibility. In the last case study, for instance, couldn't it be argued that the engineer was entirely master of his own destiny? However there are steps an employer could – and currently would – be expected to take. Preparing a risk assessment along the following lines might provide a defence.

Example	Roof work risk assessment

The employer could stipulate that:

1   Roof work is restricted to competent personnel and there would need to be an assessment of competency before permitting a person to work on a roof.

2   The work to be done must be assessed and the dangers identified and minimised or removed. Those that remain must be brought to the attention of those involved and a plan of work prepared.

3   Roof access is only possible via possession of a key, retained by a manager.

4   The manager, when asked for the key, must:
    (a) ensure the person is competent to undertake the work;
    (b) accompany the person to the roof (i.e. not simply hand him the key).

5   Before opening the door, the manager must state that access is only granted on condition that the crawling boards provided are used. (The employer would need to be able to show that these were in good condition and fit for their purpose, to avoid liability.)

6   The manager must instruct the person to put on a full protection harness which, if he did fall through the roof, would prevent him suffering serious injury.

7   The person might even be required before stepping on the roof to sign a statement that all the foregoing had been explained to him.

8   Whilst the roof door was open, the manager might be required to remain there to ensure no other person (unless under the requirements set out above) went onto the roof.

Obviously the manager would not be able to force the employee once on the roof to wear the harness (or to stop him removing it, if donned prior to access) or to use the crawling boards, but should an accident occur in those circumstances it seems likely that the court would feel that the occupier had done as much as they reasonably could have done to protect the person, and thus liability might be avoided – or at least minimised.

(Note: This is an example only – a detailed risk assessment would be needed, guidance to preparing which is available on the HSE website.)

Recent developments

The Health and Safety Executive recently stated that, enforcing authorities should *'prosecute ... individuals ... if they consider that [it] is warranted. In particular they should consider the management chain and the role played by directors and managers and take action against them where the investigation reveals that the offence was committed with their consent or connivance or [is] attributable to neglect on their part. Where possible enforcing authorities should seek the disqualification of directors under the Company Directors Disqualification Act 1986.'*

Nigel Turnbull himself, speaking at the launch of the annual Risk Management Survey, stated: *'Boards should review risk management processes on a monthly process.'* However, according to a recent survey (conducted by the Institute of Chartered Accountants in England & Wales), only 47 per cent of boards review risks monthly, most boards look at the issue once every four or six months and 10 per cent consider it only once a year. The top three general risks identified by finance directors were:

- reputation;
- operations and markets; and
- strategic challenges;

whilst the bottom three they identified were:

- terrorism;
- accounting; and
- non-compliance with rules and regulations.

Ironically, many commentators would argue that the likely incidence of these risks is actually the reverse.

Corporate Manslaughter

The Corporate Manslaughter (in Scotland, Corporate Homicide) Act came into force in April 2008 and created new offences relating to killing or injury effected by corporate bodies. If found culpable, substantial fines (possibly starting at £1 million) would be the penalty. In the event of a death, a company/employer can be held to be guilty if either:

- the way in which its activities were organised amounted to a gross breach of a duty of care owed by it to the deceased; and
- it causes the death of the deceased;

or

- the way in which its activities were managed or organised by its senior management was a substantial element in the breach.

Sanctions include unlimited fines (and even imprisonment), a requirement to remedy a failing and a requirement for the company to publicise the offence in its own annual report (i.e. to 'name and shame').

The Government has stated that employers have no fear of prosecution under this Act where they have 'conscientiously':

- ensured safe working practices (that is, employees are trained and equipment is safely maintained);
- maintained premises safely (e.g. taken adequate fire precautions); and
- complied with health and safety legislation.

And, one might add, provided also that the employer can *prove* that they have 'ensured ..., maintained ..., and complied ...'. Hence safety should be a regular item on the board agenda, whilst using safety folders (i.e. accessible folders containing data detailing all safety requirements, which are widely promulgated throughout the organisation and concerning which all employees are briefed) may be one way of assisting in the provision of safe working practices and demonstrating the company took its responsibilities seriously and protecting the personal position of those in charge.

Reinforcing the above legislation, the Health and Safety (Offences) Act came into effect in January 2009. It:

- raises the maximum fine that can be levied in the lower courts to £20,000;
- allows the cases concerning some offences (currently heard in lower courts) to be heard in higher courts (meaning the penalties can be enhanced);
- allows both lower as well as higher courts to impose a custodial sentence.

Case study	Fines increased
	In *HM Advocate v Munro & Sons (Highland) Ltd*, as a result of faulty securing, a heavy wheeled loader fell off its trailer and flattened the following vehicle, killing a passenger. The contractor pleaded guilty and was fined £5,000. However HM Advocate felt that the penalty was too low and appealed. On appeal the High Court increased the fine to £40,000. Had the Health & Safety (Offences) Act been in force, the penalty could have been even greater.

Driving on company business

Research indicates that each year, five times the numbers of work-related fatalities take place on the roads than in workplaces. A campaign has been launched by the police attempting to reduce the 1,000 fatal crashes each year. There are three million company cars plus around a million privately owned cars used for employers' business on the roads of the UK. The priority is on checking private cars used for company business, on the basis that these are less likely to be maintained properly. The tests are whether the employer carried out basic checks – ensuring the car is regularly and properly serviced and maintained, that there is a valid MOT certificate for any vehicle that is three or more years old, that the driver/vehicle is insured for business use and the driver has a valid driving licence. The Corporate Manslaughter Act makes it easier for the authorities to prosecute for death caused by negligence, which could include requiring employees to drive for too long a time (without a break). It is estimated that around 300 people (i.e. roughly a third of the total) are killed each year simply as a result of drivers falling asleep at the wheel. The use of vehicle folders (required to be carried at all times on all cars used for an employer's business) with contents stipulating legal adherence to the above points, giving guidance on what to do in the event of an accident, maintenance requirements etc., may become essential as a means of proving that the employer took their responsibilities seriously and took 'reasonable' precautions to try and ensure that vehicles being driven on their behalf (and the drivers) were legally compliant in all respects. (The April 2009 budget contained proposals to hold senior accounting officers in 'larger' companies personally responsible if their companies' accounting systems are 'inadequate'.)

INTRODUCTION

The concept of using a seal originated over a thousand years ago, when few people could read or write. If an illiterate person was required to evidence their agreement to a contract, instead of writing their signature, they could impress their signet ring into hot wax at the foot of the document (literally 'making their mark'). Similarly, a company cannot physically sign a document, so its 'signature' can be effected by using a seal bearing its name. The use of hot wax was discontinued some years ago and replaced by adhesive red wafers, but even the wafers have disappeared and nowadays the seal is usually simply impressed directly onto the page. A company is a legal person and, if it adopts a seal, the affixing of its seal acts as the equivalent of the signature of a real person. The use of the seal, evidenced by an entry in a register of seals or sealings which can be inspected by the whole board (for example at a board meeting), is an effective control over and record of the use of the seal and of the commitments entered into by the company and those acting to effect this.

Adopting the seal

Assuming the articles give authority for a seal, one should be obtained bearing the full name of the company. At a board meeting the seal should be produced and a resolution passed adopting it as the common seal of the company. The seal should be impressed on the page alongside the minute. If the company changes its name and wishes to continue using a seal, the process must be repeated with a seal with the new name.

Requirement for use

A deed is a contract under seal and is needed:

- for all freehold property transactions and for all leases that will last three years or more;
- for all sales/purchases of British ships (or shares in such ships);
- for any 'gratuitous promise', i.e. a transaction in which there is no consideration for the value being given; and
- (subject to individual company articles) to confirm the legitimacy of share certificates.

This last requirement can cause problems to a company limited by shares if it decides to dispense with using a seal. It is quite common for articles to state that a share certificate is only a valid document of title if it bears the common seal of the company. If there is no seal, share certificates cannot be validly issued unless the articles are changed – or a seal is adopted.

Sealing procedure

To ensure adequate time is allowed to gain the authority of the board to the item, the following draft procedure should be considered:

1   All documents required to be sealed should be submitted at least two weeks before any critical date.
2   The affixing of the seal can be witnessed by two directors, or a director and the secretary. A company registered in Scotland can have its seal witnessed by one director and a person authorised by the board – usually known as an 'authorised countersignatory' – but this can only be used by companies registered other than in Scotland if it is specifically allowed by the individual company's articles. In fact many large companies that need to undertake a great deal of sealing do take powers to delegate witnessing the seal to officers other than a second director or the company secretary. If documents are to be signed 'as deeds' rather than sealed, then they can only be witnessed by two directors or one director and the company secretary or in Scotland (only) by one director and an authorised countersignatory. Further relaxations regarding use of the seal are set out below.
3   At least one signatory must know personally of the content of the item to be sealed.
4   Other than for the approval of the following items, a brief synopsis of the content of the document must be prepared and initialled by the director ultimately responsible for the commitment of resources, etc., evidenced by the document. This synopsis should be kept in the register of seals or sealing until the sealing has been approved by the board, and will be preserved elsewhere subsequently for three years.
    (a) Share certificates. Many companies use a securities seal which is affixed by the company registrar (i.e. the person looking after the share registration work of the company) under terms of authority granted by the board from time to time.
    (b) Renewals of leases, or new leases the terms of which have already been approved by the board.
    (c) Agreements where the capital value in total (either separately or, should the document be one of a series, cumulatively) is less than (say) £5,000.
5   The register of seals or sealing (and/or of documents signed as deeds) will be completed for every item sealed – each being given a sequential

number. The same number will be placed on the document itself and also on any synopsis. Using such a register is not a legal requirement but has many practical advantages not least being a record of all the items sealed or signed as deeds and it avoids having to give details of all items sealed at a board meeting – the register can provide the details to interested parties.

6   The register of sealing will be produced at each board meeting so that all members (if they wish) can inspect details of all items sealed between board meetings. With board approval the chairman will initial under the latest entry in the register.

Control and security

The affixing of the seal to a document grants the authority of the company to the item and thus the seal needs to be adequately protected.

1   Is the seal kept secure – both in a secure place and its use restricted by a padlock on the seal jaws? (The modern lightweight portable seals do not have this protection, making the security of the whole seal essential.)

2   Is the register of sealing also kept secure, entries being made only (but always) when the seal is used, and submitted for authorisation to the next following board meeting?

3   Is every item sealed inscribed with the seal number given to the entry in the register?

4   Is there a schedule of authorities, requiring adherence to levels of approval for prescribed value contracts (see AUTHORITIES, CONTROL AND DELEGATION)?

Abolition of seal

Under CA89, companies were permitted to dispense with (or not adopt) a seal. If a seal is not to be used it might be advantageous to consider the following:

1   Are there adequate procedures for ensuring items needing the equivalent of the affixing of the seal do receive the degree of authority they require?

2   Are there procedures in place to provide evidence of the authority of those who will sign deeds, instead of these being sealed?

3   Has explanation of the relaxation been given to those used to receiving a sealed document (for example, those located overseas)?

4   Have we incorporated a rule such as the following to provide back-up authority for those actually signing documents which would otherwise be sealed?

'Every six months, the board will approve a resolution authorising (named) directors and the company secretary to sign on behalf of the company, documents which otherwise would have been sealed. Copies of such a resolution, authenticated by the chairman, will accompany each document signed to avoid any questioning re the authority.'

This should also help avoid questions from those who are not aware of the option to dispense with the seal and have been accustomed to receiving documents that have been sealed. Requiring a six-monthly repeat/update of the authority itself, should negate any challenge to its currency.

5 To ensure appropriate drafting, all solicitors must be briefed to refer to documents as a deed, if they are to be regarded as deeds and not to be sealed. A wording such as *'Executed as a deed, for and on behalf of Any Company Ltd by [two directors or one director and the company secretary or authorised countersignatory]'* should be incorporated.

Whilst nothing in the company articles can prevent the abolition of the seal (the Act overrides the articles on this subject), before deciding to dispense with it the articles should be checked for the effect of such dispensing.

Further relaxations

Under the Regulatory Reform (Execution of Deeds and Documents) Order 2005 the requirement was further diluted. The principles are that:

- sealing a document no longer makes it a deed (reversing the previous long-standing presumption that this was the case);
- a third party can rely on a document signed by two directors (or a director and the company secretary) – the same indication of authority to 'signing a document as a deed' under CA89; or by a director and a person authorised to be the second signatory;
- solicitors signing 'on behalf of the company' are now assumed to have the authority to bind the company in all transactions (not only transfers of land, as they could previously);
- a corporate director (that is, a 'company that is a director'), can bind the company for third parties if a representative of the corporate director signs a deed.

There are further relaxations in CA06. The Act allows a sole director of an LTD where there is no company secretary to appoint an 'authorised signatory' so that a second signature is available for documents requiring dual signature.

In addition, under s. 47 of CA06 the company can by deed empower a single person (either for a specific purpose or generally) as its attorney to execute deeds or other documents on its behalf.

If using these relaxations, proper control of the delegated authority is essential (see AUTHORITY CONTROL AND DELEGATION).

Register of Seals or Sealing

The recording of the affixation of the seal (or the signing as a deed) in a register is referred to above. There is no legal requirement to keep such a register, although many companies do so since it not only provides a record of the act of seal affixation (or 'company signature'), but also requires the completion of brief details of the contents, the date of approval, and the destination of the item after sealing/signing. If entries are numbered in the register, subsequent approval of the board to the affixation/signing can be achieved by a simple board minute:

> *'Approval was granted to the affixation of the seal (signing as a deed) of items numbered [X] to [Y] in the Register of Sealings. The Chairman initialled the register under item [Y].'*

Cross-referencing can be obtained by inserting the register number against the seal or signatures on the document itself.

WARNING

 If conducting business in the BRIC countries (Brazil, Russia, India and China – the four fastest-growing worldwide economies), UK companies may often find that their opposite numbers prefer contracts to be sealed – and may insist on additional confirmation by a notary public. Retention and usage of the seal may avoid a considerable waste of time trying to explain the diluting legislation referred to above. Usage of the seal is simple, time efficient, inexpensive (a seal can usually be obtained for less than £25), and subject to few challenges. Removing it negates these advantages and may create time-consuming – but avoidable – problems.

Shadow directors

INTRODUCTION

Within a few years of the passing of the first Companies Acts of 1856 and 1862, it was realised that there were people 'directing' such companies but without any formal and outwardly acknowledged relationship with the companies – unlike the directors of those companies, whose details as required by statute had to be lodged at CH. Very often such persons were the real controlling force of the company, acting through others (who might best be described as 'front men') who had no real power. Individuals operating in this way became known as 'shadow directors'. Such persons act as a kind of *'eminence grise'*, unseen (and unknown by third parties, including creditors, dealing with the company), moving behind the board, and exercising control over the directors – thus negating the principle that those dealing with the company should always know the identity of those who are running it. Virtually repeating earlier legislation, s. 251 CA06 defines a shadow director as '*a person in accordance with whose directions or instructions the directors of the company are accustomed to act'*. The need to define and control such individuals reflects a continuing concern at a tendency of some major shareholders, creditors or others (even including customers) effecting control over of the company and directing it (without any liability) whilst sheltering behind the appointed board (who could be held liable). Without requiring such shadowy operators to be declared, the impact of the Insolvency Act 1986 (i.e. making directors personally liable to contribute to any shortfall due to the creditors in the event of WRONGFUL or FRAUDULENT trading), would have increased the appeal of this 'hidden power' type of relationship with 'shadows' escaping liability.

Definition

The above definition of a 'shadow director' can cover a number of relationships – but there are exceptions. Thus, if a major creditor, instructed (or 'suggested') that the board should carry out a certain act on a one-off basis and the board did so, that person would probably not be a 'shadow director', as *'accustomed to act'* implies a regular relationship, rather than a one-off suggestion. But if such control was ongoing (i.e. 'suggestions' were made regularly and the board complied regularly) a shadow directorship probably exists. Similarly, if a major customer regularly required the board to act in a certain way and they did so, the customer could also become a shadow director. A company doctor – a person brought in to try to assist the company's survival – would almost certainly be a shadow director (if not properly appointed to the board) simply because of the control they would need to exercise. This was the decision reached in the case of *Tasbian Limited* by the Court of Appeal, where a company doctor negotiated with creditors, countersigned all the cheques and set up a new corporate organisation.

However, a bank manager requesting certain action as a result of power or influence gained because the company has borrowing facilities with his bank would not normally be a shadow, since this would be regarded as advice given in a professional capacity, which is excluded by s. 251(2), even if the board regularly acted upon such advice. In the same way, auditors or solicitors, despite sometimes having considerable influence and power, are unlikely to become shadow directors.

In the *Deverall* case the Court of Appeal stated that *'directions or instructions'* needed to be interpreted objectively and can include both words and conduct. There was no need to show that there was an expectation that the communication would be complied with. Neither was it necessary to show that the board was subservient to the shadow. Courts will therefore seek to determine whether a person was a shadow director or not, by establishing the extent of their control or influence.

Liability

If the company becomes insolvent, the insolvency practitioner(s) appointed will wish to seize as many assets as they can to try to repay the creditors. If it is felt that the directors have been guilty of WRONGFUL TRADING there is a possibility that their personal assets could also be seized to acheived this end. The existence of a shadow director is obviously of interest in such an situation, since such a person can, if proved to have been giving the board instructions or requests, be treated in the same way as the directors whose details are lodged at CH.

Whilst they are not legally appointed, shadow directors are still obliged to comply with all requirements of company law. Full personal details should be entered in the register of directors and filed at CH (which would of course legitimise the 'shadowship'), and any contract between the company and the shadow must be made available for inspection. If it is not possible to legitimise the directorship, for example because the director refuses to sign the 'consent to act' line on the appointment form, those officers aware of the situation should consider their position very carefully since they too have obligations – and potential personal liability – particularly if they act in accordance with the wishes of the shadow. Since they know the person is acting as a shadow and are deemed to know that this is illegal, they too could be held liable.

Any indication of a shadow director operating should be brought to the attention of the board, and if they do not wish to rectify the situation (or they do but the shadow is unwilling to be properly appointed), it would be

Case study	Out of the shadows – and liable
	In *HMRC v McEntaggart*, the Inland Revenue sought to recover £73,000 from the wife of a disqualified director. Since he was disqualified, he could not act legally as a director and was giving instructions to his wife who thus *'acted on his instructions'*, meaning that under s. 15 of the Company Directors Disqualification Act 1986 she too could be held liable. In the same case the Revenue successfully claimed £154,000 from her husband since – although disqualified – he was still regarded as a *de facto* director. (A director acting whilst disqualified has unlimited personal liability for his actions in relation to the company.)

safest to bring this to the attention of the auditors (who may refuse to sign the audit certificate, since that certificate is required to cover the report of the directors in which must be stated the names of all directors during the period under report) or a regulatory body (e.g. CH, BERR, etc).

The person in breach is liable for both an initial fine and a daily fine (which continues until the breach is remedied). If the company secretary (or anyone else) has tried unsuccessfully to legitimise the matter internally first and then reports it externally, should a sanction be applied against him, he should be protected by the Public Interest Disclosure Act (PIDA or, as it is more widely known, the 'Whistle-blowing' Act). He could claim unfair dismissal at an Employment Tribunal for which (in this case) there is no limit on compensation. Since the PIDA came into force there have been around 3,000 claims and over £10,000,000 has been paid in compensation.

Should the 'shadow' have a service contract (which would really make a nonsense of them not being acknowledged as a director), then such a contract must be dealt with in exactly the same way as other directors' contracts, and the place where such contracts can be inspected must be advised to CH.

Parent company

If the board of a subsidiary company are accustomed to act in accordance with the advice or instructions of employees of the parent company (whether these be directors or senior management), there is a possibility that such persons could be shadow directors of the subsidiary. It may be preferable to make the parent company itself a director. Any personal liability, in the event of failure of the subsidiary, that could otherwise have attached to such senior staff by reason of them acting, however unwillingly, as shadow directors, will then be borne by the parent company. Of course, this negates part of the reason for setting up a subsidiary in the first place. Under current law there is nothing to stop a holding company allowing a subsidiary to go into insolvent liquidation whilst having no obligations to that company's creditors – unless it has guaranteed the debts of the subsidiary. However, a parent company itself will not normally be regarded as a shadow director even if it directs the activities of the directors of its subsidiary(ies).

Case study	Disqualified for riding roughshod
	In *Re Mea Corporation, Secretary of State for Trade & Industry v Aviss*, A was director and sole shareholder of a parent with two subsidiaries. B could not be a director of any company (since he had already been disqualified). Both A and B required all monies received from any of the three companies to be placed in a central fund from which B would determine payments. Large payments were made from this fund to companies (in which A had a substantial interest) outside the group. Directors of the subsidiaries protested at this procedure, but A and B overrode their objections.
	The court decided that A was a shadow director of the subsidiaries and that B was a shadow director of all three companies. In the application of trading income and the payment of creditors, both A and B failed to respect the 'separate legal identity' of all three companies, and this led to a substantial increase in the deficiency of all three companies to the detriment of the creditors.
	A was disqualified for seven years and B for 11 years (a longer term, since he was acting whilst disqualified).
	Here, the personal liability of the directors of the subsidiary companies was protected since they had tried to protest against their instructions. Had they not done so then they too could have been held liable (as happened in the *McEntaggart* case).

Volunteer directors

Many charitable companies operate with a board comprised entirely of non-executive directors who, since they are often also trustees of the charity and thus cannot be paid, are essentially volunteers. Ignoring the question *'Can an entire board really be composed only of non-executives – mustn't there be at least one executive?'*, the situation of the chief executives of such entities prompts examination.

Case study	Charities and shadows
	The Association of Chief Executives of Voluntary Organisations (ACEVO) took legal advice on the position of chief executives (CEs) of charities and other voluntary organisations. Since the non-executive boards of these organisations often do exactly what their CE suggests, this is surely tantamount to the CE being a shadow. In any event such CEs are almost certainly officers of their companies and/or 'de facto' directors. The advice was that this was almost certainly the case.

Such companies might wish to consider converting their company into a 'charitable incorporated organisation', once the final structure and delineation of which has been finalised. As noted, often such directors are (required to be) unpaid volunteers – yet as company directors they have all the normal potential liabilities under company and insolvency law. In addition they have to operate under both charity and company law – which are often in conflict – a dichotomy that the CIO seeks to avoid.

Capacity to act

Some people have multiple directorships which, if these are many, must raise the question of whether they are able to carry out their responsibilities properly.

Case study	The Sark Lark
	More than one inhabitant of the island of Sark in the Channel Islands, were, some years ago, making a lucrative business by acting as 'front men' directors of UK companies which were actually being run by others operating in the background – shadow directors. One person was a director of 1,300 companies, which the judge understandably found, in disqualifying him, an impossibility in terms of his being able to act properly in relation to all those companies! Obviously if any of the companies failed this was potentially very dangerous as the director would be personally liable – acting in accordance with the directions of a shadow.

Shareholder agreements

INTRODUCTION

Companies are required by company law to have articles of association, and under CA06 these are to be regarded as the company's constitution (with the memorandum for such a company containing little more than evidence of the company's incorporation). If a company does not adopt a set of articles, then the pro forma articles apply. These are either comprised in the appropriate table within the Act under which the company was formed, or, for a company formed under CA06, in the articles which accompany the Act. However, in addition to the publicly available detail set out in the articles, the shareholders may wish to agree between themselves certain items which they do not wish to be made public. They can do this by entering into a shareholders' agreement which, since it is not required to be lodged at CH, does not form part of the publicly available information. Care is needed to ensure that provisions in these two separate contracts are not in conflict, and that the content of the shareholders' agreement does not breach company law. If there is inconsistency between articles and such an agreement, it can be argued that generally the articles (being publicly available and the document required by law) should prevail; however, this can be disputed and some commentators feel it is the shareholders' agreement which should be given precedence.

Contents

Most shareholder agreements contain provisions regarding the protection of the continuation of the status quo in terms of control of voting powers. This can be a valuable method of protecting the interests of minority shareholders:

Agreement to discuss the possibility of selling the shares

Clauses could stipulate that should one or more member(s) wish to withdraw from the company, the other members should have the right to purchase, or find purchasers for, the shares (i.e. a right of pre-emption or first refusal on the shares), rather than them being sold to an outsider. This is particularly important where the voting strength is heavily unbalanced. Reference should first be made to the articles, as some degree of protection may already be included there. For example, many articles of LTD companies give the directors powers to refuse to register a transfer of shares (hence the description of these companies as 'private'). However it might be preferable to address the possibility in advance, as the following draft illustrates. This version does not, subject to the wording of the articles, prevent the actual barring of any sale or transfer of the shares (as the board of an LTD usually can) but simply requires the member to discuss the situation with the other members.

Example	Deed of agreement
	This Deed of Agreement is made this day of 2XXX between XYZ, ABC, DEF and GHI, all of whom are shareholders in ANY OTHER COMPANY LTD (a limited liability company registered in England under number 1112223334).
	It is hereby expressly agreed by and between all four parties hereto that none of them will sell (individually or collectively) all or any of the shares he holds in the company without first discussing it fully with, and to the satisfaction of, the other members.
	In witness whereof this Deed of Agreement is signed this day of 2XXX
	Signatures of all members and witnesses

Since an agreement is unenforceable unless there is consideration, such a document (and the following alternatives) should always be described and signed as deeds, or alternatively incorporate a nominal consideration.

Right of pre-emption

Effectively this gives a right of first refusal to the other members to buy any shares that another member may wish to sell on each occasion a sale is contemplated.

Example	Deed of pre-emption

This Deed of Pre-emption agreement is made this ... day of ... 2XXX between all the members of ANY COMPANY LTD (the company) a limited liability company registered in England No 112233445566, whose registered office is at [address] namely XYZ (owning approximately 70 per cent of the issued shares of the company) and ABC (owning approximately 30 per cent of the issued shares of the company).

Both the parties hereto, namely Messrs XYZ and ABC, hereby voluntarily, mutually separately and expressly agree that in the event of either wishing to dispose of his shareholding (or any part thereof) in the company, he will first offer it for purchase by the other party hereto.

The offer must be in writing specifying a price per share, and any other conditions of sale and must be posted by recorded delivery to the last known private residential address of the shareholder (the recipient). The recipient will have 56 days to make a decision whether to accept or reject the offer. If at the end of 56 days from the date of posting of the offer (as evidenced by the recorded delivery slip) no agreement or rejection of the offer has been received then the offer will lapse and the offering shareholder will be at liberty to offer the shares elsewhere at a price not below that used in the offer to the other shareholder. In the event, and on each and every occasion, if the shares have subsequently to be offered at a lower price than that originally calculated, the shares will first be offered to the other shareholder (in the manner, and under the time restrictions, set out above).

In witness whereof, etc.

Signatures of both parties and witnesses to each.

Date

It is important that the exact basis of the appointment of a valuer of shares is set out in the agreement or articles and that those requirements are strictly adhered to.

Case study	Exact obligations required
	In *Cream Holdings Ltd & Ors v Stuart Davenport*, a director who owned 25 per cent of the shares in the company was removed from office. The articles stipulated that the shares should be valued by an accountant to be chosen by the parties. Although the parties agreed the name of an accountant, his letter of appointment was signed only by the company – not by the director whose shares were to be valued. The director disagreed with the valuation and successfully argued that it should not be binding, since he was not a party to the appointment. The judge held that an appointment could not be completed until all the parties had agreed the terms of engagement, and thus the valuation was invalid.

Agreement allowing for calculation of value and veto on alternative member proposed.

This version involves the auditors as witness to the negotiations which may help clarify the events in the event of dispute.

Example	Deed of agreement for calculation of value and veto on alternative member
	This Deed of Agreement is made this day of 2XXX between XYZ and ABC (the parties) both of whom own and control shares in ANOTHER COMPANY Ltd, a company registered in England No 111122223333.
	It is hereby expressly agreed between the parties that should either party wish to dispose of the shares held in their name or the name of their spouses as their nominees, or of any of such shares, that they should first offer such shares to the other party, and will only be able to dispose of such shares elsewhere after the other has indicated in writing that he does not wish to acquire the shares.
	The valuation to be placed on the shares shall be calculated by the auditors to the company, Messrs Accountant & Auditor, ➡

Example	**Deed of agreement for calculation of value and veto on alternative member** – *continued*

or such other valuer as the parties may jointly agree, or in the absence of agreement, by a person appointed to carry out such valuation by the president for the time being of the Institute of Arbitrators.

In the event of such shares being offered at the price stated by the auditors, the member will have 56 days (from the date that the disposing member confirms the intention to dispose in writing to the other member, a copy of such offer being sent to the auditors) to consider the offer. If at the end of this period no acceptance has been received, the member may offer the shares elsewhere. On receipt of an offer from a third party full details of such third party will be given to the remaining member, who shall have a right to veto in writing the person to whom the shares would otherwise be transferred. Any veto shall be sent by post within seven days of the remaining member being made aware of the identity of the third party, a copy of the veto will be sent to the auditors.

In witness wherefore the parties have signed this Deed of Agreement this [number] day of [month] 2XXX

Member Member

In the presence of

Witness (Name) ....

(Address) ....

(Occupation) ....

Case study	Costly ignorance

In *Cottrell v King*, Mr King's motor business needed capital and Cottrell agreed to refinance it, taking 75 per cent of the shares in consideration of his investment. When Cottrell died, the company gave the shares under transmission to Mrs Cottrell. Then someone noticed that in the company's articles there was a requirement that if one shareholder died, their shares had first to be offered to the surviving shareholder and therefore that King's interest had been overlooked. After a High Court action (with attendant costs incurred) the shares had to be transferred from Mrs Cottrell back to her husband's estate, the executors of which then had to have the shares valued and offered to King. If King wanted the shares he would have to pay for them, the money going to Cottrell's estate; if not the executors would then be able to deal with the shares in accordance with Cottrell's will.

Ironically, whilst he was alive Cottrell (since he had 75 per cent of the shares) could easily have passed a special resolution changing that requirement. However, there might have been a clause in a shareholder's agreement under which Cottrell undertook not to seek to change the articles in this way.

Other clauses

In addition to the above examples, clauses could be included covering:

- the granting of enhanced voting rights to some directors if the board is deadlocked (a device sometimes used in joint venture companies). Since one of the joint venturers effectively has control of the board, this may mean that the results of the joint venture company itself have to be consolidated with those of the principal with board control. (Advice from the auditors should be sought);
- other methods (than the foregoing) whereby a member can realise the value of the shareholding;
- situations where unanimity of shareholders is required before action can be taken;
- a mechanism whereby if the shareholders are deadlocked, a decision can be arrived at.

This last item reflects fairly numerous instances where there is an equality of votes (two shareholders each holding 50 per cent of the shares, which can be described as a 'quasi-partnership'). This may have seemed fine when the company was set up, since the parties were then in agreement. Should they later fall into dispute, deadlock can result – which is even more problematic if they are also the only directors. The logical result here would be for one shareholder to sell his holding – ideally to the other, although that in turn may give rise to a dispute as to the value to be placed on the shares. Without agreement at the time and/or in the absence of a shareholders' agreement regarding share price valuation, it may be necessary to apply to the court for determination of the situation. The court has wide-ranging powers – it can order that the company's conduct be regulated; require the company to refrain from certain activities; or authorise civil proceedings to be brought in the name of the applicant. The court could also order that one party's shares should be bought by the other, and, if the parties cannot agree a valuation, the court itself will determine this. Alternatively, the party in dispute could apply for the company to be wound up since obviously the 'quasi-partnership' has come to an end.

Obviously any recourse to the court means (win or lose) that there would be legal fees – which could be expensive. Some kind of negotiated settlement would probably benefit both parties.

WARNING

1 Experience indicates that in some cases, shareholders' agreements whilst freely entered into may create a situation which breaches the law. One agreement sought to indicate that certain directors would be 'special' directors, and only they would have a vote at a board meeting, even though all directors were 'statutory' directors (i.e. their details were registered at CH!).

2 Any agreement which allows the shareholders to change the articles in certain circumstances will probably need to be lodged at CH (since it overrides the provisions in and thus effectively changes the articles).

Single member companies

INTRODUCTION

Until 1992 all UK limited companies were required to have at least two members. So that subsidiaries could comply with the legislation and yet the parent company could retain control, the practice was very common when setting up a 'wholly owned' subsidiary that 100 shares would be issued, with the parent company holding 99 shares whilst the remaining share was held by an individual (often a director) as a NOMINEE of the majority shareholder. This gave the company the legally required second shareholder whilst the parent retained total control. Following the enactment of the Companies (Single Member Private Limited Companies) Regulations 1992, companies were and are allowed to have only one member.

Administration

When incorporating a single member company (SMC), only one signature is required on the memorandum, and only one member's name will be shown in the register of members. If, however, additional members are generated by an allotment or transfer of shares, (which may need ordinary resolutions to increase the share capital and to authorise the director(s) to ALLOT shares, to be passed and lodged with CH within 15 days), not only do new accounts need to be opened in the register of members, but also the fact has to be drawn to the attention of anyone inspecting the corporate records. Thus in the share account of the original single member, a note: 'This company is no longer an SMC' needs to be written, together with a note of the date that this occurred.

Conversely, should a company with two or more members become an SMC, then in the account in the register of members for the remaining member, a note 'This company is an SMC' needs to be entered, together with a note of the effective date.

Meetings and resolutions

At general meetings of an SMC, obviously the sole member forms a quorum. Despite the apparent absurdity of the situation, decisions taken at 'meetings' of the single member should be recorded in writing (i.e. by compiling minutes of each meeting) if not effected by means of a WRITTEN RESOLUTION (which, since a record has to be placed in the minute book, amounts virtually to the same thing). Contracts between the sole member and the company (particularly if the sole member is also the sole director which is very common) should also be recorded in writing or set out in the minutes of the board meeting(s). There are initial and daily fines for every officer in default of these requirements.

Whilst the creation of these companies does, in theory, reduce the amount of administration required where formerly a nominee shareholder was used, the particular requirements of the administration need to be adhered to carefully to avoid those responsible becoming liable for fines.

Multi-member company becoming sole member

Where a company which is not an SMC carries on trading with only one shareholder, after six months the remaining shareholder loses their limited liability protection and thus has potential personal liability for the debts should the company fail.

Inability to continue in business?

It is thus legal for there to be just one shareholder, and that person could be (and often is) the sole director. This means however that should the sole director/shareholder be killed (or, in some other way, become unable to act e.g. is declared bankrupt or sectioned under the Mental Health Act), there is no one with capacity to appoint someone to replace the director. The company will be unable to continue to trade until the ownership of the share(s) is determined – a process which could take several weeks (or more) during which time the company could fail.

However for companies formed under CA06 (i.e. new companies from October 2009 adopting the new pro forma articles accompanying the Act), this is to some extent overcome, since article 17 states that *personal representatives ... have the right ... to appoint a person to be a director'*. This implies that it would not be necessary to wait for probate or letters of administration to be granted to such personal representatives. It would be wise for the company to check the authority of the 'personal representatives' claiming to act. If there is a will, this is relatively easy; however, if the shareholder has died intestate there may be difficulties proving the authority of the person wishing to act. Where there is a company secretary at least there is an officer of the company who could carry out these checks – without this appointment the situation is even more problematic. The company might be wise to insist the person claiming to act signs a form of indemnity protecting the company should they act on his instructions which turn out later to be unauthorised. Legal advice should be taken.

Guarantee companies

Other than a few guarantee companies formed under legislation prior to 1980 (from which time a guarantee company has only been able to be an LTD, i.e. it cannot be a PLC), guarantee companies do not have a share capital. Their members are persons who have given guarantees (usually for a nominal sum, e.g. £1) that in the event that the company becomes insolvent they will pay the amount of their guarantee to the insolvency practitioner appointed to wind up the company affairs. The situation where there is just one guarantor is even more problematical than for an SMC limited by shares. Where a sole shareholder dies, whilst it may take time to determine who now owns the shares, at least they still exist and can be passed to the inheritor(s) of the deceased shareholder, but a guarantee cannot be transferred in the same way. Subject to legal advice it might be preferable to form an SMC limited by shares but with just one share, so that the amount to be invested is small. Alternatively (and again subject to legal advice) it might be suggested that the guarantor find a substitute who could step into the position should anything happen to the original guarantor. The substitute would have to sign the same guarantee as the original guarantor (presumably made in advance but only coming into effect in the event of the original guarantor's death).

The same proviso referred to above for companies limited by shares formed under CA06 applies to guarantee companies where a sole guarantor who is also the sole director dies. Article 17 similarly states that *'personal representatives ... have the right ... to appoint a person to be a director'*. Once again this implies that it would not be necessary to wait for the grant of probate or letters of administration. Legal advice might best be taken.

Social responsibility

INTRODUCTION

The Corporate Social Responsibility (CSR) Academy was set up to provide education, training and development for managers in both public and private sector organisations to help them, in turn, incorporate CSR activities into their business practices. The launch followed the recommendations of a report issued by a working group including representatives of Business in the Community (BITC), Confederation of British Industry, the Trade Union Congress and the Chartered Institute of Personnel and Development. Deputy Chief Executive of BITC, Peter Davis, commented on the Academy's launch: *'This is an initiative to fill the gap that exists between corporate strategy on social/environmental responsibility and management practice.'* Listed PLCs are required under the Stock Exchange listing agreement to state their social responsibility commitment in their annual reports. In addition, all companies required to produce a business review (see OPERATING and BUSINESS REVIEW) must report the impact of their operations on the environment and employment.

Power and control

Over 50 per cent of the top 100 wealth-controlling 'economies' are corporations rather than countries. Although like is not really being compared with like (since the comparison is between a corporation's turnover and a nation's gross domestic product, which are not the same animals) there is no doubt that such corporations wield enormous power. Obviously the bigger the corporation the greater the power and the greater the risk of such power not being exercised legitimately. Amalgamations and takeovers will continue to create even larger corporations so that it may not be many years before there will be a corporation which 'rivals' a first ranking country. The control of such corporations is vested in boards of directors which themselves are largely self-perpetuating. Recent scandals involving leading companies raise a worrying scenario of the power of such corporations either being used less than ethically or in what is apparently a negligent fashion. The Institute of Business Ethics (IBE) stated recently that companies will come under increasing pressure to demonstrate that they are *'good citizens'*. The IBE aims at establishing a network of companies demonstrating socially and ethically responsible policies by becoming 'good corporations' (see www.good-corporation.com). One method of demonstrating this can be achieved by companies adopting a social responsibility policy which listed PLCs must publish in their annual report. However what is required is much more than a couple of printed pages – hence the commitment should be to ensuring everyone connected with the company knows, and above all, adheres to it.

Using society's resources

Employers operate within society and, since they use society's resources, create scarcity by such consumption. Nowadays there is an increasing expectation that such resources should be used wisely and efficiently. Many processes not only use resources but in the process create by-products and emissions which may harm the ENVIRONMENT. Increasingly operations and operators (companies and their boards of directors) are required to take account of environmental matters – not least, since this an explicit requirement under CA06. Employers also create two of the most important necessities of society – employment and wealth (without the taxation of which, none of society's public services could be provided). Increasingly not only listed PLCs but also larger/higher profile companies provide public statements (usually set out within their annual report) of their attitude to, and means of attaining a level of social responsibility. This is a trend which is likely to continue not only for such companies but also for far more employers since it will come to be expected not least by the 'best employees' – that is, those whom progressive employers should most wish to recruit and retain.

An initiative was recently published by the EU, *'Promoting a European Framework for Corporate Social Responsibility'* (reference COM/2001/366). This echoes previous appeals to businesses to adopt and promote:

- lifelong learning for employees, to maximise their talents;
- improved work organisation;
- equality of opportunities for everyone;
- social inclusion; and
- sustainable development.

Employers are expected not only to adopt such guidelines but also to use them as a base and to go beyond them to develop corporate social responsibility in the widest sense of those words.

The aim is to make the EU *'the most competitive and dynamic knowledge-based economy in the world, capable of sustainable economic growth and with more and better jobs and greater social cohesion'*. The current paper is aimed at moving ahead the principle underlying that statement by:

- promoting social responsibility of corporations and employers within the EU and world-wide;
- using existing (best) practices and encouraging their adoption on a universal basis;

- encouraging the development of innovative policies for the future;
- promoting the concept of transparency of the concept and their adoption of policies and practices to develop this; and
- evaluating the impact of the policies.

Appeal

In a competitive employment market, those applicants, who for ease of reference we can call the 'best' employees (i.e. applicants who many employers will wish to attract) will want to know:

- what the organisation stands for;
- how it wishes to trade (attitudes on safety, value, quality etc.);
- how it interacts (i.e. with society as a whole, as well as with suppliers, customers, employees, shareholders etc.);
- what it will not do (i.e. operations/countries in which or with which it will not trade);

and so on.

Companies that fail to address this need may find they cannot attract those with the skills they wish and, as a result, could lose their cutting edge. This is not meant to imply that a few words in an annual report are all that is needed – a paper commitment must be evidenced in practice, and at all levels throughout the company (particularly if it is one with a high public profile).

Case study	Real commitment needed
	Tesco PLC is a rightly admired leading UK company whose annual reports each include a double page outlining its CSR commitment – features which have won awards as best practice. Further, in the Sunday Times 'Companies that count' survey (which seeks to rank companies in terms of continually improving the impact that they have on society), the company scored the highest ranking of 'Platinum'. However, neither the prize-winning reports nor the Platinum award prevented the company selling 'pole dancing kits' as Christmas presents aimed at eight-year-old girls.

Case study	**Real commitment needed** – *continued*
	Immediately the attention of senior management was drawn to this 'toy', it was withdrawn. The question begged of course is where was the intelligence of the buyer representing a leading company committed to high standards of social responsibility, giving a supplier a contract for such items? CSR is a far wider commitment than saving energy and the environment. Sony, the electronics giant, launched its 'God of War II' game for its PlayStation 2 console with a video that featured the corpse of a freshly slaughtered goat, into the entrails of which guests at the launch were invited to reach. When challenged, Sony immediately issued an apology and recalled the print run. But why should it be necessary for a challenge to be made, before consideration is given of the effect of such an obscene episode on the company's corporate reputation? Sony also annoyed the Christian church by setting one of the mass assassinations in a violent 'game' in a replica of Manchester Cathedral, without any input or permission from the church. When challenged, no apology was forthcoming. The company replied that had it needed permission, it would have applied. Regardless of wondering whether they would have dared to use a replica of a mosque to stage such a bloody massacre, one must question whether these are the actions of a responsible management in the twenty-first century?

The first essential of such a programme is a willingness to commit to the principle of having a duty to trade in a way that enhances society, uses materials in as 'non-wasteful' a way as possible, treats all-comers with respect, and so on. NOP conducted a survey for the Institute of Directors and discovered that:

- in roughly 50 per cent of the 500 organisations contacted, the board discussed social responsibility (66 per cent of large companies);
- 60 per cent discussed environmental issues (66 per cent in large companies and 85 per cent of those engaged in manufacturing);
- 36 per cent had a board member whose responsibilities included social issues;
- 48 per cent had a board member whose responsibilities included environmental issues.

Under CA06 all boards have been required since October 2007 to take into account environmental matters in reaching their decisions.

Adverse publicity

Failing to appreciate the power of public opinion or customer perception can be dangerous and costly, and there may be a temptation to stick with old attitudes etc. However, directors/owners of organisations are paid (sometimes very highly) to drive companies forward, which must entail a willingness to embrace the new and the unknown. Legal and regulatory changes are often unwelcome, and whilst resisting change may be understandable, those who 'oppose' this trend may do their companies a disservice. The changes cannot be resisted and it might be more beneficial (and economic) to accept the new requirements and to assess whether there are ways in which the company can use them to its own advantage.

Directors may be excused for antipathy towards legislation (particularly given the output of new laws over the last few years – around 36,000 between 1997 and 2009) – and arguing against it with the lawmakers may assist changes being made – but refusing to work within it is foolish and costly, as well as being a breach of the duty that the directors owe to their shareholders. This is part of their social responsibility and challenge: to run with the changes and use them to their organisation's advantage. This is a point that it is even more pertinent in the aftermath of the 'credit meltdown' of 2008 and the exposure of unnecessary risk-taking, and downright faulty decisions made by extremely well-rewarded and probably over-paid executives.

Stakeholders

In introducing CA06, the concept of there being several 'stakeholders' in the success or life of a company was much to the fore. It was argued that directors should be responsible not only to:

- the company itself (as a legal person entirely separate from its owners and its officers);
- its shareholders;
- its employees; and
- its creditors;

(which were already requirements under CA85 and the Insolvency Act 1986), but also to:

- society (or the community) as a whole;
- future generations;
- customers and suppliers;
- the environment;

and so on.

The difficulty of directors arriving at decisions whilst balancing the interests of such a plethora of stakeholders (some of whose interests could be diametrically opposed) led to some criticism of the concept. These are, however, the legal requirements.

Advantages

The benefits of companies adopting social responsibility principles are outlined by proponents as:

- being able to market the organisation as a 'responsible entity', thus attracting the best applicants, leading in turn to improved productivity and profitability, and thus to greater investment in socially acceptable activities;
- improving safety performance for both employers and members of the public (and thereby minimising the massive costs of accidents, deaths and suffering in the workplace);
- generating a better environmental performance via sustainable use of resources, minimising pollution and adverse impacts on natural habitats; and
- meeting human rights, the development of which is assuming a greater importance in the minds and expectations of many employees.

The requirements

This initiative involves the company:

- monitoring all its activities, e.g. checking that its suppliers are themselves socially responsible and ceasing relationships with those who are not and will not commit to such principles;
- ensuring its employees abide by the tenets at all times;
- taking decisions having considered the impact on all the stakeholders' interests (which may require a not inconsiderable balancing act – see DIRECTORS: OBLIGATIONS);
- aligning itself in areas such as aims, vision and values, with best business practice and demonstrating that its management team works to such criteria, and the criteria are promulgated throughout the organisation (including on recruitment and during training and promotion) as well as in supplier relationships;
- ensuring that where performance does not meet these expectations, that differences are examined and rectified;
- adopting an ethical code covering its relationships both internally and externally;

Case study	Embracing the concept
	● Farrelly Engineering and Facilities had high employee turnover and came to the conclusion that the main cause was the long hours being worked. The company decided to cut working hours to 8.30–5.00p.m. (4.00 on Fridays), with complete flexibility for family and domestic commitments. Company director/owner Stephen Farrelly stated that *'People aren't stressed – they're more refreshed and staff turnover has been dramatically reduced – sales figures have now more than doubled – we don't compete on price we compete on people.'*
	● It was reported recently in the *Sunday Times* that there is a company in Chesterfield which has 35 employees – and 35 different shifts. The employer has managed to create a situation where every individual's preference regarding hours worked can be met. Over the five years that the scheme has been working, productivity has doubled. The owners might echo the comment made above.
	● From one of the country's smaller employers to one of the largest: Tony DeNunzio, chief executive of Asda claims that that company's flexible working practices had contributed greatly to a £4 million reduction in absenteeism costs, and have acted as a key retention tool. They are claimed to be a significant inducement in attracting recruits. Asda employees can swap 'shifts' for family or domestic reasons, 'swap stores' where students (e.g. at university) work in one shop and during the vacations return to their main home (and local store), and even have 'grandparent's leave' for older workers. De Nunzio claims that the success of the process is simply due to the fact that it is *'based on what colleagues want and need'*.
	● McDonalds has introduced a 'family' shift. They employ several members of a family to cover one shift. They are not worried which family member works the shift, as long as one of them does!

■ ensuring that checks are implemented to monitor progress towards the above aims, etc.

At present the requirements are in embryonic form but this will swiftly change and boards should be prepared to comply with such additional requirements and the challenges that are inherent in them.

The pertinent questions

A board could look at its activities on two levels and ask the following questions at the macro level:

- What are ethical investments and/or activities? Do they include tobacco, alcohol, defence equipment, gambling etc.?
- How ethical does the organisation wish to be? Will it permit a small amount of turnover/profit to be derived from otherwise 'unacceptable' activities?
- Will we trade with organisations that themselves are involved with what we regard as unethical activities – e.g. animal experimentation etc.?
- How susceptible should we be to pressure regarding the above matters from shareholders, Government, campaigning lobbies, society etc.?

And at the micro level:

- How concerned are we concerning the health and safety of our workforce, beyond our legal obligations?
- Are we concerned for their welfare and/or their pensions?
- Are we concerned for the welfare of our customers (e.g. not selling them food items with high salt and/or cholesterol etc. levels that might cause them long-term harm?)
- Are we concerned how we source our raw materials? Do we ensure that those working for our suppliers are treated fairly – or is there 'sweated' or child labour?
- Do we actively try to take account of health risks inherent in our business (e.g. running an airline without concern for deep vein thrombosis)?

The determination of organisational attitudes to these and other questions may be helpfully focused as a result of recommendations contained in the Association of British Insurers' (ABI) Disclosure Guidelines on Social Responsibility. These encourage institutional investors to require the boards of companies in which they invest to answer questions such as the following in their annual reports:

- Does the board regularly review social, ethical and environmental (SEE) matters?
- Has the board reviewed both short- and longer-term risks arising from SEE matters?
- Has the board adequate information for this purpose and is there training of directors and managers in SEE matters?

In addition it is recommended that companies should state such information in their annual reports. The ABI suggests that institutional investors should work with their companies to develop joint understandings reflected in statements in their annual reports. It would prefer boards as a whole to consider these matters regularly.

(See also GIFTS, ETHICS AND INTERESTS and WHISTLE-BLOWING.)

Statutory books

INTRODUCTION

To evidence the existence of the company as a legal person, company law requires details of those who own and direct it, etc., to be entered in registers required to be kept and made available for inspection. These registers are collectively known as the statutory books, and must not just be kept (and protected), but also be kept updated. As part of their audit, the AUDITORS will usually check the registers, providing a means of ensuring that at least once a year the books are brought up to date. However, the obligation to bring them up to date is 'on occurrence' (and to notify the changes to CH within specific time limits) – and these obligations are placed on the directors, albeit usually delegated by them to the company secretary. The statutory books are the official records of the company – although CH must be told of changes, the records at CH are purely copies of the entries in the company's statutory books.

The registers

Register of members into which must be entered the name and address of each member. A company limited by guarantee must enter the amount of the guarantee given by the member whilst a company limited by shares must enter the number of shares held (and the transfers into and out of their holding), calls on, and the nominal value of the shares. If it is a single member company the sheet in the register relating to their sole holding should bear the phrase: 'This is a single member company'. Companies with large numbers of members usually keep their register in a computerised form, in which case the Registrar of Companies must be informed of this. Companies limited by guarantee who have only one guarantor should take legal advice concerning the administration of the company should the guarantor die, although a guarantee company formed under CA06 which adopts the articles accompanying the Act can accept the requirements of the personal representatives of the sole member (e.g. to give a new guarantee).

Similar details must be filed with the Registrar of Companies (i.e. in the ANNUAL RETURN each year) however, because of justified fears of identity theft, unwanted mailings etc., public information is restricted. Thus in listed PLCs, addresses of shareholders with less than 5 per cent of the shares will not be disclosed, whilst for LTDs no private addresses of shareholders at all are shown.

Register of directors and secretaries. Full details (name, and any former name, address, date of appointment and date of resignation/removal) must be given for both directors and secretaries. In addition, dates of birth and nationality must be stated for the directors. Formerly only directors who considered themselves to be subject to genuine and serious physical threats (e.g. from terrorists such as animal rights protesters) were able to apply to use a service address rather than their real address. Under CA06 all directors (from October 2009) can opt for not allowing their private address to be made public. Both company and CH must be told the private address and a service address but only the latter will be made available publicly.

Register of directors' previous directorships. The requirement for each company to keep records of all the companies of which their directors have been directors during the previous five years has been abolished under CA06 (mainly since CH records are available to provide this information automatically).

Register of directors' share interests. Although holdings of shares in the PLCs of which a person is a director must be recorded, this register is no longer required for LTD directors. However if a director of an LTD has an interest in a third party which does business with their company then that interest should be recorded (and could usefully be placed in this register – renamed omitting the word 'share'). If the interest arises after appointment then as soon as the director is aware of it, he should make that information known. Similar entries could be made for any indemnities given to the director, any loans made to him and so on.

Register of substantial interests. Where a member holds a beneficial interest of three per cent or more, a non-beneficial interest of 10 per cent or more, or a combined (beneficial and non-beneficial) interest of 10 per cent or more, in the shares in a listed PLC, that fact must be disclosed to the company and recorded in this register. Changes through each percentage point (up or down) must also be notified. Non-beneficial interests of 5 per cent are also now required to be disclosed (but not the variation of percentage points between 5 and 10 per cent).

Register of debenture and/or loan stockholders must contain details of name, address, holding (and changes thereto) of each and every stockholder.

Register of charges. Regardless of whether the company has created any charges (i.e. a mortgage of the company assets) or not such a register must be set up. It must contain full details of all charges over assets of the company and by whom they have been taken.

Register of seals or sealing. There is no legal requirement to maintain such a register. However, many companies find this an essential and efficient way of recording in one place, details of how and when the seal was affixed to deeds, who witnessed the affixation of the seal, and a brief synopsis of the content covered in the deed, and its ultimate destination. Even where a company has dispensed with the use of a seal, such a register may be a valuable method of recording such salient details of documents signed on behalf of the company as deeds – not least as a means of exercising control of the delegation of authority.

Compilation

Traditionally these registers have been held in hard copy format – and many still are, particularly in smaller LTDs. Combined registers giving all the required rulings can be bought from law stationers (or will be supplied by formation agents when they form a company for a client). Formerly some registers were required to be held at the registered office, which would mean when using a combined register that it had to be held at that office. A problem may arise when the place of work of the company secretary (or whoever is responsible for their updating and security) is not at the registered office. Under CA06, if the company notifies CH of an alternative address (known for short as a SAIL) using form AD02, all the registers can be held at that office.

In addition, the registers can be held in electronic format which, if there are linked computers in the office where the books are kept and the registered or SAIL office, would both comply with the legal requirement as well as meeting the administrative requirements of a choice of inspection locations (although those wishing to inspect these records would probably opt for electronic inspection of the duplicate records at CH).

Access and charges

From 1 October 2007 the charges for inspection and copies were increased as follows:

(a) Register of members:
   Inspection: £3.50 each hour or part thereof.
   Copies: £3.50 for first 50 entries, £31.50 for next 950 entries or part thereof, £20 for next 4,000 entries or part thereof and £25 for every subsequent 5,000 entries or part thereof.
(b) Directors' service contracts and/or indemnity provisions, resolutions and meetings, report under s. 805: 20p per 1,000 words or part thereof.

Retention and inspection

All these registers must be kept safely by the company and preserved for at least the life of the company (but see also RESURRECTION OF COMPANIES). Historically for two hours every working day, any member of the public could walk into the registered office of a company and demand to see its register of members. The creditors could demand to see that register and the register of charges, and the members could demand to see all the registers.

However the right of inspection of the register of members has been curtailed by CA06. Since 1 October 2007, any person (including a shareholder) wishing to inspect the register of members has been required to give notice to the company stating their details and the purpose for which they wish to inspect. The board must within five days allow the inspection or apply to the court (telling the person wishing to inspect that it has done so) for permission to resist the inspection because they feel it is 'not a fit purpose'. It is suggested that the reasons for resisting an inspection could include purposes that:

- are unlawful;
- would breach the Data Protection Act;
- are to enable a third party to check credit or identities of shareholders;
- are to market investments or commercial products;
- might result in the threatening, harassment or intimidation of shareholders.

There is further guidance as to *'proper purpose'* tests on the ICSA website (http://www.icsa.org.uk). If wishing to resist an inspection, taking legal advice may be appropriate.

Of course the register of members is also available at CH, since the data it contains is included in the annual return although the addresses of private shareholders will progressively not be available there.

The inspection rights of the other statutory books are unchanged (see RECORD RETENTION and INSPECTION).

Certificate of incorporation

Although not usually regarded as one of the statutory books, the certificate of incorporation issued by the Registrar of Companies should be kept with these books.

The certificate is issued when the Registrar places the company on the company register and evidences its incorporation. The certificate bears the company name, date and place of incorporation, and company number. If a company changes its name a fresh certificate bearing the new name will be issued. Whilst some years ago companies had to display their certificates of incorporation in the registered office this is no longer the case. However the certificate should be kept safely as it evidences the existence of the company, and, if, for example, the company wishes to borrow money, a bank will insist on seeing the certificate. If the certificate is lost, CH can issue a duplicate.

Certificates of employers' liability insurance

It may be prudent to keep one copy of each successive year's certificate with the statutory books, in case there is a claim against the company many years after the claim is stated to have originated.

Types of companies

INTRODUCTION

Most corporate bodies in the UK are formed under company law, which originated in the mid-nineteenth century when, for the first time under law, the liability of their entrepreneurial (i.e. risk-taking) owners was limited to the amounts of their shareholding. Prior to that, owners could only escape personal liability to creditors if and when their company failed, if it was constituted under Royal Charter or an Act of Parliament (a statute company) some of which are still in existence. Examples of all the 'original' types of companies formed under law still exist although more recently new types of corporate bodies have been and are still being made available.

Unincorporated businesses

Sole trader

This is the simplest form of business – and the most numerous – often run from the trader's own home, which keeps overheads low and enables lower prices to be charged. Approaching four million people work from home in the UK – a figure which was (before the credit crunch and recession) projected to rise to nine million by 2010 since, to some extent, the move is being supported by Government. This projection may still be achieved as there are large numbers of redundant employees, thrown out of work as a result of the recession, who are using their redundancy payments to set up their own operations. A sole trader is an unincorporated body and as such the owner has personal unlimited liability for the debts of the business. If the business fails, the owner's personal assets can be seized to pay off the creditors of the business.

Committees

Those elected to a committee (for example of a social or sports club etc.) have personal liability for the debts of the business they are carrying on – a situation rarely understood by their members. Although such persons may not feel they are operating a business as such, many employ bar stewards, gardeners and other staff. Breaching employment legislation in relation to those people could create personal liability on the part of those serving as committee members at the relevant time. If the offence was discrimination, a Tribunal can award unlimited compensation. The committee members' personal positions could (and should) be protected by making such a body into a company limited either by shares or guarantee.

Partnership

If two or more people go into business together they form a partnership, whether or not they enter into a partnership deed (which is advisable). Individually their situation is similar to the sole trader and the club committee – that is, they have joint and several liability for the debts of their business and should it fail, the partners can be held jointly responsible for the debts. Since 2001 partnerships have been able to limit the liability of their principals by becoming a limited liability partnership (LLP). This option is widely used by auditors, solicitors and other professionals who formerly traded as partnerships. There are over 10,000 LLPs registered at Companies House. An LLP is a hybrid, being neither a company nor an unincorporated partnership. They are not required to have a 'company' secretary, but since the filing requirements (including the need to file accounts within set periods) are similar to those for LTDs, there is an obligation for someone to perform very similar duties.

As a result of CA06, it has been noticed that the compliance requirements of LLPs are less onerous than LTDs or PLCs, and some of those running the latter have been considering converting the status of their organisation from a limited liability company to an LLP. This may be unwise, since legislators are now considering tightening the compliance requirements for LLPs.

Business names

Formerly anyone (e.g. a sole trader or partnership) using a 'business name' or trading name rather than the name(s) of their principals had to comply with the Business Names Act 1985 (BNA85). CA06 repealed BNA85 but replicates its requirements in ss. 1200-1208. The legislation stipulates that, in running a business, if individuals use a trading name other than their own personal name(s), then on all notepaper, orders, invoices etc., the name(s) of the principal(s) using the business name must be stated. This is required so that those that deal with the business know the identity of the person (real or legal person) with whom they are trading. Legal action cannot be taken against a 'name' – only against a person. Repealing the separate Act and inserting its requirements into CA06 seems odd in terms of requiring legal compliance – after all, a sole trader or other unincorporated organisation is unlikely to think of referring to the Companies Act for legal requirements affecting their (non-company) organisation.

Incorporated bodies – becoming a company

There are some very large sole trader businesses. As businesses grow larger, however, so too do the debts of the organisation, and to protect personal liability many sole traders, club committees, and partnerships decide to incorporate as limited liability companies.

(a) Private company limited by shares (LTD)

Such organisations constitute the largest proportion of all the companies registered at CH. The company can issue from one to many million shares although around 80 per cent of such companies have a share capital of under £100 and around 90 per cent of LTDs have five or fewer shareholders. The shareholders' duty (and legal obligation) is to appoint officers to run the company and to delegate to them the day-to-day control and operation of their company. Very often the articles, approved by the shareholders, allow the directors to restrict who owns the shares (that is, the directors have the right to block a share transfer to a person they do not wish to be a shareholder) thus those running the company to a large extent can control the ownership of the company – hence the description of this body as a 'private company'. Other than in cases of their personal fraud, once a shareholder has paid for their shares in full then they cannot be asked to pay more into the company even if it fails with massive debts. An LTD can be formed with just one shareholder owning one share – a SINGLE MEMBER COMPANY.

(b) Private company limited by guarantee

Where there is no real need for a share capital – for a company which will not trade in the normal sense of the word and/or is thus unlikely to fail in an insolvent manner (e.g. a club, chamber of commerce, flat management company, charity etc.) the entity can be formed by members who do not subscribe for shares (and thus create a fund of share capital) but simply undertake that should the company fail they are prepared to contribute (say) £1 each to pay off the creditors. Normally the company will be required to state 'Limited by Guarantee' at the end of its name but, with permission, the last two words can be dispensed with. The word 'Limited' can also be omitted from the name under s. 60 of CA06. This is carried out by submitting form NE01 to CH.

In a guarantee company, the subscribers are members not 'shareholders', and if and when the company is wound up in deficit the members (the guarantors) contribute (and are liable to contribute for up to a year after they have ceased to be a member). Since there are no shares, there are no dividends.

However, some guarantee companies formed prior to 1980 do have a share capital. Thus there might be a few shareholders who have contributed a small amount of capital to the company and, in addition, a further number of guarantors who have not contributed anything. Since 1980 a guarantee company has not been able to be a PLC. (See SINGLE MEMBER COMPANY re the potential problem where there is just one guarantor.)

(c) Company with unlimited liability

Such a company (normally formed to take advantage of tax concessions available to UK subsidiaries of USA owners, or for businesses involved in farming or forestry work) does not seek to limit the liability of its members – hence in any insolvent failure unpaid creditors can sue the shareholders themselves. The shareholders here have the same exposure to debt should the company fail as have sole traders, club committee members or partners of an unlimited liability partnership. Unlimited companies are not obliged to file accounts unless they are members of a group which also comprises limited liability companies. In addition such a company can reduce its share capital without either of the processes required of other types of companies.

(d) Royal Charter companies

Such companies formed under a charter signed by the monarch are nowadays mainly used by professional bodies which do not trade in the accepted meaning of the word, although they may often be the parent company owning trading subsidiaries limited by shares or guarantee. However the charter company could be regarded as the oldest type of company as it is a form used since the thirteenth century, when obtaining a Royal Charter was the only method of incorporation. Royal Charters were originally used to 'create cities' – raising them from town status to one where they could 'conduct commerce' (however, the first two charter companies were the Universities of Oxford and Cambridge). There are now just under 1,000 Royal Charter companies.

(e) Statute companies

These are companies formed under a specific statutory enactment. Such companies mainly pre-date the innovation of limited liability company law in the 1850s, since (other than by Royal Charter) this was formerly the only method by which members' liability could be limited should the company fail. Whilst they must comply generally with company law, they are also bound by the particular terms in their constitution.

(f) Public limited company (PLC)

Subject to a company having:

- an issued share capital, of £50,000 of which at least 25 per cent (i.e. £12,500) is paid up; and

- excluded from the articles any directors' right to reject a share transfer (which gives them control of who owns the shares); and
- from the Registrar a certificate or licence to commence trading, evidencing that he is satisfied that the required share capital has been subscribed; and
- changed its name to end in 'PLC' or 'Public Limited Company',

then an LTD can re-register, or a new company can be formed, as a PLC.

The external perception may be that this is a corporate body of considerable value and prestige, even though its share capital is in fact tiny. Indeed many PLCs are smaller than some LTDs. Such a company should not be confused with a listed or quoted PLC, although it must be said this confusion is very widespread – and actually is often the reason some LTDs become unlisted PLCs (i.e. to give to the outside world an impression of being far more substantial than they really are). They have all the legal obligations of a listed PLC (e.g. must file accounts within six months of their year end etc.), but obviously not the listing agreement requirements.

(g) Listed or quoted public limited company

A PLC formed as above can apply either for a full 'listing' on the Stock Exchange or for a quotation on the Alternative Investment Market (AIM). To obtain permission to join either, the share capital will have to be increased considerably and the company will have to commit itself and its officers to the appropriate rules for each market. Obtaining a listing is termed 'flotation' and is a route chosen so that either existing shareholders may be able to realise their investment and/or so that the company has access to additional share capital other than that sourced by existing owners.

(h) Community interest companies

Since July 2005 any LTD or PLC company formed for social enterprise and/ or those entities which intend to use their profits for the benefit of the local community or public have been able (unless they are charities) to apply to be a community interest company or a CIC as it is known for short. A CIC is:

- subject to objective and transparent eligibility tests;
- required to produce an annual report placed in the public domain (via filing at CH) showing how they are attaining their objective(s); and is
- allowed to transfer assets to other similar bodies.

A CIC can not only issue shares but also pay dividends, subject to limits set from time to time by the Bank of England, since most of its profits are expected to be ploughed back into attaining the company's social activities. In addition a 'CIC' can also pay its directors.

If a company becomes a CIC its name must be displayed everywhere as (for example) 'J Bloggs CIC PLC' or 'J Bloggs CIC LTD'.

(i) Charitable incorporated organisations

At time of writing these are proposals only, although the concept (similar to a CIC) was enacted in the Charity Act 2006. CIOs will be available to charities and have to register with the Charity Commissioners (CC), but not with the Registrar of Companies (which might simplify matters for those running charitable companies since in some areas charity and company law are in conflict). A CIO will need to adopt a constitution, and have a trustee body, and members. Whether the members will have an obligation to contribute on winding up as members of guarantee companies do, may be optional. A CIO will be required to:

- keep registers of its trustees and members;
- make the above details available publicly;
- file accounts and annual returns with CC;
- advise CC of any charges it has created over the charity's property.

Final details of such a body are still awaited; however, the Government has stated that a CIO may not be an appropriate vehicle for charities whose work entails giving grants and/or which do not enter into significant contracts.

(j) Foundation

This is not strictly a company, but can be described as a corporate entity for the roughly 100 foundation hospitals which have their own regulator and emerging requirements which are very similar in many ways to those applicable to companies.

(k) Societas Europaea (SE)

Since October 2004 it has been possible to form an SE, which is a European PLC formed under the European Company Statute (ECS). The ECS contains a regulation allowing the formation of such a company under core company law provisions which apply throughout the European Union. An SE must have a minimum share capital of €120,000 and is available to commercial bodies with interests in more than one European country. An SE allows UK companies to engage in cross-border mergers with companies from other EU member states. Thus rather than taking over a company in another member state, a UK company can agree with the other company to form a jointly owned SE subsidiary or holding company.

(l) European Private Company

SEs are only available for public companies. Paralleling that development, however, is a proposal for private companies – set out in the European Council Regulation on the Statute for a European Private Company. Assuming the proposal goes ahead allowing such a new legal entity, it is unlikely that it will be available before 2011.

(m) Oversea company

Under s. 1044 of CA06, any 'company incorporated outside the United Kingdom' (rather than the previous definition which was 'a company incorporated elsewhere than in Great Britain) is an 'oversea company', and within one month of it establishing a place of business here it must send the following information (using form BR1) to CH:

- the Charter or articles;
- names of the directors and secretary;
- list of persons in the UK authorised to accept service of notice on behalf of the company etc.

Under CA85 a 'place of business' was usually deemed to be one where only administrative functions are conducted. Any other activity (e.g. 'trading' or functions central to the operation of the business) usually meant that the location was defined as a 'branch'. However, under CA06 there is to be no difference between the two definitions – any place of business will be deemed to be and required to register as a branch.

(n) Dormant

Possibly as many as 25 per cent of all companies registered at CH are not trading – they are dormant – sleeping and inactive. They are nevertheless required to submit an annual return and accounts each year (although instead of an actual set of accounts – which might be fairly skeletal – they can submit Form DCA). At any time the company can be reactivated.

It is widely thought that keeping a company on the Register (active or dormant) automatically protects its name. Whilst it may stop another company with an identical name being registered as a company (although even this is not impossible), it may not stop another trader using the name without 'Ltd' at the end. In this instance company law is of no assistance, and the recourse is an action for passing off or possible trade mark infringement. The rule is that if a new company has been placed on the register with a name which an existing company feels is too like its own name, the original company has only one year to object. If an objection is raised, this will generate an investigation and if the complaint is upheld the new company will be required to change its name. However, if a year or more has expired there may be nothing that can be done.

Example	Parallel protection advised
	IBM registered 'Websphere' for software products as a community trade mark in 1998 – that protects it from other parties using an identical mark in relation to identical (and even similar) products throughout the EU. In 1999 Publiweb Ltd changed its company name to Web-Sphere Ltd and registered three domain names using that corporate name. IBM sued but in response the former Publiweb Ltd contended that it was merely using its new corporate name. This argument failed and Web-Sphere Ltd was not only found to have infringed IBM's trade mark, but also the High Court felt it had authority to require 'Web-Sphere Ltd' to change its name.

Companies using names etc. as trade marks may find it advisable to also register a private company with that name.

Within the UK the protection given to companies whereby another company cannot have the same name may actually be of limited protection. For example, a company registered in the Isle of Man, or Jersey, Guernsey etc. could have the same name as a company registered at CH at Cardiff. The mainland Registrar is unable to prevent this, provided the 'externally registered' company does not establish a place of business on the mainland (in which case it would be required to comply with the 'oversea' company provisions), but merely operates via third parties (solicitors, agents etc.).

A new website (www.businesslink.gov.uk/nameandtrademark) has been launched by Business Link (incorporating data from both CH and the Intellectual Property Office), which enables users to check registers of company names and trade marks simultaneously, to avoid unnecessary applications or subsequent challenges.

(o) Joint venture companies

To develop a new product or concept, two or more bodies (not necessarily companies) may agree to set up and operate a jointly owned subsidiary company. In addition to framing the ARTICLES OF ASSOCIATION they will normally enter into a SHAREHOLDERS' AGREEMENT setting out their relationship and the relationship they may have with those nominated to serve on the board. Most joint venture companies are LTDs, although there is nothing to stop one being a PLC. If there is a shareholders' agreement, care should be taken to ensure it does not conflict with the requirements of the articles. Where a joint venture company is an LTD, it is most unlikely that it can dispense with holding an AGM, although of course either (or any) of the shareholders could requisition a(n) (extraordinary) general meeting at any time to call the directors to account.

Voting and taking a poll

INTRODUCTION

Most of the proceedings at the general meetings of companies are decided by a show of hands and, since there is often a consensus, rarely may there be a need for the chairman of the meeting even to count the hands. Occasionally, however, there will be opposition to a proposal and it is as well to be prepared for the eventuality. Several listed PLCs have altered their articles so that all business requires ratification by poll (not by show of hands) which, since it reflects the true voting power of their shareholders, is a true application of shareholder democracy.

Authority to vote

There are three ways in which shareholders' power can be exercised:

1   By attending and voting in person. Such attendance gives the shareholder complete freedom of action to speak and vote at the meeting.
2   By appointing a PROXY. For members of an LTD, a proxy may be able to speak but (subject to the articles) may not be able to vote on a show of hands. The proxy can, however, demand (or join in the demand for) a poll. For members of a listed PLC, usually the proxy cannot speak but can only vote. Institutional shareholders of companies should not use a proxy but appoint a representative.
3   By appointing a representative. Such a person – appointed by a corporate body – is for all intents and purposes a member (since effectively the corporate body is actually 'present') and can exercise all the rights of an individual member.

Preparation

It is rare for antipathy to surface at a meeting without there having been some indication in advance. If antipathy is expected or evident the company needs to prepare for it. The following approach could be utilised:

■ negating the impact by advance discussion with those wishing to raise a matter;
■ arranging for sufficient support to be garnered so that opposition can be outvoted;

- ensuring only those entitled to speak do so – but are allowed to do so with courtesy;
- ensuring that meeting administration (see below) is sound; and
- ensuring those in the media who may report what happened at the meeting are given an adequate (and accurate) briefing.

Media

It is important that those who are to deal with the media are coached in such work, particularly in dealing with hostile or critical questioning. Unless well-prepared and well-briefed for this type of examination, reputations (of both person and company) can be irreparably damaged and unnecessarily bad impressions created.

Out-thinking the opposition

Not only is it important to contact supportive shareholders to obtain their proxy (and thus support) if they are not attending, and to arrange tame 'proposers' and 'seconders' to avoid silences at the meeting when the chairman invites nominations, etc., but also it is essential that if hostility is expected, it is prepared for.

CHECKLIST   Preparing for hostility

✓ Identify source and extent of support and of opposition.

✓ Check if 'hostiles' have a right of attendance (if not, seek to exclude them).

✓ If time allows, consider possibility of an advance private meeting to avoid public confrontation.

✓ Monitor arrivals and arrange for security to be nearby to deal with any physical disruption. Ensure visitors sit apart from shareholders, to aid accurate 'show of hands' counting.

✓ Canvass proxies sufficient to ensure overcoming any potential opposition.

✓ Prepare a list of the questions least wished to be asked – and, more importantly, a crib of suitable answers. Take advice.

✓ Brief the directors concerned of the source of the problem and the steps taken to control/deal with it.

✓ Brief media contacts and provide media-trained spokesman to answer follow-up queries.

✓ If hostile shareholders wish to make a point, they should be allowed this courtesy, answering the points made as far as possible and offering subsequent discussions if this is feasible.

Voting

1   Reference should be made to the articles of association to check QUORUM requirements, rights of attendance, who is to chair the meeting and any special rules re voting

2   If a large number are expected and/or attend the meeting, it may be helpful to arrange shareholder seating in blocks of (say) 20 or 50, and to arrange for representatives of (say) the company auditors to take responsibility for a block of seats each. The use of such representatives (announced by the chairman at the commencement of the meeting) seeks to show that an independent force is in control of the numbers. The scrutineers could also act as receptionists, asking shareholders to sign in, checking voting strength and ensuring that only shareholders sit in 'shareholder areas' to aid ease of counting votes (if necessary).

3   If a show of hands is required, each scrutineer should note the result from his section and hand it to the chief scrutineer (two such persons may be advisable for checking purposes) to provide the chairman with totals.

Poll

A poll can usually be demanded or called by:

- the chairman;
- any two members (which includes representatives of corporate shareholders); or
- any member(s) holding one-tenth or more of the share capital.

Reference should be made to the articles for guidance regarding calling and administering a poll.

The chairman needs to:

- check that the person making the demand has the required authority;
- appoint scrutineers to administer the poll; and
- set the date, time, and place for poll to be taken.

Administration

1   Scrutineers can be arranged before the meeting as set out above. Since proxies are usually required to be deposited 24 hours or more prior to the meeting, the first task of the scrutineers should be to check these proxies for authenticity and voting strength for each resolution. Proxies should provide a space for the insertion of the number of shares/votes applicable.

2   At the meeting, the list of proxies lodged must be compared with those shareholders present, to ensure there is no double-counting. For example a shareholder has a right, even having lodged a proxy, to attend the meeting. In such circumstances, clarification of the authority and scope of the proxy must be sought (i.e. is the proxy to act or will the shareholder act in person, or are they each to act in relation to part of the holding?).

3   On receiving a demand for a poll to be taken, the chairman usually has authority to require it to be conducted immediately, or at the end of the meeting or at some other date (in which case the meeting may have to be adjourned). Once again the articles should be referred to for guidance.

4   If a poll is demanded then the proxy cards provide evidence of the preferences of those not present in person. Additional voting cards (identical in most respects to the proxy card) need to be made available for those shareholders present at the meeting. Each scrutineer responsible for a shareholder seating area, should distribute voting cards to shareholders present and not represented by a proxy – and after voting collect and total them. The results from each area should be passed to the chief scrutineer(s) who will summarise the returns and pass the result to the chairman, to declare the result. Under CA06 shareholders have a right to inspect details of a poll vote.

The future

In *PNC Telecom plc v Thomas* the court held that it was valid to serve notice of a meeting by fax. This was the first occasion on which this matter was challenged in court. However, companies are now permitted to communicate electronically with their shareholders. They have to first submit a resolution to their members (having checked that there is nothing to prohibit the use of electronic mail in their articles). Once the resolution is passed they must

Case study	Using technology
	In *Byng v London Life* the court stated that that a general meeting could be validly held in several locations, provided there were 'fully functional mutual audio-visual links' – i.e. so that everyone could see and hear and interact with all others. Whilst holding the meeting in two or three locations might be feasible, attempting to use more locations than that and trying to ensure everyone can see and hear everyone else must be virtually impossible at least with current technology.

write to their shareholders stating that they have the option of continuing with hard copy or opting for an electronic version. They must be advised that if they do not reply within 28 days they will be deemed to have opted for the electronic option. However even if they do not reply (or do not give an electronic address), they must still be sent a hard copy notification of a meeting with reference to the company website carrying full information re the meeting. They would not be sent (for example) the report and accounts – the shareholder would need to request these. Those who do not opt for electronic communication can be reinvited to do so once a year.

Taking the above developments further, it is possible to foresee a situation where AGMs could be held with shareholders remaining in their homes (connected via the Internet to the location where the AGM is physically being held) and being able to exercise their voting power in 'person' having heard any points made in favour or against a particular proposal, rather than signing a proxy well in advance of the meeting and without the benefit of such arguments. However this would only be a realistic possibility under current requirements if everyone was able to see and hear everyone else, which poses a logistic/practical difficulty with current technology.

Whistle-blowing

INTRODUCTION

As suggested in the code of ETHICS, adoption of a whistle-blowing code for employees (required under the listing agreement for listed PLCs in any event) may be advisable so that those aware of wrongdoing are not only encouraged to report it, but also (and perhaps more importantly) know that if they do so, they will suffer no detriment and their position will be protected. There is no doubt that in some companies the position of company secretary (being the person trying to ensure that the company complies with legislation) can be difficult particularly if there is a dictatorial managing director or chairman who wishes to drive the company forward virtually regardless of legal restrictions. The Public Interest Disclosure Act (or PIDA, colloquially known as the 'Whistle-blowing Act') seeks to protect individuals placed in such difficult positions.

Application

Under the requirements of the listing agreement, listed PLCs are required to have a 'whistle-blowing' policy and it may be advisable for other organisations to adopt such a code. PIDA provides protection for those that report or bring to the attention of the authorities, wrongdoing or the covering up of wrongdoing in their organisations if or after their internal protestations have been ignored. PIDA has been described as a 'whistle-blowers' charter', although in fact relatively few may be able to rely on the protection it provides. It covers 'workers' – thus including employees and the self-employed, as well as agency workers and the like, and Crown servants. Protection is given to those making certain 'qualifying disclosures'. A qualifying disclosure is any information which tends in the reasonable opinion of the worker (which is an objective test in each case) to show a relevant failure. Relevant failures include:

- a criminal offence has been, is being or is likely to be committed;
- a miscarriage of justice has occurred, is occurring or is likely to occur;
- someone has failed, is failing or is likely to fail to comply with a legal obligation to which they are subject;
- health and/or safety of any individual has been, is being or is likely to be endangered;
- the environment has been, is being or is likely to be damaged;

■ information relating to any of the above has been, is being or is likely to be deliberately concealed.

Course of action

The first resort of a potential 'whistle-blower' will usually be to the employing organisation, and if a qualifying disclosure is made in good faith to an employer (or some other person, in the belief that they are responsible for the matter) or to a third party in accordance with a procedure authorised by the employer, then it will be a 'protected disclosure'. If the employee reasonably believes that if he discloses internally he will be subject to a detriment, or that the evidence will be concealed or destroyed, or he has previously made a similar disclosure without any remedial reaction, or it is reasonable for him to do so, the initial disclosure may be made externally.

Where disclosure is to be made to a regulator then not only must the matter comply with the above requirements, but also the complainant must:

(a) believe that the information is substantially correct;
(b) believe the failure lies within the remit of the regulator; and
(c) not be making the disclosure for personal gain.

Any clause in a contract which prohibits workers from exercising these rights (i.e. a gagging clause) is void, and any employee (there is no minimum service requirement) who suffers a detriment has a right of action. In the event of dismissal, this will be regarded as being automatically unfair by an employment tribunal. If the detriment falls short of dismissal then any employee or worker can also complain to a tribunal. Unlike compensation for unfair dismissal, there is no limit on compensation if a dismissal results from whistle-blowing. Although it is stated that the reason for not imposing a compensation limit is to encourage such disclosures (since breaches are not in the public interest), there is no doubt that a more fundamental reason is that a person who has blown the whistle on a previous employer may find it difficult to find future employment.

A policy

It may be good practice (whether required or not) for companies to adopt a whistle-blowing policy with an indication of to whom suspicions etc. should be reported.

Obviously if the person disclosing wrongdoing is under pressure – whether deliberate or latent – not only are few likely to come forward, but also the purpose of the Act is lost.

Case study	Protect the whistle-blower

The (then named) Abbey National made a payment of £25,000 to a manager who voiced his concerns regarding collusion over payments made to suppliers. As a result, the bank's then marketing services director was found guilty of and jailed for receiving bribes for authorising invoices in respect of goods which had not been delivered or which had been delivered only in part, and seven other employees were also found guilty and jailed. In referring to the award the bank had made to the whistle-blower, a spokesperson said *'We hope this will set an example for all our employees and for other employers. Staff should feel able to speak out if they think something is wrong.'* However at that time Abbey National (then an independent listed PLC) did not have a whistle-blowing policy and the person who made the disclosures felt so isolated within the company that he felt he had to resign, although he later rejoined the company.

Example	Whistle-blowing policy

1   [As stated in its GIFTS, ETHICS policy] [the organisation] operates within the country's laws and regulations and expects all employees to co-operate in this by adhering to all external laws and regulation and all internal policies and procedures.

2   Every employee is expected to advise [specify a named person or position] should he become aware of any matter or act which seems not to be in accord with the general aim set out in 1 above. Specifically all employees are expected to make such notification immediately they become aware that an employee or agent of the organisation seems to be responsible for:

   (a) the breach, breaking or proposed breaking of any law or regulation;

   (b) the breach, breaking or proposed breaking of the organisation's procedures or policies;

   (c) any wrongdoing;

   (d) any matter which seems likely to harm an employee, customer, member of the public, the environment etc.;

→

Example	Whistle-blowing policy – *continued*

    (e) any possibility or suggestion that one of the items set out in (a) to (d) has occurred and is being covered up.

3   Assuming these requirements have been met (i.e. the initial report is to [specify name/position] rather than to an outside body), the [organisation] undertakes to hold the reporting employee harmless and to protect them from any personal claims and from any victimisation, harassment or bullying occasioned as a result of their acts. The aim is that the career and income of any notifying employee should not in any way be harmed or hindered as a result of their act (whether the item reported proves to be true or not provided the reporting was carried out in good faith).

4   The action of any other employee against an employee who has made disclosure under this policy and as a result of such disclosure, whether they are affected by the disclosure or not, will be regarded as gross misconduct which could render them subject to summary dismissal.

5   Anyone, including an elected safety representative, who becomes aware of a hazard or dangerous occurrence is expressly required to notify [specify] before making any other report – e.g. to an outside body – not least so that immediate action can be taken if necessary to remove or limit the hazard.

6   Failure to notify when reasonably aware or certain of an occurrence covered by 2. above is regarded by the organisation as misconduct since effectively it makes the employee an accessory. Failure to notify internally before notifying externally is also usually regarded as misconduct. Only if an employee has reasonable grounds for believing that no notice will be taken of the report internally (or he may suffer detriment if he reports the matter internally) may he contact an outside body in the first instance.

If the organisation has a compliance officer, then it may be logical to insert the name of that person in such a clause. However in safety reporting it may be important that a person is designated for this purpose on each site, so that urgent investigation and rectification can be implemented.

Legal actions

Since PIDA came into force there have been over 2,000 claims for compensation as a result of sanctions imposed following whistle-blowing. Around £15,000,000 has been paid in compensation in total. The average payment is around £100,000 and the highest amount awarded so far was £805,000.

Case study	Theft and fraud
	Antonio Fernandes was the financial controller of Netcom. His managing director gave him petty cash slips on two occasions without any supporting receipts. The amounts claimed were in excess of £200,000. When he protested that such claims were almost certainly a fraud on the Inland Revenue, since they could not be properly claimed as being wholly and exclusively in the proper execution of his duties, he was told by the managing director, and subsequently by the American owners of the company to *'keep your nose clean and pay it'*. He refused and was told to resign. When he did not, he was dismissed. In one of the first claims under PIDA, he was awarded £293,000 compensation.

The Law Commission has proposed new laws concerning the practice of giving bribes. There would be two entirely new laws – one prohibiting the giving of bribes and another prohibiting the taking of bribes. In addition there would be new laws prohibiting the bribing of a foreign official residing or doing business in the UK and negligently failing to prevent bribery by an employee or agent. The latter is particularly relevant to companies, which would need to ensure that their internal rules outlaw such practices – and that such rules are stringently policed.

Winding up

INTRODUCTION

The annual turnover in companies registered at CH is considerable – there is a net gain each year of around 200,000 companies, with around 100,000 companies being removed from the register. Some companies are removed from the register by default. For example, if all the directors and the secretary resign simultaneously, the Registrar has no one to chase for filing documentation, and after a certain period, and advertising the fact, may strike the company off. Alternatively if the company does not file an annual return the Registrar can take action to strike the company off the register. These are not ideal methods of removing a company and should only be used for dormant companies which have never traded, that is those where there is no possibility of subsequent claims from creditors, employees and other injured parties, etc., leading to RESURRECTION. Most companies are removed following a winding-up order or for failing to file accounts. In recent years, efforts have been made to encourage companies in financial trouble to adopt voluntary arrangements to try to support the recovery, rather than the winding-up of the company.

Types of orders

Members' voluntary winding-up

Where the purpose(s) of the company has/have been achieved and the assets are such that they are able to meet all claims likely to be made against the company, and the directors can swear a declaration of solvency to this effect, this method of ceasing the company's existence can be utilised. Within five weeks of the directors swearing the declaration of solvency, the members must pass a resolution winding up the company, and advise the Registrar accordingly.

Procedure: the directors swear declaration of solvency and convene an (E)GM at which a liquidator is appointed. A notice regarding this event is posted in the *London Gazette* and details are given to the Registrar within 14 days of the appointment. The liquidator proceeds to sell the assets and settle the debts. A director has liability for the debts of the company (regardless of any earlier resignation) for 12 months from the date of a declaration of solvency.

Creditors' voluntary winding-up

In this instance if the directors are unable to swear a declaration of solvency, the company decides to wind itself up and calls a creditors' meeting

Procedure: an (E)GM is convened to pass a winding-up resolution. The meeting nominates a liquidator, and authorises the convening of a meeting of creditors giving at least seven days' notice. A notice is placed in the *London Gazette*. At the creditors' meeting, those present endorse a liquidator – or appoint an alternative. When the liquidator's appointment is confirmed by the creditors, the powers of the directors terminate. The liquidator proceeds to sell the assets and settle such debts as are possible.

The court orders a winding-up

This occurs when:

- the company passes a special resolution to this effect; or
- a judgment creditor has a debt of £750 or more and has petitioned for the winding-up; or
- the company has failed to comply with certain requirement; or
- the court feels it is just to do so.

Procedure: in this instance the Official Receiver becomes the liquidator.

Striking off

Under the Deregulation and Contracting Out Act 1994, provided a company has not in the previous three months:

- changed its name;
- traded or conducted business;
- engaged in any activity (other than that connected with this application); and
- made a disposal for value of property rights,

then the directors can apply to the Registrar for it to be struck off.

Procedure: a form DS01 (under s. 1003 CA06) (formerly form 652A CA85) must be filed, with copies sent to all directors (who do not sign the form) and all other interested parties.

Notice re intent to strike the company off is inserted in the *London Gazette*. Three months after *London Gazette* notice, provided there are no objections, the Registrar can strike the company off the register. (Reference should be made to the Registrar's Guidance note on the subject.)

Resurrection

A company which is dissolved, wound up, or struck off, for example, for failure to file accounts, can be reinstated by court order for up to six years (recently increased from two). This could, however, entail substantial costs, since filing penalties for items that should have been filed during the period it was off the register may need to be paid.

Administrative receivership

Until the passing of the Enterprise Act 2002, a creditor (usually a bank holding a charge over the company's assets or undertaking) could be invited by the board to appoint an administrative receiver, whose sole aim was to liquidate the assets as quickly as possible, pay his own fees, pay the creditor holding the charge and, if there was anything left, pay the creditors. The Enterprise Act altered the priority, by requiring companies to use the administration route, and permitting administrative receivership only in a few instances.

Administration

The Enterprise Act now requires most companies approaching insolvency to apply for administration. As a result of the credit crunch there have been a number of well-publicised and household-name companies – particularly retail chains – that have had to do so. Under this arrangement an administrator is appointed (usually by the creditors) to try to save the company or part of it; possibly selling assets (often at a discount to their true worth, to gain a swift sale) to raise cash to keep the company going. Should the administrator be successful the company may be able to emerge from administration and resume its previous status, usually as a smaller organisation. Voluntary arrangements (i.e. agreements with the creditors) are also encouraged under the Enterprise Act (which has also diluted the stigma of bankruptcy for individuals). Wherever the name of the company is used, the words 'in administration' must be added to bring its situation to the attention of all third parties – particularly creditors and potential creditors. This is also important to customers – after all, a customer wishing to return goods if they are faulty needs to be made aware of the state of the company, since it may not exist in the near future.

Unfortunately administrative receivership (AR) and administration have similar names, but have completely divergent aims:

- The aim of an AR is to generate as much cash for the assets of the company as quickly as possible, which will entail the cessation of the company trading whilst the assets are sold – often at a considerable discount, since purchasers, knowing the situation, may be able to strike a hard bargain. This was certainly the case in the recession of the early 1990s, and banks particularly were heavily criticised (since usually it was banks that had the right to appoint ARs) for 'pulling the rug' from organisations which might have survived had they been supported on a short-term basis. (Sadly a similar situation is being experienced as this edition was being updated. Once again, despite government pressure, the banks are refusing to support some businesses hit by the recession – a situation ironically precipitated by the banks themselves.) The AR takes his own fees, pays the organisation (usually a bank) which has taken a CHARGE over the assets, and then, if there is anything left, pays the unsecured creditors and shareholders.

■ Conversely, however an administrator tries to keep the company (or at least part of it) trading for at least a limited time, possibly selling some assets and trying to trade out of the situation, with at least part of the original company surviving.

Voluntary arrangements

Under a voluntary arrangement the creditors agree to support the company – normally by agreeing not to press for payment of their debt for a set period to relieve pressure on cash flow etc. This may allow the company time to 'trade out' of its current solvency problems. Very often the creditors may be placed in the position of being virtually forced to agree to a 'voluntary' arrangement, since otherwise (i.e. if the company fails) they are likely to receive nothing for the value of their invoices. As a further development, if the creditors wish to avoid the company failing, they may even be prepared to exchange their debt for shares in the company – a 'debt-equity swop'. In this way, should the company survive they can share in its recovery, whereas if it fails they have probably lost no more than their already incurred debt.

Case study	Saved by the creditors
	The Queens Moat House Hotel group was saved from insolvency in the late 1980s by the actions of its bankers, mainly because the credit they had advanced to the company was so great they could not afford to let their debtor go under – in which event the credit they had allowed would have become their bad debt, thus affecting their own accounts and possibly their solvency.
	Similarly in 2003 the Marconi Group (formerly the highly respected GEC) was saved from insolvency by its creditors, who agreed to a debt:equity exchange and finished up owning over 99.5 per cent of the share capital of a listed PLC.

WARNING

 The section on WRONGFUL and FRADULENT TRADING suggests actions that could be taken by the officers if the company is approaching insolvency – inactivity in such a situation is certainly not an option, if personal liability is to be avoided.

These are difficult and involved areas and legal advice should be taken promptly.

Written resolutions

INTRODUCTION

In an attempt to reduce the perceived time and resources that LTDs 'wasted' in convening meetings to gain their shareholders' agreement to business, CA89 introduced the concept of such business being effected by members signing resolutions to deal with business which otherwise would have been required to be conducted at general meetings. However, for a written resolution to be passed, total unanimity was required (i.e. all 100 per cent of votes had originally to be in favour), in practice only companies with few shareholders, or those where all the shareholders were on the board, could use this process. (The total unanimity rule has been diluted under CA06 – see below.)

Notice

To take advantage of this relaxation (i.e. not needing to convene a meeting), all the members must be sent a copy of the required RESOLUTION with a request to sign and return it. They do not all have to sign the same piece of paper – or even the same wording. Where the members are distant from the company (or are not known well) it may be advisable to send the copies by recorded delivery so that some record of posting exists, and possibly to suggest that the same precautions are taken when returning the signed copies. With shareholders who are not known personally to the company, it may also be prudent to request that the shareholder's signature be witnessed. These are administrative suggestions, however, since neither of these points is required under the law.

As noted, originally, written resolutions required unanimous agreement – if just one member did not agree or simply did not reply, then the resolution failed. However unanimity has been dispensed with under s. 288 CA06. Ordinary written resolutions can now be passed if there is a simple majority (50 per cent plus one or more) of ALL those entitled to vote. Special written resolutions are passed if there is 75 per cent support from ALL those entitled to vote. Even this is a higher level of agreement compared to the situation where the same resolutions are considered at a meeting. At a meeting a simple majority for an ordinary resolution or 75 per cent for a special resolution is needed but only of the votes *cast*.

Copies of the proposed resolution must be sent to all members (either electronically or in hard copy) with a note of how to indicate agreement

(s. 296) and a cut off date. after which, if not ratified, the resolution will fail. If no cut-off date is specified, the proposed written resolution will fail 28 days after the date (the circulation date) the resolution is dispatched.

Under the original rules, the company's AUDITORS' views on the resolution needed to be sought, as they had seven days in which to state whether the business covered by the resolution 'concerned them'. If it did, then they stated this to the company, and the written process had to be abandoned and a meeting convened. Under the Companies (Resolutions of Private Companies) Order 1995 this 'policing' role of the Auditors was abolished. However the auditors must still be sent a copy of the resolution – failure to do so attracts a £500 fine for those responsible.

Recording and filing

Once the resolution is passed, a copy certified by a director or the company secretary must be recorded in the minute book. If the resolution is such that, had it not been passed using the written process it would need to have been passed as a special resolution, or would have been passed as an ordinary resolution which was required to be notified to the Registrar of Companies, then the Registrar must be notified within 15 days.

Prohibitions

A written resolution cannot be used to remove a director (s. 168) or auditor (s. 510) from office. Such a proposal can only be effected at a meeting with the resolution subject to the special notice requirements.

In addition, there are special rules (mainly relating to the need to provide full explanation) regarding using written resolutions in the following circumstances and legal advice should be sought:

- disapplication of pre-emption rights;
- financial assistance for the purchase of own shares;
- purchase of own shares;
- payment out of capital;
- approval of directors' service contracts.

Requesting a written resolution

Members holding five per cent or more of the voting strength of the company can request that a written resolution be put to the members. A lower percentage can be required if the articles so permit.

Wrongful and fraudulent trading

INTRODUCTION

Before the creation of limited liability companies under the Companies Acts of 1856 and 1862, owners (entrepreneurs, or risk-takers) and directors (if they were owners as well) of companies had unlimited liability for the debts of their failed companies, unless the company had been formed under a Royal Charter or an Act of Parliament – (i.e. a statute company). The formation of a statute company was an expensive process and hence few took this route. Since most promoters were wary of taking on potential liability in excess of the funds they could afford to lose, having to accept unlimited liability tended to inhibit the growth of commercial entities – and thus limited liability from such potential debts was introduced to protect the shareholders (who were very often also directors of the companies). This was criticised at the time as being a 'rogue's charter' and 'encouraging overtrading' – in short, it was accused of being a blueprint for unscrupulous directors who could run the company into the ground, knowing that they had no personal liability for the debts if their company failed. Liability for failure thus passed from the shareholders to the creditors. True to the criticism referred to above, some shareholder/directors did abuse the new protection by carrying on their businesses to the ultimate detriment of the creditors. To rectify this imbalance, the Insolvency Act 1986 extended a director's personal obligations and responsibilities materially. The concepts of 'wrongful' and 'fraudulent' trading were introduced, and where these offences are proved, directors can be fined, imprisoned and/or required to make good any deficiencies personally. This is particularly pertinent at present, when there are so many company failures: in fourth quarter of 2008, company insolvencies increased by 52 per cent over the corresponding quarter of 2007. In at least some of these cases there could have been wrongful trading. In addition, the number of companies placed in administration, from which some (or parts of some) may emerge in the same period, was three times that of the previous year.

Wrongful trading

A director can be held to have traded wrongfully, if he knew or (the really important requirement) *ought to have concluded* that there was no reasonable prospect of the creditors being paid on their due dates or within a reasonable time of those dates, or of the company avoiding insolvency, and yet he allowed the company to continue to trade (and to take on credit). A director found guilty of wrongful trading can be made personally liable to contribute to any deficiency in assets available to satisfy the creditors of the company. In addition, the person can be disqualified from acting as a director for a maximum period of 15 years. Whether at any time a company is insolvent (and should, therefore, cease trading rather than continuing to trade 'wrongfully') may be able to be judged fairly accurately with hindsight, but may be difficult to assess at the time, particularly as the directors may genuinely be working to try to save the company. The following outline tests should be used merely as a first examination of the position, before taking competent advice:

1   Is the company capable of paying its debts as they fall due (or shortly afterwards)?
2   Do the assets of the company exceed the value of its liabilities?
3   Would the realisation of assets be sufficient to pay all liabilities?

If the answers to any of these questions are 'no', then unless there is knowledge of an influx of cash within the period until the debts are due, the company is almost certainly insolvent (or is approaching that position) and unless the situation can be or is reasonably expected to be rectified swiftly (or there is demonstrable evidence that the situation is about to change), it should cease trading. To do otherwise may involve the directors being held to be personally culpable. In assessing culpability, the court will bear in mind the expertise of the persons concerned. Thus, a personnel director might be held to be liable to a lesser extent than a finance director, who might normally be deemed to be more knowledgeable in this area by virtue of training and experience in that field. Liability can be reduced or avoided, if it can be shown that everything that could be done, was in fact being done to minimise the potential loss.

Case study	Qualifications enhance liability

In *Dorchester Finance Co Ltd v Stebbing* there were three directors (all qualified accountants), of whom two left the running of the company to the other. The former often signed blank cheques for use by their colleague and made no enquiry of how the funds were used by him. When the company failed owing substantial sums to its creditors, all three directors were prosecuted. The court found that the two 'sleeping directors' had failed to apply the necessary skill and care in the performance of their duties (and indeed that they had failed to perform *any* duties in their positions as directors).

In the judgment the court stated that a director must in the exercise of his duties:

→

Case study	Qualifications enhance liability – continued

- show the degree of skill and care reasonably be expected from a person of his knowledge and experience (hence the expectations of qualified accountants – as was the case here – would be high in view of their professional training and qualification);

- take such care that a person might be expected to take on their own account;

- use the powers granted to him in good faith and in the interests of the company of which he is a director.

Directors must be proactive in the exercise of their responsibilities (inactivity is not an option, if personal liability is to be to be limited). The decision in this case also demonstrates that there is no difference in liability between executive and non-executive directors.

Action required

Boards should ensure that there are regular assessments and projections of future cash flow so they can always know the state of solvency (and predicted solvency) of their companies. Immediately it is known that a company is insolvent, or it appears that it is approaching this state, the directors must take action – inactivity is not an option.

Whenever a company is wound up, an insolvency practitioner must investigate the records of the company and the actions of its officers. Each officer is required to and MUST complete a very lengthy questionnaire – the answers to some of the questions (e.g. *'When were you first aware the company was trading wrongfully?'*) being potentially self-incriminating. If transactions were effected at under-value or at preferential rates, or a creditor was given preferential treatment, this can result in a report being made to the Director of Public Prosecutions who will decide whether to prosecute for fraud. If the company is being wound up under a court order, the report must be made to the Official Receiver. If the insolvency practitioner or the Official Receiver feels that the conduct of a director has been such that he is unfit to run a company, then a report must be made in case legal action should be taken against those culpable. The body responsible for the initiation of action in such instances has recently been privatised and one can expect an increased number of prosecutions in this area – not least due to the considerably increased numbers of company failures.

Case study	Fraudulent concealment?

In *Contex Drouzhba Ltd v Wiseman*, W caused the company of which he was a director to enter into an arrangement with a creditor whereby the company would pay the creditor within 30 days of invoice. However the company's financial position was so poor that the director knew there was no way in which the requirements of the arrangement could be met. The judge held that there had been deceit on the part of the director and that it was 'inconceivable' that the status of director should protect him from personal liability. Accordingly the director was held personally liable for the amount promised to the creditor.

Actions that the board could take, include:

I   Ceasing to trade and calling a creditors meeting to consider a voluntary arrangement (see WINDING UP). Whilst this may completely remove what confidence remains in the company, in many respects the last thing most creditors would wish is for the company to fail, as often they have a great deal (more possibly than directors or shareholders) at stake. If there is a chance that the company could trade out of the position, the creditors (or a 75 per cent majority of value of them whose wishes could be binding on all creditors) may be prepared to accept a moratorium on their debt (or even a debt:equity exchange, that is taking shares in the company in exchange for extinguishing part or all of their debt).

2   Appoint an administrative receiver. In fact this right belongs to a creditor – usually a bank – which has a first floating charge over assets of the company. The directors' action is to invite the creditor to appoint an administrative receiver. As a result of the Enterprise Act 2002 this course of action is increasingly discouraged in favour of trying to save the company by means of a voluntary arrangement or administration.

3   Petition the court for the appointment of an administrator. This is only possible if the company has access to funds and it is thought possible that the company – or a profitable part of it – could trade out of the situation. Using this alternative is encouraged under the Enterprise Act 2002.

The first quarterly insolvency report after the impact of the changes introduced by the Enterprise Act showed that the number of company administrations had soared by 131 per cent against the comparable period whilst the number of administrative receiverships had fallen by 54 per cent. It would appear that the effort to try to bias actions towards recovery rather than liquidation seems to be working although the acid test of course is how many of the administrations were successful.

4 Raise loans (i.e. additional capital) from bankers or others.

5 Source additional shareholder (i.e. risk) capital or loans. Although sourcing loans may be a solution to the immediate cash situation, care needs to be taken, since taking on a loan creates a further liability and may increase the company's inherent insolvency. New capital for an LTD could be sought from family and/or friends of the officers, and possibly even offering shares to employees. If considering inviting employees to invest, it would be wise for the company to offer to fund financial advice for them, since the risk of failure may be high. When the former Rolls-Royce company failed in 1971, the employees suffered a 'triple-whammy' of loss, since as well as losing their jobs, many had invested personally in the company, and in addition the company pension fund had also invested heavily in the company.

Other sources of funds include loans from national and/or local government and even the EU; by advertising in the media for investors or even, if it is the only way the company can survive, approaching a competitor or supplier with a view to a merger.

6 Seek to amalgamate with another business.

7 Seek a 'white knight' to take over the company as a going concern. ('White knight' is a term mainly used when listed PLCs are subject to a hostile takeover bid, and depicts a company whom the board of the target company feel would be a more acceptable new parent – more welcome than the predator.)

8 At all times, record (on an ongoing basis) full details of every action taken, by whom it was taken, the date on which it was taken, and the result. Whilst the recording of such actions may not save the company, it may, since it is evidence of the positive action of the directors to regard the interests of the creditors as 'paramount', save them (the officers) from being required to contribute to the assets available to the creditors. Advice should be taken.

If genuine refinancing steps are being actively taken (even if these subsequently prove unsuccessful), liability on the directors may be minimised or avoided. It is worth repeating that if it is thought that a company might be nearing the point at where it could be held to be trading wrongfully, it is **essential** that the directors take action and record details of their actions in this respect on a daily basis. Inactivity is not an option if personal liability is to be minimised or avoided.

Under recent initiatives, a company in financial difficulties, can use a process under which creditors claims can be frozen for 56 days during which period efforts could be made to save the business. At the end of 56 days a creditors' meeting must be held at which the creditors could (subject to gaining a 75 per cent agreement) extend the moratorium for a further month.

Directors' and officers' liability insurance policies should be checked to see whether, if found guilty of wrongful trading (which almost certainly would involve a degree of dishonesty), there is any cover under such a policy. The best policies cover the defence costs – even of those found guilty but only until that verdict and obviously cannot pay out regarding any personal liability.

Case study	Creditors' interests are paramount
	In *Gwyer & Associates v London Wharf (Limehouse) Ltd*, a director made no effort to ascertain what were the interests of his company (which was approaching insolvency) before voting on a board resolution. The court held he was not only negligent, but also in breach of his fiduciary duty to exercise his discretion independently and *bona fides* in the interests of the company. It went on to state that where a company was on the brink of insolvency, the directors owed a duty *'to consider as paramount'* the interests of the creditors.

Penalties

Although there have not been many such actions, a recent court case found two directors personally liable to contribute £75,000 each to the assets available to the creditors of their insolvent company because they knew before the liquidation that it was likely to happen and yet continued trading to the obvious detriment of the creditors.

Judgment in a similar case required a husband and wife to contribute £431,000 to the creditors of their failed company.

In one of the greatest value cases, a director was required to contribute £2 million to help pay off the creditors of his failed company.

It is expected that the number of actions should increase mainly since the responsibility for action has been passed from the Department of Business, Enterprise and Regulatory Reform (when operating as the Department of Trade and Industry) to an independent company – Forensic Investigation and Recovery Services.

Fraudulent trading

The essential difference between wrongful and fraudulent trading is intent. Whereas under wrongful trading the director could be held culpable by negligence or even ignorance, under fraudulent trading intent needs to be proven. Here directors will be held responsible when the business of a company has been carried on for fraudulent purposes and/or with the intent to defraud its creditors. Those responsible can be:

- held personally liable to an unlimited extent;
- disqualified from acting as a director for a maximum period of 15 years;
- fined and/or imprisoned (for a term increased by CA06 from October 2008) to ten years).

Index